A Dictionary of False Friends

Robert J. Hill

First published 1982

Published by
THE MACMILLAN PRESS LTD
London and Basingstoke
Associated companies throughout the world

ISBN 0 333 27784 8

Typeset by Santype International Ltd, Salisbury

Printed in Hong Kong

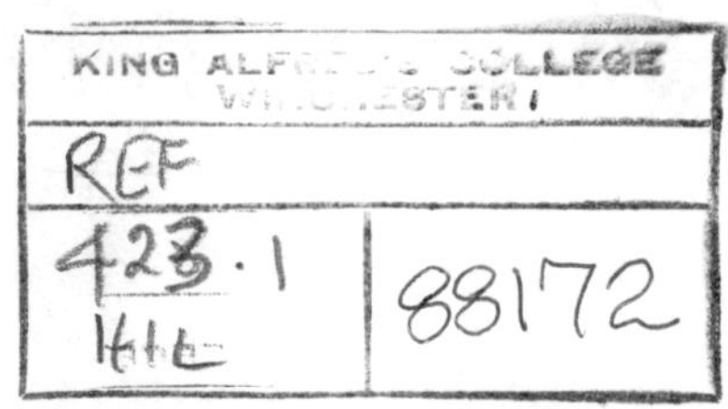

DEDICATION

To Frank and Elisabeth Bell

Contents

Introduction

Since the early 1960s, when I began teaching English as a foreign language, there has been a marked shift in emphasis in the way we teach, from detailed studies of texts, to methods which encourage the students to talk more. From the beginning, I remember noticing how the meaning of certain English words was repeatedly misunderstood: the context might offer no hint of the fact that words like *sympathetic*, *smoking*, or *control* meant something quite different in English from the similar word in other languages. I am ashamed too, when I think how many times I had used *fastidious* as a reasonable synonym for *fussy*, before I discovered that the former was likely to be understood by all the Latins (i.e. speakers of Portuguese, Spanish, French, and Italian) as *irritating*, *troublesome*, or *annoying*.

Then, as now, a good deal of time is spent in trying to get students not to say 'I am here since two weeks' or 'I like very much the ski.' If they express themselves like that, they will lose marks in an exam, but an English speaker will understand what they are trying to say. If I make the comment to a North European that a house has *stark walls*, (s)he may well suppose I mean *strong walls*, while if I mention a *partition* to a Frenchman, he may think I'm talking of a musical score. On the other hand, we must remember that huge numbers of users of English as a second language (e.g. Africans or Indians) will probably not have these difficulties. An Italian telling a Swede that he is looking for his *billet* may not be misunderstood, as both may suppose it means *ticket*, but the African or Indian (like the native English speaker) would be quite misled.

A striking discovery was that English frequently has a meaning or use for a word which differs from the meaning of its cognates in most (if not all) of the other languages where it occurs. Even when a bilingual dictionary gave the correct translation, it rarely contained a note to warn the user of possible misunderstanding. The first time a student comes across such a word in the dictionary, the reaction is one of surprise and disbelief. A dictionary dealing with this aspect of vocabulary directly was an evident need, especially in the light of the teaching methods now so widely in use.

Sources

I initially relied on standard bilingual dictionaries. Many items first became evident as false friends in the classroom; in addition, I have worked through the books listed below. My subsequent method has been to check any item found in one language in virtually all the West

European language dictionaries, especially in those of its associated language family.

The following comments apply specifically to the individual languages.

Portuguese

The entries are more concerned with Brazilian usage than European. There are roughly ten times more speakers of the former than the latter. Here I had a valuable source in a dictionary which was the exception to the rule: James L. Taylor's *Portuguese English Dictionary* (Harrap), in which false friends have clear notes of warning in square brackets. I think I can say (Lusitanian) Portuguese speakers should scarcely find the present dictionary less useful than Brazilians.

Spanish

An important source was an anonymous list of words which came my way through a Spanish student; this was backed up by *Cassell's Colloquial Spanish* by A. Bryson Gerrard (Cassell) and finally by the *Spanish-English, English-Spanish Dictionary* by Colin Smith (Collins). These two take great care in explaining differences in vocabulary in Latin American countries and Castilian. There is scarcely room for such guidance in the present work and as a rule of thumb, items are only included if they affect several countries.

Italian

Cassell's Colloquial Italian by P. J. T. Glendening and his *Cassell's Colloquial English for Italians* (Cassell) are the only relevant books I have found.

French

From my own student days, I remembered Anderson and Harmer's *Le mot juste* (Dent). It is out of print but still to be found in libraries. Sadly, it seemed out of date, not because words had changed, but because of a vast number of neologisms and cases of *franglais* which it lacked. Moreover, it contained many entries in English (and presumably French) so obscure and specialised, and distinctions in usage so slight as to distract the user from what was important. However, I did find a good deal of worthwhile material from it. *Cassell's Colloquial French* by M. and E. Levieux (Cassell), though shorter, was considerably more valuable. More recently, in 1975, M. Koessler's *Les faux amis* (Vuibert) came out. It is a vast work beyond the pocket of most students, and like *Le mot juste*, differs in one important respect from the present work, in that many cases are included where an English word has a wider number of meanings than French. (See 'Criteria for exclusion' below.)

Dutch
Only a few short lists in dictionaries have come my way. They were far from complete. There has been some difficulty where spelling and pronunciation of shorter words suggested two distinct entries.

German
Anderson and North's *Cassell's Colloquial German* (Cassell) was a useful source early on; at a much later stage, I had the good fortune to be put in contact with Miss M. L. Goodbody of the Department of German in Bristol University (see acknowledgments).

Danish
Helge Schwarz's *False Friends* (Samfundslitteratur, de Studerendes Forlag, 1973) was most helpful.

Norwegian
No book seems to have been produced, though of course the above Danish work set me on the trail for a good many items. Entries diverge in Danish and Norwegian sometimes because of the differing final consonants.

Swedish
As a useful initial source, I used P. J. T. Glendening's *Cassell's Colloquial English for Swedish students* (Cassell).

Japanese
Toru Matsumoto's *Random Dictionary* (Japan Times Ltd., 1974) lists many words taken into Japanese from English. Not surprisingly, a good many turned out to be false friends.

Swiss German
Bernese has been the basis for the majority of these entries: it has upwards of a million speakers and more High Alemannic survivals in its vocabulary than the Central, Zürich, and North Eastern dialects. Of course, all Swiss German speakers will need to take note of the (High) German entries too. My wife has been my main source here.

For the remaining miscellaneous languages, modern Greek, Arabic, and Turkish, I have mainly relied on items which have cropped up in lessons, though I searched a Turkish dictionary for French borrowings. Greek I have pursued when a Greek-based word in English struck me as a potential false friend: I suspect more Greek items await identification.

Criteria for inclusion

1. Words which are false friends in spelling and/or in pronunciation. It is assumed that *-ly* is readily associated with *ment(e)* in the Latin languages, and *-y* with *-e*, *-ig*, *-ick*, *-ich* etc. in North European languages. It is also assumed that many final vowels in Latin languages are lost in English.
2. Words where the foreign language has a broader range of meaning(s) than English, though one (or more) meanings may be identical, e.g. *etiquette* has the 'correct manners' meaning in many languages (so this is not mentioned in Part 1, but can be verified in Part 2). However, it also means 'label' in the same languages, but not in English. This easily leads to EFL students making mistakes.
3. Words causing trouble in the same part of speech.
4. Words not related semantically or etymologically are included as they really help the learner to increase his vocabulary. Relatively speaking, more Latin entries are cognates, while shorter North European entries sometimes are not, because of the effects of Grimm's law and similar sound shifts.

Criteria for exclusion

1. Words where the foreign use is narrower than English, since these do not lead to EFL mistakes. The student may gradually discover this for himself as he progresses.
2. Words apparently coinciding, but in different parts of speech. (There are a few exceptions to this since some borrowings have clearly changed function, e.g. *campari* in Japanese and *vendetta* in Greek.)
3. A word may appear in a standard dictionary looking like a false friend, but if it was not known to my informants, I have omitted it as being too rare or old-fashioned to matter.
4. Very few taboo words are included. (I have had a list published in *Modern English Teacher*, vol. 6, no. 1, page 31, though words in differing parts of speech were included.) They are also given very sensible treatment in Kay and Strevens' *Cassell's Colloquial English* (Cassell).

Conclusion

In its very compilation, there has been a great risk of errors in this dictionary. When the usual dictionaries failed me, I have repeatedly asked my students and colleagues on points of translation. Only now that it is available to more people, can it really be checked for errors and omissions. I shall be most grateful to you, the reader and user, for any corrections and new entries you can offer me; please write c/o the publishers. They will be invaluable for any possible future editions. Meanwhile I hope this unorthodox dictionary will help in a better understanding between the nations of the world.

Using the dictionary

Part 1

What do the entries mean? Let us take:

to **control** ≠ to check P E I F Nl, etc.

This says basically that the verb *control* does not mean 'check' and the following languages are affected ...; the letters are taken from the international vehicle registration plates. We can develop this a little:
1. for the speaker of any of the languages indicated on the right, the verb resembling *control* in their language is expressed in English by *check*. By referring to Part 2, the English meaning of *control* can be found.
2. for the speaker of English who is learning any one of the languages shown on the right, to express the verb *check*, a word resembling *control* is needed. Its precise form can be found in a conventional dictionary, and perhaps even safely guessed!
3. a zero entry in a column on the right means either:
- **a** the words are totally dissimilar in that language and English, or
- **b** the words coincide so closely in meaning and form that no serious problem exists.

(Reference to Part 2 will indicate which to the foreign student.)

A second sign is also occasionally used:

diverted → amused P I F

That is to say, where Portuguese, Italian, and French speakers may be tempted to say: *His story diverted us*, it is preferable to say: *His story amused us.* → is used then where the left-hand word is just possible, but the right-hand is more natural in English; the left-hand word is usually too formal or old-fashioned in this meaning

Italics used for the languages in the right-hand columns indicate that
1. the word in that language is less close in appearance than in the other languages listed, or
2. if the pronunciation is less close, or
3. if the word indicated is relatively obscure.

Grammatical markers are kept to a minimum. Verbs are marked by *to*; adjectives, adverbs, and the occasional preposition are unmarked; nouns are normally marked by an article: *a* or *an* for countable nouns, and *the* if the noun is countable in other languages, but uncountable in English (see the Appendix) and also in the rare case of an entry in the plural.

Part 2

This part of the dictionary has been written to show the foreign student how British and American English uses the false friends given in Part 1. The entries are in part a synthesis of several current EFL dictionaries, but to avoid making this part too long, only the major meanings are given and/or those showing the false-friend aspect. The presentation is usually in the order: verb, noun, adjective, where the same word has more than one function. Definitions are mostly within the 2000 most common words, though there was less need for this restraint in the case of entries affecting the Latin languages only.

All entries have these indicators by them:

A very important
B of medium importance
C of minor importance

These are based not only on word counts but partly on how relatively troublesome these words are.

Suggestions for the foreign student

You are advised to go carefully through every page of Part 1 marking all the words affecting your language, then check each one in Part 2 for status. As your knowledge of English grows you will gradually move from A and B words to C words. You may then like to write in the translations from a good bilingual dictionary. The more you mark your copy of the dictionary in this way, the sooner you will become familiar with the contents relevant to you.

Little has been published for multi-lingual EFL-classes as yet, but my *Get it right* (Longman) may be found useful.

Acknowledgments

I received valuable help in the past from the following, though they had no chance to check the final manuscript: Issam Al Khayyat for Arabic; Sinan Bayraktaroglu for Turkish; Sylva Gethin and Lena Hindmarsh for Swedish; Arne Juul for Danish; Peter Mansfield for Greek; the Rev. Eckhardt von Rabenau for German; Reiko Yamanuchi for Japanese.

I am heavily indebted to the following three for their continued help over a long period and for checking the final manuscript, though I must emphasise that I accept ultimate responsibility for the entries myself: Mieke Champernowne for Dutch, Ann Cronin for Swedish, Åse Fozzard for Norwegian; and, in a special way, to Margaret L. Goodbody of the Department of German in Bristol University. She generously allowed me full access to her 900 cards of research material bearing on German-English false friends, and granted me permission to publish any of her material. Her research in this field is very substantial and would have resulted in many more entries if I had not had to apply my criteria for exclusion.

Finally, I am indebted to a large number of students at the Cambridge Bell School who patiently answered my queries.

Abbreviations

Abbreviations of languages

Ar	Arabic	I	Italian
Ch	Swiss German	J	Japanese
D	German	N	Norwegian
Dk	Danish	Nl	Dutch/Flemish
E	Spanish	P	(Brazilian) Portuguese
F	French	S	Swedish
Gr	Modern Greek	Tr	Turkish

Other abbreviations:

adj	adjective	*n*	noun
adv	adverb	s/o	someone, somebody
AE	American English	s/th	something
BE	British English	u	uncountable noun
c	countable noun	*v*	verb
e.g.	for example		
esp.	especially, above all		
etc.	et cetera, and so on		
i.e.	that is (to say)		

Status markers (see page vi)

A	very important
B	of medium importance
C	of minor importance

PART 1

False Friends

a

to **abandon**	≠ to let s/o down, fail to keep promises	F
	≠ to go home from	E
to **abate**	≠ to pull down, demolish, shoot down	P E I F
	≠ to slaughter	P I F
	≠ to discourage, depress	P E I F
abated	≠ depressed	P E I F
	≠ despicable, contemptible	E
the **abatement**	≠ the depression, dejection, low spirits	P E I F
	≠ the discount	P
an **abortion**	≠ a miscarriage	E I
to **abrade**	≠ to burn, scorch	P E
an **absence**	≠ a faint, black-out	D
absolute	≠ domineering, tyrannical (of temperament)	E F
	≠ absolved	I
to **absolve**	≠ to complete/finish (a course)	D
	≠ to pass (an exam)	D
the **abstinence**	≠ the fasting	E F
to **abuse**	≠ to use too much of, misuse, treat wrongly	P *I* F
	≠ to deceive, delude	F
an **abuse**	≠ a mistake, error	F Nl
abused	≠ quarrelsome	P
abusive	≠ unofficial, illegal	I
	≠ incorrect, contrary to usage, unlawful	F Nl
	≠ corrupt, unjust	E
	≠ extortionate (of prices)	P
an **academic**	≠ a professional (e.g. a lawyer)	D
(an) **academic (point)**	≠ (an) elegant/harmonious (point)	F
an **academic question**	≠ a question dealt with in an academy	E F D
an **access**	≠ an outburst, attack, fit	E I F
the **accessories**	≠ the minor parts in a play	F
	≠ the props for a play	E F

an **accident**	≠ a (medical) complication	F
	≠ a faint, swoon	E
	≠ an apoplectic fit	I
acclimatised	≠ air-conditioned	I F D
to **accommodate**	≠ to sit down, make oneself at home	E I F
	≠ to add sauce to, season	F
	≠ to settle a bill	I
	≠ to mend, put right, adapt, repair	E I
	≠ to fit, suit	E F
the **accommodation**	≠ the conversion, adaptation of s/o to s/th	F
the **accomplishment**	≠ the completion	F
to **accord**	≠ to wake up, rouse	P
	≠ to remember, recall	P E
	≠ to decide, resolve	E
	≠ to tune an instrument	E I F
	≠ to acknowledge, concede, admit	P
the **accord**	≠ the piece-work	D Dk N S
	≠ the chord (in music)	P I F Nl D Dk N S
	≠ the commercial agreement	D S
	≠ the tune, melody	I F
to **accost**	≠ to come alongside, attach	P
	≠ to go to bed	E
	≠ to approach (s/o)	I F
	≠ to board a ship	I F
an **account**	≠ a deposit (i.e. part payment)	F
an **account rendered**	≠ a review, discussion	F
accurate	≠ painstaking, demanding	P
to **accuse**	≠ to complain of	I
	≠ to show up, accentuate	F
	≠ to show, reveal, betray, denote	P E
	≠ to acknowledge (a letter)	P E I F
accused	≠ accentuated, noticeable, marked	P E F
an **ace**	≠ an axle, axis, spindle, shaft	Nl
	≠ a big guy	F
	≠ a wing, fin, handle	P E

the **ace**	≠ the ashes	Nl
to **achieve**	≠ to end, complete, finish off	F
the **achievement**	≠ the completion, conclusion	F
the **acquaintance**	≠ the familiarity, intimate link	F
to **acquit**	≠ to keep (a promise)	F
	≠ to satisfy one's conscience	F
	≠ to carry out/fulfil (a task)	F
an **acre**	≠ a field	Nl D
to **act**	≠ to be careful	*Dk* N S
an **act**	≠ a share in a business	Dk
in **the act**	≠ straightaway	E
the **acts**	≠ the documents, deeds, certificates	*P* E I F Nl D Dk N S
	≠ the nudes (in painting)	D Dk N S
	≠ the ceremonies	Dk N S
	≠ the intentions, purposes, designs	N
	≠ the records, transactions, minutes, proceedings	P E I F
an **action**	≠ a special offer (on sale)	I *D* Ch
	≠ a campaign, drive, plan	Nl D
	≠ a share in a business	P E I F *D*
the **actions**	≠ the events, activities, things going on	D
the **active and the passive**	≠ the assets and liabilities	P E I F Nl D Dk N S Tr
an **active citizen**	≠ a citizen with full political rights	I F
an **activist**	≠ a canvasser, voluntary helper	I
actual(ly)	≠ now, present-day, topical, up-to-date	P E I F Nl D Dk N S Tr
the **actualities**	≠ the news, current events/affairs	P E I F Nl Dk N S Tr
an **addict**	≠ a supporter	E
an **addition**	≠ a bill	F
to **address**	≠ to recommend, refer s/o to s/th	F
the **address**	≠ the skill, cleverness, cunning	F
adequate	≠ suitable, appropriate	P E I
an **adherent**	≠ a supporter	F
to **adjourn (a meeting)**	≠ to postpone (a meeting)	I F
	= /to bring up to date	I

to **adjudge**	≠ to knock down s/th at an auction	F
to **adjudicate**	≠ to knock down s/th at an auction	E I
	≠ to hand/take over (responsibilities)	P
the **adjudication**	≠ the tender (for contract)	F
	≠ the allocation of contract	F
	≠ the sale, knocking down by auction	E
the **adjunct**	≠ the secondary school teacher	N S
	≠ the (junior) university lecturer	Dk
the **adjustment**	≠ the settling, agreement (of accounts)	P E F
	≠ the garb, attire	F
the **(point of) admiration**	≠ the exclamation mark	P E
admired	≠ astonished	P E
to **adopt**	≠ to make use of	*P* I
to **advance**	≠ to project (of a building)	F
an **advance**	≠ a projection of a building	F
	≠ a profit margin, rate of profit	Dk
an **adventure**	≠ a fairy tale	Dk *N*
to **advertise**	≠ to warn, caution	E I F
	≠ to observe, instruct, advise, consider, admonish	P E *F*
	≠ to be on the alert, watch out	I
an **advertisement**	≠ a warning	P E I F
to **advise**	≠ to explain	P
	≠ to admonish	P E
	≠ to give heed to	P
	≠ to warn	P E F
	≠ to take notice	P E
	≠ to point out	E F
	≠ to instruct	E
	≠ to state, observe, perceive, look at	E
	≠ to remind	P
an **advocate**	≠ an egg-nog	Nl
	≠ a barrister	P E I F D N S
	≠ a lawyer	Nl S
an **aeon**	≠ a century	Gr

an **affair**	≠ a shop	S
to **affect**	≠ to be cut and sliced	I
the **affect**	≠ the emotion, passion	D Dk
an **affection**	≠ an illness, trouble, disease	E *I* F D
	≠ an affectation	Dk
the **affluence**	≠ the poll percentage	I
	≠ the influx, crowding of people	P E I F
	≠ the tributary	P *E*
	≠ the eloquence, fluency	E
	≠ the flowing, rush	E I F
	≠ the rush hour	F
affluent	≠ copious, flowing, abundant	P E I
to **affront**	≠ to confront, face, defy	P E I
	≠ to tire	P
	≠ to strike, attack	P I
	≠ to cheat, deceive	F
affronted	≠ out of breath	P
Afrikaans	≠ African(s)	Dk N S
an **Afrikaans**	≠ an African girl	Nl
after	≠ behind	*Nl* Dk *N* S
the **afternoon**	≠ the evening, night	Dk N S
the **afterthought**	≠ the meditation, reflection	Dk *N* S
an **agenda**	≠ a diary, pocket notebook, an engagement book	*P* E I F Nl Ch Gr
an **agent**	≠ a policeman	*E* F Nl
	≠ an employee	F
an **agglomer-ation**	≠ a built-up area	F
an **aggregate**	≠ a diplomatic attaché	E
	≠ a university assistant	E
	≠ a mechanism, device	Dk N
	≠ s/o living with a family	P
	≠ a member	I
an **agnostic**	≠ a stranger	Gr
agnostic	≠ foreign	Gr
agonising	≠ dying	P E I F
the **agony**	≠ the act of dying, death struggle	*P* E *I* F D Gr
to **agree**	≠ to approve/accept (an idea)	F
the **agreement**	≠ the charm, grace, pleasure	F
the **air(s)**	≠ the wind	Gr
	≠ the resemblance	F
an **aisle**	≠ a wing (of a bird)	F
	≠ a clove of garlic	*P* *I* F
an **alarm**	≠ a noise, din, uproar	Dk N S

an **alcove**	≠ a simple bedroom	P E
alias	≠ besides, moreover	P
	≠ otherwise	E
alienated	≠ insane	*P* E I F
all day	≠ every day	Nl D
to **allege**	≠ to plead; enclose; set on edge	I
	≠ to mitigate, ease, allay	F
allegro	≠ cheerful, bright, pleased, tipsy, merry	*P E* I
an **alley**	≠ an avenue	F Nl Dk N S Ch
	≠ a walk, drive, path	F
an **alliance**	≠ a wedding ring	P E F Tr
the **allure(s)**	≠ the gait, behaviour, rate, speed	F
	≠ the eccentric/conceited behaviour	D
	≠ the airs, ways	Nl D
an **almoner**	≠ a chaplain	F
the **alms**	≠ the souls	P E *I*
	≠ the alpine pastures	D
aloud	≠ time-honoured, ancient	Nl
also	≠ thus, so, consequently, therefore	Nl D Dk N S
to **alter**	≠ to grow, old, decline	D
	≠ to impair, falsify, distort, forge	I F
	≠ to get tense/worked up/ angry	P E I
the **alterations**	≠ the deterioration	F
	≠ the upset, change of character	P E
alternatively	≠ alternately	P E F
(an) **alto (voice)**	≠ (a) loud (voice)	P E I
alto	≠ important, high, excellent	P
to **amass**	≠ to crush, crumble	P E
an **amateur**	≠ s/o fond of something	F
an **ambassador**	→ a messenger	I
an **ambulance**	≠ an out-patients' department	D
	≠ a surgery	I
	≠ an imbalance	J
an **amendment**	≠ an improvement (esp. in farming)	F
the **amends**	≠ the fines, forfeits, penalties	F
an **amenity**	≠ a kindness (spoken)	F

amorous	≠ kindly, affectionate	E
an **amphitheatre**	≠ a university lecture room	P F Tr
	≠ a theatre dress circle	*P* E
Amphitryon	≠ a host(ess)	P E
ancient	≠ former	F
the **ancients**	≠ the former members	F
an **androgyne**	≠ a married couple	Gr
the **angel**	≠ the hinge, axis	D
	≠ the fishing tackle	D
	≠ the sting, hook	Nl
the **anger**	≠ the remorse, regret(s)	Dk N S
	≠ the (village) green, meadow, lawn	D
the **angina**	≠ the tonsillitis, throat inflammation	E I F D Tr
an **anniversary**	≠ a birthday	*P I* F
to **announce**	≠ to advertise in a newspaper	I D Dk N
	≠ to herald, foretell, prophesy	E I F
an **announce-(ment)**	≠ a (written) advertisement	P E I F Nl D Dk N S Tr
an **announcer**	≠ an advertiser	Dk S
to **annoy**	≠ to bore, be wearisome	*P* E *I* F
an **ant**	≠ a duck	Nl Ch
an **antenna**	→ an aerial	P E I F Nl D Dk N S Tr Gr
to **anticipate**	≠ to bring forward, come before	I
	≠ to pay in advance	P I *F*
	≠ to encroach (on s/o's rights)	F
in **anticipation**	≠ in good time, in advance	P E I
an **antiphon**	≠ a difference of opinion	Gr
anxious	≠ greedy, ambitious	E
apart	→ distinctive, attractive	NL D
	≠ private, independent, attractive	Nl
	≠ odd, eccentric	Dk N
an **apart(ment)**	≠ a room for renting	J
	≠ a hotel room with private W.C.	P
	≠ a (usual) flat (in BE)	
an **ape**	≠ a monkey	Nl *D Dk* N S
the **aperitives**	≠ the food eaten with aperitives	*P* E
the **aplomb**	≠ the uprightness	I F
	≠ the balance, equilibrium	F

the **Apocrypha**	≠ the mysteries	Gr
an **apology**	→ an apologia, defence, vindication	P E I F Nl
an **apostrophe**	≠ a reprimand, rebuke	E F
to **apostrophise**	≠ to detest, dislike	Gr
the **apparatus**	≠ the display, pomp, magnificence, array	P E I F
	≠ the decoration, furnishings, fittings	P E I F
	≠ the camera, electric razor	D
	≠ the contraption, gadget, appliance	D Dk
apparent	≠ clear, easily seen/understood	F
	≠ suitable, proper, fit	E
an **apparition**	≠ an appearance, coming into view	E F
	≠ a publication date for a book	P E
to **appeal**	≠ to summon, call by name	F
an **appeal**	≠ a parade, roll-call	I F Nl D Dk N
to **appear**	≠ to show off	P
to **appoint**	≠ to note down, point (to)	P E
	≠ to hint (at), indicate	P E
	≠ to sharpen	P I F
	≠ to pin up	I
	≠ to prompt (in the theatre)	E
	≠ to aim a gun	P E
the **appointments**	≠ the salary	F
appreciable	≠ valuable, noteworthy, esteemed	E
to **appreciate**	≠ to be fond of	E *I*
	≠ to estimate	F
to **apprehend**	≠ to dread, fear	F
	≠ to learn	P E I
to **appropriate**	≠ to fit, make appropriate	I F
to **be approved**	≠ to pass an exam	P E I
to **approximate**	≠ to move near (physically)	P *E* I
the **après-ski**	≠ the warm (fur) boots	E *I* F
	≠ the after-ski fashions, clothing	*I* F D S
	≠ the walk taken after skiing	Ch
apt	≠ fit, capable	P E F
an **aqueduct**	≠ a water main	P E I
	≠ a water works/company	I

an **arc, ark**	≠ a bow (curved shape)	P E I F
	≠ an arch(way)	P E I
	≠ a goal (in football)	P
	≠ a chest, coffer	P E
	≠ a tank, reservoir	E
an **archive**	→ a filing system (for office letters)	P E I *F* Nl D Dk N S Tr Gr
the **arena**	≠ the sand	E *I*
an **argument**	≠ a subject, topic, theme	P E I
	≠ a plea	Nl
	≠ a token, sign	P
	≠ a basis/reason offered in proof, or for an opinion	F D
	≠ a plot of a play	E F
to **arm**	≠ to assemble, put together, make	E I
	≠ to fit out, reinforce, rouse up, excite	F
the **Armada**	≠ the Army	E
	≠ the Fleet	P E
the **armament**	≠ the fitting out of a boat	F
the **armature(s)**	≠ the shipping magnates	*E* I Tr
	≠ the car instruments	D
	≠ the armament	Dk N
	≠ the lamp fitting	S
	≠ the mountings, fittings	Nl Dk N
	≠ the brace, reinforcement, framework	P F
	≠ the animal's teeth, claws	P
	≠ the key signature in music	*E* F
	≠ the suit of armour	P *E* I
an **aroma**	≠ a flavour	I F D
to **arrange a room**	≠ to decorate/do up a room	F
the **arras**	≠ the pledge, deposit, down-payment	E
to **arrest**	≠ to stop, hinder, censor	F
	≠ to delay, detain, hire (a room/servant)	I F
	≠ to fix a date	I
	≠ to confiscate	P
an **arrest**	≠ a guard-room/house	S
	≠ a decree, judgment	F
	≠ a prison, jail	Dk N
to **arrive**	≠ to happen	F Nl
	≠ to understand, grasp	I
	≠ to convalesce, get better	E

the **art**	≠ the type, sort, kind	Nl D Dk N *S*
	→ the skill, knack, workmanship	P E
	≠ the cunning, deceit, mischief	P E
the **art nouveau**	≠ the new art	F
an **artist**	→ a circus/theatre performer, actor/actress	P *F* D Dk S
arty	≠ polite, courteous	D Dk S
	≠ entertaining, amusing, interesting	Nl N
	≠ nice, pleasant, agreeable	Nl
the **asbestos**	≠ the (quick) lime	Gr
the **Ascension**	≠ the climb, ascent	P E I F
	≠ the promotion	P E
the **asp(s)**	≠ the inverted comma(s)	P
the **asparagus**	≠ the greenery ferns (with a bouquet)	F
the **aspersions**	→ the sprinkling(s)	P E
the **aspiration**	≠ the breathing in	P I F
to **aspire**	≠ to breathe in	P I F
	≠ to make an 'h' sound	I F
an **ass**	≠ an ace (in cards)	P E I F Nl D *Dk N S* Gr
	≠ a shaft	Nl
an **assault**	≠ a match, bout (in sport)	F
an **assent**	≠ a seat, foundation	P
	≠ an absentee	I
to **assent**	≠ to be on the scent/track of	F
to **assert**	≠ to hit on, find, guess correctly; achieve, be successful	P *E*
	≠ to hit the nail on the head	P *E*
an **assessor**	≠ a qualified teacher, etc., not yet appointed to a post	D
to **assimilate**	≠ to compare	F
to **assist**	≠ to be present, to attend	P E I F
the **assistance**	≠ the audience	P F
	≠ the board and meals	E
the **public assistance**	≠ the public ambulance service and first aid	P F
	≠ the state medical service	E
an **assistant**	≠ a batman, a charwoman	E
	≠ a midwife	P
the **assistants**	≠ the audience, those present	P E I F
the **assize(s)**	≠ the foundations, building course	F

	≠ the layer, stratum	F
	≠ the livery, uniform	I
assorted	≠ matched, paired, (well-) stocked	F
	≠ preoccupied, distrait	I
astute	≠ cunning, sly, crafty	E
an **asylum**	≠ an old people's home	P E I
the **Atheneum**	≠ the secondary school	Nl
an **athlete**	≠ a strong/robust man	*D* N S
an **atom**	≠ a person	Gr
to **attack**	≠ to attach, stick on	I
to **attain**	≠ to affect, wound, hit, catch s/o up	F
to **attend (to) s/o**	≠ to wait for s/o	F
	≠ to answer the phone/door	P
an **attic**	≠ a penthouse, top-floor flat	E *I* D
to **attire**	≠ to attract, entice	I F
	≠ to throw, shoot, aim	P
the **attitude**	≠ the aptitude	I
an **audience**	≠ a court (civil or military)	P E I F
an **auditor**	≠ a magistrate, judge	P E
	≠ a member of the audience	I *F*
	≠ a listener	P F
the **auditorium**	≠ the audience	P E I D Dk N S
the **auguries**	≠ the good wishes, best luck	I
an **author**	≠ a creator, maker, inventor	P E I F
the **average**	≠ the damage	Nl
to **avert**	≠ to warn, inform	I F
	≠ to advertise	Dk N
an **aviator**	≠ a provider	E
	≠ a (rubber) warehouse	P
an **avocado**	≠ an avocate	P E I
to **axe**	≠ to found/base the economy on	F
an **axe**	≠ an axis, axle	F D Dk N
	≠ an ear of corn	Dk N S
an **axle**	≠ an armpit	Nl
	≠ a shoulder	P D Dk N S

b

the **baby foot**	≠ the table football game	F
a **baby grand**	≠ a large infant/baby	*P* F
a **bachelor**	≠ s/o who has passed school leaving exams	F
a back	≠ a box, tin, trough, etc.	Nl
	≠ a cheek	D
	≠ a ship's forecastle	Dk N S
	≠ a hill, slope	N S
	≠ a tray	N
	≠ a joke	Nl
	≠ a backside	N S
	≠ a crate	S
	≠ a ferry boat	F
a **backbone**	≠ a hind leg	Dk N S
a **backside**	≠ a back, reverse side	NL Dk N S
a **bag**	≠ a ring	F
	≠ a behind, seat, bottom, backside	Dk
the **bagatelle**	≠ the trifle, small matter	P *E* I F Nl D Dk N S
	≠ the flirting	F
the **baggage**	≠ the rabble	D
	≠ the (stock of) knowledge	F
	≠ the trouble, difficulty	Ch
an **old baggage**	≠ an old suitcase	P E I F
the **bail**	≠ the lease (hold)	F
to **balance**	≠ to swing, hesitate	P E F
a **balance**	≠ a swing	P F
a **balcony**	≠ a shop counter, hotel reception desk	P
a **ball**	≠ a bullet	P E F
to **give s/o a ball**	≠ to tell/tick s/o off	Dk
a **ballad**	≠ a to-do, hullabaloo, row	Dk N
	≠ a stroll, saunter	F
a **balloon**	≠ a football	E F
	≠ a carboy, retort	D
to **ballot**	≠ to shake (about), rattle, swing to and fro	F
a **ballot**	≠ a bundle, pack(age); duffer	F
the **balsa**	≠ the pond; obstacle	E
	≠ the raft	P E
	≠ the ferry	P

to **ban**	≠ to banish	P F
a **ban**	≠ a (magical) spell	D
to **ban(d)**	≠ to swear	Dk N
a **band**	≠ a ban, excommunication	Dk *N*
	≠ a restraint	Nl S
	≠ a tyre	F Nl
	≠ a volume	D S
	≠ a magnetic tape	F Nl D Dk N S
	≠ a ship's side	E F
	≠ a proclamation	P E
	≠ a link, tie, bond	Nl Dk N S
	≠ a dog's lead	Dk N *S*
	≠ a shoe lace	*D* S
	≠ a sling for the arm	S
	≠ a trouser belt	J
	≠ a binding	Nl D
	≠ a piece of string	Dk
	≠ a ribbon	Nl D Dk S
a **bane**	≠ a railway track; ice rink; field/ground	Dk N S
	≠ a death	S
a **bank**	≠ a bench	P E I F Nl D Dk S
	≠ a knock, tap, beat, throb, thrashing	Dk N S
a **banquet**	≠ a stool	E
	≠ a side-table	P F
	≠ a counter, stall	I
	≠ a narrow path	F D
	≠ a stone window-ledge	F
	≠ a golf bunker; bench seat in a theatre	F
to **bar**	≠ to make a clean sweep of, sweep, brush	E
	≠ to smear with mud	P E
a **barb**	≠ a chin	E
	≠ a beard	P E I F
	≠ a bore (i.e. thing or person)	I
	≠ a villain in a play	E
the **barb**	≠ shut up!, let me alone!	F
the **barbarity**	≠ the lot/mass (of)	E
	≠ the nuisance, bore	P
barbarous	≠ awful, nasty, maddening	E
	≠ super, terrific	E
barbed	≠ shaved	Dk N
the **bark**	≠ the lightning	Ar
the **barmaid**	≠ the hostess; prostitute	F

the **barn**	≠ the child	Dk N S
the **barrack(s)**	≠ the hovel, hut, shed, shanty cabins	P E I F Nl D Dk N
	≠ the warehouse	E
	≠ the booth/stall at a fair	P E I F
	≠ the tent	P
	≠ the blessing	Ar
	≠ the small shop	Gr
	≠ the small shop on a farm	P
	≠ the temporary building	N Tr
a **barrage**	≠ a road block	F
	≠ a crossing of a cheque	F
	≠ a dam (across a valley)	F Tr
	≠ a limit (to actions etc.)	Ar
a **barrier**	≠ a quarter/part of a city	E
a **base**	≠ a (female) cousin	D
a **basin**	≠ a pond, pool (ornamental)	F Nl N
a **basis**	≠ a pedestal	Gr
	≠ a base	Nl Gr
the **basket**	≠ the basketball	F
	≠ the running/exercise shoes, sneakers	F
a **bassoon**	≠ a trombone	Dk N S
a **bastard**	≠ a hybrid, crossbreed, mongrel	Nl D Dk N S
a **bat**	≠ a dressing gown; simpleton	E
	≠ a smock; duster	P
	≠ a relief, benefit	Nl
the **bathos**	≠ the depth(s)	Gr
a **batman**	≠ a building-site worker	F
a **baton**	≠ a piece of chalk, stick, etc.	F
to **batter**	≠ to hit	P *E* I F
	≠ to flap (of wings)	P *E* I F
the **battery**	≠ the percussion, drums	P E I F Tr
	≠ the kitchen utensils	E I F
	≠ the heat (in athletics)	I
	≠ the footlights	E
	≠ the dance band	P
a **bazaar**	≠ a (cheap) toy shop	E
	≠ a market place	Tr
	≠ a mess, confusion	F
beach	See **beech**	
a **beam**	≠ a tree	D

a **bean**	≠ a bee	D
	≠ a bone	*Nl* Dk N S
a **beast**	≠ a silly ass, blockhead	P E I *F*
to **become**	≠ to obtain, receive	Nl D S
	≠ to suit, agree with s/o	Nl Dk N S
becoming	≠ worried, anxious, happy-go-lucky	Nl
the **bedding**	≠ the slipway	Dk N
to **bedeck**	→ to cover	Nl D Dk N
	≠ mask	Nl
a **bedstead**	≠ a cupboard-bed	Nl
a **beech, beach**	≠ a spade (for digging)	F
the **beef**	≠ the cutlet, fillet	E
	≠ the beefsteak	P Dk N S
a **beer**	≠ a whim	P
to **befall**	≠ to order, command	Dk N S
	≠ to please, suit; be confined	Nl
behalf	≠ except(ion)	Nl
to **behold**	≠ to keep	Nl Dk N S
beige	≠ natural, undyed, untreated	F
the **beige**	≠ the heap, pile	Ch
to **believe**	≠ to please	Nl *D*
a **bend**	≠ a band, group, gang; untidy heap	Nl
a **benefit**	≠ a profit, gain	*P* E I F
a **Bengali**	≠ a walking-stick, cane	P
the **benzine**	≠ the petrol	I F Nl D Dk N S Tr Gr Ar
	≠ the paraffin, the motorboat	Gr
a **benzine tank**	≠ a filling station	Dk
to **berate**	≠ to advise	D
	≠ to inform, relate	S
a **Berliner**	≠ a doughnut	*D* Ch
to **beseech**	≠ to visit	Nl D *Dk N S*
beset	≠ occupied	Nl D Dk N S
to **besiege**	≠ to conquer, defeat	D S
the **best man**	≠ the leading seaman	Dk
to **bet**	≠ to pray	D
	≠ to graze	S
	≠ to bathe, dab (the eyes)	Nl
a **bevel**	≠ an order	Nl
to **beware**	≠ to keep, preserve	Nl D Dk N S
a **bible**	≠ a book	Gr
to **bid(e)**	≠ to pray	Nl
	≠ to bite	Dk

a **bier**	≠ a beer	Nl D
a **bill**	≠ a taxi	N
	≠ a beetle	Dk N
	≠ a (motor) car	Dk N S
	≠ a buttock	Nl
a **billet**	≠ a ticket	P *E* I F Dk N S Tr Ch
	≠ a banknote	*P* E F Nl
	≠ a handbill, poster	Nl
a **billion** (in BE)	≠ a thousand million	P I F Nl Tr Ar
a **bind**	≠ a volume binding	Dk N
	≠ a book jacket	Dk N
	≠ a sling for the arm	Dk N
	≠ a bandage	Dk N S
to **bind up**	≠ to unbind	Dk N
a **biography**	≠ a cinema	Dk S
a **biscuit**	≠ a sponge cake	E
	≠ a cake mixture	D
	≠ a rusk	Nl
	≠ a small biscuit made with almonds	S
a **bit**	≠ a request, prayer	D
a **bitch**	≠ an insect, grub, worm; beast	P E
	≠ a hind, doe	F
bizarre	≠ gallant, smart, dashing, noble	P E
	≠ generous, splendid	E
	≠ tall and handsome, well-groomed	P
black	≠ drab, grey, faded	S
	≠ pale, pallid	*Dk N* S
a **blade**	≠ a leaf	Nl D S
to **blame oneself**	≠ to put one's foot in it, disgrace oneself	Dk N S
to **blame s/o**	≠ to shame	D
	≠ to disgrace, make s/o look a fool	Dk N
bland	≠ mixed, blended, miscellaneous	Dk N S
to **blandish**	≠ to brandish, wield	E
blank	≠ bright, shining, glossy	Nl D Dk N S
	≠ white	E F
	≠ broke, pennyless	Dk N
	≠ flooded, waterlogged	Nl
a **blanket**	≠ a form (to fill in)	Dk N S
	≠ a stew (of lamb or veal)	F

the **blast**	≠ the wind	Dk N
	≠ the fuss (made by s/o)	Dk
	≠ the top of a vegetable	S
to **blaze**	≠ to blow (of the wind)	Nl D Dk S
bleak	≠ pale	Nl *D* N S
to **blemish**	≠ to turn pale, faint	F
to **blend**	≠ to glare, dazzle, shade, blind	D S
	≠ to hoodwink	D
a **blend**	≠ a camera shutter; sham door, etc.	D
to **bless**	≠ to wound, injure, offend, hurt	F Nl *S*
blind	≠ sham, blank, fake, hidden	Nl D
a **blind passenger**	≠ a stowaway	Nl D Dk N
blinded	≠ encased, armoured, bomb-proof	F
the **blinds**	≠ the shutters	Nl
to **blink**	≠ to flash, glitter, twinkle	Nl D Dk N S
	≠ to wink	Dk N S
a **blinker**	≠ a decoy metal fish	D
the **blinkers**	≠ the trafficators, winkers	Dk N
a **blitz**	≠ a flash of lightning	D *S*
	≠ a flashlight bulb, etc.	Nl D Dk N *S*
a **block**	→ a writing pad	P E I *F* D Dk N S Tr Gr Ar
a **blockhouse**	≠ a conning tower	F
	≠ a log hut	Dk S
	≠ a signal box	Nl
	≠ a block of flats	N
to **blot**	≠ to hide away, nestle/ snuggle down	F
a **blouse**	≠ a smock, white coat	F
	≠ a sweater	Gr Ar
blue	≠ drunk	*F* D
	≠ boiled (of food)	D
	≠ poached (egg)	*F* NL D
a **blue**	≠ a novice, a first-year recruit	F
the **Blue Book**	≠ Who's Who	Dk
to **board**	≠ to embroider	P E
a **board**	≠ a table (any kind)	Dk N S
	≠ a plate (for meals)	Nl
	≠ an edge, rim, border, brim	P E I F D
	≠ a shore, river bank	P F
	≠ a dress hem	E F
	≠ a shirt collar	Nl

a **boat**	≠ a rumour; night club	P
	≠ a tin, can, container	E
a **bobbin**	≠ a(n electric) coil	P E I F Nl Tr
	≠ a spool of film	P I F Tr
	≠ a reel of tape	I Tr
	≠ a head, face (informal)	F
a **Boer**	≠ a jack/knave (in cards)	Nl
	≠ a smallhold farmer	Nl
a **bog**	≠ an arch, bow	Nl D S
	≠ a shoulder	N
	≠ a book	Dk
a **boil**	≠ a blister	P
	≠ a dent, bulge	D
a **boiler**	≠ a clothes hanger	Dk
to **bomb**	≠ to pump (water)	P E
	≠ to spy	P *E*
a **bomb**	≠ a pump	P E
	≠ a gas container	J
	≠ an exam failure	P
	≠ a lie, fib	I
	≠ a binge, spree	F
	≠ an aerosol spray	F
bombed	≠ curved, bulged, humped, convex	P F
a **bomber**	≠ a fireman	P E
	≠ a glassblower	F
	≠ a spy; plumber	P
a **bon viveur**	≠ s/o living it up/going the pace	F
a **bonanza**	≠ a time of fair calm weather (at sea) and of tranquillity	P *E*
a **bond**	≠ a peasant	Dk N S
	≠ a tram	P
	≠ a plug hole	F
	≠ a jump, leap, bounce	F
	≠ a (trade) union, league, federation, association	Nl
a **bone**	≠ a bean	Nl D Dk N S
a **bonnet**	≠ a cap, brimless for the head	P F
	≠ a mortar-board	E
	≠ a biretta	E
	≠ a bathing cap	F Tr
to **book**	≠ to swot	Dk
a **bookcase**	≠ a box for holding books or for displaying books	Dk
the **bookholder**	≠ the accountant, accounts	Nl *Dk* N S

a **boom**	≠ a tree	Nl
	≠ an owl	Ar
	≠ a student's party	F
a **boot**	≠ a boat	Nl D *S*
	≠ a fine, penance	Nl
	≠ a messenger	D
to **bore**	≠ to blot, stain, daub	P *E*
	≠ to erase	*P* E
to **boss**	≠ to swot, slave, work hard	F
the **boss**	≠ the chaff	N S
a **boss**	≠ a gimmick, s/th attractive	P
	≠ a knack	P F
	≠ a hump(ed back)	F
	≠ a forest, wood; bunch	Nl
	≠ a gun; a money box; a gay	Dk
the **bounty**	≠ the kindness, goodness	*P E I* F
a **bout**	≠ an end, scrap	F
	≠ a drumstick (of a chicken); soldering iron	Nl
to **bow**	≠ to build	Nl D
a **bow**	≠ a shower, squall	Nl
	≠ a building, construction	D
a **bower**	≠ a smallhold farmer	D
	≠ a (bird) cage	D
	≠ a (chess) pawn; jack (in cards)	D
a **bowl**	≠ a wine-cup, punch	Nl D
the **bowling**	≠ the bowling alley	P I F Dk N
the **box**	≠ the boxing	P F
a **box**	≠ a safe, strongroom	Dk N
	≠ a tin	D N
	≠ a covered parking place	F
	≠ a (motor-racing) pit	P
the **boxer**	≠ the trousers	Dk N *S*
a **boy**	≠ a buoy	*P* E I *Nl* D Dk N S
the **boy(s)**	≠ the cattle	P
the **brace**	≠ the arm	P *E* I *F*
	≠ the hot/live coals	E
	≠ the embers; flight of steps	I
	≠ the wing of a building	I
	≠ the crawl (swimming stroke)	F
	≠ the span of the arms	F
	≠ the fire(side); bonfire	S
	≠ the rubbish, trash, junk	Dk
the **bracket**	≠ the flies (in clothing)	E F
to **brag**	≠ to crash	Dk

to **branch**	≠ to plug in (electricity)	F
a **branch**	≠ a trade, line of business	Nl D Dk N S
a **brand**	≠ a(n unintended) fire	Nl D Dk N S
	≠ a folding/camp bed	I
the **branding**	≠ the surf	Nl D Dk N
the **brass**	≠ the brace (See **brace**)	D Dk
a **brasserie**	≠ a brewery	F
a **brassiere**	≠ a life jacket; baby's vest	F
brave	≠ good, well-behaved	F Nl D
	≠ clever	I
	≠ wild, fiery	P E
	≠ rude, uncivilised, rugged	E
	≠ excellent, luxurious	E
	≠ honest, upright, worthy	F Nl D Dk
the **bravura**	≠ the bravery	*P* E I *F*
the **breast**	≠ the chest, lungs	D
a **brew**	≠ a daughter-in-law	F
the **bribe**	≠ the truancy; rascal	E
the **bribes**	≠ the left-over pieces of cloth, fragments, remnants	F
	≠ the smattering	F
a **brick**	≠ a man/piece in a board game	Dk N S
	≠ a mat, doily	Dk N S
	≠ a disc; tray	S
	≠ a tin	J
	≠ a brig	F
	≠ a coffee jug	I
	≠ a kettle	Gr
a **bride**	≠ a fiancée	D
	≠ a flange; bridle, rein, ribbon, strap	F
a **brief**	≠ a letter (correspondence)	Nl D *Dk N S*
briefly	≠ shortly, soon	P
bright	≠ wide, broad	*Nl* D
to **bring**	≠ to take s/o or s/th somewhere	Nl D N S
a **briquet(te)**	≠ a cigarette lighter	F
	≠ an artificial stone slab	F
	≠ a brick	I
a **brochure**	≠ a paperback (edition)	Ch
the **bronze**	≠ the brass (in music)	E
	≠ the toughness, insensibility	P
the **brood**	≠ the bread	Nl *Dk N* S
	≠ the bride	Dk N S
the **brook(s)**	≠ the trousers	Nl
	≠ the bridge(s)	Nl D

to **browse,**		
bruise	≠ to rush; fizz, froth	Dk N
	≠ to roar (of water)	Dk N S
brutal	≠ super, fantastic, smashing	E
	≠ uncouth, stupid	E
	≠ impudent, insolent, rude	Nl
to **brutalise**	≠ to be rude to	Nl
	≠ to treat brutally, bully	P F
the **brute**	≠ the crude oil	E F
	≠ the total capital	P
a **buck**	≠ a belly	N S
	≠ a bow (bending forward)	Dk N
a **bucket**	≠ a bouquet	Nl D Dk N S
a **buckle**	≠ a shield; loop	F
	≠ a curl/lock of hair	F Tr
	≠ an earring	I *F*
	≠ a hump(back)	D
a **bud**	≠ a messenger; message	Dk N S
	≠ a bid, offer, tender	Dk N S
	≠ a commandment	*Dk* N S
	≠ an order, command	Dk N S
a **Buddha**	≠ a workshop	Ch
a **buffet**	→ a sideboard	F
a **bug**	≠ a belly	Dk
	≠ a bend; bow (bending forward)	D S
a **bugle**	≠ a coat hanger; stirrup, strap, hoop	D
to **build**	≠ to form, educate	D S
a **build**	≠ a picture	*Nl* D S
	≠ a statue	Nl
the **building**	≠ the form, shape, development, training, education	D S
	≠ the organisation (of s/th)	D
	≠ the building site	F
	≠ the block of flats	F
a **bull**	≠ a noise, row, disturbance	E
	≠ a mess; lot	Nl
a **bulldog**	≠ a tractor	D
a **bulletin**	≠ a school report	P F
	≠ a small written note	P
	≠ a theatre ticket	I
a **bungalow**	≠ a hovel	P
to **burst**	≠ to brush	*Nl* D Dk N S
a **bus**	≠ a box	Nl
the **buses**	≠ the buzzards	F

a **bust**	≠ an envelope	I
	≠ a corset	I
	≠ a bristle	N
a **butt**	≠ an aim, goal, intent	F
	≠ a knoll, mound	F
a **butterfly**	≠ a bowtie	*Nl* Dk
the **buttons**	≠ the pimples; buds; door-handles	F
by now	≠ almost	Nl
to **bypass**	≠ to pay extra/the difference	Nl
a **byword**	≠ an adverb	Nl Dk N

C

a **cab**	≠ a headland, cape	P E
a **cabal**	≠ a patience game (in BE), solitaire game (in AE)	Dk N
a **cabaret**	≠ a night club	E
	≠ an inn, tavern, a small smart restaurant	F
	≠ a cheap bar	Gr
	≠ a striptease (show)	
a **cabinet**	≠ an office, small room	F *Nl* D
	≠ a W.C., loo; surgery	F
a **cachet**	≠ a seal on a letter, postmark	F *Nl*
	≠ a tablet (medical)	F
a **cadaver**	≠ a carcass of an animal	D Dk N S
the **cadence**	≠ the pace, rate	P F
the **cadet**	≠ the youngest of the family	F
	≠ the caddie (in golf)	F
	≠ the smallest part of s/th	F
	≠ the soft bread roll	Nl
the **cadre**	≠ the board of a firm	F
	≠ the professional classes	F
	≠ the payroll, staff; team	Tr
the **café**	≠ the coffee	P E I F D Dk N S Tr Gr
	≠ the brown colour	Nl
to **cajole**	≠ to comfort, be kind to	F
a **cake**	≠ a fruit cake	F

the **cakes**	≠ the biscuit(s)	D *Dk N* S
to **calculate**	≠ to weigh up to see one's own interests	P E F
a **calendar**	≠ an appointments diary	D
callous	≠ bony, hard(ened)	D
	≠ fine, honest, kind, good	Gr
a **camel**	≠ a fool	*F* D
Camelot	≠ (a) pedlar, news vendor	F
	≠ rubbish, trash	I F
a **camera**	≠ a room	I Nl
	≠ an inner tube of a tyre	P E I
a **camera obscura**	≠ a (photographer's) dark room	I
to **camp**	≠ to stand out, excel; graze	E
	≠ to reconnoitre (military)	E
	≠ to make (a book character) convincing	F
	≠ to search for cattle	P
a **camp**	≠ a field, ground, pitch	P E I
	≠ a theme, subject, sphere	P E I
	≠ (the) countryside	P E
	≠ a side in a game	E F
	≠ a struggle, fight, strife	D Dk N S
	≠ a small square (e.g. of a village)	P *I*
	≠ a background of a painting	P E
	≠ a scope; opportunity	P E
	≠ a flat field; caterpillar; bend, curve, angle	Gr
	≠ a tombstone	P
Campari	≠ cheers!, bottoms up!	J
the **camping**	≠ the camping site	P E I F Nl Dk N J Gr
	≠ the caravan site	D
	≠ the sports team meeting	Tr
a **can**	≠ a jug	Nl D Dk S
	≠ a jail; policeman	E
	≠ a gun barrel	I
	≠ a mug, tankard, a tea/coffee pot	D N S
a **canal**	≠ a gutter, spout, drainpipe	E
	≠ a channel (water)	P E I *Nl* D N S Tr
	≠ a TV channel	P E I Nl Dk N S
	≠ a sewer	E *I* D
	≠ a narrow valley	E
	≠ a conduit	P E I F

the **canalisation**	≠ the sewerage system	P E F D Tr
	≠ the electric mains wiring	P E F
	≠ the water mains supply system	P F
	≠ the oil pipeline	P F
the **canasta**	≠ the basket, shopping bag	E
the **cancan**	≠ the gossip, talk	F
to **cancel**	≠ to rub/cross/scratch/wipe out, erase	P I
	≠ to efface from the memory	E
candid	≠ white	P E I
	≠ simple, gentle, sincere, innocent, naive, disarming, pure	P E I F
a **candidate**	≠ a teacher trainee	Dk S
	≠ a final-year university student (in some faculties)	D
	≠ a houseman, a partially qualified doctor	Dk N S
a **candle**	≠ a sparking plug	I *F*
the **candour**	≠ the innocence, naiveté, ingenuousness	P E *I* F
	≠ the whiteness	P E I
a **cane**	≠ a (female) duck	F
	≠ a sledge	Dk
a **canon**	≠ a barrel, nozzle of a rifle	F
	≠ a (small) glass	F
	≠ a tax, levy, toll	E
to **be a canon**	≠ to be good (at)	D
a **canopy**	≠ a settee, sofa	P E I F Nl D Dk N Gr Ar
the **cant**	≠ the lace	Nl D
	≠ the edge, border, margin	F Nl D Dk N S
	≠ the region	D
	≠ the way, direction	Nl
a **canteen**	≠ a cellar	I
the **canto**	≠ the song, singing	P E I Tr
	≠ the edge, rim, border, end, corner	P E
	≠ the stone, rock, pebble, boulder	E
	≠ the bread crust	E
a **cantor**	≠ an office	Nl *D*
a **canyon**	≠ a pipe, tube, shaft	E
	≠ a gun, cannon	E
	≠ a gun barrel	E
	≠ a chimney stack, flue	E

a **cap(e)**	≠ a cover, cloak, wrapper	P E
	≠ a boss, manager	I
	≠ a thatched roof	Nl
	≠ a private (TV) detective	J
	≠ a raincoat	J
a **capacity**	≠ an authority, expert	D
	≠ a first-rate/able person	Dk N S
	≠ a qualification (legal/ educational)	F
capricious	≠ painstaking; selfish	P
a **car**	≠ a fellow, chap	N S
	≠ a horse-drawn cart	P *E* Nl
	≠ an inter-town coach	F Nl
	≠ a front, surface, face	E
	≠ a large truck/lorry	I
	≠ a vessel, container, vat	Dk N
my **car(s)**	≠ (the) privately owned car(s)	J
the **carbon**	≠ the coal	P *E* I *F*
	≠ the charcoal (sketch)	P E
to **be carbon-ised**	≠ to be burnt to death (e.g. in an accident, house, etc.)	P *I* F
	≠ to be electrocuted	E
	≠ to be burnt down	E
a **card, cart**	≠ a charter; a thistle	P E I
	≠ a letter (correspondence)	P E
	≠ a map, chart	I F Nl D *Dk* N S
	≠ an agenda	N
	≠ a ticket	Nl D
	≠ a playing card	Nl J
a **card game**	≠ a pack of cards	Nl D Dk N
a **cardinal**	≠ a bruise	E
a **career**	≠ a street, avenue, road	E
	≠ a rapid advance in a profession	D
	≠ a (horse) race	P E
	≠ a racecourse	P E *F*
	≠ a ladder in stockings	E
the **careers**	≠ the studies for a degree	E
a **cargo**	≠ a duty, office, responsibility	P *E*
	≠ a post, position, job	P
	≠ a cargo ship	F
the **carillon**	≠ the quarter-hour chimes	F
the **carnation**	≠ the flesh tint/colour	P F
a **carousal**	≠ a carousel, (road) roundabout	P E I F D Dk N S

a **carpet**	≠ a folder, file, briefcase	E
	≠ a cloth to cover a table (e.g. for cards)	P E
	≠ a flatterer	P
	≠ a (gambling) casino	P
	≠ a floor rug/mat	P F
	≠ a blanket	Gr
a **carrot**	≠ a diamond (in cards)	D
	≠ a cherry	Ar
	≠ a casserole dish	S
to **cart**	≠ to play cards (See also **card**)	Nl
a **cartel**	≠ a school wall-chart	E
	≠ a poster hoarding	E
	≠ a group of student societies	D
	≠ a notch	Nl
	≠ a label	P
	≠ a hanging wall-clock	F
	≠ a government bond; lottery ticket; medical file; folder, writing pad, piece of manuscript paper; satchel	I
a **carter**	≠ a postman	P E
the **carto(o)n**	≠ the cardboard	P E I F Nl *D* Dk N S Tr
the **case**	≠ the buttonhole	P
	≠ the cheese	Nl D
	≠ the house, institution, etc.	P E I
	≠ the point (is that...)	P E
	≠ the way, means	I
	≠ the pigeon hole	F
	≠ the (last) resort	E
	≠ the cash/pay desk	P I *F* Nl D Dk N S
	≠ the hot/glass-house	Nl
	≠ the funds	Nl S
	≠ the firm, business	I
the **casement**	≠ the wedding, marriage	P E
	≠ the tenement house/building	I
the **cash**	≠ the cashmere pullover (See also **case**)	F
a **casino**	≠ a brothel	I
	≠ a social club	E
	≠ an officers' mess	P D
	≠ a night club	D Tr

	≠ a card game	Dk N S
a **cask**	≠ a husk, peel, rind, shell	P
	≠ a cap	S Gr
	≠ a (crash) helmet	E I F S
	≠ a setback	I
	≠ a skull; inner part of a city	E
	≠ a hull	P E Dk N
	≠ an animal's hoof	P E
a **casket**	≠ a peaked cap	P E F Dk Tr
	≠ a helmet, cap, wig	E
a **casserole**	≠ a saucepan	E I F
a **cassette**	≠ a cash box	Nl
	≠ a writing desk	Nl
	≠ a jewel box	Nl
a **cassock**	≠ a (man's) jacket	P
	≠ a dress coat; wedding	E
	≠ a jumper, sweater	Tr
	≠ a one-piece dress	I
a **cast**	≠ a cupboard, wardrobe	Nl D
to **cast up**	≠ to vomit	Dk N S
a **caste**	≠ a rank (e.g. in the army)	E
	≠ a type, sort, kind	P
a **caster, castor**	≠ a beaver (hat/skin)	P E I F
	≠ a sponge cake	J
casual	≠ fortuitous, accidental, unexpected	P E I F Nl
the **casuals**	≠ the incidental fees	F D
the **casualty**	≠ the chance event, coincidence	P E
	≠ the contingency	F
a **cat**	≠ a silly person/mistake	P
	≠ a hangover; a tied cottage	D
a **catalog(ue)**	≠ a menu, list	Gr
to **catch**	≠ to hide	F
	≠ to hunt	I
the **catch**	≠ the all-in wrestling	P E F D
(of) **category**	≠ (of) high rank/importance, good standing/distinction	P E
a **caterpillar**	≠ a caterpillar tractor	P E I F Tr *Gr*
(not) **catholic**	≠ (not) up to much	P E
a **catkin**	≠ a kitten	Nl
to **cause**	≠ to chat	F

a **caution**	≠ a pledge, security, guarantee	P E I F D Dk N
	≠ a bail	P E Dk N
	≠ a guarantor	F
	≠ a deposit on a bottle	F
	≠ a deposit on property	P
	≠ an escort	N S
a **Cavalier**	≠ a dancing partner	F
	≠ a (horse) rider	F
	≠ an escort	N S
a **cave**	≠ a cellar, vault underground	P *E* F
	≠ an arm hole	P
	≠ a ditch	P
	≠ a quarry, pit, mine, mould, hollow	I
	≠ a rope, cable	I
to **cavil**	≠ to puzzle, ponder (over), be absorbed (in)	E
	≠ to divide into lots	Nl
to **celebrate**	≠ to hold (a meeting)	E
	≠ to be delighted about	E
	→ to speak highly of, extol, praise	P E I F
the **celery**	≠ the celeriac	Nl D S
a **cell**	≠ a (phone) booth/kiosk	Nl D
the **cement(s)**	≠ the foundation(s) of a building; glue	E
a **censor**	≠ an external examiner	Dk *N* S
the **censure**	≠ the exam results sheet	D Dk N S
	≠ the censorship	F Nl D Dk N S
to **censure**	≠ to give marks	D Dk
a **centimetre**	≠ a tape measure	Nl Ch
to **certify**	≠ to register (a letter)	E
the **chair**	≠ the flesh, meat	F
	≠ the desk, rostrum, pulpit, throne	F
	≠ the steel for sharpening knives	P
a **chaise longue**	≠ a deckchair	*P* I F Tr Gr
the **chalk**	≠ the limestone	Nl D Dk N S
	≠ the mortar, plaster	Nl Dk S
	≠ the whitewash	Dk N
a **chamber**	≠ a bedroom	F
	≠ an inner tube of a tyre	F
	≠ a hoop	Tr

	≠ a military barracks	F
a **champ**	≠ a field	F
a **champion**	≠ a mushroom	P E Nl N S
the **chance**	≠ the luck, prospect, outlook, hazard	I F D Dk S Tr
a **chandelier**	≠ a (branched) candlestick	F
	≠ a candle maker	F
(the) **chandler**	≠ Candlemass	F
to **chant**	≠ to praise s/th; sing	F
	≠ to appeal, attract	F
to **make s/o chant**	≠ to blackmail s/o	F
the **chant**	≠ the singing	F
a **chap**	≠ a licence plate	P *E*
	≠ a disc, tally	E
	≠ a panel, board, sheet	P E
	≠ a bottle-top, a door-handle/lock	E
the **chap**	≠ the good sense, prudence	E
	≠ a band (musical)	S
a **chapel**	≠ any equipment used in the mass	F
	≠ a mortuary	Dk
	≠ an orchestra, small band	S
a **small chapel**	≠ a clique, coterie	F
a **chaplain**	≠ a curate	Dk N
the **character**	≠ the characteristic	E
	≠ the school marks	Dk N
	≠ willpower	S
character-ised	≠ competent, reliable, distinguished	E
	≠ made up for the stage	P
a **character-istic**	≠ a study/sketch of a character	D
	≠ a literary appreciation	S
character-istic	≠ quaint, special (of food)	P I F
a **charge**	≠ a parody, joke, trick, caricature	F
	≠ a load, cargo, freight	F Nl
	≠ a rank, situation, post, employment	F
	≠ a small part in a play	D

charged	≠ busy, occupied	F
	≠ loaded, filled, exaggerated (of a story)	F
a **chariot**	≠ a porter's four-wheeled trolley, wagon	F
	≠ an aircraft's undercarriage	F
	≠ a typewriter carriage	F
the **charisma**	≠ the good point, talent, gift	Gr
a **charlatan**	≠ a gossip, chatterbox	E I
a **charm**	≠ a hornbeam	F
a **chart**	≠ a charter	F
to **chase**	≠ to hunt, go shooting	F
the **chase**	≠ the hunt(ing)	F
a **chassis**	≠ a forcing frame for plants	F
	≠ a window frame	F
a **chat**	≠ a cat	F
a **chauffeur**	≠ a lorry driver	Ar
	≠ a driver of any vehicle	E F Nl S Tr
a **chef**	≠ a chief, boss	P F Nl D Dk N S
	≠ a heading	F
the **chenille**	≠ the (hairy) caterpillar	F
	≠ the caterpillar track	F
a **chevron**	≠ a rafter	F
chic	≠ generous, nice, decent	F
a **chick**	≠ a cigarette stub/end	I
the **chiffon**	≠ the scrap, rag, ribbon; duster	F
a **chiffon(n)ier**	≠ a rag and bone man	F
a **chimney**	≠ a hearth, open fire	E F Ch Tr
	≠ a funnel of a boat	F
	≠ a stove	F
a **chin**	≠ a cheek	Dk N S
the **chips**	≠ the potato crisps	F Nl D Dk N S J Tr Gr Ar
a **chock, choke**	≠ a shock	Dk N S
to **choke**	≠ to shock	Dk N S
the **cholera**	≠ the anger	P E I
a **chore**	≠ a choir, chorus; church chancel	D
a **chorus**	≠ a dance	Gr
Christ	≠ a Christian	D
to **christen**	≠ to christianise	Dk N S
Christendom	≠ Christianity, religious instruction	Dk N S
a **Christmas**	≠ a Christmas card	E
the **chrome**	≠ the colour; paint	Gr

the **cider**	≠ the soft fruit drink	J
a **cigar**	≠ a cigarette	P E Tr Gr
	≠ a cicada, locust	P E
a **cinch**	≠ a girdle, sash	P E
the **cinders**	≠ the heavy furnace-coke	Dk
the **circle**	≠ the out-of-school activities	J
to **circulate**	→ to move/pass along/on	E I F
the **circulation**	→ the traffic	P E I F
to **cite s/o**	≠ to make an appointment with s/o	E
a **citron**	≠ a lemon	I F Nl D Dk N S
the **city**	≠ the business section of a town	D
	≠ the inner core (e.g. walled part) of a town	F
	≠ the housing estate	F
civil	≠ refined, civilised	I
	≠ civilian clothes	D Dk N S
the **civility**	≠ the civilisation	I
clairvoyant	≠ shrewd, perspicacious	F
to **clamour**	≠ to fasten, clamp	D
	≠ to squeeze, pinch	S
	≠ to cling to, clutch	Dk N S
to **clamp on**	≠ to buttonhole, accost	Nl
	≠ to clomp, stamp	N S
the **clams**	≠ the brackets (in writing)	Dk *N S*
a **clang**	≠ a sound, ring, clink	D Dk N S
to **clap**	≠ to clatter, flap, rattle	D
	≠ to suit s/o well; succeed, go well	D
	≠ to smack the tongue	F
	≠ to beat, slap, throb	S
	≠ to gossip; to fold together sharply	Nl
a **clap**	≠ a flap, valve	D Dk N
	≠ a trap, hatch	D
	≠ a mouth; bed (both slang)	D
	≠ a pat	Dk N S
a **clapper**	≠ an index; cracker (firework)	Nl
the **clapper**	≠ the rubble, shingle (building)	S
	≠ the clatter, rattling	Dk S
a **class**	≠ a kind, sort, type	E
classic	≠ classical	P E I F Nl Dk N S J
classic books	≠ school books	F

the **clavier**	≠ the piano	Dk N S
	≠ the piano keyboard	F
	≠ the piano action	Tr
the **clay**	≠ the key (for a lock)	F
	≠ the clover (plant)	D
clean	≠ small	Nl *D* Ch
cleanly	≠ narrow-minded, mean	D
to **clear**	≠ to manage, cope	Nl Dk N S
clear	≠ ready, prepared	Nl
clever	≠ cunning, crafty	D
a **cliché**	≠ an illustration, plate	F
	≠ a printing block	P I F Nl D Dk N S Tr
	≠ a photo negative	E F Nl
	≠ a stencil skin	E I F D Tr
	≠ a master copy of a text (to be copied)	E F Ar
	≠ a rough description of s/th	F
to **click**	≠ to misfire (of a gun)	Dk N
a **click**	≠ a clique	F
	≠ a dab, blob	S
to **cling**	≠ to ring, sound	D Dk N S
a **clinker**	≠ a vowel	Nl
a **clip**	≠ a rock, cliff	Nl D Dk N S
a **cloak**	≠ a cesspool, sewer	*P* E I *F* D Dk N S
a **cloche**	≠ a bell; cheese cover	F
a **clock**	≠ a wise old man	N
	≠ a bell	Nl Dk N S
	≠ a blister	F
to **clock in**	≠ to put one's foot in it	Dk
to **clog**	≠ to clomp, stamp	Dk
a **cloister**	≠ a monastery, friary	*F* Nl D Dk N S
a **close**	≠ an enclosure; vineyard	F
	≠ a clod, lump; dumpling, meatball	D
close	≠ enclosed	F
a **closet**	≠ a W.C., loo	Nl D Dk N S
a **clover**	≠ a club (in cards)	Dk N S
a **clue**	≠ a nail	F
a **clump**	≠ a clog (shoe)	Nl
	≠ a lump (of matter)	D S
a **coach**	≠ a car	E
	≠ a nick, notch	F
the **coal**	≠ the carbon	D
	≠ the cabbage	E Nl D Dk N S
a **coal tit**	≠ a great tit	Nl D
the **coat**	≠ the coast	F

a **cobra**	≠ any type of snake	P
a **cock**	≠ an egg shell; ship's hull	F
	≠ a cook, chef	Nl Dk N S
a **cocktail**	≠ a cocktail party	P E I F Tr Gr
a **coda**	≠ a tail, queue, end, finish	I
	≠ an angle; elbow	E
	≠ a frost	P
a **coffer**	≠ a suitcase	F Nl D Dk *N* S
	≠ a car boot	E F
the **cognoscenti**	≠ the acquaintances	I
coherent	≠ consistent	P E I
a **coin**	≠ a corner, angle, nook	F
a **coincidence**	≠ a travel connection	I
cold	≠ hot, warm	I
a **collaborator**	→ a contributor (to a periodical)	P E I F
the **collage**	≠ the adherence, binding to	F
	≠ the TV miscellany programme	P
the **collar, collier**	≠ the necklace	P E F *Nl* Dk Tr Ch Gr
	≠ the bodice, jerkin	D
a **collation**	≠ a packed meal	F
	≠ a snack	E Nl
	≠ a stomach medicine	E
	≠ a job, position, place	*P* E
	≠ an investment	E
	≠ a granting of a degree	P
a **collect**	≠ a collection (of money), whip-round	P E I F D Dk N S Gr
	≠ a collar	I
a **collector**	≠ a conduit, drain	E
a **college**	≠ a colleague	*P* Nl D
	≠ a course of lectures	Nl D
	≠ a state school	P E F
	→ a boarding school	I
a **collocation**	≠ a job, position, post	P *E* I
	≠ a placing in a firm, or in an exam	P E
	≠ an investment	E *I*
	≠ a positioning of a building	E I
a **colon**	≠ a convoy of vehicles	D
	≠ a queue of cars	I Dk Ch
	≠ a colonist, settler	*E* F
	≠ a column (architecture)	I
	≠ a contract coffee-worker	P

(the) **colony**	≠ the (elegant) suburbs	E
	≠ Cologne/Köln	E I
a **colour**	≠ a type, sort, kind	I
	≠ a suit in cards	*I* F *Nl*
the **school colours**	≠ the atmosphere of a school	J
coloured	≠ soft pinky red	E
	≠ ruddy, reddish	P
a **coma**	≠ a comma	*P* E
	≠ a tuft, a mane	P
	≠ a pause, rest (esp. in music)	P
	≠ a miserichord	E
a **combination**	≠ an agreement	P
	→ an arrangement of things (e.g. flowers)	P
	→ a woman's underslip	P E F Tr
	≠ a cocktail, esp. gin and vermouth	E
	≠ a rail, connection	P E
	≠ a plan, project, scheme	P E F
	≠ a coincidence, chance, occurrence	P I
	≠ a flying suit	D
	≠ a means of transport	E
	≠ an overall, dungarees	F
to **combine**	≠ to (manage to) do s/th	I
	≠ to think out, scheme, devise	F D
	≠ to arrange, fix up	P I
to **come out**	≠ to make do with, manage	*Nl* D
a **comedian**	≠ an actor/actress, player	E I F
a **comedy**	≠ a play (of any type)	E I *F*
	≠ a fuss, to-do	F Nl
the **comic**	→ the quality of being comical/humorous	D Dk N S
comic(al)	≠ strange, odd	D
	≠ theatrical, dramatic	E
a **comma**	≠ a (political) party, faction	Gr
	≠ a paragraph or a section in law	I
a **commando**	≠ a small detachment of soldiers	F D
	≠ a duffel coat	E
	≠ a (military) command	P E I Nl D Dk N S
a **commentary**	≠ a comment, remark	P E Nl D Dk
a **commissariat**	≠ a bus conductor	Ar

the **com-mission(s)**	≠ the shopping	F Ch
a **commission-aire**	≠ a selling/commission agent	*E I* F Dk N
a **commode**	≠ a comfort, convenience, opportunity	I
	→ a chest of drawers	P E F Nl D Dk N *S*
the **commodity**	≠ the comfort, ease, convenience	P I F
	≠ the profit, advantage	E
	≠ the facilities, amenities	E I F
	≠ the W.C., loo	F
the **commotion**	≠ the excitement	I F
	≠ the concussion, shock	P E I F D
	≠ the riot	P
	≠ the feeling	E
communal	≠ municipal, local	D Dk N S
the **commune**	≠ the parish	F
	≠ the municipality	I Dk N S
a **companion**	≠ a partner in business	Nl D Dk N S
	≠ a (communist) comrade	I
	≠ a booze-up	J
a **compartment**	≠ a room	P
	≠ a department, office of a firm	I
to **compass**	≠ to weigh up, consider, measure	F
the **compass**	≠ the time, beat, tempo, measure in music	P E F
compassed	≠ measured, precise, formal, dignified, not showing feelings	P E I F
a **compendium**	≠ a textbook	P
	≠ an abstract, summary, abridgment	E
a **compere**	≠ a godfather, accomplice, comrade	F
	≠ an old crony	I
the **competence**	≠ the competition	P E
	→ the area, province, line of country	F Nl D
competent	≠ authorised, official	*I* F D
the **complacency**	≠ the delight, satisfaction	E *I*
	≠ the desire to please	P *I* F
complacent	≠ obliging, desiring to please, accommodating, indulgent	P E I F

	complete	≠ full up, sold out, all places sold	P E I F
a	**complex**	→ collection, group	D
a	**complexion**	≠ a temperament, disposition, build, constitution	P E I F
		≠ a combination, complex	P
to	**compliment**	≠ to fulfil, execute	E
to	**compliment s/o**	≠ to greet s/o, shake hands	P
to	**compose**	≠ to fix, adjust, arrange	P E
		≠ to mend, repair	E *I*
a	**composition**	≠ a school test/exam	F
a	**compositor**	≠ a composer	P E I F S
the	**compost**	≠ the stewed fruit	I Tr
		≠ the fruit salad	Gr
to	**comprehend**	≠ to include, consist of	*P* E I F
	comprehen-sive	≠ understanding, sympathetic	P E I F
a	**compromise**	≠ a promise, undertaking, agreement	P E
		≠ an appointment, date	P E
to	**compromise oneself**	≠ to commit oneself, promise, undertake	P E I *F* Nl
	compromised	≠ engaged, as a fiancé(e)	E
		≠ ashamed	P
to	**commute**	→ to (exchange)	P E I
a	**comrade**	≠ a dormitory, barrack room	I
		≠ a colleague	D
		≠ a (fascist) companion	I
a	**con**	≠ an idiot; vagina (both slang)	F
a	**concept**	≠ a rough copy, draft	D Dk N S
the	**concepts**	≠ the mental equilibrium, (keep/lose one's head/'cool')	Dk N S
a	**concert**	≠ a concerto	P E I F D Dk N S J
		≠ a road repair/mending	P
a	**concession**	≠ a TV or radio licence	D
a	**concordance**	≠ a grammatical agreement	P I *F*
the	**concourse**	≠ the competitive exam, contest	P E I F Nl
		≠ the bankruptcy	I D Dk N S
		≠ the crowd, throng	*P* E F
		≠ the help, cooperation, collaboration	*P* E F
		≠ the coincidence	F

to **concrete**	≠ to summarise, finalise, fix up	E
	≠ to fulfil, carry out	I
concretely	≠ in short, precisely	E
to **concur**	≠ to compete	Nl D Dk N S
	≠ to gather together	E
concurred	≠ crowded	E
the **concurrence**	≠ the rivalry, competition	P I F Nl D Dk N S
	≠ the throng, crowd	E
the **concussion**	≠ the extortion	E F
	≠ the (public) graft	F
	≠ the embezzlement	I F
to **condescend**	≠ to submit, be obliging	P E
condescending	≠ helpful, obliging, submissive	P E *I*
the **condition**	≠ the origin, extraction	P E
	≠ the nature, temperament	E
the **conditions**	≠ the ability, working order	P E
	≠ the qualifications	E I
the **conduct**	≠ the funeral cortège	D
	≠ the electrical conductor	D
a **conductor**	≠ an electric lead	E
	≠ a driver (of any vehicle)	E F
	≠ a leader, guide	E *F*
the **conduit**	≠ the presence of mind	Dk
	≠ the management, judgment, wisdom	N
	≠ the behaviour, conduct	F
	≠ the military record of a soldier	Nl
the **cone**	≠ the personal contacts, connections	J
a **confabulation**	≠ a plot, conspiracy	E
the **confection**	≠ the assembling, putting together	E
	≠ the making, drawing up, preparation	F
	≠ the make, manufacture	I
	≠ the ready-made suit	E I F
	≠ the ready-made clothing	P Nl Dk N S Tr Ch
	≠ the ready-made clothes shop	P
	≠ the dressmaking	E
the **confectioner**	≠ the outfitter, clothier	F D
	≠ the mixer of any ingredients	P

to **confer**	≠ to compare, collate, tally	P F
a **conference**	≠ a lecture	P E F Nl Tr
	≠ a phone call; interview	E
the **confetti**	≠ the pills, sweets, sugared almonds	I J
confident	≠ trusty, trustworthy	*P* E
a **confinement**	≠ a restriction, limitation	E
a **conflagration**	≠ a war	E
	≠ a wild, disorderly mob	P
to **conform**	≠ to agree (about)	E
conformed	≠ formed, shaped	F
(it) **conforms**	≠ (it) depends	P
to **confound**	≠ to merge, mix up, blend, get blurred	P E I F
	≠ to lose	E
to **be confused**	→ to be embarrassed	P E F
	≠ to be brought together, amalgamated	I
the **confusion**	≠ the embarrassment	P F
to **congeal**	≠ to freeze up	P E I *F*
the **congestion**	≠ the bad digestion	P
	→ the traffic jam	I
the **conglomerate**	≠ the building complex	P
	≠ the conglomeration	F
	≠ the hardboard	P
to **conjugate**	≠ to blend, combine	E
a **conjugation**	≠ a union, juxtaposition	P
the **conjunctive**	≠ the subjunctive	I Nl D Dk N S
to **conjure**	≠ to speculate, conjecture	P
	≠ to blend	P
	≠ to conspire, plot	E F
	≠ to entreat, implore	E F
a **conjuror**	≠ a conspirator	*P E* I F
the **consent**	≠ the electric plug/socket	J
consented	≠ spoilt (of a child)	E
the **consequence**	≠ the consistency, agreement	Nl D Dk N S
consequent	≠ consistent	*E I* Nl D Dk N S
	≠ important	F
conserved	≠ (well-) preserved, looked after	P *E* I F Nl
the **conserves**	≠ the tinned food	*P E F* D Dk N S Tr
	≠ the dark glasses	F
to **consign**	≠ to state, put down, record	E

the **consistency**	≠ the stock/cash in hand	I
	≠ the firmness, steadiness, stability	P E I F
consistent	≠ firm, compact, solid, dense, stiff	P E I F D
	≠ firm-bodied (wine)	Nl
a **consolation prize**	≠ a booby prize	P E I F
the **consorts**	→ the partners, associates, accomplices	P E I F Nl D Dk
conspicuous	≠ eminent, famous	E
	≠ distinguished, prominent	P *E*
a **constellation**	≠ a juxtaposition of events	D
to **be constipated**	≠ to have a cold	P E *I*
the **constipation**	≠ the blocked nose	P E I
a **constituent**	≠ a constituent assembly	I
a **constructor**	≠ a designer, designing engineer	Nl D N S
	≠ a film director	Dk
to **construe**	≠ to construct	P E I F Nl D Dk N S
the **consummation**	≠ the refreshments/drink consumed	P E I F N
the **consumption**	≠ the refreshments/drinks consumed	*Nl*
	≠ the catering	Nl
the **contact(s)**	≠ the contact lenses	J
	≠ the electric switch, wall-socket, etc.	Nl Dk N S
to **contend**	≠ to contain, hold in check	P E I F
the **contention**	≠ the holding back	E
to **contest**	≠ to answer	*P* E
	≠ to agree, confirm	P
a **contest**	≠ a context	I
a **contingent**	≠ a quota	P I F D *S* Tr
	≠ a subscription	Dk N
	≠ a year's call-up of recruits	E
a **continuo**	≠ a continuum	E I
	≠ an office boy, messenger	P
a **contour**	≠ an office	Dk N S
a **contour line**	≠ an outline, silhouette	*P* F D Dk N S
to **contract**	≠ to acquire (customs)	P *E* F
	≠ to negotiate, bargain	I

to **contrast**	≠	to discourage, put (s/o) off	I
a **contra-vention**	≠	a traffic/parking ticket	I F
a **contretemps**	→	a delay, mishap; inconvenience	P E I F
	≠	a syncopated beat/note	E I F
the **contributions**	≠	the taxes, rates	P E I F
to **control**	≠	to check	P *E* I F Nl D Dk N S Tr Gr
to **convene**	≠	to agree	E F
	≠	to suit, be convenient	E I F Nl
	≠	to be profitable, advantageous, advisable	I F
a **convenience**	≠	an expediency	P E *F* D
the **conveniences**	≠	the propriety, decorum, social conventions	P E I *F* D Dk N S
convenient	≠	fitting, desirable, expedient, useful, advisable, appropriate	P E I
	≠	profitable, advantageous	P E I
	≠	cheap	I
a **convent**	≠	an assembly, a convention	D Dk N S
	≠	a monastery	P E I
	≠	a priest's house	E
the **converse**	≠	the conversation	P *E*
	≠	the lay brother/sister	I *F*
a **convict**	≠	a monastery, Catholic hostel	D
	≠	a boarding school; banquet	I
a **convoy**	≠	a train, funeral procession; a loaded vehicle	F
to **cook**	≠	to boil (water)	*P* E Nl D *Dk* N S
a **cook**	≠	a gingerbread	Nl
the **cooling**	≠	the breeze, wind	Dk N *S*
coordinates	≠	name, address, and particulars	F
the **cop**	≠	the pantry; cupboard	P
	≠	the heart (in cards)	P E
	≠	the snowflake	E
	≠	the rolled oats	E
	≠	the cup	Nl Dk N S J
	≠	the headline	Nl
the **copper**	≠	the brass (in an orchestra)	E
the **cops**	≠	the glasses (for drinking)	P E
a **coquette**	≠	a sleeping berth	Gr
a **cord**	≠	a rope	P I F Nl
	≠	an electric flex	E J

a **cordon**	≠ a shoelace	P E
	≠ a flex, string	E
a **cordon bleu**	≠ an outstanding/skilled person	F
the **corn**	≠ the barley	S
	≠ the seed, kernel; rifle sight	D S
	≠ the horn	P E I F D Tr
a **cornet**	≠ a pennant	I
	≠ a bugle(r)	P E *I*
	≠ a car hooter	P *F* D Gr
the **corona**	≠ the crown, garland, wreath; tonsure	P E
a **coroner**	≠ a colonel	P
a **corporation**	≠ a student society	D
a **corps**	≠ a (living) body	P E I F D S
	≠ a corpse	F
	≠ a type of student society	Nl D
the **corps**	≠ the strength, substance, matter, etc.	F
	≠ the brass band	Nl N S
corpulent	≠ burly	E
the **correction**	≠ the manner, breeding, behaviour	E
	≠ the reproof, telling-off	*P* E I F Nl
a **corrector**	≠ a proofreader	Nl D
to **correspond**	≠ to be fitting for, belong to, concern	E
	≠ to pay, remit (in commerce)	I
the **correspondence**	≠ the travel connection	E F
	≠ the response	E
	≠ the newspaper reporter's article	D
a **correspondent**	≠ s/o on the other end of the phone	F
a **corridor**	≠ a runner, racer	P E I
	≠ an agent, broker	E
	≠ a racehorse	I
a **corsage**	≠ a woman's blouse	F
	≠ a corset	E
a **cosh**	≠ a thigh	P
cosmic	≠ sociable	Gr
the **cosmos**	≠ the world	Gr

the **cost**	≠ the food, fare, board	Nl D Dk N
a **cost**	≠ a coast	P E I *Nl*
	≠ a hillside	P I
	≠ a brush, broom	Dk N
to **cost**	≠ to try out, taste	D
costly	≠ delicious	Nl D
	≠ beautiful	Nl D
	≠ delightful	Nl D Dk *N*
	≠ very amusing	D Dk *N* S
the **costs**	≠ the back (of anything)	P
a **costume**	≠ a man's suit	P I Nl D S
	≠ a custom, habit	P *E*
a **cot**	≠ a shed	Nl D
the **cot**	≠ the dung, filth	D
	≠ the vertebra	S
the **cotton**	≠ the cotton wool	I F
	≠ the shirt, vest	E
to **couch**	≠ to go to bed; put s/o to bed	F
a **couch**	≠ a layer, coating, stratum, covering	F
	≠ a cake filling	F
	≠ a coat of paint	F
a **council**	≠ a piece of advice	P E I F
the **countability**	≠ the accounts office; bookkeeping	P E I *F*
the **countenance**	≠ the capacity, content	F
to **counterfeit**	≠ to produce a likeness, depict	D
a **counterfeit**	≠ a (human) face	Dk
a **country**	≠ an area, region	F
a **coupé**	≠ a railway compartment	Nl Dk N S Ch
	≠ a ship's gangway	F
a **couple**	≠ a dome, cupola	Nl D
	≠ a dog's lead	S
a **coupling**	≠ a (car) clutch	Nl D Dk *N* S
the **courage**	≠ the anger, temper	E
	≠ the act of colouring or bleaching	P
the **courier**	≠ the post, mail	*I* F
a **courier**	≠ a circular (letter)	F
	≠ a runner	F
the **course**	≠ the rate of exchange	Nl D *Dk* N S Tr
	≠ the circulation of currency	D
a **course**	≠ a disc; lozenge	Tr
	≠ a race (in sports, etc.)	E I F
	≠ a trip, journey	F

	≠ a price, commercially quoted	F Dk N S
	≠ a cross	Dk N S
	≠ a taxi	Gr
to **do some courses**	≠ to do some shopping/ errands	F
a **court**	≠ a card	Dk N S
a **courtier**	≠ a share broker	F
the **courting**	≠ the discount, reduction offered	Nl
a **cove**	≠ a grave, pit	P
to **cover**	≠ to collect one's wages	E
	≠ to charge (money)	E
a **covert**	≠ an envelope, cover	Dk N S
	≠ a place set at a table	F Nl Dk N S
	≠ a cover(ing), shelter	F
the **cow**	≠ the cold (weather)	Nl
a **cox**	≠ a thigh	P
a **crab**	≠ a prawn	D
the **crabs**	≠ the crayfish; cancer	D
a **crack**	≠ a crack sportsman	P F
	≠ a failure, bankruptcy, crash, crack-up	E Nl Dk N
the **craft**	≠ the strength, power (i.e. electricity)	Nl D Dk N S
crafty	≠ powerful, strong, hefty, energetic	Nl D Dk N S
a **crag**	≠ a collar	D
to **cram**	≠ to crush, crumple	Dk
	≠ to fumble, rummage	D
	≠ to hug	S
a **crammer**	≠ a hawker, pedlar	Nl Dk
	≠ a haberdasher	D
	≠ a tradesman, retailer, shopkeeper	D Dk *N S*
a **cramp**	≠ a convulsion, fit	Dk N S
a **crampon**	≠ a bore	F
a **crane**	≠ a skull	*P E I* F
	≠ a (water) tap	Nl S
cranky	≠ ill	D
	≠ morbid	S
crass	≠ blatant	D
	≠ pungent, acrid, intransigent, radical, extreme	Dk
	≠ vigorous	Nl

a **cravat**	≠ a tie	I F D *S* Tr
to **crave**	≠ to claim, demand as a right	Dk N S
the **cream**	≠ the shoe polish	*D* Dk
	≠ the custard	D Dk
	≠ the fruit pudding	S
the **creation**	≠ the breeding (of cattle, etc.)	P E
the **creator**	≠ the (cattle) breeder	P E
the **creatures**	≠ the livestock, cattle	Dk N S
a **crèche**	≠ a Christmas crib	F
the **credence**	≠ the sideboard	I F D
to **buy on credit**	≠ to buy on hire-purchase	F
a **real credit**	≠ a mortgage	P
the **crème de la crème**	≠ the also-rans	F
the **crêpe**	≠ the pancake	F
a **crick**	≠ a car jack	Nl D
the **crime**	≠ the murder, manslaughter	P E
crippled	≠ lame	Nl N S
a **crisis**	≠ an attack, fit	P I F D
	≠ a breakdown (mental)	E
crisp	≠ puckered, wrinkled, clenched, twitching	P E F
a **critic**	≠ a criticism, write-up, review	P E I *F* Nl D Dk N S
a **crochet**	≠ a hook; sharp turn	F
a **crock**	≠ a crutch (for walking); a doorhandle	Nl
	≠ a car crash	S
	≠ a corner, nook	*Dk* N S
	≠ a hook	*Dk* N S
the **crock**	≠ the croquet	S
the **crocket**	≠ the croquet	P F Nl D Dk N
a **crone**	≠ a crown	Nl D Dk N *S*
a **crop**	≠ a body	Dk N S
a **crotchet**	≠ a quaver	F
the **crowd**	≠ the herb	Nl
crucial	≠ cross-shaped, formed like a cross	P
crude	≠ raw (of food)	*P* E I *F*
the **crudities**	≠ the raw vegetables/fruit	F
	≠ the indigestible food(s)	F
to **cruise**	≠ to cross, traverse	Nl
a **cruise**	≠ a cross	Nl
the **crumb(s)**	≠ the chaff	Dk
crummy	≠ crooked, curved, twisted	*Nl* D Dk N
a **crusade**	≠ a crossword	P

the **crystal**	≠ the glass (material)	E
the **crystals**	≠ the window-panes	E *I*
a **cube**	≠ a wheel hub	P E
	≠ a mill pond	P E
	≠ a cask, barrel, tub, bucket	P E
	≠ a bastion, fortress, tower	P E
a **cuckoo**	≠ a second cousin	Ch
a **cue**	See **queue**	
the **cuisine**	≠ the kitchen	F
a **cult**	≠ a (church) service	P E F
the **culture**	≠ the manners	E
cunning	≠ cheating (in exams)	J
a **cup**	≠ a glass (tumbler)	P E J Tr
	≠ a quota, share	E
	≠ a heart (in cards)	E Tr
	≠ a scoop in the newspaper	Dk N
	≠ a good hand in cards	Dk N S
	≠ a coup d'état	Dk N S
	≠ a summit, knoll, mound of s/th	*Nl* D
	≠ a head	Nl
a **curate**	≠ a vicar	F
a **curator**	≠ a probate lawyer	Dk
	≠ a student counsellor	N S
to **curb**	≠ to bend down, stoop, kowtow	F
to **cure**	≠ to dress a wound	P E I F
	≠ to treat s/o (medically)	E I
	≠ to recover from an illness	P E
	≠ to take care of (s/o)	P I
	≠ to revise/edit a book	I
	≠ to remedy a wrong	E
	≠ to pick one's nails/teeth; trim a tree	F
	≠ to dredge a river, clean out a drain	F
	≠ to slide	Dk
	≠ to sit and brood	N S
the **cure**	≠ the treatment, care	I F N
	≠ the priest	E *F*
	≠ the vicarage	F
	≠ the whim, tantrum	Nl
cured	≠ treated/by a doctor	I
the **current**	≠ the electorate	D
	≠ the newspaper	Nl
	≠ the (iron) chain	P

current	≠ usual, routine, ordinary, everyday	P E I F
	≠ cursive (of handwriting)	D
	≠ saleable, marketable	Dk N S
currently	≠ fluently (of speech)	P E I F
a **curse**	≠ a course, path, career, running race	P E Nl
	≠ a year of students	E
	≠ a choice	Nl
	≠ a rate of exchange	Nl Dk N S
curt	≠ short, brief	P E I F Nl *D* Dk N S
a **cushion**	≠ a pillow	P E Nl *Ch*
	≠ a mattress	P
a **cylinder**	≠ a top hat	I D S
a **cynic**	≠ a selfish/unprincipled/ egocentric person	E I
cynical	≠ hypocritical, casual	E
	≠ shameless, brazen	P E F
	≠ unprincipled	E I
	≠ ironic, untrustworthy, impudent, audacious	P
the **cynicism**	≠ the effrontery, barefaced hypocrisy	E
	≠ the shamelessness	F
	≠ the indecency, obscenity	P F
a **cyst**	≠ a bladder	Gr

d

a **dado**	≠ a die/dice	P E I
	≠ a (screw) nut, lock-nut	I
	≠ a datum; proviso	P
a **dale**	≠ a part (of s/th)	Nl Dk *N* S
	≠ a thrashing floor	Nl
a **dam**	≠ a pond	Dk N S
	≠ a puddle	N
	≠ a dyke, embankment	Nl D
	≠ a queen (in cards)	P D Dk N S
	≠ a flat roof	Tr
	≠ a king (in draughts)	E I Nl
	≠ a queen (in chess)	P E
	≠ a lady	F Nl D Dk N S
	≠ a lady dancing partner	I F Nl D Dk N S

the **dam**	≠ the game of draughts	E I *Nl* D Dk N S
	≠ the dust	S
the **damage**	≠ the beating down of (snow)	F
the **damask**	≠ the apricot	P E
a **dame**	See **dam**	
a **damp**	≠ to chat(ter), gossip	Ch
the **damp**	≠ the smoke, fume(s), vapour, steam	Nl D Dk N
a **damper**	≠ a steamship	D Dk N
	≠ a dancing partner	J
the **dance**	≠ the dancing	F
the **dancing**	≠ the dance hall	P F Nl D Tr
dapper	≠ brave, valiant, gallant	Nl
the **data**	≠ the date	P
a **date**	≠ a tip, information, advice	E
a **datum**	≠ a date	Nl D *Dk* N S
a **daub**	≠ a stew	F
a **deal**	See **dale**	
the **debit**	≠ the sale of goods	D
	≠ the flow (of a river)	F
	≠ the strength, intensity, output	F
	≠ the delivery (of speech), utterance	F
	≠ the duty (financial)	I
	≠ a retail shop	F
to **debit**	≠ to retail goods	F
	≠ to utter, recite, spout	F
a **debutante**	≠ a beginner (in a general way)	F
a **decade**	≠ a period of 10 days	I F
	≠ a set of 10 things	P E F
the **decadence**	≠ the decay, decline, deterioration	*P* E I F
decadent	≠ decaying, declining, deteriorating	*P* E I F
the **decani**	≠ the deans (of cathedrals)	I
to **deceive**	≠ to disappoint, let down	P *E* F
decent	→ quiet, unobtrusive, plain (of clothes, manners, music, etc.)	D
a **deception**	≠ a disappointment, let-down	P E F Nl
a **deck**	≠ a ceiling	D
	≠ a blanket	Nl D
	≠ a tyre	Dk N S
to **decorate**	≠ to learn s/th by heart	P

the **decoration**	≠ the (theatrical) scenery, décor, setting	E Nl D Dk *N* S
	≠ the window-dressing	D Dk S
a **decorator**	≠ a window-dresser	D Dk N S
to **dedicate oneself to s/th**	≠ to concern/apply oneself to s/th	P
a **deer**	≠ an animal	Nl Dk N *S*
defended	≠ forbidden, prohibited	F
the **defiance**	≠ the mistrust, suspicion	F
defiant	≠ mistrustful, wary, suspicious	F
to **defile**	≠ to file off (in pairs), make off, clear out	F
	≠ to march past	Nl Dk S
a **defile**	≠ a procession, march-past, parade	F S Ch
a **definition**	≠ a clue in a crossword	*P* F
	≠ a commercial settlement	I
deformed	≠ uneven, bumpy (of a road)	F
to **defraud**	≠ to let s/o down, dash s/o's hopes	E
to **defray**	≠ to divert (a conversation) skilfully	F
deft	≠ correct, proper	Nl D
	≠ capable, strong, sound	D
	≠ dignified, stately, grave	Nl
the **degradation**	≠ the decline, wear and tear, weathering, eroding	F
	≠ the demotion	P E I
the **degree**	≠ the stair, step	F
dejected	≠ warped, lopsided, buckled	F
the **dejection**	≠ the evacuation of the bowels	P E F
	≠ the volcanic debris	E
to **delay**	≠ to dilute, stir in, water down; spin out, pad out, waffle (on)	F
a **delay**	≠ a time limit, notice (given); respite; extension of time	F
delicate	≠ polite, courteous	P
	≠ refined, tactful, fussy (about food)	F
	→ critical, arguable	F
	≠ delicious, exquisite (of food)	Dk N S
a **delicatessen**	≠ a delicacy (to eat)	Nl D Dk N S

delicious	≠ charming	F
a **delight**	≠ a crime	E I
	≠ a minor offence	F
a **habitual delinquent**	≠ a (hardened) criminal	E I
to **delude**	≠ to disappoint	I
a **delusion**	≠ a disappointment	I
the **dema(gogue)**	≠ the false rumour, propaganda	J
to **demand**	≠ to ask, request, want, inquire, invite	*I* F
a **demand**	≠ a question	I
to **demean oneself**	≠ to struggle, fling oneself about, bestir oneself	F
demented	≠ contradicted, denied, disclaimed	F *Nl* D Dk N S
the **dementia**	≠ the denial	F Nl *D* Dk N *S*
a **democracy**	≠ a republic	Gr
to **demur**	≠ to tarry, delay	P *E I* F
	≠ to live, stay	F
a **demur**	≠ an abode, dwelling	*I* F
a **denomination**	≠ a name, designation, title	P E I F
to **denote**	→ to show (emotions on the face)	P *E* F
the **denouement**	≠ the outcome, result, upshot	F
to **denounce**	≠ to indicate, reveal, denote (emotions on the face)	*P* E *I* F
a **dentist**	≠ an unqualified dentist	D
to **depart**	≠ to chat	E
the **depart(ed)**	≠ the department store	J
a **department**	≠ a compartment (e.g. in a train)	E
	≠ a flat, apartment	E
a **dependant**	≠ a shop assistant	E
the **dependence**	≠ the outbuilding, annexe	P E I F
	≠ the personnel, employees	E
	≠ a (subsidiary) branch (office)	P E
to **deploy**	≠ to display, unfold	F
to **depose**	≠ to leave/drop s/th with s/o	F
	≠ to drop s/o off by car	F
	≠ to leave off, lay down, abandon	P I
	≠ to testify under oath	P I

the **deposit**	≠ the fuel tank	*P* E
the **deposition**	≠ the faeces, stool	E
	→ the testimony, evidence	P E I
a **depot**	≠ a deposit on a bottle	F
	≠ a prison	F
a **deputy**	≠ an MP (in BE)	P E I F
to **derange**	≠ to bother, disturb, trouble	F Nl
deranged	≠ down at heel	Dk
to **deride**	≠ to unwrinkle; cheer up	F
a **derivation**	≠ a detour, digression, diversion	*I* F
to **derive**	≠ to divert (a stream)	F
	≠ to drift (of a boat)	E F
derogatory	≠ derogating/repealing of a law	E
to **descend**	≠ to stay (at a hotel)	F
	≠ to derive from	P
	≠ to take/get/bring down (luggage)	P E F
a **descent**	≠ a bath/bed rug/mat	F
to **descry**	≠ to disbelieve	P E
desert *adj*	≠ deserted, abandoned, empty	P E I F
to **deserve**	≠ to serve (of transport or a restaurant)	F
	≠ to clear away	F
	≠ to be harmful to	F
to **design**	≠ to designate	P E I F
a **design**	≠ a drawing	P E I F J
a **desk**	≠ a table laid for dinner	I
desolate	≠ very sorry	P E I F
a **despot**	≠ a bishop	Gr
the **destination**	≠ the purpose of a building	F
the **destiny**	≠ the destination	P E
	≠ the post, job (esp. military)	E
destitute	≠ dismissed, deposed	P E I
the **destitution**	≠ the dismissal from office	P E I F
a **detail**	≠ a gesture/token of appreciation	E
detail	≠ retail	E *I* F Nl D Dk N S
to **detain**	≠ to possess, keep	*E* I F
the **detention**	≠ the holding in possession	I F
to **deter**	→ to detain, stop, check, restrain	P
	≠ to dig up, unearth, bring to light	F
determined	≠ fixed (of associations)	P E
	≠ given (of time)	P E

the **determined case**	≠ the particular/given case	P E *F*
the **detritus**	≠ the refuse, rubbish	F
a **deviation**	≠ a detour	I F
	≠ a swerve	I F
	≠ a bypass	I
a **device**	≠ a foreign currency	P E I F *Nl* D Dk Tr
	≠ a ship's name	F
	≠ a spoken order	*D* Ch
	≠ a uniform	I
	≠ a coat of arms	E I
	≠ a (hair) parting	I
	≠ an estimate for work to be done	F
to **devise**	≠ to distinguish, make out	P E
	≠ to chat, gossip	F
the **devolution**	≠ the refund, repayment	P E
	≠ the drawback	E
to **devolve**	≠ to return s/th, hand/give back, refund	P E
devout	≠ submissive, humble	D
a **diabolo**	≠ a devil	I
the **diacritic**	≠ the discretion, discernment	Gr
diagonally	≠ cursorily, superficially	D
a **diagram**	≠ a timetable, schedule (esp. for trains)	J
a **diapason**	≠ a tuning fork	P E I F
the **diapason**	≠ the range of a voice (in singing)	I F
	≠ the music pitch	F
a **diary**	≠ a daily expense, wage, allowance	P E
	≠ a newspaper	E
	≠ a (child's) autograph book	I
the **Diaspora**	≠ the religious minority (in any community)	*Nl* D
a **diatribe**	≠ a (written) thesis	Gr
	≠ an office, function, responsibility, position	Gr
to **dictate**	≠ to read out aloud	E
a **dictate**	≠ a dictation	*P E* D
to **differ**	≠ to defer, put off	P E I F
difficult	≠ unlikely (to happen)	E I
dilapidated	≠ misappropriated, squandered, wasted	P E I F
a **dilettante**	≠ an amateur	P I Dk N S

a **diplomat**	≠ a graduate, anyone with a diploma	I
direct	→ straight	*P E* I
	→ straightaway, directly	Nl D Dk N S
a **directive**	≠ a director, executive	E
a **director**	≠ a (school) headmaster	P E I F Nl D
a **disagreement**	≠ an unpleasant occurrence, source of annoyance	F
to **disarm**	≠ to exhaust (s/o)	I
	≠ to dismantle	P E
a **disaster**	≠ an accident	P
disastrous	≠ clumsy, awkward	P
a **disc**	≠ a phone dial	*P E I* F
	≠ a shop counter	Dk N S
	≠ a pay/cash desk	Dk
the **disc**	≠ the dish; washing up	Dk S
to **discharge**	≠ to relieve/ease (a weight)	*P E* F
a **disciple**	≠ a school pupil	P E
the **discipline**	≠ the self-discipline	D Nl
	→ a subject studied, branch of instruction	P E I F
a **disco**	≠ a disc, gramophone record	P E I *F*
the **discount**	≠ the national bank rate	Dk N S
to **discourage**	≠ to lose courage	P
	≠ to irritate, annoy	E
a **discourse**	→ a speech, conversation, talk	P E I F
to **discover**	≠ to uncover, expose, lay bare	*P E* F
discreet	≠ average, middling, not bad	*E* I
discreetly	≠ reasonably, tolerably	*E* I
at **discretion**	≠ to one's heart's content	F
a **discussion**	≠ an argument	*P* E I
a **diseuse**	≠ a fortune teller	F
a **disgrace**	≠ a misfortune, calamity	P E I F
disgraced, disgraceful	≠ unlucky, wretched, accursed, unpleasant, ugly, graceless, gauche	P E F
the **disgust**	≠ the dislike, disappointment, sorrow, grief	P *I F*
	≠ the trouble, sorrow, dissatisfaction, quarrel, shock, annoyance, upset	E
to **disgust**	≠ to enjoy (the flavour of)	F
	≠ to annoy, upset	P E
disgusted	≠ squeamish, fussy	F
dishonest	≠ improper, immodest, shameless, unseemly	E F

to **dislocate**	≠ to visit, go to	P
	≠ to remove, shift	P
	≠ to slip (of soil)	P
	≠ to dismember (a state)	F
dislocated	≠ ungainly, loosely built	F
	≠ disjointed (of speech)	F
	≠ not integrated (in a group)	P
the **dislocation**	≠ the being swept away by floods, etc.	P
	≠ the landslide; fault (in rocks)	E
to **dismay**	≠ to faint, swoon	P E
the **dismay**	≠ the faint, swoon	P E
to **dismount**	≠ to dismantle, knock down, take to bits	P E *F*
to **dispatch**	≠ to hurry	*P* E *F*
	≠ to deal with, attend to	P E
	≠ to issue (tickets)	P E
	≠ to settle/complete (affairs/business)	P E
a **dispatch**	≠ a study, office; village shop	E
a **dispensary**	≠ an outpatients' department	F
	≠ a consulting room	E
	≠ a butler, a caterer	E
the **dispensation**	≠ the sharing out (of favours)	F
	≠ the dispensing (medically)	F
the **dispersion**	≠ the (commercial) distribution	F
to **dispense**	≠ to excuse, release from, exempt from	P E I F D
to **displace**	≠ to shift, alter (train times)	F
	≠ to move	E
displaced	≠ awkward, out-of-place, uncalled for	E F D
a **displacement**	≠ a distance, journey	E F
	≠ a removal; transfer of employment	F
to **dispose of**	≠ to have available	P E I F
the **dispositions**	≠ the preparations, steps, measures	*P* E I F D
	≠ the arrangements, plans	*P* E I F D
a **dispute**	≠ an academic discussion/debate/disputation	*F* Nl *D* Dk N
to **disrobe**	≠ to steal	F
to **disrobe oneself**	≠ to steal/slip away	F

distinct	≠ distinguished, eminent, outstanding	P
	≠ different	E
	≠ refined	I
a **distinct post**	≠ a reserved seat	I
the **distortions**	≠ the troubles, things going wrong	P
to **distract**	≠ to break a contract/ agreement	P
	≠ to relax, amuse, entertain	E
distracted	≠ casual, absent-minded, inattentive	P E I F Nl
	≠ entertaining, amusing	E
a **distraction**	≠ a slip, blunder, oversight	E
	≠ an embezzlement, misappropriation	E I F
	→ an entertainment, amusement	P E I F Dk N S
the **distress**	≠ the dexterity	P E *I*
a **dive**	≠ a muse	P
	≠ a star (in entertainment)	I
	≠ a prima donna	E Nl D Dk N S
the **diversion**	→ the amusement, entertainment	P E
to **divert**	→ to amuse	P E I F
diverted	≠ laughable, jolly, merry	P E
	→ amused	P I F
to **divide**	≠ to share (a room)	I F
a **division**	≠ a foreign currency	Nl
to **divulge**	≠ to make (s/th) known, broadcast	*P* E I
to **do up**	≠ to get, acquire	Nl
the **dock**	≠ the medical examination	J
a **dog**	≠ a bulldog, mastiff	E F Nl Dk N
	≠ a Great Dane	D
	≠ a bobby (policeman)	J
a **domain**	≠ a stretch of crown/government-owned land	Nl D S
a **dome**	≠ a cathedral	I *Nl* D N *S*
the **dome**	≠ the Doom	Dk N S
to **domineer**	≠ to dominate	Dk N S
a **don**	≠ a gift, present	F
to **doodle**	≠ to play the bagpipes	Nl D
the **Doom**	≠ the judgment, verdict	Dk N S
	≠ the curse	Nl
a **door**	≠ a doorway	Dk N S
a **dormer**	≠ a sleepy person, sleeper	F

a **dormitory**	≠ a bedroom	P E
the **dormitory**	≠ the bedroom furniture	P
a **dose**	≠ a box	Nl D Dk N S
a **dot**	≠ a dowry	*P E I* F
	≠ a darling	Nl
to **double**	≠ to overtake another vehicle	F
	≠ to line a dress; understudy a part	F
	≠ to repeat a year at school	F Nl
	≠ to dub a film	E F
a **double**	≠ an understudy, stand-in	*F* D
	≠ a duplicate (copy)	F Nl Dk
double	≠ downright, regular, absolute	F
a **double-decker**	≠ a biplane	*Nl* D Dk N
doubled	≠ gold-plated	Nl D N
	≠ failed in an exam	Nl
a **dove**	≠ a moat, ditch	F
	≠ a deaf person	Nl
the **Downs**	≠ the dunes	Nl
to **doze**	≠ to dose	Nl
to **drag**	≠ to carry, wear, bear	Nl
	≠ to go, move, set out	Dk N *S*
	≠ to go out looking for girls	F
	≠ to dredge a harbour	F
a **drag**	≠ a kite (to fly)	Dk
	≠ a (cold) draught; facial feature; stroke	N S
a **dragon**	≠ a dragoon	P I E F Dk N S Gr
a **drake**	≠ a dragon	Nl *D* S
	≠ a kite (to fly)	*D* N S
dramatic	≠ ending unhappily	P E I F *Nl*
to **draw up**	≠ to educate, bring up	Dk N
to **dress**	≠ to bring up (a child)	F D Dk
	≠ to train (an animal)	F Nl D N S
	≠ to set (a table)	F
	≠ to summarise (a report)	F
to **dress oneself**	≠ to stand up straight	F
the **dress**	≠ the special clothing (e.g. for sports)	D
the **drift**	≠ the angry passion	Nl
	≠ the instinct, impulse, inclination	Dk N S
	≠ the running, management	Dk N S

to **drill s/o**	≠ to tease, vex s/o	Dk
	≠ to trill, warble	S
to **drive**	≠ to drift	Nl Dk N S
	≠ to float on water	Nl Dk N
	≠ to stroll, saunter	Dk N
	≠ to operate, manage, run, carry on	Nl Dk N S
a **drive**	≠ a pile, heap, snowdrift	S
to **drone**	≠ to bang, crash, roar	Dk N
	≠ to vegetate, drowse, idle	
to **dry**	≠ to turn, wind (round)	Nl
a **dry**	≠ a Martini	F
a **duenna**	≠ an owner, mistress, proprietress	E
dumb	→ stupid, silly	Nl D Dk N S
to **dump**	≠ to fail (an exam)	Dk N
	≠ to tumble, flop down	Dk N
a **dune**	≠ an eiderdown	Dk N
a **dungeon**	≠ a castle keep	F
to **dupe s/o**	≠ to make a good impression on s/o	Dk N
the **Durex**	≠ the Sellotape	P
the **dusk**	≠ the tuft of hair	Dk N
	≠ the tuft of grass	Dk
	≠ the tassel	N
dusky	≠ drizzly	*N* S
the **Dutch**	≠ the German(s)	*Nl* D
the **duvet**	≠ the (feather) down	F
	the fleece-lined jacket	I
to **dwell**	≠ to wander, err	Nl
a **dwelling**	≠ an error	Nl

e

eager	≠ bitter, tart, shrill (of a sound), raw (of wind)	F
an **eagle**	≠ an owl	Dk *N*
	≠ a hedgehog	Nl D
	≠ a leech	Dk N S

the **earl**	≠ the beer, ale	Dk N S
an **easel**	≠ a donkey	Nl D Dk N
an **easy person**	≠ a well-to-do person	F
an **éclair**	≠ flash of lightning	F
the **economies**	≠ the savings, money put by	F
to **economise**	≠ to save money, put money by	P E I F
to **edify**	≠ to make up, invent (stories)	P
	≠ to enlighten, instruct	F
	≠ to erect, build up	F
to **edit**	≠ to publish	P E I F
an **editor**	≠ a publisher	P E I F *Nl*
an **editorial**	≠ a publishing house	P E
to **educate**	≠ to bring up	P E I F
well-educated	≠ polite, well brought up	P E I F
badly educated	≠ rude, impolite, badly brought up	P E I F
the **education**	≠ the upbringing, breeding, good manners	P E I F
effective	≠ real, actual, in power	P E I F D
	≠ efficient, efficacious	Dk N S
effectively	≠ really, in fact, actually	P E I F
the **effects**	≠ the stocks and shares, securities	Nl D
an **egg**	≠ a harrow	Nl D
egregious	≠ distinguished, honoured, worthy	E
to **elaborate**	≠ to perfect, develop; organise	P
	≠ to work out details	E I F
the **elaboration**	≠ the compilation, putting together	P
	≠ the finishing off, completion	E F
the **elastic**	≠ the elastic band	P I F Nl Dk *N*
	≠ the car tyre	Gr
	≠ the spring mattress	I
the **elders**	≠ the parents	*Nl* D
elders	≠ elsewhere	Nl
to **elect**	≠ to choose (in a general way)	P E *I* F
the **election**	≠ the choice, preference, option	P E *I* F
elementary	≠ elemental, basic	D *N* S
the **elements**	≠ the (pieces of) evidence	F
	≠ the battery	Dk

an **embargo**	≠ a sequestration	E
	≠ a hindrance, impediment, disturbance	P *F*
the **embarkation**	≠ the craft, vessel	P E I F
to **embarrass**	→ to hinder, obstruct	P F
embarrassed	≠ pregnant	E
	≠ tangled, muddled	P
embarrassing	≠ cumbersome, inconvenient	P E F
an **emission**	≠ a broadcast	P E F
	≠ an issue of shares/tickets	Nl D Dk N S
to **emit**	≠ to broadcast	P E F
an **emotion**	≠ an excitement, thrill	E I F Nl
	≠ a bother, concern, anxiety	F
the **emphasis**	≠ the bombast, grandilo-quence	I F
emphatic	≠ bombastic, grandiloquent, elaborate	*E* I F D
the **emporium**	≠ the church choir loft	D
	≠ commence, trade	Gr
the **enamel**	≠ the patent leather	J
the **encaustic**	≠ the wax floor-polish	F
to **encounter**	≠ to find (in a general way)	P E
encrusted	≠ die-hard, in a rut, stick-in-the-mud	F
energetic	≠ forthright (of a person)	E D
	≠ drastic (of a remedy)	E I F
	≠ resolute (of a decision)	E
	≠ decided, having willpower	D S
the **energy**	≠ the willpower, verve, determination	D S
to **enervate**	≠ to madden, annoy	F
enfolding	≠ easy (of work)	Nl
	≠ stupid, dull, limited (of mentality)	Dk N *S*
to **engage**	≠ to pledge, pawn, involve, entangle, commit	F D S
engaged	≠ enthusiastic	F
	≠ committed (to an action, etc.)	F D Dk N S
the **engagement**	→ the agreement, promise, liability, commitment	F D *Dk* N S
the **English steak**	≠ the rare steak	D Dk
to **engrave**	≠ to dig in	Nl
to **enliven**	≠ to take in, annex (e.g. territory)	Nl
to **entail**	≠ to cut a slot/notch; gash	E F
	≠ to engrave, carve	P E

an **enterprise**	≠ a building firm	F Nl
to **entertain**	≠ to delay, detain	E
	≠ to maintain, support, keep up	P E F Nl
	≠ to talk to s/o about s/th	F
entertained	≠ amusing	E
the **entourage**	≠ the surroundings, setting, environment	F
the **entrances and exits**	≠ the credits and debits	I
an **entrée**	≠ a way in; entrance hall	F Nl Dk N S Tr Ch
	≠ an entrance fee	F Dk N S Tr
	≠ s/o's first appearance	Dk S
an **entrepreneur**	≠ a contractor, manager	F Dk N
	≠ an undertaker	S
an **envoy**	≠ a sending-off (ceremony)	F
to **envy**	≠ to send	P E
the **ephemera**	≠ the newspaper	Gr
episodic	≠ occasional	F
	≠ argumentative	Gr
an **epithet**	≠ an adjective	Gr
an **epoch**	≠ a season; age; time, stage	P E I F
equal	≠ smooth, even	Nl Dk
	≠ (the) same	P E Nl
	≠ level, steady, uniform	P E *I* F
equally	≠ as well, too	P E *I* F
	≠ '(the) same to you'	E
to **equip**	≠ to man a boat	I F
the **equipment**	≠ the fitting out	F
to **equivocate**	≠ to be wrong	P E
ersatz	≠ spare, replacement	D
especial(ly)	≠ special(ly)	P E
the **essence**	≠ the petrol (in BE), gas(oline) (in AE)	F
	→ the toilet water	I F Tr
the **estate**	≠ the summer	I
	→ the state, condition	F
	≠ the list, report	F
to **esteem**	≠ to consider, assess, estimate, appraise	F
	≠ to be glad	P
the **etiquette**	≠ the label	P E I F Nl D Dk N S Tr Gr
	≠ the trademark	P
to **evade**	≠ to escape	F
evangelical	≠ Protestant	D
an **evangelist**	≠ a Protestant	P

an **evasion**	≠ an escape, flight	P E I F
even	≠ flat, level	D
	≠ just (*verb*) a moment, equally, as much as	Nl
	≠ just (+ *present perfect tense*)	Nl
the **event**	≠ the issue, outcome	I
	≠ the open air, air-hole	F
eventual	≠ occasional, temporary, possible	E I F Nl D Dk N S
the **eventual work**	≠ the casual labour	E
eventually	≠ possibly, if needed	E I F Nl D Dk N S
	≠ by chance, fortuitously	P E
the **evidence**	≠ the clarity, obviousness	D
evidently	≠ of course, naturally	F
	≠ obviously	P E F
to **evince**	≠ to evict, turn (s/o) out, oust	F
	≠ to recover possession (legally) of	I
evolved	≠ sophisticated, refined, civilised	F
	≠ holding advanced views	I
to **exaggerate**	≠ to overdo, overrate, go too far	F
exaggerated	≠ excessive, absurd, wild (of speed, etc.)	P E I F
to **exalt**	≠ to become irritated	P
	≠ to excite, work up, enthuse	P E I F
	≠ to be enhanced by	P E
exalted	≠ hot-headed, quixotic	P E I F S
	≠ impassioned (of a way of speech)	P E I F
	≠ heated (of discussion)	P E S
	≠ highly-strung, (over) excited	D Dk N S
an **example**	≠ a copy, specimen	Nl *D*
exceeded	≠ exasperated, tired out	F
to **excite**	≠ to upset	P E
an **exceptional child**	≠ a handicapped child	P
an **excuse**	≠ an apology	E I F Nl
to **excuse oneself from doing s/th**	≠ to apologise for having done s/th	I F Nl

excused	≠ superfluous	E
exempt	≠ free from (an illness)	*E* I F
to **exercise**	→ to drill (soldiers)	F Nl D Dk N S
an **exercise**	≠ a military drill	Nl Dk N S
the **exercise**	≠ the premises, establishment (e.g. café)	I
	≠ the financial year	F
the **existence**	≠ the livelihood, income	D
	≠ the human being	D
an **exit**	≠ a success	P E
an **exodus**	→ an exit	Gr
to **exonerate**	≠ to dismiss from a post/job	P I
the **expedient**	≠ the opening hours (of premises)	P
	≠ the legal proceedings; red tape	E
	≠ the (contents of a) file/dossier	E
	≠ the shop assistant	Dk *N*
	≠ the dispatch clerk	D
expedient	≠ resourceful	P
to **expedite**	≠ to serve in a shop	Dk N S
	≠ to issue (documents), draw up	E F
	≠ to dismiss from work	F
	≠ to get (s/th) out of the way, get rid of	F
an **expedition**	≠ an office; counter	*D* Dk N S
	≠ an undertaking, enterprise	I
	≠ a dispatch department	D S
	≠ an office of a newspaper	D
the **expedition**	≠ the forwarding/shipping (of goods)	Nl
an **experience**	≠ an experiment	P F
to **experiment**	≠ to feel (an emotion), undergo	*P* E I F
	≠ to try on (clothes), try out	P E I F
experimented	≠ experienced	P E I F
	≠ tested	P
an **expert**	≠ a valuer	F Nl
expert	≠ alert, smart, nimble, sharp, crafty	P
the **expertise**	≠ the expert's report, investigation, assessment; surveyor's certificate	F Nl D

the **expiration**	≠ the breathing out, exhalation	I F
to **expire**	≠ to breathe out, exhale	I F
to **exploit**	≠ to function, operate, serve	F
	≠ to explode	E
an **exploit**	≠ a writ, summons	F Nl
to **explore**	≠ to exploit, ransack	P
an **exposition** (in BE)	→ an exhibition	P E I F Nl S
the **exposition**	≠ the aspect/orientation of a building	I F
	≠ the exposure of film	I
	≠ the lying in state	F
an **express**	≠ a black coffee, espresso	F
	≠ an express letter	I F Tr
	≠ a (swift) boat/ship	Tr
	≠ a stopping train	E
the **expression**	≠ the greetings, regards	E
exquisite	≠ odd, strange, peculiar	P
	≠ affected, precious (of manners)	E
an **extension**	≠ an expanse, stretch	P E I F
	≠ a compass, range (in music)	I
to **extenuate**	≠ to exhaust, overdo, weaken, wear out	P E I F
extra	≠ on purpose	D
	≠ of top quality, outstandingly good	E I F *Nl*
an **extract (of an account)**	≠ a (bank) statement	*P* I
extraneous	≠ odd, strange, peculiar	E
	≠ shy, timid	P
the **extravagance**	≠ the oddity, peculiarity, whimsy, eccentricity	P E I F
extravagant	≠ odd, unusual, weird, eccentric, outlandish	*P* E I F Nl D
	≠ moody, erratic	P I
the **extreme(s)**	≠ the side, end, extremity (of a town, etc.)	P E

f

a **fabric**	≠ a factory	P E I F Nl D Dk N S Tr Gr Ar
	≠ a sample	F Ar
to **fabricate**	→ to produce, manufacture	P E I F Nl N S
the **fabrication**	≠ the make, manufacture	Nl D Dk S
	≠ the ready-made clothes	Tr
	→ the workmanship, making, construction	P E I F N S
the **façade**	≠ the title-page of a book	P
	≠ the corruption	Ar
facile	≠ simple, easy	P E I F
	≠ likely, probable	E I
	≠ moderate, reasonable (of prices)	S
to **facilitate**	≠ to supply, provide, let (s/o) have	E
	≠ to reduce (prices)	I
	≠ to expose oneself to danger	P
all **facilities**	≠ all methods of payment (are available)	P E I F
a **facility**	≠ a weakness, compliance	E F
	≠ an informal manner	P
the **factions**	≠ the (facial) features	E
	≠ the picket duty, sentry guards	F
	≠ the military duties	E
a **factor**	≠ a postman, delivery man	F
	≠ a department manager	D *S*
	≠ an agent; middle man	Nl D
	≠ a farmer	I
a **factory**	≠ a farm	I
	≠ a trading post, agent's office	E Nl
a **fad**	≠ a dish	Dk
faded	≠ stale, insipid, dull, boring	F D Dk S
a **fag(g)ot**	≠ a bassoon	P I Nl D Dk N S
	≠ a silly story, bit of nonsense	F
to **fail**	≠ almost to do something	F
	≠ to make a mistake, be absent/lacking	Nl D
	≠ to auction	Nl
a **fail**	≠ a mistake, error	*D* Dk N S
a **failing**	≠ an auction	Nl

a **fair(y)**	≠ a holiday	I Dk N S *Ch*
	≠ an open-air market	P E
a **fall**	≠ a leak (of liquids)	I
	≠ a trap	D
in **this fall**	≠ in this case/instance	*Nl* D S
to **fall in**	≠ to occur/strike s/o (mentally)	Nl D Dk N S
	≠ to be due	N S
	≠ to join in (esp. in music)	Nl Dk S
to **fall out**	≠ to fall to pieces	D
	≠ to (have as a) result	Nl S
	≠ to burst out	Dk
false	≠ feigned, pretended	E
the **fame**	≠ the rumour	E
	≠ the hunger	I
familiar	≠ of the family	E D
famous	→ splendid, super	E F Nl D
	≠ notorious, infamous	I F Dk S
a **fan**	≠ a flag (to wave)	D
	≠ a devil	S
a **fang**	≠ a tusk	D
	≠ a lap (on the knees)	N
the **fantasy**	≠ the fancy dress	P
	≠ the imitation jewellery	E
	≠ the (work of) fiction	E I
	≠ the fancy goods	Tr
	→ the imagination, fancy, whim	P E I F Nl D Dk N S Gr
the **farce**	≠ the stuffing (to eat)	F Nl D Dk
	≠ the minced meat/forcemeat	D Dk N S
a **farce**	≠ a practical joke	F
	≠ a fake, sham, trick	E
	≠ a company of players/actors	E
to **fare**	≠ to go	D S
	≠ to sail	Nl
	≠ to do/make	I
a **fare**	≠ a danger, peril, hazard, risk	Nl Dk N S
a **farmer**	≠ a colonial settler	D
to **fart**	≠ to satiate; indulge in	P
the **fart**	≠ the speed, hurry	Nl Dk N S
	≠ the journey	D
the **fashion**	≠ the shape, style, appearance, look	F
	≠ the decency	Nl

the **fashions**	≠ the fuss, pretence, affectation	F
fast	≠ certain, definite	Nl
	≠ solid, regular, permanent, compact	Dk N S
	≠ almost, practically	D
	≠ favourable, propitious	I
to **fasten**	≠ to seize, grasp	D
fastidious	≠ tiresome, boring, tedious	P E I F
the **fasts**	≠ the display, pageantry, pomp, ostentation	E I F
	≠ the annals	*P* E F
	≠ Lent	Nl S
a **fat**	≠ a serving dish	N
fat	≠ greasy	*Nl* D N S
	≠ conceited, selfish, cocky	F
fatal	≠ disagreeable, annoying, awkward, tricky unlucky, unfortunate	D Dk N S
	≠ ghastly, rotten, awful	E Nl
	≠ inevitable	F
a **fatality**	≠ a calamity	P F
	≠ a fate, destiny, ill-luck	P E I F
a **fate**	≠ a fact	P E I Nl
	≠ a feat, deed	P I
	≠ a ridge, top, summit	F
fatty	≠ poor, needy	Dk N S
fatuous	≠ conceited, smug	P E I
a **fault**	≠ a lack/need	P E *I F*
	≠ a wrinkle	D
to **fear**	≠ to lower (a flag)	Dk N
	≠ to slacken, pay out, loosen, release	Nl D
	≠ to celebrate	Nl N S
a **feast**	≠ a festival	D
	≠ a holiday, party	P E I Nl S
	≠ a celebration	Dk N S
a **feather**	≠ a spring (coil, etc.)	*Nl* D Dk *N S*
a **fee**	≠ a fairy	F D
to **feed up**	≠ to educate, rear, bring up	Nl S
the **felicities**	≠ the good luck, success(es)	E
	≠ the congratulations	P
a **fell**	≠ a hide, skin, pelt	*Nl* D N
	≠ a fault, defect, short-coming	Dk N S
	≠ a trap	N

a **fen**	≠ a paddock, pasture	Dk
the **fern**	≠ the far distance	D *Dk N S*
to **fetch**	≠ to date (e.g. a letter)	E
	≠ to close	P
a **fête**	≠ a holiday; birthday	*P E I* F
the **fetters**	≠ the shoelaces	Nl
	≠ the (male) cousins	D Dk N
a **fever**	→ a temperature	P *E* I F *D* Dk N S
a **fibre**	≠ a temperature	D
a **fiend**	≠ an enemy	Dk N S
fierce	≠ proud	I F Nl
a **figure**	≠ a face	I F
to **file**	≠ to escape, get away	I F
	≠ to spin (wool, etc.)	I F
	≠ to pinch, nab; cheat in exams; cut lessons; seize hold of	P
a **file**	≠ a line/queue of vehicles	E I Nl
	≠ a wire, thread	I F
	≠ an arrow	D
	≠ a cutting edge	E F
	≠ a lane on a motorway	S
to **fill up**	≠ to fulfil (duties/promises, etc.)	Dk N S
a **fillet**	≠ a (piece of) net(ting)	F
	≠ a thin thread	I F
a **fin(e)**	≠ an end, close; purpose	E I F
final(ly)	≠ utterly, totally	Nl
to **find**	≠ to end, finish	P
to **find out**	≠ to invent (e.g. excuses)	Nl S
a **fire**	≠ a festival, celebration	D
	≠ a chap, fellow	Dk N *S*
	≠ a lighthouse	Dk N S
	≠ four	Nl Dk N *S*
a **firm**	≠ a signature	E I
firm	≠ well-versed	D
	≠ clever, smart	Dk
the **first**	≠ the ridge, peak; roof ridge	D
the **first house**	≠ the best establishment of its kind	D
the **first jet**	≠ the first draft/version	I F
a **fish**	≠ a bill (to be paid)	F Tr
	≠ an electric plug	F Tr
	≠ a slip of paper, voucher, ticket, etc.	F
	≠ a counter in a game	F Nl Tr

a **fishline**	≠ a small fish	D
a **fit**	≠ a tape, band; aim, purpose	P
to **fix**	≠ to stare	P *I* F D
a **fixation**	≠ a fastening, fixing	P
fixed (in)	≠ keen (on)	P
a **flair**	≠ a sense of smell	F
flamenco	≠ Flemish	E
a **flan**	≠ a caramel custard	E F
a **flash, flask**	≠ a pulley block	D
	≠ a bottle	Nl D Dk S
the **flask**	≠ the pork, bacon	Dk S
to **flatter**	≠ to flutter	D
to **flay oneself**	≠ to flatter oneself	Nl
the **flesh**	≠ the meat	Nl D
	≠ the pork, bacon	*Dk* N S
to **flick**	≠ to darn, mend, patch up	D Dk N
	≠ to manage	Nl
a **flick**	≠ a patch (in mending)	Dk
	≠ a torn flap	N
	≠ a girl	S
	≠ a wink	S
	≠ a chocolate drop	Nl
the **flicks**	≠ the cops, police	F
flighty	≠ busily, diligently, in a lively way	Nl Dk N S
a **flint**	≠ a shotgun	D
a **flip**	≠ a collar	Dk
a **flipper**	≠ a pinball table	P E I F Nl D N S Gr
a **flirt**	≠ a flirtation	E I F Nl D Dk N S Gr
to **float**	≠ to rain (slang); waver	F
a **float**	≠ a fleet, navy	*E I* F Nl *D Dk* N S
a **flock**	≠ a flake (of snow)	Nl D
a **flood**	≠ a river	Dk *N* S
	→ a flood/high tide	Nl D *Dk* N S
the **flood**	≠ the cream (whipped)	Dk
the **floor**	≠ the blossom, flower	P E D N S
	≠ the crêpe, gauze	Nl D N S
	≠ the pile of a carpet	D
florid	≠ thriving, flourishing	I
	≠ full of flowers	P
the **floss**	≠ the raft, buoy; fin, flipper	D
a **flow**	≠ a flea	Nl D
the **flu, flue**	≠ the fly, the bow tie	Dk N S
fluent	≠ discharging (medical)	F
a **fluke**	≠ a curse, an oath	Nl

to **fluster**	≠ to whisper	Nl D
a **flute**	≠ a whistle	Nl Dk N
a **fog**	≠ a fire	P
a **föhn**	≠ a (hand-held) hair-dryer	Nl D
a **folio**	≠ a sheet of paper, a leaf	P I
	≠ a foil (background)	S
	≠ a bank account	N
a **folly**	≠ a (piece of) (metal) foil	D S
	≠ a lark, bit of merry-making	P
the **folly**	≠ the madness, lunacy, mania	I F
to **fool**	≠ to feel	Nl *D*
a **fool**	≠ a lazybones	Ch
the **footing**	≠ the running practice, jogging	E I F Nl
	≠ the evening promenade	P
the **forage**	≠ the drilling/sinking of a well	F
one's **force**	≠ one's strong point/forte	Dk N
by **force**	≠ necessarily	I
to **ford**	≠ to challenge, claim, demand	Nl D *Dk N S*
a **foreman**	≠ a front-rank man	Dk N
	≠ a president, chairman, speaker	Dk N
to **foresee**	≠ to take care, guard against; consider	D
	≠ to furnish/provide with	Nl
the **foresight**	≠ the prudence, care, caution	*Nl* D Dk N S
to **forestall**	≠ to represent, play a part	S
	≠ to introduce	S
	≠ to imagine	*Nl D* S
to **foretell**	≠ to recount, tell	Dk N S
	≠ to count out	Nl
a **forfeit**	≠ an all-in fee	F
by **forfeit**	≠ by/in bulk (contracts)	I
a **forfeiture**	≠ a fault, error, evil act	F
	≠ a case of maladministration, etc.	F
a **forger**	≠ a fabricator of lies	F
to **forgive**	≠ to poison	Nl *D* Dk *N* S
to **forgo**	≠ to take place, go on	Dk N
	≠ to disappear, fade, vanish	S
	≠ to perish, die	Dk N S
	≠ to come/go first	Nl D
forlorn	≠ lost, mislaid	Nl D S
	≠ false, sham, mock	Dk N
	≠ non-returnable (bottle, etc.)	Nl

the **forlorn hope**	≠ the lost expedition	Nl
the **forlorn son**	≠ the Prodigal Son	Nl D Dk N S
a **form**	≠ a way, method	P E
	≠ a mould, s/th giving shape to s/th else	Nl D Dk N S
	≠ a running/track suit	Gr
formal	≠ reliable, dependable, steady, inspiring confidence, business-like	E
	≠ definite, categorical, strict (promise/denial)	F
a **format**	≠ a (good) quality	D
	≠ a stature, size (of an object)	Nl
	≠ an importance	D S
a **formation**	≠ a training	P E I F Tr
formed	≠ graduated (academically)	P
the **Formica**	≠ the ant	I
formidable	≠ marvellous, super	P E I F Nl *D* Dk *S* Ch
a **formula**	≠ a printed form	*E Nl* D Dk N S
forte	≠ strong	P I *F*
fortunate	≠ wealthy	Nl
the **fortune**	≠ the storm	Gr
of **fortune**	≠ makeshift, chance *adj*	I F
a **forward**	≠ a condition, term, stipulation	Nl
foul	≠ lazy, rotten (of fruit)	D
a **fowl**	≠ a bird	Dk N S
a **fox**	≠ a fox terrier	D
a **foyer**	≠ a hearth, home, hostel; lens focus	F
	≠ a lobby, a crush-room	Nl
	≠ a desire, craze	I
a **fracas**	≠ a failure, breakdown, collapse, fiasco	P E
	≠ a din, clatter, crash	I F
a **fraction**	≠ a (political) faction	E F Nl D Dk N S
	≠ a suburb	I
the **fracture**	≠ the Gothic type	D Dk N S
the **franchise**	≠ the freedom of a city	F
	≠ the sanctuary, diplomatic immunity	F
	≠ the frankness, candour; exemption from duty (tax on goods)	F
to **frank a letter**	≠ to put a stamp on a letter	Nl D Dk N S

to **free**	≠ to woo, court	Nl D Dk N
	≠ to propose (marriage)	S
freely	≠ indeed, admittedly, of course	D
the **freeze**	≠ the fear	Nl
to **frequent**	≠ to go to/attend regularly	P E I F S
fresh, frisky	≠ healthy	N S
	≠ light, thin (of clothes)	P E
	≠ cool (of drink)	P E I *F* D S
	≠ gay, effeminate	P
the **friction**	≠ the (car) clutch	I
	≠ the massage	P
a **Frigidaire**	≠ a frying pan	P
(the) **frivolities**	≠ a kind of lace	Ch
frivolous	≠ obscene, indecent, improper, immoral	Nl D Dk N S
	≠ irreverent, profane	S
	≠ flighty	F
	≠ indifferent, cold, impolite, unmoved	P E
a **front**	≠ a forehead	P E I F
	≠ a (hotel) reception desk	J
the **fruition**	≠ the (legal) use, enjoyment (of s/th)	P E I
a **fugue**	≠ a joint, seam, groove, juncture	D *Dk N*
	≠ a flight, escape	P E I *F*
full	≠ drunk, sozzled	D Dk N S
	≠ unsightly	S
full-blooded	≠ thoroughbred	Nl D Dk N S
the **fume**	≠ the tobacco; smoke	P
a **function**	≠ a spectacle/performance in the theatre	E
	≠ a position, office, duty, official post	E I F Nl D Dk S
a **functionary**	≠ a civil servant	P E I F Nl
	≠ a domestic servant	P
a **fund**	≠ a discovery	D
the **funk**	≠ the radio	D
	≠ the spark	N
a **fur**	≠ a fir (tree)	N S
a **furnace**	≠ a stove, cooker	F Nl
the **furniture**	≠ the supply, requisite, fitting, equipment	I F
	≠ the print (typography)	E
a **fuse**	≠ an axle, spindle	P I

a **fusion**	≠ a merger	P E I F Nl D Dk N S
futile	≠ worthless, trifling, trivial, frivolous	P E I F

g

a **gable**	≠ a fork, pitchfork	D
a **gadget**	≠ a novelty, knick-knack	I
a **gaffer**	≠ a bystander	D
the **gaffes**	≠ the glasses (for the eyes)	E
a **gag**	≠ a gimmick	D
a **gage**	≠ a wage	F *Nl* D Dk N S
gallant	≠ capital, first-rate	S
	≠ erotic	I
	≠ smart, elegant	P F
	≠ wanton, licentious	E
the **gallantry**	≠ the fancy goods/articles	Nl *D* Dk N
	≠ the compliments	E I F Dk N
	≠ the politeness (to ladies)	E I F
a **gallery**	≠ a tunnel	I
	≠ a rim, border, cornice	F
	≠ a changing hut/cubicle	E
a **gallon**	≠ a strip of braiding (to show rank)	P E I F Nl
	≠ a white coffee in a glass	P
the **galoshes**	≠ the clogs	F
a **gang**	≠ a corridor	Nl D Dk N S
	≠ a gait, step, mechanism, movement	D Dk N S
	≠ a speed, rate	Nl D Dk N S
	≠ a gangster	J
	≠ a gear of a motor	D
	≠ a time, occasion	Dk N S
the **garb**	≠ the grace(fulness), poise	P E
	≠ the gallantry	P
	≠ the glamour, allure	E
	≠ the sheaf of corn	D
a **garden**	≠ a curtain	*D* Dk N S
garnished	≠ furnished (of rooms)	I F
	≠ fitted, provided, strengthened, stocked	I F
the **garrison**	≠ the recovery, cure, healing	F

the **gate**	≠ the street	Dk N
	≠ the hole	Nl
	≠ the clamp, vice, jack	E
	≠ the cat	P E I
	≠ the mistake	P
a **gauge**	See **gage**	
a **gaze**	≠ a net, cheesecloth	D
	≠ a gauze, chiffon	P F
	≠ a medical gauze	J
	≠ a stretch of wire netting	Nl
the **gazette**	≠ the truancy	P
a **gazetteer**	≠ a truant	P
	≠ a journalist	P *E I F*
the **gelatine**	≠ the jelly (to eat)	P E I *Nl*
a **gender**	≠ a son-in-law	*I* F
the **generalities**	≠ the name, address, etc., as for the police	I
genial	≠ having genius; gifted, ingenious	*E* I *F* Nl D Dk N S
the **geniality**	≠ the ingenuity, creativity, brilliance	I Nl D Dk N S
a **genie**	≠ a genius	Nl D Dk N S
a **genre**	≠ a gender	P F
genteel, gentle	≠ kind, thoughtful, pleasant	P I F
	≠ elegant, attractive, pretty	E
	≠ refined, noble	P
a **geometer**	≠ a land surveyor	I D
	≠ a land-measuring instrument	P E I
a **real German**	≠ a mallard (duck)	I
the **gestalt**	≠ the shape, figure, form, size	Nl D S
a **ghost**	≠ a soul	D
the **gift**	≠ the poison	Nl D Dk N S
	≠ the anger	D
gifted	≠ married	Dk N S
a **Gillette**	≠ a bisexual	P
	≠ any razor blade	E
a **girder**	≠ a (railway) bridge	J
a **giro**	≠ a hinge; short walk	P
	≠ a rotation; tendency	E
	≠ a lap in racing	I
	≠ an endorsement (e.g. on a cheque)	D N Tr Ar
the **gist**	≠ the yeast	Nl

to **give out**	≠ to spend	Nl D Dk S
	≠ to publish	Nl Dk N S
to **give a task up**	≠ to set a task	Nl
to **give up**	≠ to provide, supply	Nl
	≠ to state, mention, declare	Dk N S
glace	≠ frozen, icy, glossy	F
to **glance**	≠ to shine, glitter	Nl D S
a **glance**	≠ a gleam, shine, lustre	Nl D Dk N S
the **glance**	≠ the splendour, glory, brilliance	Nl D Dk N S
a **glass**	≠ an ice cream	F S Ch
the **glass eyes**	≠ the glasses (for the eyes)	S
a **globe**	≠ a toy balloon	E
glorious	≠ conceited, boastful, vain	E
a **gloss**	≠ a language	Gr
	≠ an ironic commentary	D
	≠ a sneer	D
to **gloss over**	≠ to comment on	D
a **glow**	≠ a trifle, silly matter/thing	Ch
to **glue**	≠ to glow	Nl
the **glue**	≠ the glow	N
	≠ the birdlime	F
a **glut**	≠ a glow	D
to **go after**	≠ to (go and) fetch	N
to **go off**	≠ to retire from work	Dk N
a **goal**	≠ a goalkeeper, goalie	F
the **God**	≠ the goth	P E
	≠ the pebble	P
golden	→ endearing (of a person)	D
the **golf**	≠ the sweater, cardigan	I
	≠ the golf course	F Gr
	≠ the wave (radio and water)	Nl
	≠ the gulf	P E I F Nl D Dk N S Gr
a **gondola**	≠ a Venetian canal	Ar
the **goods**	≠ the property, estate, possessions	Nl D Dk N S
a **gorge**	≠ a throat, gullet	F
gorgeous	≠ expensive, costly, dear	J
to **grab**	≠ to dig	Nl D
gracious	≠ comical, witty	P E
	≠ pleasing, graceful, dainty, elegant	P E I F Nl
	≠ graceful	D Dk N S
to **grade**	≠ to refine/purify (metals)	D

a **grade**	≠ a degree (in temperature, etc.)	E I F Nl D Dk N S
	≠ a railing, grill, grating, bar; electric grid	P
	≠ a step, row (of seats); rate	E
	≠ willingness	P E I
	≠ a military rank	E I F Nl D Dk N S
	≠ a fish bone	Nl
the **graffiti**	≠ the prehistoric rock/ancient tomb mural/painting(s)	I
a **grain**	≠ a spruce (tree)	Dk N S
	≠ a seed	F
the **gram**	≠ the grief, distress	D
	≠ the wrath	Nl
the **grammar**	≠ the letter (correspondence)	Gr
	≠ the glamour	J
grand	≠ big, tall, large	P E I F
a **grand person**	≠ an adult	*I* F
a **grand ensemble**	≠ a comprehensive housing scheme	F
a **grape**	≠ a bunch, cluster	I F
	≠ a joke, hoax	Nl
	≠ a paper-clip	E
the **graph**	≠ the writing; letter (of recommendation)	Gr
graphic	≠ picturesque	Gr
the **grass**	≠ the fat (on meat)	F
	≠ the grease	E I
	≠ the greasiness, fattiness; filth	E
a **gratification**	≠ a bonus payment	P E *I* Nl D
	≠ gratuity, reward	Dk S
to **gratify**	≠ to bestow s/th on s/o	F
	≠ to attribute s/th to s/o	F
	≠ to reward, tip, give a bonus	P E I
gratis	≠ congratulations	S
the **gratuity**	≠ the gratuitousness	F
a **grave**	≠ a moat, ditch, trench	Dk N S
the **grease**	≠ the groats, semolina	*Nl* D
	≠ the gravel, grit	D
a **grenade**	≠ a pomegranate	E F *Nl*
	≠ an explosive	Nl
	≠ a garnet	Nl D Dk N S

a **grid**	≠ a shout, cry	I
the **grief**	≠ the grievance, grudge	F Nl
to **grieve**	≠ to hurt, offend	Nl
	≠ to burden, encumber	F
to **grill**	≠ to fit gratings to (a window)	F
a **grill**	≠ a cricket (insect)	P E I D
	≠ a caprice, whim	Nl D
the **grills**	≠ the low spirits, melancholy	D
grim	≠ enraged, fierce, wrathful	D
	≠ ugly, hideous, plain	Dk N
	≠ cruel	S
the **grime**	≠ the (theatrical) make-up	Nl
to **grin**	≠ to laugh, guffaw	Dk
	≠ to be cross; nag, fret	N
	≠ to gape, stare; pull faces; cry	S
the **grip(e)**	≠ the dislike, aversion	F
	≠ the influenza, flu	P E I F Nl D Tr Gr
to **grip**	≠ to catch, capture; concoct, make up; interfere	N S
	≠ to seize, grasp, clutch	F Nl
	≠ to pinch, steal	F
the **grit**	≠ the shout, cry	P E
a **grocer**	≠ a wholesaler, merchant	Dk N
the **groin**	≠ the (pig's) snout	F
a **groom**	≠ a page (boy), buttons	F
	≠ a (c)lump, clot	P E I
gross	≠ fat, stout, big	E I F
	≠ large, tall, good (at)	D
the **ground**	≠ the core, heart, essence	D S
	≠ the foundations (of a building)	Dk *N* S
gruesome	≠ cruel, callous	Dk N
to **guarantee**	≠ to insure, protect	F
to **guard**	≠ to keep, hold onto	P E F
	≠ to look at, watch	I
a **guardian**	≠ a watchman, (security) guard	F
	≠ a prior	D
the **guer(r)illa**	≠ the guer(r)illa warfare/activity	P E I F Nl *D* *Dk* S
a **guesthouse**	≠ a pub, restaurant	D
	≠ an old people's home	Nl
to **guide**	≠ to drive (a car)	*P* I
guilty	≠ valid	*D* Dk N S

a **gulf**	≠ a floor	Dk N S
the **gull**	≠ the gold	Dk N
	≠ the gluttony	P E
a **gulley**	≠ a street drain	D
the **gulp**	≠ the flies (in trousers)	Nl
the **gum**	≠ the rubber, eraser	*E* I *F Nl* D Dk N *S* J
	≠ the elastic	E J
	≠ the condom, contraceptive sheath	S
to **gurgle**	≠ to gargle	Nl D Dk N S
a **gusset**	≠ an arm-pit	F
the **gust**	≠ the taste, inclination, relish	E I
a **gymkhana**	≠ a sports competition	P E
	≠ a sort of driving or motor-cycle competition	I F
	≠ a treasure-hunt	P
a **gymnasium**	≠ a grammar/secondary school	P E I F Nl D Dk N S

h

a **habitat**	≠ a bedsitter	E
the **habitation**	≠ the room, bedroom	E
the **habits**	≠ the clothes, dress, attire	*P I* F N
to **hack**	≠ to attack verbally, quarrel, bully	Dk S
	≠ to stutter	N
	≠ to mince (meat) up	D
a **hag**	≠ a hedge	Nl D
a **half**	≠ a child of mixed parentage	J
half six, etc.	≠ half past five, 5.30, etc.	Nl D Dk N S
a **hall**	≠ a sound, resonance	D
	≠ a covered market-place	F Nl Tr
to **halt**	≠ to hold	D
	≠ to limp	Dk N S
a **halt**	≠ a foothold, support	D
a **halter**	≠ a dumbbell (for exercises)	F Nl
a **hamburger**	≠ a person from Hamburg	D Dk
a **handicap**	≠ a good start in life; helpful background; advantageous position	P

the **handicraft**	≠ the manual power	Dk N S
to **handle**	≠ to treat	D Dk S
	≠ to deal (in business)	Nl D Dk N
a **handle**	≠ a trade, business, bargain	Nl D Dk N S
	≠ a vehicle steering wheel	J
the **handles**	≠ the cycle handlebars	J
the **handling**	≠ the action, story, plot	Dk N S
the **hang**	≠ the inclination, bent, bias, propensity	Dk N
to **hang on**	≠ to ring off, hang up	D
a **hangar**	≠ a (garden) shed	F
a **hank**	≠ a handle	Dk N
to **harass**	≠ to tire out, exhaust	F
hard	≠ loud, harsh	Nl
hardy	≠ bold, impudent, audacious	F
to **hark(en)**	≠ to rake	Nl D
to **hark back**	≠ to rake back	Nl D
the **harm**	≠ the grief, affliction, sorrow, distress	D
	≠ the indignation, resentment	Dk N S
harmful	≠ indignant, angry, resentful	Dk N
the **harmony**	→ the peacefulness, orderliness	Gr
the **harness**	≠ the (suit of) armour	Nl D Dk N S
the **Harpic**	≠ the resin	Dk N
the **haste**	≠ the rod, pile, stem, (tree) trunk	P
hateful	≠ spiteful	*Dk* N S
a **haven**	≠ a pot, saucepan	D
	≠ a harbour	Nl
the **hazard**	≠ the chance, luck, accidental event, fluke	E F
a **health centre**	≠ a (community) sports centre	J
hearty	→ friendly, warm, sincere, cordial (of greetings)	Nl D Dk N S
to **heckle**	≠ to crochet	Dk N
a **heckler**	≠ a hypocrite	*Dk N* S
hefty	≠ passionate, boisterous, tumultuous, passionate	D
	≠ violent, impetuous, vehement	Nl D Dk N S
	≠ furious	D S
	≠ fierce	Nl D S
	≠ intense acute (of pain)	D Dk N S
	≠ heated (talk)	Nl Dk N S

heinous	≠ full of hatred	F
a **helix**	≠ a propeller	P E F Gr
a **helm**	≠ a helmet	Nl D Dk N S
a **hen**	≠ a cock(erel), rooster	Nl D Dk N S
the **herb**	≠ the grass	E I F
a **herd**	≠ a (cooking) stove, hearth, fireplace	D *S*
the **heritage**	≠ the inheritance	F
the **hide**	≠ the heath(er)	*Nl* D
high collar	≠ upper class style (said of smart clothing)	J
a **high school**	≠ a college, university (esp. technological)	Nl D Dk N S
a **high street**	≠ a flyover	D
to **hinder**	≠ to bother, trouble	Nl D *N*
hindered	≠ handicapped	D
Hindi	≠ (a) turkey (bird)	Tr
a **Hindu**	≠ an Indian	F
a **hint**	≠ a clue	J
a **hip**	≠ a scyth, sickle, reaping hook; breadroll	D
the **hire**	≠ the chauffeur-driven car	J
	≠ the fillet of meat	J
to **hiss**	≠ to hoist up	F Nl D
a **hiss**	≠ a pulley	D
	≠ a lift, elevator	Dk N S
the **history**	≠ the story	P E F Nl *D* Dk N S
	≠ the fuss, to-do, trouble	P E F Nl
	≠ the rubbish	F
a **hob**	≠ a crowd, lot, heap	Nl Dk
a **hobo**	≠ an oboe	Nl
a **hold**	≠ a (sports) team	Dk
	≠ a stitch	N
to **hold out**	≠ to bear, tolerate	Nl D Dk N
to **hold over**	≠ to have (s/th) left (over)	Nl
	≠ to observe, obey, comply with	Dk N
to **hold under**	≠ to entertain	Nl D Dk N *S*
a **hole**	≠ a halt, stop	Dk
	≠ a cave	Nl D
	≠ a furnace, Hell	D
the **homage**	≠ the free gift (commercial)	I
a **home**	≠ a station platform	J
my **home**	≠ a future home of my own	J
homely	≠ secret, private, clandestine	Nl *D Dk* N S
honest	≠ chaste	P E

	≠ decent, decorous, proper, respectable	P E I F
the **honesty**	≠ the chastity	F
	≠ the politeness, decency, respectability	F
a **hood, hoot**	≠ a hat	Nl *D* Ch
a **hook**	≠ an angle; corner	Nl
a **hoop**	≠ a siren, horn, hooter, buzzer	D
	≠ a heap, pile, lot; hope	Nl
to **hop**	≠ to jump, spring	Dk N S
	≠ to hope	S
a **hop(e)**	≠ a crowd, lot, heap	Nl N S
to **hope**	≠ to heap	Nl
a **horn**	≠ an oven, furnace, kiln	E
the **hose**	→ the trousers	D
a **host**	≠ a guest, lodger, visitor	*E* I F
a **hotel**	≠ a (town) hall	F
a **particular hotel**	≠ a large private town house	F
a **hound**	≠ any kind of dog	Nl D Dk N S
an **hour**	≠ a clock	D
an **hourglass**	≠ a watch/clock glass (in BE)/ crystal (in AE)	D Dk N S
to **house**	≠ to reside/live/dwell in	D Dk N S
a **house**	≠ a building (of any kind)	D
a **householder**	≠ a housekeeper	*Nl D* Dk N S
a **houseman**	≠ a cottager	Dk N
a **housemaster**	≠ a caretaker, warden	Nl D
the **housework**	≠ the homework	Nl *D*
a **huddle**	≠ a rag, tatter; tramp, ragamuffin	D
a **hue**	≠ a bonnet	Dk N
to **hug**	≠ to cut/slash (wood)	Dk N S
the **hug**	≠ the mind, mood	N
huge	≠ high	Nl *D S*
a **hulk**	≠ a sob	Dk N
hulking	≠ sobbing	Dk N
human	≠ humane	P E I F Nl D Dk N S
the **humour**	≠ the state of mind, (bad) mood	F
to **hurl**	≠ to howl, moan, whine	I F
to **hurt**	≠ to steal, pinch	E
to **hurt oneself**	≠ to stumble, collide with, come up against	I F
	≠ to withdraw, steal away	E

a **hurt**	≠ a theft	E
hush!	≠ quick!	D
a **hustler**	≠ a coward	Ch
a **hut**	≠ a hat	D
	≠ a protection, guard	D
	≠ a passenger cabin on a ship	Nl
	≠ a forge, kiln, foundry	D
a **hymn**	≠ an anthem	Dk N S
	≠ a national anthem	D
	≠ an ode	D
a **hypothesis**	≠ a possible course of action, suggestion	P *E* I F

i

an **icing**	≠ a shudder	Nl
the **iconography**	≠ the illustrations (of a book)	Gr
an **idiom**	→ a language	E
an **idiosyncrasy**	≠ an aversion	I D
	≠ an allergy	Dk
	≠ an animosity	D Dk
	≠ a temperament	Gr
	≠ way a group/society thinks	E
idiotic	≠ private	Gr
idle	≠ pure, sheer, mere (of an absurdity)	S
to **ignore**	≠ to be ignorant of, not to know	P E *I F D*
illumined	≠ visionary, crazy	*E* I F
the **illusions**	≠ the hope(s), joy, pleasure(s), wish(es), intention(s)	E
	≠ the delusions	F Dk S
to **illustrate**	≠ to teach, enlighten	P E
	≠ to make illustrious	*P* E I F
the **person illustrated**	≠ the learned/educated person	P E
the **illustration**	≠ the learning, enlightenment	P E
	≠ making illustrious	F
an **image**	≠ a picture, illustration	P F
the **imago**	≠ the image, idol	I
an **imbecile**	≠ a silly person	*P* E *F*

to **imbibe**	≠ to steep, soak (up), drench, impregnate	*P* F
immediate	≠ adjoining (of a room)	*P* E
imminent	≠ coming soon/shortly	I F Nl
an **immortal**	≠ an everlasting flower	F D
an **impasse**	→ a cul-de sac, close, dead-end	F
the **imperative**	≠ the demand, requirement	F
imperfect	≠ not yet finished, incomplete	E I F Nl
the **impetus**	≠ the violence, impetuousity	E
to **impinge**	≠ to inflict, impose (on)	P
implicit	≠ implicated, involved	Dk N
to **import**	≠ to matter, be important	P E I F
an **import**	≠ a price, cost, amount	E
important	≠ considerable, big; thick (of fog), serious (of damage); heavy (of traffic)	P F
to **impose on s/o**	≠ to trick s/o, take s/o in, , deceive	F Nl
	≠ to impress, inspire s/o with respect	F Nl D
the **imposition**	≠ the depositing of money in the bank	E
	≠ the tax, duty	P E I F
	≠ the laying on of hands	F
an **imposter**	≠ a tax	I
impotent	≠ lacking use of the arms and/or legs	F
impregnable	≠ capable of being impregnated	P F
	≠ waterproof(ed)	*D* N S
an **impresario**	≠ a contractor (for any kind of work)	I
the **impress**	≠ the form (to be filled in)	P E
	≠ the printed matter	P E
to **make an impression**	≠ to be a shock (distressingly)	E
improper	→ incorrect, wrong, mistaken, unfit	P I F
	→ inappropriate, unsuitable	P E I
the **impropriety**	→ the incorrectness	E F
	→ the unsuitability	E
inadequate	≠ unsuitable, inappropriate	P E I F
inadmissible	≠ intolerable, unthinkable	P E I F
incarnate	→ /flesh-coloured	Nl
an **incendiary**	≠ a fire (of a building)	P E I F

	incensed	≠ flattered, praised	P E I *F*
	incessantly	≠ at once	F
an	**incident**	≠ an accident	I
		≠ a (legal) objection, difficulty	F
an	**incitement**	≠ a stimulus, incentive (good or bad)	Dk
an	**inclination**	≠ a bow, an invitation to a dance, an attachment, love for s/o	Dk
to	**incline**	≠ to ask a girl for a dance	Dk
	inconsequent	≠ inconsistent, contradictory in itself	Nl D Dk N S
	inconsistent	≠ insubstantial, flimsy	*P* E
	incontinent	→ unrestrained, lacking self-control	P I
		≠ right away, immediately	P E *F*
an	**inconvenience**	≠ an impropriety	P I F
		≠ an impoliteness, silly remark	P E
	indelicate	≠ dishonest, unscrupulous	I
an	**index**	≠ an indication, clue, hint, token	*P E I* F
		≠ a forefinger	E I F Nl
to	**indicate**	≠ to recommend, suggest (e.g. a hotel)	P E I F
	indicated	≠ obvious, suitable, appropriate	P E I F
an	**indication**	≠ a crossword clue	E
the	**indicative**	≠ the theme tune (of a programme)	F
an	**indicator**	≠ a forefinger	P
	indifferently	≠ equally well, equally correctly	P E I F
	indignant	≠ wicked	F
		≠ outrageous, humiliating, infuriating	E
the	**indignity**	≠ the vileness, scandalous action	F
the	**industrial action**	≠ the industrial activity	P E I F
	inexcusable	≠ inevitable, unavoidable	E
		≠ essential, indispensable	E

the	**infatuation**	≠ the self-conceit, vanity	E F
	infect(ed)	≠ disgusting, loathsome	P E F
		≠ corrupted, perverted	E I
	inferior	≠ lower, placed below	P E I F
	infirm	≠ ill, unwell	P E I
	inflammable (in BE)	≠ burnable	F Nl
	influenced	≠ having the flu	I
the	**influenza**	≠ the influence	I
to	**inform**	≠ to inquire	Nl D
		≠ to give lessons	N
	informal	≠ unreliable, ill-behaved	E
the	**information**	≠ the news (bulletin)	F
an	**infusion**	≠ an injection	D
	ingenious	≠ witty	E
		≠ shrewd, astute	P
the	**ingenuity**	≠ the ingenuousness, candour, simplicity	P E I F
	inhabited	≠ empty, uninhabited	P E I F Nl
to	**inhale**	≠ to overtake (of traffic)	Nl
an	**initiation**	≠ a general introduction (to a subject)	F
to	**injure**	≠ to abuse, insult, wrong, damage, harm; call s/o names	P E I F
	injurious	≠ offensive	P E I F
the	**injury**	≠ the insult, abuse	P E I F D Dk N
		≠ the defamation, slander	P F D Dk N
an	**inn**	≠ a hymn	I
the	**inning(s)**	≠ the collection of money	Nl
		≠ the guild, corporation	D
	insane	≠ unhealthy	E I
to	**inscribe**	≠ to enrol, register (e.g. at a school)	P E I F Nl *D* Dk N S
an	**inscription**	≠ an enrolment, registration	P E I F
	insensate	→ insane, mad	F
		≠ lifeless	I
to	**inset**	→ to put in, insert	Nl Dk N
		≠ to install, arrest, deposit	Dk N
		≠ to devote (time)	Nl
an	**inset**	≠ a stake (in gambling), employment	Nl
an	**insight**	≠ an inspection, perusal, judgment	D
the	**inspiration**	≠ the inhalation, breathing in	P I F

to **inspire**	≠ to inhale, breathe in	P I F
an **instance**	≠ an entreaty, request, plea, petition	P E I F
	≠ a military court	Nl *D* Dk N S Tr
the **instances**	≠ the registered mail awaiting collection	F
	≠ the authorities	Nl
instant	≠ urgent, pressing	P I F
instantly	≠ strictly, formally, insistently	E I F
	≠ urgently	E
an **institute**	≠ a state (grammar) school	E
an **instructor**	≠ a producer, stage manager	Dk N
intact	≠ unaffected	P E I F
to **intend**	≠ to understand, superintend	P
	≠ to get s/th straight; hear	*E* I
	≠ to mean; understand	E I
intensive	≠ intense	D Dk N S
interested	→ biased, prejudiced	E F
	→ having ulterior motives, calculating	*P* E I F
interesting	≠ profitable, worthwhile	P E F
an **interloper**	≠ a shady/suspect person	*P* F
to **intern**	≠ to put/place (eg in hospital)	P
	≠ to penetrate	E
to **interpret**	→ /to perform (music)	P E I F
the **interpretation**	≠ the interpreting, translation	E
an **interpreter**	≠ a performer	P E I F
an **interrogation**	≠ a (school) comprehension test	F
an **interrupter**	≠ a light switch	P E I F
to **intervene in**	≠ to act a part in, join in	E I
	≠ to be present at	I
	≠ to arise, happen	F
the **intervention**	≠ the attendance, presence, coming	I
	≠ the speech	E
	≠ the surgical operation	*P* E
	≠ the administrative check	E
intimate	≠ private, (of the) family	F D
intoned	≠ in tune	I
	≠ filled with pride	P
intoxicating	≠ poisonous	P E I F

the **intoxication**	≠ the poison	P E I F
to **invent**	≠ to take stock; make an inventory	D S
the **inventory**	≠ the furniture, equipment	Dk N S
	≠ the effects, stock, stores, plant	D S
an **inversion**	≠ an investment of money	*P* E
to **invest**	≠ to attack, rush on, assail	P I *F*
	≠ to collide	I
the **investi-gations**	≠ the academic research	E
an **investment**	≠ an accident, collision	I
involved	≠ developed	P
	≠ wrapped up, surrounded	P E
to **irritate**	≠ to disconcert, confuse, distract	D
	≠ to disturb, make less calm (e.g. water)	F
(the) **Island**	≠ Iceland	P E I F Nl D Dk N S Tr Ar
to **isolate**	≠ to insulate (See Part 2)	P I F Nl D Dk N S
the **isolation**	≠ the soundproofing	I F
an **isotherm**	≠ a refrigerator	E
an **issue**	≠ an exit, outlet, solution, way out	F
Italian	≠ Italy	D
item	≠ (well) as I was saying	Ch

j

to **jabber**	≠ to speak	J
a **jack**	≠ a jacket	Nl D Dk N S
a **jacket**	≠ a morning suit/coat	P F Dk N S
a **jail**	≠ a cage	P
the **jargon**	≠ the slang	I
the **jealousy**	≠ the Venetian blind	P I F Nl D Dk N S Tr
	≠ the sweet william (flower)	F
jejune	≠ (connected with a period of) fasting	P
the **jelly**	≠ the (better quality) jam	P
a **jest**	≠ a gesture	P E I F D S Tr
	≠ a look, appearance	P E
a **Jew**	≠ a funny bone	F

the **joint**	≠ the tongued and grooved board	F
	≠ the gasket	*P E* F
jolly	≠ pretty	F
a **journal**	≠ a newspaper	P I F
	≠ a day's wages	P E
a **journey**	≠ a (whole) day('s work/travel)	F
a **joy**	≠ a jewel	P E
	≠ a weed	P
the **jubilation**	≠ the retirement (pension)	P E I
	≠ the dismissal (for some slight offence)	P
	≠ the retirement of a sports-man	Tr
the **jubilee**	≠ the happiness, cheers, cheering	P I
	≠ the comings and goings	E
the **jug**	≠ the juice	E
a **jumper** (in BE)	≠ a casual-wear top (leather or cloth)	J
a **junkman**	≠ a bachelor; young man	Nl
a **junta**	≠ a small (informal) meeting	E
	≠ a board, council, committee	P E I
	≠ a congress, conference	E
	≠ a pair, couple	P
	≠ a joint, coupling; gasket	P E
	≠ an addition, appendix, surplus	I
the **Jura**	≠ the law (as a study)	Dk
a **jurist**	≠ a lawyer	Nl Dk N S
	≠ a law student	Nl Dk
just *adj*	≠ close-fitting (of clothes)	*P* E F
	≠ correct, without errors	I F Nl S
	≠ in tune (musically)	E F
justly	≠ exactly, just so	P E F
	≠ suddenly, by chance	F

k

a **kaffir**	≠ a (rural) security guard	Ar
	≠ a (religious) enemy	Tr
	≠ a beetle	D
	≠ an oaf, lout	Nl
a **kayak**	≠ a sledge	Tr
the **kayak**	≠ the skiing	Tr
a **keel**	≠ a throat	Nl
keen	≠ bold, audacious	Nl D
a **kerb**	≠ a notch	D
a **kernel**	≠ a pip (in fruit)	D *Dk* N S
a **kettle**	≠ a boiler	Nl D N *S*
to **kick**	≠ to look	*Nl* Dk N S
a **kick**	≠ a look, peep	Dk N S
a **kicker**	≠ a frog	Nl
the **kicks**	≠ the biscuit	Dk *N* S
	≠ the miss, misfiring	Dk
a **kid**	≠ a calf	Dk
to **kill**	≠ to tickle	Dk N S
a **killer**	≠ a hired assassin	P I D
a **kind**	≠ a child	Nl D
	≠ a cheek	Dk N S
	≠ a chin	D
kindly	≠ childish, childlike	D
kinky	≠ fussy	S
	≠ awkward, invidious	N
a **kip**	≠ a chicken	Nl
	≠ a calf (child's language)	Dk
	≠ an edge, brink; dangerous situation	D
a **kipper**	≠ a dumper bucker, skip; tip-lorry	D
a **kiss**	≠ a pillow, cushion	*Nl* D
the **kit**	≠ the putty, cement	D Dk N S
a **kitchen**	≠ a prison, clink, jug	D
a **knack**	≠ a crease	Dk
	≠ a crack, break, crackle	D Dk N S
	≠ a knock, blow, shock	Nl Dk N S
	≠ a setback	Nl
	≠ a bend, angle	Dk *N*
	≠ a toffee	S

the **knickers**	≠ the marbles	Nl
a **knight**	≠ a farm labourer	D
	≠ a servant	Nl
	≠ a knave/jack (in cards)	Dk N S
	≠ a rascal	Dk N
	≠ a fellow, chap	N
a **knob**	≠ a knot (nautical speed)	Dk N
a **knock**	≠ a bone	Nl D
a **knoll**	≠ a bone	Dk
	≠ a farmhorse	Nl
a **knot**	≠ a bone	S
	≠ a midge	N S
	≠ a bun (hair-do); skein of wool	Nl
a **knuckle**	≠ a (school) swot	Dk

l

a **label**	≠ a spoon	Nl
laborious	≠ hard-working, diligent	E I F
	≠ elaborate, intricate	P E F
to **labour**	≠ to plough	F
the **labour**	≠ the laboratory	D
	≠ the ploughing, tillage	F
a **labourer**	≠ a ploughman	F
the **lack**	≠ the lacquer	Nl D Dk S
the **lacquer**	≠ the wax	P
a **lad**	≠ a stable boy	F
	≠ a side, position	P E
a **ladder**	≠ a slope	P E
the **ladder**	≠ the leather	S Ch
the **lager**	≠ the bearings (mechanical)	Nl D *S*
	≠ the deposit seam (in rocks)	D
	≠ the store/stock (of goods), depot	Dk N S
	≠ the layer (of skin)	*Nl* D Dk N S
	≠ the couch, camp bed	Nl D
	≠ the dregs, sediment	D
	≠ the laurel(s)	S
a **lagoon**	≠ a gap, hiatus, lacuna	E
the **lamb**	≠ the cripple	S
	≠ the mud, slime	P E
	≠ the blade of a sword/knife	I

lame	≠ numb	S
	≠ paralysed, crippled	Nl D Dk N S
to **lament**	≠ to complain	*P* E I
	≠ to deplore, be critical	P
the **lamp**	≠ the (flash of) lightning	I
to **lance**	≠ to launch, issue, set (s/o) up	*I* F
a **lance**	≠ a stroke, fling; critical attack	P
	≠ a stretch of road	P
	≠ an event, episode, occurrence; row, quarrel	E
	≠ a hose nozzle	I
	≠ a launch	I
a **land**	≠ a region, province, county,	D
	a field	Nl
a **landsman**	≠ a compatriot	Nl D Dk N S
a **lane**	≠ an avenue	Nl
	≠ a loan	Dk
to **lap (up)**	≠ to mend, patch (up)	Nl Dk N S
a **lap**	≠ a rag, cloth, patch	Nl D
	≠ a scrap, strip, patch	Dk N S
the **lard**	≠ the bacon	F
large	≠ wide, broad, vast	P I F
	≠ generous	E I F Dk
	≠ long	E
	≠ broad-minded	Dk
a **larva**	≠ a mask	D
the **last**	≠ the blame, vice, bad habit	Dk N S
	≠ the load, burden, cargo	Nl D Dk N S
	≠ the bother, nuisance; instructions	Nl
the **last post**	≠ the nuisance	Nl
the **last taxi**	≠ the hired van	D
a **Latin**	≠ an Eastern Catholic	Tr
the **lattice**	≠ the lath-work	F
	≠ the latex	P I
the **lauds**	≠ the verdicts, decisions, findings	P E
	≠ the book pages	P
	≠ the lutes	E
a **laureate**	≠ a graduate	I
a **lavatory**	≠ a washbasin	P
the **lavender**	≠ the laundry (building and process)	P *E I*
to **lay out**	≠ to explain	Nl Dk N S

to **learn**	≠ to teach	*Nl* D Dk N S
a **learner**	≠ a teacher	*Nl* D *Dk* N S
to **lease**	≠ to allow, leave, let	F
a **lease**	≠ a lead, leash	F
a **leather jacket**	→ a hooligan	Dk
the **lecture**	≠ the reading (matter)	P E I F Nl D Dk N S
a **lecture table**	≠ a record-player console	F
a **leek**	≠ an onion	N S
	≠ a layman	Nl
to **leer**	≠ to empty	D
the **leer**	≠ the leather	Nl
a **leg**	≠ a game	Dk
	≠ a fold, tuck, crease, pleat	Dk N
(it's) **legal**	≠ (it's) all right, O.K.	P
a **legend**	→ a text, caption, inscription, map-key	F D
the **legs**	≠ the legacy, bequest	F
the **lemon**	≠ the ooze, slime, mud	F
	≠ the lime (fruit)	F D
	≠ the lemming	N
Lent	≠ Spring	Nl *D*
the **lentils**	≠ the (small) lenses	E
to **let up**	≠ to look after, pay attention to	Nl
the **letters**	≠ the words of a song, lyrics	P E
	≠ the handwriting	P E
	≠ the (printed) label	J
a **levee**	≠ a collection of the mail	F
	≠ a closing/adjourning of a meeting	F
	≠ a trick (in cards)	F Tr
to **lever**	≠ to deliver, supply	Nl *D* Dk N S
the **lever**	≠ the liver	Nl Dk N S
the **liaison**	≠ the binding, fastening, join(t)ing, link	F
	→ the affair, love affair	F
	≠ the involvement	S
to **libel**	≠ to draw up/word a document	F
the **libel**	≠ the wording (e.g. in a document)	F
	≠ the small book	P
	≠ the dragonfly	Nl

the **liberation**	≠ the settlement of a debt	*P* E *I* F
a **libertine**	≠ a freethinker	F
a **library**	≠ a bookshop	P E I F
	≠ a bookcase	E I
a **libretto**	≠ a booklet, notebook	I
the **licence**	≠ the (military) leave	P E I
	≠ the permission (to do s/th)	P E
	≠ the (academic) degree	F Tr
licensed	≠ having a degree	P E F
	≠ having a school-leaving exam	I
	≠ disbanded, sacked, dismissed	I F
a **lid**	≠ a limb; member of the family	Nl
	≠ a member, subscriber	Nl
the **lieder**	≠ the songs (any type of)	D
a **life**	≠ a body	Nl
to **lift**	≠ to hitchhike	S
a **light article**	≠ a leading article (in journalism)	D
to **like**	≠ to look like, resemble	Nl
the **lime**	≠ the glue	Nl D Dk N S
	≠ the file, rasp (a tool)	P E I F
	≠ the polish, finish	I
	≠ the mud, slime	P E I
to **limp**	≠ to clean (out)	P E
the **limp**	≠ the (strip of) bare land	P E
limp	≠ clean, neat, trim, tidy	P E
	≠ penniless, broke; honest, above-board	P E
	≠ bare	P
	≠ bright, clear	P *I*
the **line**	≠ the flax, linen	D
the **ling**	≠ the lime tree	Ch
the **lingerie**	≠ the linen cupboard	F
links (drive/go to the links)	≠ (go/drive to the) left	Nl D
the **lino**	≠ the linen, flax	E I
the **lint**	≠ the ribbon	Nl
the **liquidation**	≠ the annual clearance sale	P E I F
	≠ the bonus paid on leaving a job	I
a **lira**	≠ a pound sterling	Tr

to **list**	≠ to steal (away), move stealthily	Dk N
	≠ to worm (s/th out of s/o)	S
a **list**	≠ a trick, device, dodge	Nl D Dk N S
	≠ a menu	P E I
to **listen**	≠ to hear	S
a **lithograph**	≠ a lithographer	P E I F Nl D Dk N S
to **litigate**	≠ to quarrel	I
livid	→ blue-grey	I F
	≠ envious	I
	≠ lively, animated	P
	≠ pallid, pale	E
a **living**	≠ a drawing/living room	P E F
the **load**	≠ the lead (metal)	Nl
	≠ the weight (as in measurements)	Dk
a **loan**	≠ a salary, reward, payment	Nl D *Dk N* S
the **local**	≠ the premises, hall, café, etc.	E I F Nl D Dk S
	≠ the classroom	*F* Nl
	≠ the phone extension	Dk
to **localise**	≠ to locate, discover, track down, pinpoint	P E I F
a **locality**	≠ a seat in a theatre	P E
the **locals**	≠ the home team (in sport)	E
the **location**	≠ the letting, hiring, leasing	P E I F
a **loch, lock**	≠ a hole	D
	≠ a lid	Dk N S
	≠ a rag; ship's log	F
	≠ a locomotive	D S
to **lock**	≠ to entice, lure, draw	Nl D Dk N
	≠ to slacken, loosen, relax	D
to **lock up**	≠ to open, undo	Dk N
a **locket**	≠ a (door) latch	F
	≠ a ticket window	Nl
a **loco**	≠ a madman	E
the **locomotive**	≠ the live wire (of a movement, etc.)	F
the **locum**	≠ the Turkish delight	Tr
	≠ the bog (slang for loo, W.C.)	Dk
a **locust**	≠ a lobster	*P* F
a **lodge**	≠ a shop	P
	≠ a loggia	*I* F
	≠ a box (in the theatre)	F Nl D Dk N S
	≠ a kennel	F

a **lodger**	≠ a lodging-house keeper; landlord/lady of furnished rooms	F
a **loft**	≠ a ceiling	Dk
logical	≠ reasonable, sensible	P E I F
long	≠ far, distant	P
	≠ tall	Nl S Ch
a **longueur**	≠ a length	F
to **look**	≠ to lock up, shut, close	Dk N
	≠ to succeed	Nl
to **look after**	≠ to look for	S
a **loom**	≠ a fire, light, flame	P I
the **loom**	≠ the enlightenment	I
to **loop**	≠ to walk	Nl
a **loop**	≠ a wolf	F
	≠ a lens	P E Nl D
to **loosen up**	≠ to solve	Nl Dk
	≠ to dissolve	N
the **lore**	≠ the pick-up lorry, open railway wagon/truck	D
the **lorgnette**	≠ the opera glasses	F
to **lo(o)se**	≠ to unload; fire (arms)	Nl N
	≠ to solve (a problem)	*D* Dk N S
a **lot**	≠ a struggle; bout of wrestling	I
	≠ a prize	F
	≠ a lottery ticket	Nl S
	≠ a plumb line	D
the **lot**	→ the fate	Nl *N* S
the **lotion**	≠ the washing/bathing of a wound	F
the **lotto**	≠ the premium bond	I D
	≠ the share, allotment, plot of land	I
	≠ the lotus	E
lovely	≠ lawful, legal, permissible	Dk N S
a **low**	≠ a silly (person)	Ch
loyal	≠ straightforward, honest	F
the **loyalty**	≠ the honesty, uprightness, respectability	*I* F D
the **luck**	≠ the happiness	Dk N S
lucky	≠ happy	Nl *D* Dk *N*
a **lump**	≠ a rascal, scoundrel	D Dk
	≠ a rag, s/th valueless	D S
lunatic	≠ moody, fickle, changeable	E I F
	≠ whimsical, capricious	F
	≠ absent-minded	P

a **lunch**	≠ a snack; wedding breakfast	E
a **lure**	≠ a nap, short sleep	Dk N S
lurid	≠ foul, loathsome, filthy	I
the **lust**	≠ the inclination, liking, wish	Nl D Dk N S
	≠ the pleasure, mirth, fun	D
a **lustre**	≠ a chandelier	E F
	≠ a deception, fake	I
lusty	≠ merry, jolly, amusing	Nl D Dk N S
	≠ strange, peculiar	S
the **lute**	≠ the mourning, grief	P E I
	≠ the wrestling	F
luxurious	≠ lewd, lustful	P E I F
the **luxury**	≠ the lust, lewdness	P E I F
lyrical	≠ vocal, involving singing	P I

m

the **macabre**	≠ the cemetery	Ar
a **machine**	≠ a car	P I
	≠ a camera; typewriter; crane, derrick	E
	≠ a fine building; crowd	E
	≠ a dynamo	F
the **machine**	≠ the engine (of a car, etc.)	D Dk S
the **Madeira**	≠ the wood, timber; wood-wind (music)	P E
a **maestro**	≠ a tutor, instructor	E I
a **magazine**	≠ a store(room)	I F Nl D Dk N S
	≠ a shop	P F S Gr
	≠ a department store	Dk N
	≠ a heap, mass	I
a **maggot**	≠ a hoard of money/savings	F
	≠ an ugly person; fright; macaque ape	F
the **magistrate**	≠ the municipal authorities, city corporation	D Dk
the **main(s) current**	≠ escalator handrail	F
to **major**	≠ to put up, increase (prices)	P *I* F
a **major**	→ an adult	*P* E I F
	≠ a chief, a superior	E
major	≠ larger, bigger	P E I

the **majors**	≠ the ancestors, forefathers	E
a **make**	≠ a match, equal, fellow	*Dk* N S
	≠ a husband	*Dk* S
	≠ a spouse	Nl
to **make out**	≠ to object, mind	D
	≠ to remove, take out (stains); finish; constitute, settle/ resolve differences	Nl
	≠ to matter, be important	Nl
to **make up**	≠ to squander	Nl
a **maker**	≠ a well-known manufacturer	J
the **malice**	≠ the prank: smart retort	F
malicious	≠ mischievous	P I F
	≠ shrewd, astute	E
a **mammy**	≠ a midwife	Gr
Man	≠ (impersonal) you, we, they	Nl D Dk N S
	≠ (a) husband	Nl D S
to **manage**	≠ to be sparing, use economically	F
	≠ to drive a car	E
the **management**	≠ the caution, care, circumspection	F
a **manager**	≠ a housekeeper	F
a **mangle**	≠ a shortcoming, need, lack	D
	≠ an almond	Nl
a **mania**	≠ a fad, idiosyncrasy, oddity, peculiarity	P E I F
a **maniac**	≠ a faddy person	E I F Nl
a **manifestation**	≠ a (public) demonstration	E I F Nl *D*
the **manoeuvres**	≠ the marshalling/shunting (railway)	P E I F
	≠ the raw materials	E
	≠ the rigging (nautical)	E
	≠ the (unskilled) labourers	F
a **mansard**	≠ a penthouse	I
	≠ an attic, garret	Nl D
a **mansion**	≠ a house	F
	≠ a flat (in a block)	J
a **mantle**	→ a cloak, coat	I F Nl D
	≠ a tablecloth	P E
the **manufacture**	≠ the drapery; dry goods (in AE)	Nl Dk N S
	≠ the factory, mill, works	E I F
a **manufacturer**	≠ a draperer	Nl

a **map**	≠ a briefcase	Nl D Dk N S
	≠ a folder, file	Nl Dk N S
to **march**	≠ to function, work, go (of machines)	E I F *Nl*
	≠ to walk	E I F
	≠ to advance, proceed	I
	≠ to leave, depart	E *D*
a **march**	≠ a gear (of a car, etc.)	I
	≠ a speed, rate	P *E*
	≠ a flight of steps	F
	≠ a fairy story	D
to **make s/o march**	≠ to trick s/o	F
the **mare**	≠ the sea	I
	≠ the poor horse, nag	D
a **margin**	≠ a river bank	P
a **marginal**	≠ a criminal; outsider; coast road	P
a **marina**	≠ a sea coast; navy; seascape	E I
the **marina**	≠ the seamanship	E
	≠ the Admiralty	I
the **marine**	≠ the navy	F Nl D Dk N S
	≠ the seascape; seamanship	F S
to **mark**	≠ to pretend to be	D
	≠ to notice	Nl
a **mark**	≠ a borderland, boundary, limit	D
	≠ a field	S
	≠ a tract, plot of land, ground	S
	≠ a picture frame	E
	≠ a maggot, worm	N
	≠ a postage stamp	D
the **mark**	≠ the make/brand (commercial)	P E I F Nl D Dk N S Tr
	≠ the strength, vigour	D
	≠ the bone marrow	Nl D
the **marmalade**	≠ the jam	E I D Dk
	≠ the fruit compote	F
	≠ the quince jam	P
	≠ the rigged-up contest	P
	≠ the sweet (of a certain kind)	S
the **Marmite**	≠ the stew pot, boiling pot	*P E I* F
a **marmo(se)t**	≠ a little urchin	F
	≠ a dunce, a lazybones	I
	≠ a vignette	E
to **maroon**	≠ to growl, grumble	F

maroon	≠ reddish/chestnut brown	P E I F D Gr Ar J
a **marquess**	≠ a sunblind, awning	Nl Dk N S
a **marsh**	≠ a (cultivated) fen	D
a **martinet**	≠ a drop hammer	E F
	≠ a car jack	E I
	≠ a strap for corporal punishment	F
	≠ a swift	F
the **mascara**	≠ the mask, disguise	P E
	≠ the scoundrel, buffoon, the masked person	Gr
to **mash**	≠ to chew	F
a **mask**	≠ a worm, maggot	S
	≠ a masked person, s/o in fancy dress	D
to **mass**	≠ to massage	*Nl* D
the **mass/Mass**	≠ the (ceremonial) mace	F
	≠ the dough	P E I
	≠ the measure(ment), size, gauge	D
	≠ the earth (in electricity)	E F
	≠ the cake mixture	N
	≠ the plaster, mortar	P E
	≠ the mallet, sledgehammer	*I* F
	≠ the capital, gross assets	F
	≠ the boulder, rock	I
	≠ the pasta	P
	≠ the material s/th is made of	D
the **High Mass**	≠ the bulk	D
massive	≠ solid, robust	F Nl D S
a **massive savage**	≠ a wild mountain (block)	F
to **masticate**	≠ to fill teeth (as at the dentist's)	F
a **mat**	≠ a mast	F
	≠ a measure(ment); companion	Nl
	≠ a forest, wood	P
	≠ a copse, tree clump	E
mat(t)	≠ dull, tame, faint, feeble, weak	Nl D Dk N S
a **matador**	≠ a murderer	P E
the **match**	≠ the squash, mud, pulp	D
	≠ the total defeat	D
the **material**	≠ the plant, working stock of a factory	F
to **materialise**	≠ to turn out (that)	S

a **materialist**	≠ a chemist	Dk
the **maternity**	≠ the maternity hospital	P I F
	≠ the giving birth	P E I
a **matinée**	≠ a whole morning	F
to **matriculate**	→ to enrol, register (s/o)	P E
a **matrimony**	≠ a married couple; double bed	E
a **matter**	≠ a subject studied at school	P E I F
a **mattress**	≠ a seaman, sailor	*Nl D* Dk N S
the **maturity**	≠ the university entrance exam	I
meagre	→ lean, fasting, skinny	F Nl D Dk N S
to **mean**	≠ to think, believe	Nl D Dk N S
a **meaning**	≠ an opinion	Nl D Dk N S
	≠ an intention	Nl Dk N S
the **meat**	≠ the rent, the hire/hiring	D
the **mechanic**	≠ the mechanics (branch of physics)	P E I F *Nl* D Dk N S *Tr* Gr Ar
	≠ the motor (of a car)	F Gr
the **medicine**	≠ the doctor	F
Medusa	→ a jelly fish	P *E* I F Gr
to **meet**	≠ to rent	D
a **meeting**	≠ a (public) demonstration	E
the **melissa**	≠ the bee	Gr
a **melon**	≠ an apple	Gr
the **memoir**	≠ the memory	F
a **menu**	≠ a complete meal	D
	≠ a set meal, table d'hôte	Dk
a **day's menu**	≠ a set meal, table d'hôte	N
mercy	≠ thanks	F Nl Tr *Gr*
a **mere**	≠ a sea	D
	≠ a mother	F
	≠ an ant; lake	Nl
a **mess**	≠ a Mass	I F D Dk N S
	≠ a tit (small bird); coward	S
	≠ a knife	Nl
	≠ a table	P E
	≠ a shop counter, landing (on stairs); presiding board, committee	E
	≠ a placing, putting up for sale	I
	≠ a trade fair/exhibition	D Dk N S
	≠ a scalpel	J
a **metaphor**	≠ a lorry	Gr
the **metaphrasis**	≠ the translation	Gr

a **metre**	≠ a metre-long ruler	P E F Nl
	≠ a lodger	I D
a **metropolis**	≠ a cathedral	Gr
	≠ a cosmopolitan city	F
	≠ a mother country	F
midday	≠ lunch (midday meal)	Dk N S Ch
a **middle**	≠ an aid, help, remedy, means	Nl *D* Dk N S
middle-aged	≠ medieval	Nl *D* Dk N
mid-week	≠ Wednesday	Nl D
a **millipede**	≠ a centipede	F
to **mime**	≠ to spoil/pamper (a child)	P E
	≠ to fondle/stroke (e.g. a cat)	P
	≠ to flatter, humour	E
the **mime**	≠ the pampering, indulgence, spoiling	E
	≠ the caress, fondling	P
the **mimic**	≠ the art of mime/acting/ mimicry	Nl D N
	≠ the (funny) facial expression	Dk N S
a **mine**	≠ a pen(cil) refill	E I F D
	≠ an expression (on the face)	F Nl D Dk N S
	→ an explosive charge	P I F Nl D Dk N S
a **mint**	≠ a coin	*Nl* Dk N S
to **minute**	≠ to draw up (an agreement/ schedule)	F
	≠ to make a bill for fees	*P* E
a **minute**	≠ a rough copy, draft	P E I F
	≠ a menu	E
	≠ a dish ordered in a restaurant	P
at **the minute**	≠ retail (selling)	I S
minutely	≠ very carefully	P E I F
a **mire**	≠ an ant	Nl Dk S
minutely	≠ very carefully	P E I F
a **mire**	≠ an ant	Nl Dk S
a **miscreant**	≠ an infidel	F
the **miser**	≠ the destitution, poverty, drudgery	F Nl
miserable	→ poor, needy, destitute	P E I
	≠ miserly, stingy	P E
the **misericord**	≠ the pity, mercy	P E *I* F
	≠ the almshouse	P
to **miss**	≠ to blink, screw up one's eyes	Dk N
	≠ to manage/do without	Nl
a **mission**	→ a job, duty, errand	E

the **mist**	≠ the dung, manure; compost heap	Nl D
a **mixer**	≠ a barman	D
the **mnemonic**	≠ the memory, ability to remember	Gr
a **moan**	≠ a poppy	D
a **mobile**	≠ a piece of furniture	P I Nl D
	≠ a motive for a crime	F
mobile	≠ changeable, fickle, unstable, restless	I
to **mobilise**	≠ to get ready	F
to **mock**	≠ to sulk	Nl Dk
the **modality**	≠ the method, condition, restrictive clause	E I F
a **mode**	→ a way, method	P E I F
	≠ a fashion	P E I F Nl D Dk N S
	≠ a tune, melody	P
	≠ a key (in music)	I
the **mode**	≠ the directions for use	F
	≠ the courage	Dk *N* S
the **modern style**	≠ (the) art nouveau	F
the **moleskin**	≠ imitation leather	F
to **molest**	≠ to bother, inconvenience	E I
	≠ to tease, vex	P
from **the moment**	≠ seeing that	F
the **money**	≠ the small change	F
a **monster**	≠ a sample, a pattern	Nl Dk N S
the **montage**	≠ the assembly, fitting (together)	P E I F Nl D Dk N S Tr Ar
the **monuments**	≠ the famous buildings, sights of a town	E I F
the **mood**	≠ the courage, bravery	Nl D Dk N S
moody	≠ brave, courageous, plucky	Nl D Dk N S
the **moonshine**	≠ the moonlight	*Nl* D *Dk* N S
a **moor/Moor**	≠ a bog, swamp, marshy area	D
	≠ a horse's bit; dead man	F
	≠ a mother	*Nl* Dk N S
	≠ a nut (for a bolt)	Nl
a **moose**	≠ a mouse	Dk N S Ch
to **mop**	≠ to pinch (the skin)	D
a **mop**	≠ a joke	Nl
the **moquette**	≠ the fitted carpet	I F
	≠ the decoy bird	F
the **moral**	≠ the morale	P E F *Nl* D Dk N S Tr
the **morale**	≠ the moral of a story	I F Nl

	≠ the moral(s) of a person	I
the **morality**	≠ the moral of a story	F
morbid	≠ soft (texture)	P E I *F*
the **morgue**	≠ the haughtiness, pride, arrogance	F
the **morning dress**	≠ the dressing gown	Nl D *Dk* N S
a **morning service**	≠ a cheap breakfast	J
morose	≠ tardy, in arrears, behindhand	*E* I
	≠ slow, dilatory, sluggish	P E
(the) **Morse**	≠ the walrus	P E F
	≠ the bite	I
the **mortal**	≠ the mortar	Nl
mortal	≠ deadly (boring), unending	E F
mortified	→ gangrened	P *I* F
	≠ declared null and void	Dk N
a **motel**	≠ a brothel	J
a **motif**	See **motive**	
a **motion**	≠ an exercise (physical)	Dk N S
to **motivate**	≠ to explain, justify reasons for s/th	P E I F Nl
the **motive**	→ the grounds, purpose, aim, explanation for s/th	P E I F Nl D
the **motor**	≠ the (prime) mover	E I F D
	≠ the motorboat	Tr
	≠ the motorcycle	*P* E
a **motorist**	≠ a motorcyclist	E
a **mould**	≠ a dress pattern	E
to **mount**	≠ to carry/take up (e.g. luggage)	F
	≠ to lift up; overlap	E
	≠ to rouse	I
	≠ to equip, furnish (e.g. soldiers)	D Dk N
	≠ to frame (a picture)	Nl
	≠ to build, construct, put together, assemble	Nl S
a **little mouse**	≠ a funny bone	D
the **mousse**	≠ the ship's boy; the moss	F
a **movement of humour**	≠ a fit/burst of temper	F
the **muck**	≠ the faint/low sound	D
	≠ the grumble	Dk N S
	≠ the mosquito, midge	Nl D *Dk*

a **muff**	≠ a musty smell	D
a **muffler**	→ a scarf	J
a **mug**	≠ a mosquito, midge	Nl Ch
	≠ a jug	Dk N
	≠ a patch of mildew/mould	Dk N
the **mug**	≠ the plebs, common people	N
a **multitude**	→ a crowd	P *E*
the **mum**	≠ the drive, energy	Ch
mundane	≠ fashionable, smart	E F Nl D
a **mundane event**	≠ a social event	P I F
the **municipal credit**	≠ the pawn shop	F
a **murder**	≠ a murderer	*Nl* D Dk N S
to **murmur**	≠ to gossip, tell tales	E I
	→ to grumble, complain	P E
to **muse**	≠ to idle, dawdle, moon about	F
	≠ to be on the alert; sniff	I
the **music**	≠ the musician, composer, player, singer	P E
a **music hall**	≠ a concert hall	D S
a **must**	≠ an ordeal	Dk S Ch
to **muster**	≠ to examine, inspect	Nl D
	≠ to pattern, bring to shape	D
the **myrrh**	≠ the (Egyptian) mummy	J
a **mystification**	≠ a hoax, deception, trick	P E
to **mystify**	≠ to hoax, cheat, deceive, mix up	P E *F*

n

to **nag**	≠ to gnaw, nibble	D
to **nap**	≠ to pinch, nip, snatch (s/th)	Dk N S
	≠ to nibble (food)	S
a **nap(pe)**	≠ a tablecloth; water table; oil slick	F
	≠ a tassel, tuft	I
	≠ a bite, nibble	Dk *N* S
	≠ a drinking cup	Nl
	≠ a baby's dummy	S
national	≠ patriotic, nationalistic	Dk

the **national economy**	≠ the economics, political economy	Dk S
to **nationalise**	≠ to naturalise	P E
a **natural**	≠ a native, inhabitant	P E F
the **(dead) nature**	≠ the still life	P *E* I F
in **nature**	≠ in kind (payment)	I F Nl D
a **nave**	≠ a boat, vessel	P E I
	≠ a church aisle	P
	≠ a large building; factory	E
	≠ a hub (on a wheel), propeller boss	Dk N S
	≠ a wheel's outer rim	Nl
the **navigation**	≠ the voyage	P E I
the **Nazis**	≠ the nationalists; nations	Nl
near	≠ to	Nl
neat	≠ clean, clear, plain	I F
	≠ kind, pleasant	D
	≠ decent, respectable	Nl
	≠ pretty, nice (esp. sarcastically)	Dk
the **necessary**	≠ the dressing case, toilet bag	E Nl S
	≠ the sewing kit	Nl S
	≠ the loo, W.C.	P
to **necessitate**	≠ to need	*P* E
to **neck**	≠ to tease	D
the **neck**	≠ the nape of the neck	Nl D Dk *N* S
	≠ the sheaf	N
the **necrology**	≠ the obituary	I F D
a **needle**	≠ a pin	D
in **a negligee**	≠ in informal/casual clothes	F
a **negro**	≠ a ghostwriter	F
nervous	→ upset, tense, irritated	P E I F Nl D Dk N S Tr Ar
a **net**	≠ a string bag a cobweb	Dk N
the **net**	≠ the mains wiring	Dk N
nettly	≠ ticklish, tricky, delicate	Nl
a **niche**	≠ a trick, prank; dog-kennel	F
to **nick**	≠ to nod (off)	Nl D Dk N S
the **nickel**	≠ the door key	*Dk N* S
a **night**	≠ a night club	I
	≠ an evening game (of spectator sports)	J
a **night club**	≠ a low/shady night spot	P
noble	≠ distinguished	Dk

	≠ generous	D Dk N
	≠ refined, genteel	S
the **noise**	≠ the quarrel(ling)	F
noisome	≠ frugal, content with little	Dk N
noisy	≠ boring	I
a **nomination**	≠ an appointment to a job/post	F
a **normal school**	≠ a teacher-training college	E F
normalised	→ standardised	P E F Nl
a **Norman**	≠ a Dane	Nl
not the way out	≠ the emergency exit	Nl D
a **notch**	≠ a night	E
	≠ a nut (to eat)	I
a **note**	≠ a nut (to eat)	Nl
	≠ an emergency	Nl D
	≠ a mark (in school tests/ exams)	P E I F D Tr
	≠ an invoice, bill, account	E F Nl Dk N
	≠ a school report	E
	≠ a trawl/fishing net	N S
	≠ a groove	Dk
a **notebook**	≠ a music book, score, song book	N S
a **notice**	≠ a note, memorandum	Nl D
	≠ a paragraph	Dk S
	≠ a news item	D S
	≠ a caption, comment(ary)	F
the **notoriety**	≠ the fame, repute	P E I F
notorious	≠ famous, renowned, well-known	P E I *F*
a **noun**	≠ a name	Dk N
a **novel**	≠ a (long) short story	P I F Nl D Dk N S Gr
the **novels**	≠ the news	F
now	≠ up-to-date, trendy, smart	J
a **nude**	≠ a knot	E
to **number**	≠ to mention (s/o)	E
a **number**	≠ a name	E
	≠ a hoax, trick	Dk
a **nut**	≠ a groove, slot	D
	≠ a use; profit, benefit	Nl

O

an **obituary**	≠ a mortuary	P I
the **obligations**	≠ the bonds, debentures, etc.	E I F Nl D Dk N S
	≠ the duties (at work)	P E
the **obliteration**	≠ the stamp cancellation	F
obscure	→ dark, overcast, gloomy	E *I* F
	≠ shady, fishy, dubious	Nl
the **obscurity**	≠ the darkness, gloom	E *I* F
obsequious	≠ kind, considerate, thoughtful	P
	≠ attentive, obedient, obliging	E
the **obstetrics**	≠ the midwives	I
an **occasion**	≠ a chance, opportunity	P E I F
occasionally	≠ by chance, accidentally	E
the **occasions**	≠ the second-hand bargains	P E I F Nl D
occult	≠ out of sight, hidden, concealed	P E I *F*
to **occur**	≠ to need, require	I
an **occurrence**	≠ a circumstance, emergency	F
	≠ a need	I
	≠ a bright idea, sudden whim	E
occurring	≠ entertaining, amusing, lively	E
of(f)	≠ or	Nl
an **off day**	≠ a day off, free day	J
to **offer**	≠ to sacrifice	*Nl* D Dk N S
	≠ to give (a present)	P I F
	≠ to hold/give (a party)	P E
an **offer**	≠ a victim, sacrifice	Nl *D* Dk N S
an **office**	≠ a job, position, post	P E
	≠ a pantry, larder; a church service	F
	≠ a chemists' laboratory/workshop	D
an **official**	≠ a craftsman, a skilled workman	P E
officious	≠ semi-official, unofficial	P E I F Nl D Dk N S
	≠ obliging, accommodating, helpful	P E I *F*
to **offset**	≠ to dismiss; earmark	Dk N
	≠ to sell, dispose of; deposit	Dk
	≠ to cut/push off, trim	Nl
an **old-timer**	≠ a veteran car	D
an **omnibus**	≠ a stopping train	*E* I F
one	≠ (impersonal) you, we, they	E F
one man	≠ (a) dictator	J

an **onslaught**	≠ an attempt (on s/o's life)	Nl D
to **ooze**	≠ to smoke, reek	Dk N S
the **ooze**	≠ the smell (of food)	Dk N S
the **opera**	≠ the (artistic) work/product	I
	≠ the opera house	P F
to **operate**	≠ to effect, accomplish, carry out	P F
an **operations room**	≠ an operating theatre	P E *I* F *Nl D Dk N* S
the **opportunity**	≠ the expediency, opportuneness	Nl
the **opposition(s)**	≠ the public competitive exams	E
an **oration**	≠ a prayer	P E I
	≠ a sentence	P E
	≠ a clause	E
an **oratorio**	≠ an oratory, a place of prayer	P E I
an **ordeal**	≠ a judgment	Nl
the **ord(i)nance**	≠ the messenger (esp. military), dispatch rider	D Dk
	≠ the batman, orderly	F Dk S
	≠ a prescription	F
ordinary	→ vulgar, base, low, cheap	P E *I* Nl D Dk N S
an **ordination**	≠ a prescription	D S
the **ore**	≠ the ear	Nl Dk N S
	≠ the gold	*E I* F
	≠ the penny	Dk N S
an **organ**	≠ any musical instrument	Gr
	≠ a music box	J
	≠ a voice	D Dk N S
the **orgasm**	≠ the excitement, nervous tension	I
	≠ s/th smashing, super	*P* F
to **orientate**	≠ to inform, instruct	Nl D Dk N S
falsely orientated	≠ wrongly informed	D
an **original**	→ an individualist	P E I F Nl D Dk N S
	≠ a subject of a portrait	D
original	≠ fussy, difficult to deal with	F
	≠ unpredictable	E
ostensible	≠ fit to be seen, open, patent	F
	≠ exuberant	P
ostensibly	≠ openly, publicly	F
	≠ exuberantly	P

the **outbuilding**	≠ the education	S
an **outcast**	≠ a draft, plan, design, sketch	Dk N
the **outcome**	≠ the living, livelihood	Dk N S
to **outdo**	≠ to quench (fire)	Nl
	≠ to cross out (words)	Nl
the **outfall**	≠ the result, outcome, issue, upshot	Dk N S
	≠ the outburst	Nl S
	≠ the fallout	Nl Dk
an **outing**	≠ an utterance, verbal expression	Nl
outlandish	≠ foreign, exotic	D Dk N S
an **outlay**	≠ a loan	D *Dk N*
	≠ an enlargement, extension	Nl D
	≠ an explanation, interpretation	Nl D
	≠ a contribution to a debate	S
	≠ a display (of goods)	D
an **outlet**	≠ an exhaust (pipe)	Nl
an **outrage**	≠ an insult, outrageous remark	F
outrageous	≠ insulting	F
an **outset**	≠ a trousseau	Nl
	≠ a delay, deferment	Dk N
outspoken	≠ really, most	D
	≠ pronounced, noticeable, striking	Nl
outstanding	≠ projecting, protruding	Nl Dk N S
	≠ on strike	D
an **oven**	≠ a stove, heater	D
an **over**	≠ an overcoat	J
	≠ a river bank	Nl
over	≠ opposite, across	Nl *Dk*
an **overall**	≠ a track/running suit	F N S
overbearing	≠ indulgent, tolerant	Dk N
to **overbook**	≠ to transfer (money)	Nl
an **overbooking**	≠ a transfer (of money)	Nl
to **overcome**	≠ to obtain, get	D S
	≠ to happen; come through/across	Nl
	≠ to manage; be equal to; afford	Dk N
	≠ to take over	S
to **overdo**	≠ to repeat	Nl
	≠ to dispose of, sell	Nl
an **overdrive**	≠ an exaggeration	Nl Dk N S

an **overflow**	≠ an abundance, profusion	*Nl* D *Dk N* S
the **overhang**	≠ the hangings	D
	≠ the surplus money	D
to **overhaul**	≠ to lurch/heel over	D N
	≠ to fetch/ferry over; pull	Nl D
	≠ to persuade	Nl
	→ to overtake (traffic)	D Dk
an **overhaul**	≠ a beating, smacking	Dk
	≠ a talking-to	Dk N S
the **overheads**	≠ the authorities, powers that be	Nl
	≠ the supreme head of state	Dk N S
to **overhear**	≠ to ignore, misunderstand, miss, fail to hear	D Dk N
	≠ to hear (lessons, etc.) learnt by heart	Nl Dk N
to **overload**	≠ to reload	Nl
	≠ to let (s/o) have, lend, hand over	Dk
an **overload**	≠ an abundance	Nl
to **overplant**	≠ to transplant	Nl
to **overreach**	≠ to hand over, present s/o with	Nl Dk N S
to **override**	≠ to run over, crush (limbs)	Nl
to **oversee**	≠ to weigh up, assess, estimate, survey	Nl N
	≠ to check, revise; indulge	N S
	≠ to fail to see, overlook, ignore, pass over	D Dk N S
the **oversight**	≠ the survey, review, summary	Nl D Dk N S
the **overspill**	≠ the adultery	Nl
	≠ the re-recording	D
to **overtake**	≠ to copy (out), oversubscribe	Nl
	≠ to take over	Dk N
	≠ to undertake (work)	N S
an **overture**	≠ an opening (up)	F
to **overwind**	≠ to subdue, overcome, conquer	D
to **overwork**	≠ to work overtime	Nl

p

English	≠	Languages
the **pace**	≠ the peace	I
to **pack**	≠ to succeed; help	D
	≠ to grab, seize, grasp, clutch, hug	Nl D
	≠ to leave, go away, move off	S
to **pack up**	≠ to unpack	Dk N S
	≠ to pick up, fetch	Nl
a **pack**	≠ a suit	Nl
	≠ a mob	N
the **package**	≠ the pasturage, grazing	F
a **packet**	≠ a woman's monthly period	P
the **packing**	≠ the seal, gasket	Nl
the **pact**	≠ the rent (payment)	Nl
	≠ the lease, tenure	Nl D
a **pad**	≠ a toad	Nl N S
	≠ an amphibian	Dk
	≠ a path, track; gangway	Nl
a **padre**	≠ a father (of a family)	E I
a **pail**	≠ a straw	F
a **pain**	≠ a loaf of bread	F
	≠ a trouble, bother	P E I F
the **pain**	≠ the grief, sorrow	P E I
to **pair(up)**	≠ to hover, soar	P
a **pal**	≠ a ratchet(wheel), pawl	Nl *D* N
	≠ a (low) stool	S
a **palace**	≠ a block of flats	I
	≠ a hard palate	F
	≠ a town house, mansion	Dk
	≠ a luxury hotel	F
a **palaver**	≠ a word	*P* E
a **palette, pallet**	≠ a stake, post	I
	≠ a shovel, trowel; fallow deer; clown	E
	≠ a quoit; table-tennis bat; paddle	F
a **pamphlet**	≠ a lampoon	P E F Nl D Dk
a **pan**	≠ a mishap, breakdown	P E F Nl D Tr
	≠ a loaf of bread	E I J
	≠ a piece of cloth/fabric	P
	≠ a flap (of clothing)	F
	≠ a forehead	*Dk* N S
	≠ a surface, section, face, side	F

a **panel**	≠ a pot, saucepan; a cushion; daily food	P
	≠ a skirting board	Dk *N S*
the **panel**	≠ the daily food	P
a **pannier**	≠ a banner, standard (flag)	D
to **pant**	≠ to seize, confiscate	Dk
	≠ to pawn	N S
the **panties**	≠ the tights	E F Nl Dk
the **pantomime**	≠ the hand/sign language	Gr
	≠ the person performing mime	D
a **pantry**	≠ a baker's shop	I
the **pants**	≠ the things pawned	*Nl* Dk
the **panzer**	≠ the coat of mail, armour (plate)	Nl D Dk N *S*
the **pap(a)**	≠ the Pope	P E I F Nl Tr *Gr* Ar
	≠ the porridge	P Nl
the **paper**	≠ the role, part	P *E*
	≠ the stock, bond	*P* E D
	≠ the goitre	*P* E
a **parade**	≠ a stop (e.g. of a bus)	*P* E
	≠ a stoppage	E
	≠ a hit parade	P
	≠ a bet, wager, stake	P E
	≠ s/th marvellous	P
the **parade**	≠ the vanity, pride, boastfulness	E
the **paraffin**	≠ the wax (e.g. as for a surfboard)	P
a **paragraph**	≠ a prescription	Gr
	≠ an item; clause	S
the **parapher-nalia**	≠ the wife's possessions	Gr
the **parasite(s)**	≠ the atmospherics/statics in radio reception	*P E* F Tr
to **pare**	≠ to stop	P E
the **parents**	≠ the relations, relatives	P *E* I *F*
the **park**	≠ the grounds (of a building, not necessarily public)	P I F
the **parking**	≠ the car park/parking place	I F Nl N S J Ch Ar
the **parole**	≠ the word	I F
	≠ the password	N S
	≠ the slogan (e.g. of a pressure group)	D Dk N
the **parquet**	≠ the (theatre) stalls	D Dk N S
	≠ the public prosecutor, etc.	F

parsimonious	≠ slow, deliberate, calm, unhurried	E I
the **parsimony**	≠ the calm(ness), deliberateness	E I
to **part**	≠ to break, smash	P E
the **part**	≠ the childbirth, confinement	P E I
	≠ the part-time worker	J
to **partake**	≠ to divide, split up, share out	F
to **participate s/th**	≠ to make s/th known, break (news)	P E
particular	≠ personal, private (lesson)	P E I F Nl
	≠ odd, strange, unusual	E F
a **particular hotel**	≠ a (private) town house	F
in **particular**	≠ in private, confidentially	P F
particulary	≠ personally	E
	≠ privately	P
the **particulars**	≠ the (private) individuals	*P* E F Nl D Dk
a **partisan**	→ a supporter, upholder	F Tr
a **partita**	≠ a match, game	I *F* Gr
a **partition**	≠ a (musical) score	F
ne s **partner**	≠ one's opposite number in a game or in business	D
a **party**	≠ a panel, shutter	I
	≠ a choice, alternative	I
	≠ a game	E *I* F Nl D Dk N S
	≠ a spouse; match in marriage	I F Nl D Dk N S
	≠ a batch, consignment (of goods)	Nl D Dk N S
	≠ a side in a game	E Dk N
	≠ a passage in a book	S
	≠ an excursion; a set in games	D
	≠ a district (in administration)	E
	≠ an advantage, profit	E I F
the **party**	≠ the support (public)	E
	≠ wholesale	S
	≠ the mind, choice, opinion	E I F Nl D Dk N S
	≠ the class at school	N
	≠ the part, section, area	D
paschal	≠ (pertaining to) Christmas	E

to **pass**	≠ to suit (of clothes)	D Dk N S
	≠ to fit (of clothes)	Nl D Dk N S
	≠ to be convenient	Dk N S Ch
	≠ to be seemly, proper	S
	≠ to happen	P E *I* F Nl D Dk S
	≠ to tolerate, endure, bear	E
	≠ to die	E I *F*
	≠ to be true	Dk
	≠ to look after	*D* Dk N S
	≠ to try on (clothes)	Nl
	≠ to iron (clothes)	P
	≠ to go bad/off (of food)	E
	≠ to sift, sieve, filter	E I *F* D
	≠ to fade	PE
a **pass (for travel)**	→ a passport	*Nl* D Dk N S
the **pass**	≠ the nursing, care, attention	Dk N S
	≠ the gait, walk	P E I
	≠ the way through, gangway	E
	≠ a raisin	P E
	≠ a footprint, pace, (foot)step	P E I F
to **pass s/o's home**	≠ to call in on s/o	P *E* I F
to **pass s/o up**	≠ to take care of s/o	Nl S
to **pass an exam**	≠ to take/sit for an exam	P E I F
a **passage**	≠ a (travel) ticket	E
	≠ a pedestrian subway	D
	≠ a pedestrian crossing	F
passé	≠ faded	F
a **passe-partout**	→ a pass/master key	I F Nl D
the **passive**	See **active**	
the **past(a)**	≠ the paste	P Dk N S
	≠ the briefcase, wallet, folder, portfolio	P
	≠ the cake	Tr
a **paste**	≠ a meal	I
	≠ a pie	Nl
	≠ a cover-board of a book	E
the **paste**	≠ the fodder, pasture	E
the **pastel**	≠ the cake	E
	≠ the tart; fried food, etc.	P
	≠ the pâté, pie	E
	≠ the ingredients of pastry (uncooked)	I
	≠ the savoury flan	D

the **pat**	≠ (the) stalemate in chess	F D
a **patch**	≠ a fix, bit of trouble	D
a **pâté**	≠ a block of buildings; pie	F
the **patent**	≠ the deed (of a flat)	P
	≠ the camp bed	P
	≠ the military commission	*P* D
	≠ the permission to do s/th	F
patent	≠ smart, clever, splendid	P Nl D
a **guide's patent**	≠ a driving licence	P I
a **master's patent**	≠ a teaching diploma	I
pathetic	≠ high-flown	N S
	≠ solemn, impressive	F D Dk
	≠ indifferent	Gr
the **pathos**	≠ the suffering	Gr
	≠ the fervour, solemnity, exuberance, animation	D
	≠ the bathos, theatricality	F
	≠ the bombast, oratorical effect	Dk *N*
a **patio**	≠ a children's (school) playground	P E
the **patron**	≠ the average size (in clothes)	F
a **patron**	≠ a dressmaking pattern	P E F Tr Gr
	≠ a patron saint	E I F Nl D
	≠ a template, design	F Nl D
	≠ a cartridge	Nl D Dk N S
	≠ a boss, employer	P E F Nl S Tr
	≠ a landlord of a bar, etc.	P E
	≠ a chap, fellow	D
	≠ a ship's master, skipper	P E I F D
a **pause**	≠ an interval	D
	≠ a pope	Nl
a **pavement**	≠ a floor (of a room)	P I
	≠ a tiled floor	E
	→ a piece of ornate paving	F
a **pavilion**	≠ a detached house	F
	→ a garden summer-house	D
	≠ a flag	P E F
	≠ a ward/section in a hospital	P
	≠ a type of café or nightclub	Tr
	≠ a stall at a fair	I
	≠ a simple-standard hotel	Gr
the **peach**	≠ the bad luck	Nl D
	≠ the pitch	D

peaked, picked	≠ quilted	F
	≠ spotted, dotted, crazy, sour (of wine), staccato (of notes in music), speckled, stippled, choppy (of the sea)	P E
	≠ stung, bitten; annoyed, irritated	P E I F
a **pear**	≠ a (light) bulb	Nl D Dk N
a **pearl**	≠ any sort of bead	D Dk N *S*
peculiar	→ special, own, unique, characteristic	P E I
	≠ appropriate	E
to **peep**	≠ to squeak	Nl D N S
	≠ to whine, whimper	N
to **peg**	≠ to stick, paste, gum, fasten (on)	P E
	≠ to hit, strike, slap, to match (of colours)	E
	≠ to seize; overtake; discover	P
a **pen**	≠ a pencil	S
	≠ a tramps' lodging house	D
to **penalise**	≠ to grieve s/o	P *E*
the **penalty**	≠ the suffering, hardship	E
	≠ the penal law	F
a **pencil**	≠ a brush	P *E* Nl Dk N S
a **pendulum**	≠ a timepiece, clock	I F Nl *D* S
penetrated	≠ earnest, serious	F
a **pension**	→ a boarding house	P E I F Nl D Dk S Gr Ar
the **pension**	≠ the board, food	N
	≠ the boarding school	F
	≠ the alimony	F
a **pensioner**	≠ a boarder (in a school); guest	I F Dk N
per se	≠ by hook or by crook	Nl
to **perceive (money)**	≠ to earn/get money/a salary	E
the **perception**	≠ the cashing/drawing of a cheque	I
perfect	≠ agreed, settled, concluded	D
a **perfume**	≠ a flavour of an ice cream	F
a **periodical**	≠ a newspaper	I E
a **perk**	≠ a flower-bed	Nl
the **perks**	≠ the bounds of decency	Nl
the **permanence**	≠ the stay, sojourn	P E *I*

	≠ the premises open day and night	F
	≠ the (weekend) duty	F
the **permission**	≠ the (military) leave (in BE)/furlough (in AE)	P E F Dk N S
the **persecution**	≠ the hunt, chase	P E
a **person**	→ a character (in a story)	Nl D Dk N S
the **persona**	≠ the person	E I
a **personality**	≠ a personal/offensive remark	F
a **personage**	≠ a character in a play/story	E I F
a **personifi-cation**	≠ an impersonation	E I F
the **perspective**	≠ the outlook, prospect(s)	P E F
	≠ the standpoint	D
to **be per-suaded**	≠ to be quite convinced	P E I F
the **persuasion**	≠ the conviction, belief	P E I F
Peru	≠ a turkey; onlooker	P
	≠ a lot of money, El Dorado	I F
	≠ a pear-shaped gem	Tr
a **pest**	≠ a plague	*P* E I F Nl D Dk N S
to **pester**	≠ to curse, storm at	F
	≠ to tease	Nl
the **pestle**	≠ the dried fruit	Tr
a **pet**	≠ a lie, fib; woodpecker	P
	≠ a cap	Nl
	≠ a fart	F
to **pet**	≠ to poke, pick, peck	S
the **petrol**	≠ the paraffin	*D* Dk N Gr
	≠ the crude/mineral oil	P E F D S
the **petroleum**	≠ the paraffin (in BE), kerosine (in AE)	D
petulant	≠ brash, brazen, saucy, shameless, insolent, cheeky, frisky	P E I F
a **phone**	≠ a sound, voice, shout	Gr
the **photo**	≠ the photography	F
a **photograph**	≠ a photographer	P E I F Nl D Dk N S
the **photo-graphic apparatus**	≠ the camera	D Dk *N* S
the **photography**	≠ the photograph	P E I F D Dk N S
a **phrase**	≠ a sentence	P E I F
	≠ a cliché, set/trite/hollow phrase	Nl D Dk N
	≠ a saying	Gr

the **physic,** **physique**	≠ the physics	P E I F D Dk N S Gr *Ar*
physical	≠ natural, not man-made	Gr
a **physician**	≠ a physicist	F
the **physiognomy**	≠ the general look/appearance	F
a **piano**	≠ a plain, plot, plan; storey, floor	I
a **piccolo**	≠ a (hotel) page-boy, bell-boy	Nl D Dk N S
	≠ a young child	I
to **pick**	≠ to sting, prick, offend	P E I F
	≠ to irritate	E I F
	≠ to tear up	P
a **pick**	≠ a woodpecker	E *I* F
	≠ a spade (in cards)	I F D
	≠ a grudge, spite	F Nl D
a **pick-up**	≠ a record-player (including turntable, etc.)	P F *Nl* Tr Gr Ar
picked	See **peaked**	
a **picket**	≠ a (tent) peg, stake	F
	≠ a local wine	F
a **pickle**	≠ a pimple	D
a **pie**	≠ a foot	E
a **piece**	≠ a room	F
	→ a gun	Dk
	≠ a booklet, pamphlet, leaflet	Dk
	≠ a (theatre) play	F N Tr
the **piety**	≠ the reverence, veneration, respect	D Dk N S
the **pigeon**	≠ the rent money	I
to **pile**	≠ to take soundings/bearings	Nl D
a **pile**	≠ an arrow, bolt, shaft	Nl
a **pill**	≠ a battery (electric)	P E I F Tr
	≠ an arrow, bolt, shaft	Dk N S
	≠ a tail side of a coin	F
a **pillow**	≠ a bolster	Nl
a **pilot**	≠ a racing-car driver	P E I F Nl Ch
	≠ a first mate on a ship	P E
a **pimp**	≠ a young lad (implying too young)	D
a **pin**	≠ a stick; perch for a bird	Dk N S
	≠ a row (ie line)	Dk
the **pincers**	≠ the clothes pegs	E
to **pinch**	≠ to puncture, pierce, prod	E
	≠ to heave (out), spring (from), reel, lurch	P

a **pinch**	≠ a spike, point	E
	≠ a kitchen boy; scullion	E
	≠ a leap, jump	P
a **pineapple**	≠ a pine cone	F *Nl*
a **pinion**	≠ a gable (end)	F
	≠ an edible pine kernel	P E
to **pink**	≠ to blink, wink	Nl
the **pink**	≠ the little finger	Nl
pink	≠ sensual, sexy	J
a **pint**	≠ a look, appearance	E
	≠ a facial expression	P
	≠ a person's mental state	J
a **pipe**	≠ a trouser leg; ship's funnel	Nl
piqued	See **peaked**	
a **piscina**	≠ a swimming pool	P E I *F*
to **piss**	≠ to trample, tread (on), crush, flatten	P E
	≠ to walk, step, tread	P E
	≠ to lie on, cover	E
	≠ to disregard, walk over, abuse	E
	≠ to humiliate, hurt	P
	≠ to pinch, steal	E
a **piss**	≠ a flat, apartment	E
	≠ the floor, ground, (stair) tread	P E
a **piston**	≠ a useful contact/connection	F
	≠ a cornet (in music)	P F Nl
a **pit**	≠ a puddle	Dk
	≠ a (fruit) pip	Nl
the **pitch**	≠ the bastard	Tr
	≠ the penis	E
a **pittance**	≠ a (monk's) daily food allowance/ration	P E F
	≠ a second course of a meal	I
	≠ a bit of grub	E
a **placard**	≠ a wall cupboard	F Ch
	≠ a panel in a door	F
a **place**	≠ a (town/village) square	E *I* F D Dk N S
the **place**	≠ the space, room	E F Nl D *Dk* N S
	≠ the instalment payment	E
the **plague**	≠ the nuisance, drudgery, bother	Nl D Dk N *S*
a **plaid**	→ a travelling rug	E I F Nl D Dk N S
a **plain**	See **plane**	

a **plan**	≠ an open space	D
	≠ a plane	F
a **fixed plan**	≠ a tail plane of an aircraft	F
to **plane**	≠ to hover	P *E* I F
a **plane/plain**	≠ a (town/village) square	Nl S
	≠ a car hood, awning	D
	≠ a plan, scheme	P E *Dk N* S
	≠ a sports ground	S
	≠ a plot of land	E
	≠ a page of a newspaper	E
a **plank**	≠ a wooden (plank) fence	D
	≠ a hoarding, poster board	S
	≠ a shelf	Nl
the **planking**	≠ the surf-riding	F
to **plant**	≠ to abandon, jilt; fix, set up	*I* F
	≠ to sack; reach	E
a **plant**	≠ a floor, storey	E
	≠ a plan, design	P E *I*
	≠ a sole of the foot	P E *I* F
the **plantation**	≠ the planted land, the planting	P E
a **plaque**	≠ a (car) numberplate	E F
	≠ a (gramophone) record	Tr
the **plaster**	≠ the pavement, paved area	D
the **plastic**	≠ the clay modelling	P
	≠ the (piece of) sculpture	E I F *Nl* D Gr
	≠ the terrorist's bomb	F
	≠ the scale model	I
	≠ the plastic surgery	Dk Tr Gr
	≠ the dance/ballet lesson/ exercise	N S
	≠ the elastic	Tr
	≠ the form of the human body	P
a **plate**	≠ a gramophone record	Nl D Dk N S
	≠ a dish of food	E
	≠ a plateau, area of upland	D
	≠ an engraving, picture	Nl
the **plate**	≠ the silver, money	E
a **plateau**	≠ a tray, a (record) turntable	F
plausible	≠ commendable, praiseworthy	E
a **play**	≠ a beach	E
a **plectrum**	≠ a morse/typewriter key	Gr
pliant	≠ folding, collapsible	F
the **plight**	≠ the (state of) bankruptcy	D
	≠ the duty	Nl *D* Dk N S

the **plinth**	≠ the vaulting horse	Nl Dk S
to **pluck**	→ to pick	Nl Dk N S
a **plume**	≠ a pen	E F
plump	≠ clumsy, awkward, coarse, heavy, rude	*Nl* D Dk N S
the **plunder**	≠ the rubbish, junk	D
	≠ the trouble, toil	N
to **ply**	≠ to bend, fold (over)	F
pneumatic	≠ witty, intellectual, spiritual	Gr
the **po**	≠ the backside	D
a **pochard**	≠ a drunkard	F
a **pocketbook**	≠ a paperback (edition)	*F* Nl Dk S
to **point**	≠ to appear, spring up	F
	≠ to collect unemployment money	F
	≠ to tick off (names on a list)	F
	≠ to sharpen (pencils); prick, stab	F
a **point**	≠ a punctuation mark	F
	≠ a baby's nappy	F
	→ a (sewing) stitch	F
a **poke**	≠ a fag (cigarette)	Nl
	≠ a poker	Nl
the **police**	≠ the (insurance) policy	F D
the **policy**	≠ the police	P E I Nl D Dk
	≠ the town	Gr
a **politic man**	≠ a politician	*P I* F
the **politics**	≠ the politician	Gr
a **political father/ mother**	≠ a father/mother-in-law	E
the **polo**	≠ the casual shirt	F
	≠ the polo-necked sweater	E
	≠ the (North/South) Pole	P E I
	≠ the focus, terminal	E
	≠ the ice lolly	E
	≠ the political leader	I
a **polygon**	≠ a rifle range	I F Tr
	≠ a building site, housing estate	E
the **pomp**	≠ the pump	E I F Nl
ich **pomp**	≠ a politician who asks penetrating questions	J
a **pond**	≠ a pound (sterling or weight)	Nl *Dk N S*

to **ponder**	≠ to speak thoughtfully	P
	≠ to eulogise, praise excessively	E
	≠ to lay (eggs)	F
a **pony**	≠ a fringe (of hair)	Nl D
a **pool**	≠ a chicken	F
	≠ a cartel, agreement to share profits	D
the **port**	≠ the bearing, poise, mien	P F
	≠ the postage, cost of transporting goods	P I F Nl D Dk N S
	≠ the door, gate(way)	P *E* I F Nl Dk N S
	≠ the load, cargo	P
	→ the porthole	N S
a **portal**	≠ a goal; vestibule	E
	≠ a landing (on the stairs)	Nl
a **portent**	≠ a marvel, prodigy, s/th wonderful	P E I
a **porter**	≠ a goalie, goalkeeper	P E *I*
a **portfolio**	≠ a wallet	I F Nl
a **portion**	≠ a (large) number/quantity	P E
a **portmanteau**	≠ a coat hanger	F
a **pose**	≠ an exposure (of film)	P I F Tr
	≠ a time exposure	E
	≠ a sediment, deposit	E
	≠ a (paper) bag	Dk N S
the **posse**	≠ the possession, ownership	P
the **possibilities**	≠ the assets, fortune	E
a **possibility**	≠ a chance, opportunity (to do/have s/th)	P E I F
possibly	≠ if possible	I
a **post**	≠ a letter box	J
	≠ a pump	N
	≠ a seat in the theatre; room; site; stake, bet	I
	≠ an item, entry (in bookkeeping)	I F Nl *D* Dk N S
	≠ a postcard	E
	≠ a slice of meat/fish	P
	≠ a berth for tying up a ship, etc.	F
	≠ a sentry, guard	Nl *D* Dk N S
	≠ an animal skin	Tr
a **post bus**	≠ a postbox (with a number, or for collecting mail)	Nl

a **poster**	≠ a picket (in strikes)	Nl
	≠ a sweet course, pudding	E
a **postman**	≠ a post office employee (of any kind)	Dk
a **pot**	≠ a students' restaurant, drink	F
	≠ a kitty (for prize money)	Nl S
a **pot-load**	≠ a pencil	Nl
the **potency**	→ the power	P E I
a **pouf(fe)**	≠ a brothel	D
to **pout**	≠ to rule (lines on paper)	P E
a **practice**	≠ an agenda	Gr
	≠ a (navigation) pilot	P E
	≠ a file, folder	I
to **practise**		
a sport	≠ to go in for a sport	P E
	≠ to bore/cut/drill (a hole)	*P* E
pragmatic (ally)	≠ usual(ly)	P
	≠ real(ly), actual(ly), genuine(ly)	Gr
the **pragmatics**	≠ the formality, social etiquette	P
	≠ the customary way of doing s/th	I
	≠ the reality, realism	Gr
a **pram**	≠ a barge, punt, lighter	Nl D Dk N S
precarious	≠ unpredictable, uncertain	E Nl
	≠ embarrassing, awkward	Dk N
precious	≠ beautiful	E
precise	≠ necessary, needed	P E
	≠ close-fitting	F
	≠ punctual	N S
precisely	≠ viz. to be exact	P I
the **precision**	≠ the need, necessity	P E
precocious	≠ early ripening (of fruit), ready to eat sooner than most varieties	F
the **predicament**	≠ the prestige, standing, status	E
	≠ the sermonising, preaching (at s/o)	I
to **predict**	≠ to preach, lecture	P E I
a **prefect**	≠ a head of a French department	F
pregnant	→ concise, pithy, terse	D Dk N

to **prejudice**	≠ to spoil, hurt, impair, detract from	P E I F
the **prejudice**	≠ the damage (in law), tort	P F
a **premium**	≠ a prize, award	P E I Nl D *Dk* N S
to **preoccupy**	→ to worry	P E I F
the **preparation**	≠ the competence, ability	E
prepared	≠ competent, well-informed	E
	≠ cultured (of people)	P
preposter-ous	≠ arranged backwards, reversed	P
the **presbytery**	≠ the short-sightedness	*P E I* F
the **presents**	≠ those present	P I
a **preservative**	≠ a condom, sheath contra-ceptive	P E I D
the **president**	≠ the chairman	P E I F Nl
the **press**	≠ the pressure, (nervous) strain	Nl Dk N S
the **pressing**	≠ the cleaners and dyers	F
the **prestige**	≠ the spell/trick in magic	E
presto	≠ soon	I
to **pretend**	→ to claim, assert	P E I F Nl
	≠ to intend, propose	P
	≠ to aim/hope/try to do s/th; woo	E *I*
the **pretensions**	≠ the intentions, ambitions	P E F
pretty	≠ pleasant, jolly, satisfying	Nl
to **prevaricate**	≠ to depart from justice; betray trust	I F
a **prevari-cation**	≠ a breach of trust; case of maladministration	I F
to **prevent**	≠ to bias	I F
	≠ to warn, apprise	P E F
	≠ to anticipate, forestall	P I F
	≠ to admonish, tell off; advise	P
prevented	≠ biased, prejudiced	I
a **prevention**	≠ a precaution; warning	P
	≠ a preparation, warning, foresight	E
	≠ a police station	E
the **prevention**	≠ the bias, prejudice	P *E* I F
	≠ the imprisonment	F J
a **preventive**	≠ a (commercial) estimate	I

a **prick**	≠ a dot, point	Dk N S
	≠ a bull's eye	N S
	≠ a dowry	Gr
a **prickle**	≠ a stimulus, incentive	Nl
prim	≠ first-class, fine, very good	P *D Dk* N S Ch
	≠ first	I
	≠ raw (of materials)	P E
a **primate**	≠ a (sport's) record	I
the **prime**	≠ the premium, bonus, reward	F
	≠ the cousin	P E
the **primers**	≠ the early vegetables	F
primitively	≠ originally, in the beginning	P E I F
a **primrose**	≠ a hollyhock	F
principal	≠ fundamental	Nl D Dk N S
the **principality**	≠ the nobleness	P E
in **principle**	≠ as a rule	F
	≠ originally, first of all	P I
a **print**	≠ a spiced biscuit	D
a **priority**	≠ a mortgage	Dk N
a **private**	≠ an individual (person)	I
	≠ a (royal) favourite, protégé	E
	≠ a W.C., loo	P *Nl*
private	≠ mad, senseless	E
to **probe**	≠ to try, experiment	E Nl D Dk
a **probe**	≠ a (theatre/concert) rehearsal	D *Dk N*
	≠ an ordeal, demonstration, experiment	D
a **proboscis**	≠ a(n elephant's) trunk	I Gr
the **proceeds**	≠ the proceedings, procedure, method, dealings	F
to **process**	≠ to sue, litigate, prosecute	P E I D S
a **(legal) process**	→ a trial	P E I F Nl D Dk N S
to **procure**	≠ to try, endeavour, contrive	E I
	≠ to look for, be in search of	P
procured	≠ sought after, desirable	P
the **Prodigal Son**	≠ the boy genius	P E I F
the **product**	≠ the produce	P E I F Nl D Dk N S
the **profane**	≠ the outsiders, laymen (i.e. those not professional)	P E I F
a **professor**	≠ a teacher (in a general sense)	P E I F
to **proffer**	≠ to utter	P E I F
	≠ to make a speech	P

the **(exam) program(me)**	≠ the (exam) syllabus	P E I F Nl D Dk Tr Gr
a **prole**	≠ an issue, progeny, offspring	P E I
a **promenade**	≠ a walk, stroll	F D S
promiscuous	→ casual, chance, random	F
	→ indistinct, mixed, confused	E I
a **promise**	≠ a promissory note	Nl D
to **be promoted**	≠ to pass an exam	I
	≠ to be graduated	D
a **promoter**	≠ a public prosecutor	P
a **promotion**	≠ a doctorate	*Nl* D N S
	≠ a year's students	E F
	≠ a year's intake/draft/ call-up of soldiers	F
a **proof**	≠ a test, experiment	Nl Dk N S
	≠ a rehearsal	Dk N
to **prop (up)**	≠ to stuff/fill up	Nl N
a **prop**	≠ a plug, stopper	Dk N S
	≠ s/th blocking a pipe	Dk S
	≠ a wad, swab; gag	Nl
the **propaganda**	→ the (commercial) publicity	P E I Nl D Gr
	≠ the write-up (in a newspaper)	P
	≠ the party political broadcast	P
proper	≠ own, individual	P *E* I F D
	≠ appropriate, fitting, real, precise	P
	≠ clean	F Nl *D* Dk S
	≠ neat, tidy	F Nl D Dk N S
properly	≠ exactly, precisely, literally, strictly	E I F
	≠ actually, in fact	P *I*
to **propose**	≠ to offer (s/th)	I F
a **proposition**	≠ a (grammatical) sentence	I
	≠ a (grammatical) clause	P *I*
a **proprietor**	→ a landowner, a large-scale farmer	Dk N
the **propriety**	≠ the property (land, buildings, etc.)	P *I*
the **props**	≠ the fuses	Dk N S
to **prosecute**	≠ to pursue, follow, continue, carry on	E I
the **prosecution**	≠ the continuation, pursuit	E *I*
a **prospect**	≠ a prospectus, brochure	P E I F D Dk N S

the **protection**	→ the help, push, pull, influence	F Nl D
	→ the patronage	P E I F Dk N S
the **protocol**	≠ the record(s), minute(s), official report	D Dk S Gr
	≠ the school (attendance) register, ledger, minute book, record	Dk N
	≠ the writing paper used for exams	I
	≠ the judicial register	P E
	≠ the formal receipt for a document	P
to **prove**	≠ to taste, sample	P Nl
	≠ to rehearse	I
	≠ to try, test, experience	P I *Nl* D Dk N S
	≠ to try on	P I Nl Dk N S
the **providence**	≠ the foresight, forethought, prudence	P E
the **provision**	≠ the brokerage, commission	Nl D Dk N S
the **provisions**	≠ the (reserve) funds	F
	≠ the deposit, sum given as security	F
to **provoke**	≠ to be sick	E
provoking	≠ challenging, tantalising	E *I* F
a **prudish man**	≠ a man of integrity	F
a **prune**	≠ a plum	I F *Nl*
a **psalm**	≠ a hymn	Dk N S Ch
the **public**	≠ the (theatre) audience, spectators, turn-out, gathering	*P* E *I* Nl *D* Dk N S
a **public school**	≠ a state school	P I F
to **publish**	→ to disclose, reveal (facts/information)	P E *I F* Nl
the **puce, pus**	≠ the flea(s)	F
	≠ the haze	Tr
	≠ the puddle	S
	≠ the finery	N
	≠ the kiss	S
a **pudding**	≠ a custard, blancmange	Nl D
the **pudding**	→ the pudding stone, conglomerate	F
a **puddle**	≠ a poodle	D Dk N S
a **pueblo**	≠ a (country) town, village; nation	E

a **puff**	≠ a bump, crash, bang, thump	D
	≠ a pillow, cushion	D
	≠ a brothel	Ch
a **puffer**	≠ a buffer	D
	≠ a potato pancake	D
	≠ a small pancake	Nl
to **pull**	≠ to polish (up), put a shine on	E I
	≠ to pinch, nick, flog	E
	≠ to clean, dust, wash	I
	≠ to jump/leap (over)	P
a **pull(ey)**	≠ a light cotton top	D
	≠ a (woollen) pullover	F Ch
	≠ a pool	Nl Dk
	≠ a jar, tankard	Nl
a **pullman**	≠ a (motor) coach	I F
	≠ a lung	P
	≠ an armchair	Tr
	≠ a cinema seat	F
the **pulp**	≠ the octopus	E
a **pulpit**	≠ a school desk	S
	≠ a church gallery, organ loft, pew	Dk
the **pulse**	≠ the energy, vigour	P I
	≠ the wrist	P E Nl
	≠ the steadiness of (the) hand	E
to **pump**	≠ to buy on tick	D
the **pump**	≠ the credit (in shops)	D
the **punctuation**	≠ the school/exam marks	E
a **puncture**	≠ an injection	I
	≠ a punch	P
	≠ a size (in shoes or gloves)	F
a **punt**	≠ a point, full stop	E I Nl
a **puny brother/sister**	≠ a younger brother/sister	F
a **pupa**	≠ a baby girl	I
	≠ a doll	P
	≠ a small scratch, pimple, blister, sore	E
a **pupil**	≠ a ward, foster child, orphan	P E I F Nl *S*
pure	≠ neat (of alcoholic drinks)	Nl D
purple	≠ dark crimson, maroon	P I D
	≠ crimson, rich red	F
to **pursue**	≠ to sue, proceed against	F
the **pursuits**	≠ the legal proceedings	F

pus	See **puce**	
to **push**	≠ to pull	P
to **put oneself out**	≠ to exhaust oneself	Nl
a **pygmy**	≠ a dwarf	Gr
a **pylon**	≠ a gateway	Gr
a **pyre**	≠ a (domestic) fire	Gr

q

a **quadrille**	≠ a gang (e.g. of thieves)	P
	≠ a group	E
to **quake**	≠ to quack	Nl D
	≠ to creak	D
	≠ to croak	Dk S
the **quaker**	≠ the porridge	Gr Ar
the **qualifications**	≠ the exam marks	E
	≠ the names, designations, titles	I F
to **qualify**	≠ to mark (an exam)	E
	≠ to describe, term s/o as	E I F Nl
a **quality**	≠ a grade, brand	D
	≠ a type, sort, kind	P D
	≠ an authority, entitlement (to do s/th)	F
the **qualm**	≠ the dense smoke	Nl D
	→ the nausea, sickness	Dk N S
	≠ the stuffiness, closeness	S
the **quark**	≠ the curds, cottage cheese	Nl D Dk S
	≠ the rubbish	D
	≠ the catarrh	S
a **quart(er)**	≠ a compass point	F
	≠ a room	P E
	≠ a block of houses	S
a **quay**	≠ a railway platform	F
	≠ a quince	Nl
queer	≠ diagonal, slanting, oblique	D
a **question**	≠ an argument, dispute, quarrel	E Nl

to **quell**	≠ to rise up, spring, expand	D
	≠ to tease, vex	Nl
	≠ to nauseate	S
	≠ to strangle, choke, smother, stifle	Dk N
	≠ to torment	Nl S
a **queue**	≠ a billiard cue	Nl D
	≠ a type of owl	P I
	≠ a tail of an animal	F
	≠ a train of a dress	F Nl
a **quid**	≠ a gist, core, crux	E
quiet	→ still, calm, at rest	E I
a **quill**	≠ a ninepin, skittle; keel	F
to **quit**	≠ to take (s/th) away	E
quit	→ lost, got rid of	Nl
the **quota**	≠ the subscription, dues, fees	P E I
	≠ the instalment payment	P E
	≠ the toll	P E
	≠ the altitude	I
	≠ the odds (in betting)	I
	≠ the mark for school work	F

r

a **race**	→ a breed	E F Nl Dk N S
	≠ a good breed/stock; sub-species	D
	≠ a ray of light; crack, fissure, slit	E
a **racehorse**	≠ a thoroughbred (horse)	P F
the **rack**	≠ the rabble	N
a **racket**	≠ a rocket	Nl D Dk N S
	≠ a snow-shoe	P *E I* F
	≠ a hairpin bend	P
the **raclette**	≠ the hoe, scraper; wind-screen wiper	F
the **racquet**	See **racket**	
racy	≠ splendid, first-class	D
a **radio**	≠ a radius	E
	≠ an X-ray	F
	≠ a radio operator (e.g. on an aircraft)	F

the **radio**	≠ the radium	P E I
to **raffle**	≠ to unravel	Nl
a **raffle**	≠ a round-up (by the police)	F
	≠ a clean-sweep (made by thieves, etc.)	F
a **rag**	≠ a cobweb	Nl
to **rage**	≠ to tower (up)	D
the **rage**	≠ the fussing, pestering, hurry	D
	≠ the acute pain/ache; rabies	F
	≠ the cashier	J
to **raid**	≠ to pull tight, stiffen	F
the **raider**	≠ the stiffness, starchiness, severity, abruptness	F
the **rain**	≠ the bank, ridge, grass strip, terrace	D
to **raise**	≠ to travel	Nl D Dk N S
a **raise**	≠ a journey, trip	Nl D Dk N S
a **raisin**	≠ a grape	F
a **rake, wreck**	≠ a row, line	Dk N S
to **ram**	≠ to row (a boat)	*E I* F
	≠ to estimate	Nl
a **ram**	≠ a window; frame	Nl
	≠ a (tree) branch	*P* E I
	≠ a bouquet	P E
	≠ a wheel rim	Nl
	≠ an oar, scull	*E I* F
	≠ a (made-up) train, rake	F
the **ram**	≠ the copper	I
the **ramp**	≠ the rogue, scoundrel, urchin	N
	≠ the handrail, bannister	F
	≠ the flight of stairs	I F
	≠ the calamity, disaster	Nl
	≠ the (theatre) footlights	F Dk *N* S
rampant	≠ crawling, creeping	F
a **ranch**	≠ a party of people	P E
	≠ a (dining) mess; hut; hamlet	E
	≠ a folk dance; barbecue	P
the **Rand**	≠ the edge, rim, brim, border, brink	Nl D Dk N S
to **range**	≠ to stow away, arrange, tidy/clear up/away	F
	≠ to creak, squeak	P

a **rank**	≠ a bend in the road	Ch
	≠ a case of crookedness; intrigue	D
	≠ a tendril, shoot, runner	Nl D
rank	≠ slim, slender	Nl D S
	≠ erect, straight, proud	Dk N
	≠ limping	I
	≠ cranky (in ideas)	Nl Dk S
	≠ climbing (of plants, etc.)	D N S
	≠ easily overturned (of a boat)	Nl
to **ransack**	≠ to bring to trial	S
	≠ to examine, probe	N S
to **rant**	≠ to rush/gad about/around	S
the **rape**	≠ the belch	N S
	≠ the rasp, file, grater	F
	≠ the turnip	Nl
raped	≠ scraped, grated	P F Nl
	≠ kidnapped	I
	≠ worn-out, shabby, seedy, threadbare	F
	≠ pinched, stolen, filched	E
	≠ cropped (of hair)	E
the **rapids**	≠ the express trains	P E I F
the **rapine**	≠ the robbery, theft	*P* E I F
	≠ the graft (money)	F
a **rapporteur**	≠ a sneak	F
	≠ a (maths) protractor	I F
the **rapproche-ment**	≠ the comparison of facts, etc.	F
	≠ the nearness, proximity, closeness	F
rare	≠ strange, odd	*P* E Nl N
	≠ exquisite	D
	≠ pleasant, kind, snug	Dk S
	≠ charming, sweet	N S
	≠ comical, amusing	Nl
rash	≠ swift, brisk, nimble, smart, lively	D Dk N S
	≠ healthy, vigorous	Dk S
a **rat**	≠ a steering wheel	Nl Dk N S
	≠ a mouse	P
	≠ a time, while	E
the **rat**	≠ the advice, counsel, consultation	Nl D
the **rate**	≠ the instalment payment	I D Dk N S
	≠ the spleen	F

to **rate**	≠ to fail, misfire	F
to **ravish**	≠ to kidnap, abduct	F
the **ray, rye**	≠ the chorus (line)	Nl
	≠ the roe(buck)	Nl D
	≠ the lightning	P E
	≠ the hair parting	E F
	≠ the line, row, stroke	P E F Nl D
	≠ the prawn, shrimp	Dk
	≠ the king	P E I
	≠ the trouser crease	E
	≠ the spoke of a wheel	P E
	≠ the frontier, limit	P E
	≠ the stripe (in fabric, etc.)	E F
	≠ the canal (within a town)	Nl
the **rayon**	≠ the area, district	Nl D
	≠ the shop department; ray of light	F
	≠ the bookshelf; spoke of a wheel, radius	F
	≠ the honeycomb; furrow	F
to **raze**	≠ to shave, skim, graze, cut close	E F
a **reactor**	≠ a jet aircraft	E I
a **reader**	≠ a copy of the Reader's Digest	J
real	≠ royal (See also **German**)	P E I
	≠ solid, respectable	D
a **real gymnasium**	≠ a science-oriented secondary school	D
a **realisation**	≠ a sale	S
	≠ an achievement, accomplishment	P E I F
a **total realisation**	≠ a clearance sale	N
to **realise**	→ to bring about, fulfil, carry out	P E I F D Dk N S
	≠ to hold, organise	P
	≠ to perform (music)	E D
the **reason**	≠ the ratio, fraction	P E F
a **rebate**	≠ an alarm	P E
	≠ a surprise attack, commotion, dispute	E
	≠ a repercussion	P
	≠ a verge/shoulder of the road	Dk
a **rebound**	≠ an unpredictable development	F

a **rebus**	≠ a muffling of the voice	P
	≠ a lapel; high collar	P
	≠ a reject	F
	≠ a mystery, puzzling situation	I
to **rebut (s/o)**	≠ to dishearten, discourage (s/o)	F
	≠ to disgust, make s/o indignant	I
a **receipt**	≠ a doctor's prescription	P E *I* Nl D Dk N S
	≠ a recipe (for cooking)	E I F Nl D Dk S
a **recension**	≠ a book review	Nl D *Dk* S
recherché	≠ in demand	F
a **recipient**	≠ a receptacle, container	P E I F
to **recite**	≠ to act a part in a play	I
	≠ to prescribe, give a prescription	P E
to **reckon up**	≠ to enumerate	N S
	≠ to rely on, count on	Nl
the **reckoning**	≠ the bill (to be paid)	Nl S
	≠ the account held with a firm	Nl D Dk N S
	≠ the arithmetic	Nl *D* Dk N S
to **reclaim**	≠ to appeal	Nl
	≠ to complain, protest, object	P E F Nl D Dk N
	≠ to require, need	P E I F
	≠ to claim back, claim a replacement	P E I F Nl D Dk S
	≠ to cry out, call for	P E F
	≠ to oppose, contradict	E
	≠ to advertise	Dk N
the **reclaiming**	≠ the advertising	Nl Dk N
the **reclamation**	≠ the complaint, objection	P E F D Dk S
	≠ the claim(ing) back for compensation	P E F Nl D Dk N S
a **recollection**	≠ a harvest	E
to **recommend**	≠ to advise	I
	≠ to pay attention	I
	≠ to register (a letter)	P E I F Dk N S
	≠ to warn	P
the **reconnaissance**	≠ the recognition, acknowledgment, gratitude	F
to **reconnoitre**	≠ to recognise	F

to **record**	≠ to remember, remind(s/o of s/th)	*P* E I
	≠ to be reminiscent of	E I
a **record**	≠ a memory (of s/th), souvenir	I
to **recoup**	≠ to cut (back) again, step back (e.g. a wall)	F
the **recourse**	≠ the resource, means, expedient	P E
to **recover**	≠ to give shelter; put in hospital	I
	≠ to hide, overlap, conceal, cover up	F
the **recreation**	≠ the school break time	*E* I F
	≠ the convalescence	Dk N
a **rector**	≠ (in BE) a vice-chancellor of a university	E Nl D
	≠ (in BE) a headmaster of a school, principal of a college	I F Nl D Dk N S
to **recuperate**	≠ to retrieve, make up for; recycle, reclaim	P E I
	≠ to get back (esp. lent money)	P E F
	≠ to find s/th (which was lost)	E I
the **recycling**	≠ the retraining	F
a **redoubt**	≠ a masked ball	D
to **redress**	≠ to set up straight again, straighten out s/th which was bent	F
reduced	≠ returned, come back	I
	≠ off-colour	F Ch
	≠ small, low, limited	E
a **reed**	≠ a marsh, bog	D
to **refer**	≠ to sum up; review (a book)	D
	≠ to report, give an account of, relate	P E I D Dk N S
refined	≠ artful, sly, crafty, calculating	Nl D S
reformed	≠ turned down, refused for military service	I F
the **reformed**	≠ the Protestant(s)	P Nl
	≠ the retired officer	P
a **refrain**	≠ a saying, proverb	P E
the **refrain**	≠ 'the same old story'!	F
the **refriger-ation**	≠ the air-conditioning	P E

to **regale s/o**	→ to give s/o a treat, to treat s/o to s/th	P E I F D
the **regalia**	≠ the privilege, prerogative	P
	≠ the perquisites	E
	≠ the gratuities, rewards; recompense	I
to **regard**	≠ to look at; concern	I F
	≠ to revise, examine closely; take care of	I
a **regatta**	≠ an irrigation ditch	E
a **regime**	→ a diet	P E I F *D*
a **regiment**	≠ a regime, government, rule	D S
to **register s/o**	≠ to search s/o for	E
	≠ to record(music, etc.)	P E I
a **register**	≠ an organ stop	E F Nl D Dk N S
	≠ a book's index, table of contents	Nl D Dk N S
	≠ a book of minutes	F
	≠ a flap, throttle, valve, damper	P F
	≠ a director, producer	I
a **registrar**	≠ a book mark	P E
	≠ a tape-recorder	I
	≠ a recording	P E
	≠ an official records office	E *D*
	≠ a police search	E
to **regress**	≠ to go/travel back	P E
the **regress**	≠ the recourse	I Nl D Dk N
	≠ the return, travelling back	P E
regular	≠ normal, typical, average, O.K.	P E
	≠ reliable (in BE)	F
to **reign**	≠ to be on heat/in rut	P
the **rein**	≠ the sand; the queen	I
	≠ the kidney; loins; the queen	F
	≠ a kingdom, realm	P E
to **reiterate**	≠ to make a mistake again	F
to **rejoin**	≠ to catch up with; meet	F
to **relate**	≠ to mention, state (facts)	F
the **relation**	≠ the ratio; list, record (kept)	P E
	≠ the contact (within an organisation), string(s) to pull	P E I F
to **relent**	≠ to slow down	I F
relevant	≠ important, conspicuous	P I
	≠ excellent, outstanding	P E
the **reliefs**	≠ the left-overs, food scraps	*E* F

to **rely**	≠ to bind, connect (again)	F
	≠ to whip	P
to **remark**	≠ to notice	F
	≠ to hallmark (silver/gold)	P
a **remedy**	≠ a device, appliance, contraption, tool, bit of paraphernalia	Dk N
	→ an aid, help, way of coping	P E I *F Nl*
	→ a medicine	P *E I*
a **remission**	≠ a cross-reference	P E
to **remit**	≠ to postpone, adjourn	E
a **remittance**	≠ a remission	P
to **rend**	≠ to trickle (down), leak, gad/scurry about	Dk N
to **render**	≠ to vomit, be sick	F
	≠ to delay	P
	≠ to surrender	P E I
	≠ to conquer, subdue, dominate	P E
	≠ to be profitable, pay (well), be successful	P E I F Nl
to **render service**	≠ to come in handy/useful	F
a **rendition**	≠ a yield, return, profit	P E
	≠ a surrender	P E
the **renovation**	≠ the refuse collection	Dk *N*
to **rent**	≠ to attract; pass close to; flirt, defy, taunt	P
	≠ to endow	F
	≠ to produce, yield	E Nl
	≠ to be profitable	D
the **rent**	≠ the income, dividends, financial returns/yield; interest on investments	E F Nl D Dk N S
rentable	≠ profitable, lucrative, remunerative	*P* E Nl D Dk N S
to **repair**	≠ to notice, observe	P E
	≠ to make amends for, make up for	P E F
	≠ to reflect, consider, heed	E
the **reparations**	≠ the repairs	E I F Nl Dk N S
	→ the amends, redress	F
to **repeal**	≠ to recall, remember	F
a **repeal**	≠ a reminder	F
to **repeat (a text)**	≠ to revise (a text)	Nl D S

to **repeat a play**	≠ to rehearse a play	P I F S
to **repel**	See **repeal**	
to **repent**	≠ to change one's mind	P I
a **repertoire**	≠ a list, catalog(ue), index	F
a **repetition**	≠ a rehearsal	*P* I F Nl Dk S
	≠ a revision for exams	Dk N
a **replica**	≠ an answer, rejoinder	P E I F Nl D Dk S
	≠ a repetition; objection	P E I F
	≠ a run of a play	Nl D
the **replicas**	≠ the lines of a play	Dk N S
to **report**	≠ to postpone	F
	≠ to carry s/th back to	I F
	≠ to fetch, carry, bring; check, restrain	E
the **report**	≠ the amount brought forward, contango	P I F
	≠ the connection, relationship	I F
	≠ the profit	F
to **repose**	≠ to put back into place	I F
the **repose**	≠ the retirement	I
	≠ no performance (at a theatre)	I
to **represent**	≠ to keep up appearances; make a show	D
	≠ to make use of an expense account	S
the **representation**	≠ the keeping up (of appearances)	D
representtative	≠ presentable	S
with **repugnance**	≠ with reluctance	*P* E I F
to **require**	≠ to write for, ask for	Dk S
	≠ to requisition	Nl D Dk N S
the **requisites**	≠ the (theatrical) props	Nl Dk N S
the **requisitions**	≠ the (theatrical) props	D
to **resent**	≠ to feel (the effects of s/th)	P E I F
reserved	≠ private, confidential, classified	P E I
	≠ stand-offish, stiff	P *E* F
a **resolution**	≠ a solution (to a problem)	E F
	≠ a dissolving, changing	F
the **resonance**	≠ the response, reaction, repercussions	D *Dk*

to **resort**	≠ to go/come out again; bring out again	F
	≠ to stand out, be evident	F
	≠ to go out again	I
the **resort**	≠ the elasticity, springiness	E F
	≠ the elastic band	E
	≠ the jurisdiction	F Nl
	≠ s/o's concern, sphere, province, area	E F Nl D Dk N
to **respond**	≠ to be responsible for	E I F
the **responsibilities**	≠ the (financial) liabilities	P E I F
responsible	→ answerable to, liable for	P I F
to **rest**	≠ to be in arrears	Dk N *S*
	≠ to stay, remain, be left over	P E F Nl Dk
	≠ to subtract, deduct, take away	E
the **rest**	≠ change (money)	I
	≠ the dregs	D
restless(ly)	≠ completely, thoroughly, entirely	D
to **result**	→ to turn out (well/badly/to be); transpire	P E I
to **resume**	≠ to condense, summarise	P E *I* F Nl Dk S
to **retain**	≠ to delay, detain, hold back	I F
	≠ to maintain (ideas), think	I
	≠ to regard, consider	I
retarded	≠ postponed, put off, deferred, put back	P E I *F*
the **retinue**	≠ the school detention, the docking (of wages, etc.)	F
to **retire**	≠ to take away, remove	P E *I F*
the **retreat**	≠ the retired person	F
	≠ the retirement	*I* F
	≠ the W.C., loo	P *E*
	≠ the portrait	P E I
	≠ the retirement pension/superannuation	F
the **retribution**	≠ the salary, pay, remuneration	P E *F*
	→ the reward, recompense	P I F
to **return**	≠ to upset (s/o); turn inside out/over, turn upside down/round	F

a **reunion**	≠ a (formal) meeting	P E I F
to **reunite**	≠ to gather/assemble/put/get together	P E *I F*
	≠ to collect, pool	*I* F
to **revel**	≠ to reveal	P E *I* F
the **revelation**	≠ the exposure (of film when photographing)	E
in **revenge**	≠ on the other hand	F
to **reverberate**	≠ to flash, glisten	P E I F
to **reverse**	≠ to pour back/out again	I F
the **reverse**	≠ the promissory note	S
	≠ the lapel	F Nl D Dk *N*
	≠ the trouser turn-up	Gr
to **revise**	≠ to recondition, overhaul	P F Nl
a **revision**	≠ an overhaul	P E I F *Nl* D Dk Tr
	≠ a re-trial, appeal (in law)	*E F* D
	≠ an audit (of accounts)	*E* I F Dk N S
	≠ a proofreading	P F
revolted	≠ insurgent, in revolt	*P* F
	≠ turned up/towards	I
to **revolve**	≠ to stir (up), mix	P E
a **rhapsody**	≠ a long poem	Gr
the **rice**	≠ the twig	Nl D
rich food	≠ delicious food	E
to **ride**	≠ to drive (a car)	Nl
a **ride**	≠ a wrinkle	F
a **rider**	≠ a knight	Dk N S
	≠ a diamond (in cards); skater	Nl
the **rind**	≠ the bark of a tree	D
	≠ the (bread) crust; cattle	D
to **ring**	≠ to struggle/wrestle with	D
a **ring**	≠ a ring road	F
a **ring road**	≠ a bypass	Nl Dk
riotous	≠ quarrelsome, sulky	I
to **risk**	≠ to strike (a match); erase, cancel	P
a **risk**	≠ a sketch	P
	≠ a steep rock, cliff	E
risky	≠ naughty, suggestive	F
a **road**	≠ a circle, ring, wheel, etc.	P
a **road show**	≠ a first night, premiere	J
a **roar**	≠ a rudder	Nl Dk N
	≠ a pipe, tube	Dk N S
a **roast**	≠ a face	P
to **rob**	≠ to creep, crawl	D

a **robber**	≠ a rubber (in cards)	P F Nl D Dk N Gr
the **robe**	≠ the stuff, material	I
	→ the dress	F
	≠ the theft	P E
a **rock**	≠ a skirt	Nl D
	≠ a man's coat	D S
a **rodeo**	≠ a roundabout way, detour	E
	≠ a cattle enclosure	E
	≠ an evasion; circumlocution	P E
	→ a cattle round-up	P E
the **role**	≠ the manners	D
	≠ the list, register, roster	F D
	≠ the riot	P
a **roller**	≠ a scooter (child's or motor)	D
a **Roman**	≠ a novel	*I* F Nl D Dk N S J Tr
Roman(style)	≠ romanesque, Norman	F
a **romance**	≠ a sentimental song, ballad	I F
romanesque	≠ romantic	F
to **romp**	≠ to break	P E I F
a **romp, rump**	≠ a trunk, body, fuselage, hull	Nl D
	≠ s/o's seat, bottom	N S
	≠ a tree stump	D
a **roof**	≠ a penthouse	F
	≠ a helter-skelter; robbery	Nl
	≠ a boat deckhouse	Nl Dk *N* S
	≠ a hatch	Dk
	≠ a call	D
the **rook**	≠ the smoke	Nl *N S*
the **room**	≠ the cream	Nl
	≠ the fame, glory	Nl D
	≠ the pile, heap	E
	≠ the bearing, direction (from a compass)	P
a **rooster**	≠ a grill, grid	Nl
	≠ an elm	D
the **rope(s)**	≠ the clothes, clothing	P E
a **rostrum**	≠ a face	E
	≠ a beak, snout	I
the **rot**	≠ the red	D
a **rota**	≠ a ship's course	P Tr
	≠ a defeat, rout, struggle	P
	≠ a course, itinerary	P
the **rouge**	≠ the red	F
the **roulette**	≠ the caster wheel	F
a **route**	≠ a road	F
	≠ a business (retail) outlet	J

the **routine**	≠ the skill, dexterity	D
to **rove**	≠ to rob	Nl Dk N S
a **rover**	≠ a robber, brigand	Nl Dk N *S*
to **row**	≠ to mourn, rue, regret	Nl
royal	≠ liberal, lavish, generous, ample; sportsmanlike	Nl
to **rub oneself**	≠ to hurry up, look sharp	Dk
the **rubric(s)**	≠ the headline(s)	Dk S
	≠ the address book, phone-number pad	I
	≠ the paragraph, section, newspaper column/item	F Nl D Dk N
	≠ the initialled signature	P E
	≠ the red chalk/ochre	P E F
	≠ the actor's instructions in a play	P
	≠ the class/group/head(ing)	Nl D S
ruby	≠ fair/blond (hair)	E
the **rudder**	≠ the window-pane	Dk
	≠ the diamonds	Dk
	≠ the oar	D *S*
rude	≠ rough/unworked (of wood), stupid, dull	E
	≠ brutal, rough, coarse (of a person)	P E I F D
	≠ stiff (of a brush), grating/harsh (of a voice), steep (of a climb), hearty (of an appetite), tough (of an opponent), dreadful (of a blunder)	F
	≠ hard (of times/blow/work)	E F
	≠ primitive (of a tribe/people)	F
rudely	≠ awfully, very, tremendously	F
the **rudiments**	≠ the vestiges, survival	Dk
to **rue**	≠ to kick/lash out	F
	≠ to spend time in the streets	P
a **ruff**	≠ a shout, cry; rumour, reputation	D
	≠ a jiffy, moment	Dk
a **ruffian**	≠ an apprentice	F
	≠ a pimp	I
a **ruffle**	≠ a rebuke	D
the **rug**	≠ the rye	Dk N S
	≠ the back	Nl *N* S
the **Ruhr**	≠ the dysentery	D

a **ruin**	≠ a gelding	Nl
the **rum**	≠ the room (to let)	Dk N S
to **rumour**	≠ to make a noise (while unseen)	D
a **rumour**	≠ an uproar, din, commotion	F I Nl D
	≠ a (small/low/slight) noise	P E F
rump	See **romp**	
a **run**	≠ a race (meeting)	Nl D
the **running**	≠ the vest	J
the **rush**	≠ the rush hour	P
	≠ one over the eight!	Ch
the **rusk**	≠ the jerk, pull, shake	Dk N
	≠ the damp/rough weather, drizzle	Dk N S
	≠ the speck of dust; trash; strong man	N
to **rust**	≠ to rest	Nl
	≠ to arm, prepare oneself	D S
	≠ to shake	Dk N
rusty	≠ quiet, peaceful	Nl
	≠ strong, robust	D
rye	See **ray**	

S

the **sable**	≠ the sand	F
	≠ the sword, sabre	Nl Dk N S
to **sabotage**	≠ to miss a (school) lesson	J
the **sabotage**	≠ the neglect	J
	≠ the botching of work	F
the **saccharin**	≠ the sugar	Gr
to **sack**	≠ to take out, extract, remove, pull/get (s/th) out	P E
a **sack**	≠ a man's sports jacket	D
	≠ a (loose) jacket; paper bag	E
	≠ a handbag, bag	*P* I F Dk
	≠ a pocket	*I* Nl D
	≠ a thing, matter, concern	N S
the **sacks**	≠ the scissors	Dk N S
sacred	≠ wretched, damned, blessed	F

to **sag**	≠ to saw	Nl D N
a **saga**	→ a fairy tale, fable	S
a **sage**	≠ a legend, myth	Nl D
the **Sahara**	≠ the desert	Ar
Saint Teresa	≠ (a) praying mantis	E
a **salad**	≠ a lettuce	*E* F *Nl* D Dk N S
a **salamander**	≠ a newt	Nl Dk N Ch
the **salary**	≠ the wages	P *E I* F
	≠ the fee	Dk
a **saloon**	≠ a drawing/living room	E *I* F Nl D Dk N S
	≠ an operating theatre	Tr
	≠ a large hall (for meetings, etc.)	P E I F
	≠ an audience (in the theatre, etc.)	S
the **salt**	≠ the shoe heel	P
	≠ the jump, leap, bound	P E I
	≠ the tent	Ch
to **salute**	≠ to greet; take leave	E I
the **salute**	≠ the greeting	E F
	≠ the salvation, welfare	I F
	≠ the health	E I
the **salvo**	≠ the safety	I
the **same**	≠ the seed, grain, semen, spawn	D
a **sanatorium**	≠ a mental hospital	P
to **sanction**	≠ to impose a sanction on	E *F*
the **sand**	≠ the sandwich	J
a **sandwich**	≠ a traffic jam	F
	≠ an open sandwich	D
sane	≠ healthy, sound, fit, wholesome	E I F
	≠ truthful, genuine	S
	≠ intact, unbroken	E
sanguine	≠ concerning the blood	*P* E F
	≠ blood-stained	I
the **sauce**	≠ the gravy	*E I F* Nl D Dk N S
	≠ the soft (drawing) pencil	F
	≠ the willow (tree)	E
to **be saucy**	≠ to tell s/o off, reprimand	F
savage	≠ uncommunicative, shy, unsociable	F
	≠ undomesticated, uncultivated (of a plant)	E F

to **save oneself**	≠ to clear off, dash away	F
a **scab**	≠ a cupboard, locker	Dk *N S*
	≠ an itch	Dk N S
to **scald**	≠ to write poetry	S
a **scald**	≠ a poet	N S
the **scale**	≠ the stairs, stairway	I Gr
a **scale**	≠ a ladder	*P* E I Gr
	≠ a (piece of) peel, husk, rind, scraping	Dk N S
	≠ a port of call, stop-over (place)	P E F
	≠ a pier, jetty	Tr
	≠ a radio dial	D
	≠ a shell, dish, plate, etc.	Nl
a **scalpel**	≠ a chisel	*E* I
a **scandal**	≠ a fuss, to-do, row	*P* E S
to **scandalise**	≠ to disgrace, expose; compromise (s/o)	Dk N
scandalous	≠ noisy, rowdy (of a child)	E
to **scatter**	≠ to dash, spring up, get agitated	I
the **scenario**	≠ the scenery	P E I
	≠ the stage in a theatre	P E *I*
	→ the scene, setting	E
the **scene**	≠ the stage in a theatre	*I* F Dk N S
sceptical	≠ thoughtful	Gr
	≠ indifferent	P
a **scheme**	≠ a form (to be filled in)	Dk N
	≠ a school timetable	Dk S
	≠ a questionnaire	Dk N
	≠ a chart, diagram	P E *I* F Nl D Dk N
a **scholarship**	≠ a training ship	Dk N S
the **schooling**	≠ the period of lectures during a correspondence course	J
a **schottische**	≠ a Scotsman	D
the **scissors**	≠ the chisels	F
to **scold**	≠ to call (so) names	Nl
	≠ to scald	Dk N
the **scope**	≠ the aim	I
to **scorch**	≠ to flay, skin, peel, scratch	P E *F*
a **scorch**	≠ a glimpse	I
the **Scotch**	≠ the Sellotape	P E I F Nl N
a **scout**	≠ a guide (person)	S
	≠ a kerchief	N

a **scowl**	≠ a shovel	Dk N S
the **scratches**	≠ the heats, eliminations (in sport)	F
scrupulous	≠ unscrupulous	D
to **scrutinise**	≠ to count a ballot	I
	→ to peer (at)	I F
the **scrutiny**	≠ the poll (at elections)	P E I F
the **scum**	≠ the foam, froth, lather	Dk N S
scurrilous	≠ absurd, farcical, strange, impish, off-beat, ludicrous, bizarre	D
a **sea**	≠ a lake	D *Dk N*
a **seal**	≠ a postage stamp	P E
	≠ a rubber stamp	E
a **seance**	≠ a meeting; (portrait) sitting	F Nl
	≠ a medical treatment (session)	F
	≠ a cinema/theatre performance	F Tr
	≠ an evening performance	Tr
to **search s/o**	≠ to look for s/o	I F
seawards	≠ sideways	Nl
a **secret**	≠ a secretion	D Dk N S
in **secret**	≠ in solitary confinement	F
the **sect**	≠ the champagne	D
	≠ the wine	S
	≠ the student political group	J
the **section**	≠ the autopsy, postmortem	Nl D
	≠ the dissection	Nl Dk
secular	≠ occurring once a century	F D
	≠ time-honoured, age-old, ancient	P E I F
security	≠ reliability (of information, etc.)	E
a **sedan**	≠ a sedan chair	F
	≠ a celery	I
to **seduce**	≠ to bribe	I F
	→ to charm, fascinate, attract	*P E* I F
to **see into**	≠ to realise, understand	Nl Dk N S
a **segment**	≠ a piston ring	*E* F Tr
the **self**	≠ the self-service café	F
to **sell**	≠ to give way, yield, conclude	P
to **sell a horse**	≠ to saddle a horse	P I F

(the) **semaphore**	≠ the traffic lights	P E I
	≠ the flag bearer	Gr
	→ the railway signal	P E I D *S*
a **semester**	≠ a (worker's) holiday	S
a **semi**	≠ a seminar	J
a **seminar(y)**	≠ a teacher-training college	F *D* Dk N S Ch
	≠ a teachers' meeting	Gr
	≠ a seed plot	P E
	≠ a university department	D
to **send up a letter**	≠ to forward a letter	Nl
a **sender**	≠ a radio transmitter	Nl D Dk N S
the **sennapod(s)**	≠ the mustard	J
a **sense**	≠ a scythe	D
to **be sensed**	≠ to be supposed (to do s/th)	F
sensed	≠ sensible, prudent, level-headed	P E I F
sensible	≠ sensitive, impressionable, susceptible	P E I F D Dk N S
	→ appreciable, noticeable, considerable	P E I F
	≠ regrettable	E
to **sentence**	≠ to pass/state/express an opinion on	P E
a **sentence**	≠ a maxim, aphorism	P E I F D Dk
the **sepia**	≠ the cuttlefish	I Gr
a **sequel**	≠ a gang, crowd	P
to **sequester, sequestrate**	≠ to kidnap	P E
serene	≠ sober, not drunk	E
a **series**	≠ a comic strip	*Dk* N S
in **series**	≠ mass (production)	P E I F *Nl* D Dk S
the **series**	≠ the heat(s) in sports	Nl
a **serin**	≠ a canary	F
serious	≠ reliable, honest, trustworthy, conscientious, genuine	P E I F D
	≠ proper, suited	E
the **Serpentine**	≠ the paper streamer	P E F Nl Gr
	≠ a winding ski piste or mountain road	D
a **servant**	≠ a member of a gun crew, gunner	I F
a **service**	≠ a job, piece of work	P
	≠ a gratuity, tip	F

it's **a service**	≠ it's free of charge	J
serviceable	≠ cooperative, helpful	F
the **services**	≠ the W.C.s, loos	E
a **serviette**	≠ a briefcase; towel;tray-cloth	F
	≠ a waiting-maid	I
a **set**	≠ a place mat (for a meal)	F Ch
	≠ a jump, bound	Dk
	≠ a sect	I
	≠ an arrow, indicator, (clock) hand	P
	≠ a fence, hedge	E
	≠ an (evening) ensemble (clothes, etc.) for a woman	D
	≠ a move (in a game)	Nl
to **set out**	≠ to expand; invest (money)	Nl
	≠ to delay, postpone, put off	Dk N
	≠ to evict	Dk
	≠ to expose (to)	Dk N S
	≠ to put in, insert	S
the **shackles**	≠ the links of a chain	Nl
the **shade**	≠ the pity, shame	D
the **shame**	≠ the modesty, bashfulness	*Nl* D
to **shape**	≠ to create	Nl N S
the **shaping**	≠ the creation	Nl N S
sharp	≠ randy; exact; keen (on)	D
a **sharp pencil**	≠ a propelling pencil	J
a **shawl**	≠ a dish, bowl	Nl D
	≠ a crust, rind	D
the **shears**	≠ the scissors	Nl D
the **sheen, shin**	≠ China	F
	≠ the railway track/line	D
a **shell**	≠ a small bell; handcuff; slap on the face; box on the ear	D
a **shellfish**	≠ a haddock	Nl D
a **shield**	≠ a sign/notice board	D Dk
	≠ a metal plate	Nl D *Dk*
to **shift**	≠ to change (clothes)	Dk N S
shin	See **sheen**	
the **shine**	≠ the appearance	Nl
the **ship**	≠ the church nave	Nl D N S
	≠ the shovel	D
the **shock**	≠ the collision, impact	F
a **shock (of)**	≠ 60, umpteen, a lot (of)	D
to **shock**	≠ to collide, knock, bump	P E F
	≠ to get broody (of hens)	P
	≠ to shuffle, shamble	Dk N

shocking	≠ silly, stupid	I
shock(ing) prices	≠ rock-bottom prices	F
the **shoe cream**	≠ the cream puff	J
to **shoot**	≠ to play football	Ch
a **shop**	≠ a stall, stand	F
	≠ a shovel	Nl
the **shorts**	≠ the apron	Ch
to **shout**	≠ to change gear	Ch
to **show**	≠ to look, view, observe	D
	≠ to survey	Nl
a **shower**	≠ a shudder, tremor, frisson, fit/attack, thrill	D
	≠ a cad, rotter	Dk
	≠ a navvy	Nl
the **shower**	≠ the terror, awe; shed, shelter	D
to **shriek**	≠ to be frightened	Nl D
the **side**	≠ the silk	*Nl* D
	≠ the page (of a book, newspaper, etc.)	*D* Dk N S
a **sidesman**	≠ a neighbour, s/o next to you	Dk N
the **siege**	≠ the chair, seat, centre	F
	≠ the harvest (time)	E
	≠ the victories, conquests; goat	D
the **Sierra**	≠ the saw	E
to **sieve**	≠ to ooze	Dk N
to **sigh**	≠ to sow	Nl
a **sign**	≠ a signature, autograph	J
to **sign oneself**	≠ to cross oneself	I F
to **signal**	≠ to point out, report, indicate, mention	*E* I F
a **signature**	≠ a label; book's catalogue number	D
	≠ a sign, mark	E
silly	≠ holy, blessed	D
simple	≠ inferior, vulgar, coarse, shameful, plain, humble, low	Dk N S
a **simple person**	≠ a straightforward person	P E I
	≠ a scoundrel, rogue	Dk N S
the **sin**	≠ the meaning, mind, opinion, inclination, sense, taste	Nl D Dk N S
	≠ the doom, fate	P E
	≠ the bell	P

a **sinew**	≠ a nerve	Nl
sinful	≠ significant, clever, logical, convenient	Nl D
the **sinus**	≠ the sine (mathematical)	F Nl D N S
a **siren**	≠ a lilac	Dk *N* S
	≠ a hooter, foghorn	E *I* F N
	≠ a mermaid	E I F
the **site**	≠ the beauty spot, lie of the land, landscape	F
	≠ the stink, stench	I
	≠ the ranch	P
	≠ the siege	P E
	≠ the page, side	D
	≠ the housing estate	Tr
a **sixpence**	≠ a cloth cap	Dk N
the **skate(s)**	≠ the taxes, local rates	Dk N S
	≠ the darling	Nl Dk N
	≠ the treasure	Dk N S
the **skin**	≠ the light, glare	Nl Dk N
	≠ the appearance	Dk N
to **skip**	≠ to hop, jump	Dk N S
a **skirt**	≠ a shirt	Dk N S
	≠ a petticoat, slip	Dk
a **skive**	≠ a slice	Nl Dk N S
the **sky**	≠ the cloud	Dk N *S*
	≠ the jelly	Dk
	≠ the gravy	Dk N S
	≠ the fear, dread	*Dk* N
a **slab**	≠ a bib	Nl
a **slack**	≠ a snail, slug	Nl
to **slacken**	≠ to heave (a sigh)	Nl
the **slag**	≠ the type, sort, kind	Nl *Dk* N S
	≠ the blow, stroke, knock	Nl D Dk N S
the **slang**	≠ the snake	Nl D Dk N
	≠ the queue	Ch
	≠ the tube, hosepipe	Nl Dk N S
to **slap**	≠ to abate, subside, flop, loosen	Nl D Dk N S
to **slate**	≠ to wear out/down; retail	Nl
the **slate**	≠ the wear and tear	Nl
a **Slav**	≠ a slave (see Part 2)	Nl D S
to **slay**	≠ to beat, strike	Dk N *S*
a **sleep**	≠ a string of barges	Nl *Dk* S
	≠ a trailer/vehicle being towed	Nl *Dk* N S
	≠ a dress train	Nl *Dk* N S
to **sleep in**	≠ to fall asleep	Nl D

to **sleep out**	≠ to sleep late/in, have a long sleep	Nl D N
the **sleet**	See **slate**	
the **slick**	≠ the mud, ooze, silt, slime	Nl D Dk
	≠ the sweets (to eat)	Dk *N*
	≠ the lick	S
slim	≠ sly, cunning, crafty, artful	Nl
	≠ bad	D
the **slime**	≠ the mucus, phlegm	Nl *D* Dk N *S*
to **sling**	≠ to spin-dry	Dk
	≠ to sway, swing, lurch	Nl Dk N
	≠ to gulp, swallow, gorge, devour	D
to **slip**	≠ to drag, pull	Nl
	≠ to release, let go; let s/o off, excuse	Dk N S
to **slip off s/th**	≠ to get rid of s/th	Dk
to **slip up**	≠ to run out of	Dk N
a **slip**	≠ a pair of (under)pants/ swimming trunks	E F D
	≠ a flap, coat tail	N L
slippery	≠ indecent	Dk
the **slips**	≠ the (neck)tie	Dk N S
to **slope**	≠ to demolish, pull down	Nl
a **slot**	≠ a (door) lock	Nl
	≠ a castle, a palace	Nl Dk N S
	≠ a ditch	Nl
	≠ a chimney, smokestack, flue	D
a **sluice**	≠ a lock in a river or canal	Nl D N S
to **slump**	≠ to sell off	S
	≠ to chance to/on	N S
the **slump**	≠ the luck	S
	≠ the remainder	N S
	≠ the dregs	N
	≠ the chance, mere accident	Dk N S
	≠ the blues, depression	J
at **a slump**	≠ at random	Dk N S
to **slur**	≠ to drag (physically)	Nl
	≠ to veil/hide (opinions)	Dk
	≠ to blur, muffle, wobble	Dk N
a **slut**	≠ an end, close, finish	Dk N S
to **smack**	≠ to taste, relish	Nl N S
a **smack**	≠ a taste, inclination, liking for s/th	Nl *Dk* N S
	≠ a bump, crash	Nl
	≠ a humiliation, insult, affront, failure	I

small	≠ narrow	Nl D Dk N S
to **smart**	≠ to ache	Dk N S
the **smart**	≠ the sorrow, distress	Nl
smart	≠ slim	J
the **smear**	≠ the butter	Dk N S
	≠ the grease	Nl D N S
a **smell**	≠ a report/crack of a gun	Dk N S
	≠ a bang on the head/of a door shutting	Dk N S
to **smelt**	≠ to melt	Nl D Dk N S
to **smite**	≠ to infect, be contagious	Dk N S
	≠ to throw	Nl
the **smoking**	≠ the dinner jacket/tuxedo (in AE)	P E I F Nl D Dk N S Tr Gr Ar
a **smut**	≠ a short trip/visit	Dk
the **smuts**	≠ the filth, mud, dung	S
the **snack**	≠ the chatter, gossip	Dk N S
	≠ the nonsense	N S
	≠ the snack bar	F
a **snake**	≠ a snail, slug	D
	≠ a worm	Dk
	≠ a darling (child)	Ch
to **snap**	≠ to understand, follow	Nl
	≠ to snatch, grab, get hold of	D Dk N S
a **snap**	≠ a press stud, snap fastener	J
to **sneer**	≠ to snarl, growl	Dk N
a **snob**	≠ a follower of fashions (esp. in art)	F
snob(bish)	≠ smart, elegant, chic	E F
to **snore**	≠ to purr (of cats)	Nl
a **snore**	≠ a piece of string/fishing line	Dk N S
	≠ a moustache	Nl
the **snore**	≠ the snot, nose dirt	N S
a **snout**	≠ a moustache	Ch
	≠ a dog's muzzle	D
to **snub**	≠ to snatch, grab, pinch	Dk
snug	≠ pretty, attractive, nice	S
	≠ clever, smart	Nl
so	≠ then	N S
the **soap**	≠ the soup	P E
social	≠ concerning the (business) firm	F
the **social news**	≠ the labour news, trade-union news	F Nl D *Dk*

a **social reason**	≠ a firm's trade name	P E F
a **sock**	≠ a clog	F
a **soffit**	≠ a ceiling	I
the **soil**	≠ the field	F
	≠ the column, pillar	D
the **sole, soul**	≠ the sun	P E I Dk N S
	≠ the brine, salt spring	D
to **solicit**	≠ to hasten, urge	I
	≠ to incite/drive (s/o) to do s/th	F
	→ to ask for, request, apply for	P E I Nl
the **solicitude**	≠ the promptness, eagerness	P E
solid	≠ healthy, sound, fit	F
	→ reliable, respectable, moderate, trustworthy	F Nl D Dk N S
the **solitaire**	≠ the hermit, recluse	P E I F
	≠ the tapeworm	P E
the **solo**	≠ the ground, soil	P
	≠ the patience (card game)	P E
sophisticated	≠ adulterated, falsified, mixed, impure	*E* I F
	≠ snobbish	E Dk *N S*
to **sort (out)**	≠ to come/go out, issue	I F
	≠ to draw lots, toss up (for it)	P E I
	≠ to swerve, dodge	E
	≠ to supply, provide	P
the **sort**	≠ the luck, fate, lot, destiny	P E I F
a **sortie**	≠ an exit, way out; excursion, departure	F
soul	See **sole**	
to **sound s/o**	≠ to fathom s/o, get to the bottom of	*I* F
sound	→ health-giving, wholesome	Nl Dk *N* S
the **English soup**	≠ the trifle (food)	I
sour	≠ hard, arduous (of work)	D
	≠ disagreeable (of work)	Nl
a **source**	→ a well	F
a **souvenir**	≠ a memory (of events)	F
a **spa**	≠ a limited company	I
a **spade**	≠ a bullfighter	P E
	≠ a bully	E
	≠ a sword	P E I

to **span**	≠ to watch on, spy, observe	S
	≠ to fit tightly (of clothes)	Nl D
a **span**	≠ a shaving	D
	≠ a splinter, chip of wood	D Dk
	≠ a bucket, pail	N S
	≠ a team of horses	Nl N S
Spanish	≠ fishy, suspicious, shady	D
to **spank**	≠ to hit, maul, whack, drive away	P
a **spanner**	≠ a span	D
	≠ an oberver	S
the **spar(s)**	≠ the savings	D
	≠ the spruce (tree)	Nl
	≠ the fir tree(s)	Nl
	≠ the spade(s)(in cards)	Dk N
to **spare**	≠ to save, economise	Nl D Dk N S
a **spark**	≠ a kick	Dk N S
to **speak against**	≠ to speak to	Nl
to **speak out**	≠ to finish speaking/talking	Nl *D*
a **speaker**	≠ a radio/TV announcer	Dk N S
a **spear**	≠ a muscle	Nl
special	≠ especial	I F Nl Dk N S
	odd, strange	F
specious	≠ neat, beautiful, carefully finished	E
a **spectacle**	≠ an uproar, row, commotion	Nl D Dk *N* S
a **speeder**	≠ an accelerator	Dk
speedy	≠ soon	Nl
to **spell**	≠ to play (a game)	Nl S
a **spell**	≠ a pack of cards; hand of cards	Nl
	≠ a game	Nl S
the **spell**	≠ the performance, acting, playing	Nl
to **spend**	≠ to distribute; yield; contribute, donate	D
	≠ to treat s/o to s/th	D Dk N
spendable	≠ open-handed	D N
a **spender**	≠ a donor, benefactor	D
spent	≠ tense, anxious, keyed-up, strained	Dk N
a **sperm**	≠ a pip (of apples/pears, etc.)	Gr
a **sphere**	≠ an atmosphere, ambiance	Nl

a **spider**	≠ a sports car	F
a **spiel**	≠ a game	*Nl* D Dk N S
a **spike**	≠ a nail	Nl *D* *N* S
	≠ a spoke of a wheel	Nl D
to **spill**	≠ to play	Dk N
a **spill**	≠ an axle	Nl
	≠ a game	Dk N
a **spine**	≠ a spot/pimple on the skin	P
	≠ a thorn, prickle	*P* E *I*
	≠ a fish bone	*P* E I
	≠ an electric plug	I
a **spire**	≠ a shoot, sprout on a plant	Dk N
	≠ a pole, sceptre	S
spiritual	≠ witty, brilliant, humorous, clever	F Dk N S
the **spleen**	≠ the depression, low spirits	E F
to **splice**	≠ to club together, go Dutch	Dk N
a **splint**	≠ a cotter pin	D
	≠ a splinter	Nl S
a **split**	≠ a cotter pin	Dk
sportive	→ fond of sport	I F Nl Tr Gr
	≠ casual (of clothes)	I Tr
	≠ sports (of a car)	I Tr
to **spot**	≠ to mock, jeer, ridicule, mimic	Nl D Dk N
	≠ to spit	S
a **spot**	≠ a butt, mockery, laughing stock	Nl D Dk N
	≠ a TV advertisement	F
a **spotter**	≠ a mocker, mimicker	Nl D Dk N
to **spring**	≠ to burst, crack, snap, split	Nl D
	≠ to run	Nl N S Ch
a **spring**	≠ a slit, chink, slot, cranny	S
	≠ a tap	N
a **spur**	≠ a clue, vestige, sign, s/th remaining; groove	D
	≠ a track; lane on a motorway	*Nl* Dk N *S* Ch
squalid	≠ penniless, very poor, poverty-stricken	E
	≠ very thin	E I
	≠ boring, dull, dreary	I
	≠ pale, wan	P E *I*
a **square**	≠ a small park; garden in a town square	F

a **stab**	≠ a staff, workers	Dk N S
a **stable**	≠ a pile, stack	Nl Dk N S
	≠ a building	I
a **stadium**	≠ a phase, stage (of development)	Nl D Dk N S
	≠ a state, condition	D
a **staff**	≠ a staff meeting	F
the **stage**	≠ the apprenticeship, probation	P F Nl Tr Ch
a **staircase**	≠ a starling's nesting box	Dk *N*
to **stake**	≠ to suspend, discontinue, cease (work)	Nl
	≠ to punt (a boat); stumble	S
the **staking**	≠ the strike, work stoppage	Nl
to **stall**	≠ to break out, split, explode, burst	P E
to **stall a car**	≠ to lay up a car (for the winter)	Nl
a **stall**	≠ a place, spot, locality	S
	≠ a stable, cowshed	D N S
	≠ a sample, specimen	Nl
the **stall**	≠ the steel	*Nl* Dk N *S*
	≠ the stalemate (in chess)	I
to **stamp**	≠ to print	P E I
the **stamp**	≠ the postmark	D J
	≠ the print, engraving	P E I *F*
	≠ the Press	I
	≠ the tub	N
a **stamp**	≠ a standstill	Dk *N*
a **stampede**	≠ a crash, sudden noise, report of a gun	P E
the **stand**	≠ the market hall	D Dk S
	≠ the status, the rank, condition, trade	Nl D Dk N S
	≠ the reading lamp	J
a **standard**	≠ a phone switchboard	F
standing	≠ de luxe quality, prestige (of a building)	F
to **staple**	≠ to pile/stack up	Nl D *Dk N S*
	≠ to stumble, totter	S
a **staple**	≠ a pile, stack, heap	Nl D *Dk N* S
	≠ a marketing centre, depot, storehouse	D
the **staples**	≠ the stocks (for a boat)	Nl

a **star**	≠ a starling	D N
	≠ a cataract in the eye	D S
a **star map**	≠ a strong portfolio/case	Nl
stark	≠ strong, vigorous	*Nl* D Dk N S
a **start**	≠ a pigtail; tail	Nl
a **starter**	≠ a choke (in a car, etc.)	F
to **starve**	≠ to die	Nl
the **stasis**	≠ the bus/railway station; revolution	Gr
a **state**	≠ a (bank) statement	E
	≠ a city, place	*Nl* D
	≠ a status	I
to **be in a state**	≠ to be pregnant	E
the **state coffers**	≠ the attaché case	Nl
a **station**	≠ a ward; stay in a place	D
	≠ a place, spot, resort, spa	F
	≠ a season	P E
the **stature**	≠ the statute	Dk S
the **status**	≠ the balance sheet	Dk N
	≠ the stocktaking	Dk
a **statute**	≠ a bank statement	P
	≠ a status (personal, political, etc.)	F
to **stave**	≠ to spell (words)	Dk N S
	≠ to confirm, substantiate	Nl
to **stay**	≠ to stand	Nl Dk *N S* Ch
a **steak**	≠ a joint of meat	*Dk* N S
to **steal**	≠ to rob	Nl D Dk N
the **steel**	≠ the handle	Nl D
a **steer**	≠ a bull	Nl D
to **stem**	≠ to vote	Nl Dk N
	≠ to be in the mood for	Nl
	≠ to do press-ups, weight-lifting, etc.	D
	≠ to prosecute	S
	≠ to tune a piano	Nl Dk N S
a **stem**	≠ a vote	Nl Dk N
	≠ a voice	S
a **stench**	≠ a touch, tinge, drop	Dk
to **step**	≠ to tap-dance	D Dk N S
	≠ to stitch, quilt	D
Stepney	≠ (a) spare wheel	Tr
the **stern**	≠ the star; forehead	D

to **stick**	≠ to embroider	D
	≠ to stitch	Nl Dk *N*
	≠ to choke, suffocate	Nl D
	≠ to pierce, stab, sting, bite, prick	D Dk N S
	≠ to engrave, print	Dk
	≠ to knit	S
a **stick**	≠ a riding whip, hunting crop	F
	≠ a lump; play (theatrical)	Dk S
	≠ a piece of music	*D* Dk N S
to **stickle**	≠ to taunt, sneer	Dk N
sticky	≠ suffocating	Nl D
a **stigma**	≠ a stain, mark, spot	Gr
the **stigma**	≠ the punctuation	Gr
the **stile, still**	≠ the style	P E I *Nl* D Dk N S Tr Gr
	≠ the composition exercise	Dk N S
	≠ the done thing	Nl
	≠ the stylus	P E I
a **stiletto**	→ a dagger	P I
	≠ a gramophone stylus	E
	≠ an engraving stylus; little knife	P
still	≠ quiet, calm, hushed	Nl D Dk N S
a **sting**	≠ a stitch	Dk N S
a **stink**	≠ a shin (bone)	I
the **stipend**	≠ the bursary, grant, scholarship	Nl D Dk N S
	→ the pay, salary	E I
	≠ the allowance (in money)	P
a **stitch**	≠ a thrust, pain	D
to **stock**	≠ to pause (in speech), stop short	D
	≠ to get held up, get stuck, clog	D S
a **stock**	≠ a stick (for walking, etc.)	Nl D Dk N
	≠ a tree trunk, bee hive, plant's stem	D
	≠ a log	S
to **stomach**	≠ to astound, take (s/o's) breath away	F
	≠ to disgust, annoy, upset	P E I
to **stomp**	≠ to shade off (as in drawing)	F
	≠ to punch, push	Nl
a **stool**	≠ a chair, seat	Nl D Dk N S
to **stop**	≠ to hitchhike	Dk
	≠ to mend, darn	Nl *D* Dk N S

	≠ to fill, stuff, cram	Nl Dk N S
	≠ to time (with a stopwatch)	D
the **stop**	≠ the hitchhiking	F
the **stoppage**	≠ the invisible mending	F
	≠ a half-back in football	D
a **stopper**	≠ a hitch-hiker	F
to **store**	≠ to bother, disturb	Nl
a **store**	≠ a shutter, blind	F Nl Tr Ch
to **storm**	≠ to wither	I
a **storm**	→ a gale	D Dk N S
	≠ a flock, group	I
stormy	≠ dizzy, giddy, confused	D
stout	≠ naughty, daring	Nl
	≠ proud	Dk N
a **stove**	≠ a living/drawing room	N
straight	≠ narrow	I
the **strand**	≠ the beach, shore	Nl D Dk N S
strange	≠ foreign	P E I F
a **stranger**	≠ a foreigner	P E I F
to **strap**	≠ to tear away, snatch; root out; extort	I
a **stream**	≠ a river	Nl D *N S*
	≠ an electric current	D *N S*
to **stride**	≠ to fight	Nl *D* Dk N S
a **stride**	≠ to fight, combat	Nl Dk N S
strident	≠ conflicting	Nl
the **strife**	≠ the strip(e), streak; patrol	D
to **strike**	≠ to iron, smooth, stroke	Nl
to **strike up**	≠ to brush up (knowledge)	Nl
a **strip(e)**	≠ a string, strap, phone line, streak	D
to **stroke**	≠ to keep in touch(with)	Nl
a **stroke**	≠ a strip of paper	Nl
strong	≠ strict, severe, stern	Nl D Dk N S
a **strophe**	≠ a curve/turn in the road	Gr
a **strudel**	≠ a whirlpool	D
to **strut**	≠ to bulge	Dk
	≠ to be bursting with life	N
a **stub**	≠ a (tree) stump	Dk N S
a **stud**	≠ a bloody fool	Dk *N*
a **studio**	≠ a bedsitter	I F
	≠ a study (room in a private house)	I D
	≠ a surgery (doctor/dentist)	I
	≠ a sketch, study, drawing	I

the **studio**	≠ the chambers of a lawyer	I
	≠ the care, preparation, skill	E I
	≠ the study (of a subject)	E I
to **study it**	≠ to think about it, think it over	P E
	≠ to worry about it	Ch
to **study a musical instrument**	≠ to practise a musical instrument	P
the **stuff**	≠ the stove	I *Nl*
stuffy	≠ dusty	Nl
a **stump**	≠ a (cigarette) stub	Dk N S
stupid	≠ idiotic	D
a **stylus**	≠ a pillar, column, prop	Gr
suave	≠ gentle, soft, smooth, meek	P E I F
to **subject**	≠ to hold in position, pin down	E
a **subject**	≠ an individual	P E D
	≠ an illustration, a picture	D
the **subsistence(s)**	≠ the provisions	F
the **suburb**	≠ the slum	E
	≠ the outskirts	P
to **succeed**	≠ to happen	P E I
a **success**	≠ an event	E
	≠ a result, outcome	P I
successive	≠ following, next, subsequent	I
the **sucker**	≠ the sugar	*D* Dk N S
the **sud**	≠ the South	I F D *Dk*
suede	≠ Sweden	F
the **sufferance**	≠ the suspense, postponement	F
suffering	≠ ill	F
the **sufficiency**	≠ the conceit, smugness, cockiness	E I F
sufficient	≠ conceited, smug, cocky	E I F
suffocated	≠ out of breath, hot and bothered	E
to **suggest**	≠ to prompt (in the theatre)	I
the **suggestion**	≠ the awe, respect, uneasiness	I
	≠ the doubt, uncertainty	P
	≠ the fascination, stimulus	E
suggestive	≠ fascinating, attractive, delightful, inspiring, stimulating	P E I Nl

	≠ easily imagined	F
	≠ picturesque	I
a **suggestive question**	≠ a leading question	Nl
a **suit**	≠ a strike	J
a **suitcase**	≠ a vanity bag	I
a **suite**	≠ a prank, trick; retinue; play's run	D
	≠ a sequel, connection, continuation, result, sequence, series	F
	≠ a retinue	F D
to **sum up**	≠ to enumerate, list	Nl
a **sump**	≠ a swamp	*D* Dk N S
the **sump**	≠ the coffee grounds	S
superb	≠ proud	I *F*
superficial	≠ unattainable	Gr
	≠ on the surface of the ground	I F
superior	≠ upper, higher	P E I F
to **supply**	≠ to beg, beseech	P E I F
	≠ to supplement, eke out	Dk
	≠ to replace	Dk
to **support**	→ to put up with, endure, stand, bear	P E I F
a **surname**	≠ a nickname	F
surrogate	→ substitute, make-shift	I Nl D Dk N S
to **survey**	≠ to supervise, watch over	F
susceptible	≠ apt (to), likely (to), open (to)	P E F
	≠ easily offended	E I
the **swamp**	≠ the sponge	Dk N S
	≠ the mushroom	Dk S
to **swarm (for)**	≠ to be infatuated (with), rave (about), daydream, enthuse (over)	D S
to **swerve**	≠ to wander (about)	Nl
to **swim**	≠ to float, drift	D
	≠ to faint, swoon	*N* S
to **swing**	≠ to vibrate	D
	≠ to soar (of birds)	N S
	≠ to brandish	D Dk N S
the **Swiss**	≠ Switzerland	P E F J
a **sycophant**	≠ a slanderer	Gr
the **syllabus**	≠ the index; summary	E
	≠ the spelling	Gr

sympathetic	≠ friendly, kind, genial	P E I F Nl D Dk N S Gr Ar
	≠ decent, presentable	S
	≠ amusing	Ar
to **sympathise**	≠ to take to s/o	P E I F
the **sympathy**	≠ the kindness, friendliness	P E I F Nl D Dk N S Gr
a **symposium**	≠ a banquet	F Gr
the **syncope**	≠ the heart attack, death	Gr
	≠ the faint, swoon	P E F
	≠ the syncopation	P F
a **syndicate**	≠ a trade union	P E I F Tr
	≠ a mayor's term of office	I
	≠ a trustee; auditor	I
a **syringa, syringe**	≠ a pipe (to blow)	Gr
	≠ a grease gun; lilac (bush)	I
to **systematise**	≠ to arrange, fix up	P I

t

a **tab**	≠ a loss	Dk
a **table**	≠ a vegetable plot	E
	≠ a slab, plank, board	E
	≠ a bulletin/notice board	P
	≠ an ashtray	Tr
a **tableau**	≠ a board, panel, roster	F
	≠ a picture, painting	F Tr *Gr*
a **tablet**	≠ a tray	D
a **tack**	≠ a quick answer	F
	≠ a branch, bough	Nl
	≠ a plug, stopper; snack	E
	≠ a pad of paper; oath	E
	≠ a golf club, mallet; bite to eat	P
	≠ a shoe heel; notch, indentation; defect	I
	≠ a point, tooth	Dk
	≠ a roof, ceiling; grasp, hold	N
	≠ a ewe lamb	S
the **tack**	≠ the thanks	Dk N S

to **tackle**	≠ to rig a ship, fit out with tackle	D Dk N S
the **tact**	≠ the (sense of) touch	P E I F
	≠ the time, beat, music measure, tempo	D Dk N S
a **tag**	≠ a day	Nl D
	≠ a roof	Dk
	≠ a hold, grasp, tug, jerk; knack	Dk S
	≠ a sharp point	N
a **tail**	≠ a size	F
	≠ a waist(line)	F Nl D
a **tailor**	≠ a woman's costume	P F Tr Ch Gr
a **taint**	≠ a complexion	Dk N
to **take**	≠ to bring	Dk N
to **take on**	≠ to suppose, assume	Nl Dk *N*
to **take place**	≠ to sit down	Nl Dk N S
the **talcum**	≠ the tinsel	P E
a **tale**	≠ a language	Nl
a **talent**	≠ a TV (pop) star	J
a **talk**	≠ an interpreter	*Nl* Dk N S
the **talk**	≠ the talcum	D S
a **talon**	≠ a heel	*P* E I F
	≠ a chequebook stub/counterfoil	*P* E I F *Nl* Dk N *S*
a **tampon**	≠ a rubber stamp	F
	≠ a shock absorber	Tr
	≠ an ink pad	E I F
	≠ a train buffer	I F Tr
	≠ a car bumper	Tr
	≠ a large cover/lid	P
a **tan**	≠ a tongue (e.g. of beef, as food)	J
	≠ a tooth	Nl Dk N
a **tang**	≠ a piece of seaweed	D Dk N S
	≠ a pair of tongs, pliers, pincers	Nl *D* Dk N S
a **tangent**	≠ a note on a piano keyboard	Dk N S
	≠ a key on a typewriter	Dk S
	≠ a straight stretch of road	P
	≠ a loophole	P
a **tap**	≠ a plug/stopper for bottles, etc.	P I
	≠ a loss	N
	≠ a lid, cover, cap	E I
	≠ a joint in woodwork	Dk N S

to **tap(e)**	≠ to type	F
	≠ to lose; fade	N S
	≠ to cover up, hide, close	P E
	≠ to fumble, grope	D
	≠ to strike, hit, beat	F
	≠ to stink; dab on paint	F
	≠ to crack (jokes)	Nl
the **tapestry**	≠ the wallpaper	I *D*
	≠ the upholstery	P I
	≠ the carpet making	P
a **tappet**	≠ a tapestry, hanging, wall-paper	D Dk N S
	≠ a carpet	Nl
a **target**	≠ a (car) numberplate	I
	≠ a (visiting) card	E
	≠ a door bolt	P F
a **tart**	≠ a cream cake	Nl *D* S
a **task**	≠ a handbag	*D* Dk
	≠ a briefcase, wallet	N
	≠ a pocket	I D
	≠ a café, tavern	P E
	≠ a satchel	I *N*
a **tassel**	≠ a plug, dowel, peg	I
to **taste**	≠ to feel for, touch, grope	I Nl D Dk
a **taste**	≠ a typewriter key	D Dk N
	≠ a note on a piano keyboard	F D Dk N
	≠ a winetaster's cup; a winetaster	F
a **tattoo**	≠ an armadillo	P F
tatty	≠ active, busy, energetic	D
to **tax**	≠ to regulate (prices)	F D
	≠ to accuse (s/o)	F
	≠ to value, assess, appraise	Nl D Dk N
a **tax**	≠ a fixed price	F
	≠ a rate (of interest, exchange, etc.)	P F
	≠ a dachshund; share, portion	Nl
the **tax**	≠ the postage due	F Tr
a **taxi**	≠ a class (of lessons)	Gr
a **teasel**	≠ a thistle	Dk
technical	≠ artificial	Gr
the **technique**	≠ the technology	F Nl D Dk N S
	≠ the technician, technologist, specialist	P E I Gr
	≠ the (fine) art (painting)	Gr

a **telephone**	≠ a telephone call	F N S Ch
to **tell**	≠ to count (with numbers)	Nl Dk N
	≠ to speak	Dk S
a **teller**	≠ a plate (for a meal)	D
	≠ a counter (in a game)	Nl
to **temper**	≠ to sharpen (a pencil)	I
the **temper**	≠ the condiment, taste, relish	P
the **tempera**	≠ the tone, timbre in music	I
	≠ the disposition, temper(ament), nature, mettle; seasoning for food	P
	≠ the dish (of traditional food)	J
the **temperament**	≠ the vivacity, liveliness	D N S
the **tempest**	→ the thunderstorm	P *E*
the **temple**	≠ the Protestant church	*E* I F
	≠ the temper, tuning, (state of) weather, mood	E
the **tempo**	≠ the weather	P *E* I
	≠ the tense of a verb	P *E* I
	≠ the movement of a symphony/concerto	E Nl
temporal	→ temporary	E
to **tender**	≠ to stretch, tighten; spread, extend, tend towards	P E I F
a **tender**	≠ a shopkeeper	P E
the **tennis**	≠ the tennis shoe(s)	P E F
	≠ the tennis court	I
a **tent**	≠ an awning	F Tr
	≠ an attempt	P
a **term**	≠ a terminus	F
	≠ an end, limit	P F
	≠ a thermos (flask)	E
the **term(s)**	≠ the spa, hot springs	P I Dk
a **terminus**	≠ a deadline; hearing in court; appointment	D
	≠ a university term	Dk N S
	≠ an expression, term (in words)	Dk
to **terrace**	≠ to overwhelm, dismay, nonplus	F
a **terrace**	≠ a penthouse	D Tr
terrible	≠ super, wonderful	F
to **test**	≠ to make a will	P F

Term	Meaning	Languages
a **test**	≠ a head	E I
	≠ a forehead, brow	P
a **testament**	→ a will	P E I F Nl D Dk N S
a **textbook**	≠ a libretto	Nl D
than	≠ then	Nl D
a **theatre**	≠ a fuss, scene, to-do, song and dance, muddle	D Dk S Tr
	≠ a play	Ch
the **theatre**	≠ (all) the dramatic works of a playwright	E I F
a **theme**	→ a translation to a foreign language	F E
	≠ an obsession, stubborness, ill-will	E
	≠ an exercise	Nl
a **thermos**	≠ a public bath; spa	*P* E *I* F
a **thesaurus**	≠ a treasure (riches)	Gr
a **thesis**	→ an assertion, proposition	D
	≠ a seat (on a train, etc.)	Gr
thick	≠ fat	Nl D *Dk N S*
thus	≠ according to	Nl
to **tick**	≠ to show emotion, wince, twitch	F
	≠ to tap; type	Nl
a **tick**	≠ a fad, fancy, whim	D
	≠ a hint/suggestion/touch of	Nl
	≠ a mannerism, unconscious habit	F
the **tide**	≠ the time (which passes)	Nl Dk N S
tidy	≠ timely, well-timed, opportune	Nl
	≠ early	Dk S
a **tiger**	≠ a jaguar	E
the **tights**	≠ the mourning suit(s)	I
a **tile**	≠ a part (of s/th)	D
	≠ a stroke of bad luck	F
till	≠ to, by, not later than	Dk N S
a **timbre**	≠ an electric bell, doorbell	E F
	≠ a postage stamp	P E I F
	≠ a crest in heraldry	P E
	≠ a seal on a document	P I F
	≠ an emblem, insignia	P
	≠ a rubber stamp	I
	≠ a postmark	I F
	≠ an embossed stamp	F

the **time**	≠ the hour; lesson	Dk N S
	≠ the team in sport	P
	≠ the swindle, trick, gag, hoax	E
timely	≠ worldly, temporal	Dk N S
the **tin**	≠ the pewter	Nl Dk N S
to **tint**	≠ to paint	P
	≠ to dye	I
a **tint**	≠ a complexion	F
	≠ an ink	P D
	≠ a paint (esp. for buildings)	P
tinted	≠ red (of wine)	P E
to **tip**	≠ to do the football pools	D Dk N S
	≠ to touch lightly; type	D
	≠ to clip, trim	Nl
to **tipple**	≠ to toddle, trot	Nl
	≠ to tramp (the roads)	D
a **tippler**	≠ a hiker, keen walker	Nl
the **tips**	≠ the football pools	S
a **tirade**	≠ a witty retort/comment	P
	≠ a journey	P
	≠ a printing, edition, circulation of s/th printed; distance, length, stretch	E
to **tire**	≠ to pull, draw (out)	I F
	≠ to take/draw out	P
	≠ to throw	E
	≠ to shoot (a gun)	F
the **tissue**	≠ the cloth, fabric, textile; texture	F
a **title**	≠ a caption	P E
	≠ a bond/stock/policy certificate	P I F
	≠ a qualification, degree, diploma	P E I F
the **titles**	≠ the headlines	E I F
a **toad**	≠ an awning	F
the **tobacco**	≠ the cigarette	J
	≠ the snuff	P *E* I
	≠ the cigar	E
	≠ the plate (for food)	Tr
a **toenail**	≠ a theatre (stage)	Nl
a **toga**	≠ a judge's or an academic's gown	P E I F
the **toil**	≠ the canvas, painting	F

the **toilet**	→ the (woman's) dress/costume/clothes	F Nl D S
	≠ the dressing table, getting dressed	F *Nl* D
a **toll**	≠ a madman	P *D*
	≠ a top (child's toy)	Nl
the **toll (house)**	≠ the customs (house)	*D* Dk N S
the **tombola**	≠ the bingo	I
to **tone**	≠ to show	Nl
a **tone**	≠ a key (in music)	P E F Nl Dk N S Tr
	≠ a note (in music)	D Dk N S
	≠ an accent, diacritic	Gr
the **tone**	≠ the etiquette, manners, good behaviour	D *Dk* N S
	≠ the energy, force	Gr
a **tongue**	≠ a sole (fish)	Nl
a **top**	≠ a rat	I
	≠ a pot	D
a **topic**	≠ a gaffe, faux pas	I
	≠ a local remedy	F
	≠ a platitude, cliché	E
	≠ a (short) newspaper editorial	P
topical	≠ local	Gr
a **torment**	≠ a violent storm, thunderstorm	P E
	≠ a blizzard	I
a **torrent**	≠ a turret	Nl
a **torso**	≠ a core of a (piece of) fruit	E I
a **toss**	≠ a fool, simpleton	Dk
a **tot**	≠ a wisp of hair; tuft of straw	Dk S
in **toto**	≠ in/at the pools (betting)	D
to **touch**	≠ to get in touch with; be related to	F
	→ to affect, influence	F
the **touch**	≠ the key of a piano/typewriter	F Tr
a **tour**	≠ a revolution of a machine	F Nl D
	≠ a tower	F
a **tourniquet**	≠ a turnstile	P E I F Nl Tr
	≠ a hairpin bend	I
	≠ a catherine wheel	F
	≠ a tough spot; gimlet	P
a **town**	≠ a garden	Nl
the **toy**	≠ the attire, trimmings	Nl

a **trace**	≠ a moth	P
to **trace a line**	≠ to draw a line	F
a **tract**	≠ a neighbourhood, district	S
	≠ a section/wing of a building	D
	≠ a treaty	D *Dk N*
the **traction**	≠ the car with front-wheel drive	F
	≠ the tractor	E
to **traduce**	≠ to translate	P E I F
the **traffic**	→ the (illegal) traffic, trafficking	P E I F
to **train**	≠ to drag	I F
a **trainer**	≠ a trawler (net)	P
	≠ a track/running suit	Ch
the **training (pack)**	≠ a track/running suit	Nl
a **trait**	≠ a stroke, line, streak; act, deed; gulp	F
the **traitor**	≠ the caterer	F
to **tramp**	≠ to tread; pedal a bike	S
	≠ to defraud, swindle	E
a **tramp**	≠ a racket, wangle, trick	E
	≠ a hitchhiker	D
a **trampoline**	≠ a spring/diving board	P E I F S Tr
a **trance**	≠ an awkward/tough situation	E
	≠ a plait of hair	P
	≠ a slice	I
in **trances**	≠ terrified	F
to **transcend**	≠ to leak/come out, spread (of news)	E
the **transcendence**	≠ the importance, important consequences	E
(the) **transit**	≠ the traffic	P E
	≠ the traffic jam	P
	≠ the stop(ping place)	E
	≠ the passageway	E
	≠ the move, transfer	E
to **translate**	→ to transfer, (re)move	*P* E I
	≠ to postpone	*P* E
the **translation**	→ the shifting, movement, removal	P *E* I F
a **translator**	≠ an authorised interpreter	Dk N
to **transpire**	≠ to sweat, perspire	P E I F Nl Dk N S
a **transporter**	≠ a protractor	E D
to **trap**	≠ to kick (out), tread/step on	Nl

a **trap**	≠ a footstep	D
	≠ a staircase	Nl Dk N S
	≠ a bustard	D
	≠ a trapdoor, sliding door, hatchway	F
	≠ a rag	P
a **trapeze**	≠ a table; dining room	Gr
a **trapper**	≠ a pedal, treadle	Nl
the **trauma**	≠ the concussion	I
	→ the wound	Gr
to **travel**	≠ to work	*P* E I F
to **traverse**	≠ to s/th across the way	*P E* I
a **traverse**	≠ a sea crossing	P E I F
	≠ a side road	E I
	≠ a railway sleeper	I F Tr
	≠ a fault, weakness	F
	≠ a short cut/road	F
	≠ a dish (for food)	P
	≠ a fork-lift truck	S
a **treasure**	≠ a strongroom, safe	D
	≠ a treasury	D
the **treatment**	≠ the salary	I F
	≠ the style of address, name, title	P E
	≠ the catering at a hotel, etc.; welcome	I
	≠ the food allowance	P I
a **treaty**	≠ a treatise	F
a **treaty of union**	≠ a hyphen	F
the **tree**	≠ the timber, wood	Dk N S
a **trefoil**	≠ a club (in cards)	F D Gr
to **trek**	≠ to pull, drag	Nl *Dk* N
a **trek**	≠ a draught in a stove; appetite	Nl
tremendous	≠ awful, terrible	P *E* I
a **trench**	≠ a trench coat	I F
the **trepidation**	≠ the thrill, delight	P
	≠ the shaking, vibration	E
to **trespass**	≠ to die, pass away	*P* I F
	≠ to cheat, fraud, tease	P
	≠ to penetrate, go through	E
a **tribunal, tribune**	≠ a grandstand	P E I F Nl D Dk N S Tr
	≠ a pulpit	P
to **trill**	≠ to vibrate, tremble	Nl

a **trilling**	≠ a vibration, trembling	Nl
	≠ a triplet	Dk N S
to **trim**	≠ to work hard, toil	F
trim	≠ well-built, exercised, in good trim	Nl *N* S
to **trim oneself**	≠ to keep oneself fit/trim	Nl D
the **trimming**	≠ the jogging	Nl
the **tripe**	≠ the gut(s)	P E
trivial	≠ immoral, risqué, vulgar	I F
	≠ boring, tedious, trite	Dk N
a **trombone**	≠ a paper-clip	F
a **trooper**	≠ a private (soldier)	*I* F
the **troops, troupes**	≠ the holes	Gr
the **trophy**	≠ the food, nourishment	Gr
the **trouble**	≠ the turmoil, confusion, hubbub, disorder	F D
the **troubles**	≠ the anxieties	F
	→ the riot(s), disturbance(s)	Nl
troupes	See **troops**	
the **trousers**	≠ the panties, briefs	Nl Dk N S
a **trousseau**	≠ a bunch (of keys)	F
a **truant**	≠ a vagabond, beggar, hooligan	F
a **truck**	≠ a trick, a thingamy, what's it	F
	≠ a stunt, dodge	*P E* Nl
	≠ a pressure, print(ing), strain, stress	Dk N S
truculent	≠ lively, outspoken, colourful	F
	≠ cruel, horrifying, fierce, savage, grim	P E I
	≠ full of strange effects	E
true	→ faithful	*Nl* D *Dk* N
truly	≠ credible	Dk N S
a **trump**	≠ a horn (in music)	P E
	≠ an elephant's trunk	E
the **trumpery**	≠ the deceit, deception, fraud, illusion	F
the **trumps**	≠ the playing cards	J
a **trunk**	≠ a drink	D
to **trust**	≠ to comfort, console, cheer up	Dk N S
the **trust**	≠ the comfort, consolation	Nl Dk N S
a **tub(a)**	≠ a tube	D S
	≠ a top hat	I

to **tug**	≠ to chew	S
a **tumbler**	≠ a tumble clothes drier	Nl D S
	≠ a porpoise, dolphin	S
a **tumult**	≠ a riot	I D Dk N S
a **tumulus**	≠ a grave	P
to **tune**	≠ to live as a vagrant	E
a **tune**	≠ a rogue; Indian fig	E
the **tunnel**	≠ the underground railway	Tr
turbulent	≠ mischievous	*E* I F
the **turf**	→ the peat	Nl D Dk N S
a **turkey**	≠ a Turkish bath, sauna	J
the **Turk's Head**	≠ the scapegoat	E
to **turn**	≠ to do gymnastics (without apparatus)	Nl D
	≠ to become, get, to make s/o (+*adj*)	P
	≠ to get out of trouble	D
a **turn**	≠ a drill (tool)	N
a **tusk**	≠ a German	Dk N S
a **tutor**	≠ a (legal) guardian	P *E* I F
	≠ a plant stake, prop	F
a **twin**	≠ a room with twin beds	J
to **twist**	≠ to dispute, quarrel	Nl Dk N S
a **twist**	≠ a dispute, quarrel	Nl Dk N S
the **type**	≠ the Press	Gr
	≠ the maths formula	Gr
	→ the chap, fellow, bloke	P E I F Nl
	≠ the rate (of exchange, etc.)	E
	≠ the build, physique, figure	E
	≠ the typewriter	J
	≠ the eccentric person	S Ch
typical	≠ formal, conventional	Gr
	≠ picturesque	E
a **tyrant**	≠ a (tie) rod	I

U

the **U.S.S.R.**	≠ the Ukranian S.S.R.	D
ulterior	≠ later, subsequent, following after	P E I F
ultimate	≠ latest, most recent	P E I

ultimately	≠ recently, lately	P E I
ult(imo)	≠ the last day of the month	D Dk
unconscious	≠ thoughtless, irresponsible, reckless	E I
unconsulted	≠ ill-advised, imprudent	I
under	≠ among	Nl D
the **underarm**	≠ the forearm	Nl D Dk N S
to **undertake**	≠ to sign	Nl
to **underwrite**	≠ to sign, endorse, subscribe one's name	Nl D Dk N S
unedited	≠ new, original, unknown till now	P E F
	≠ unpublished	P E I F
	≠ outrageous, unhear of, unprecedented	E
unhomely	≠ uncanny, haunted, sinister	D
unique	≠ strange, odd, peculiar	J
a **unique child**	≠ an only child	P E I F
unkindly	≠ unchildlike, precocious	D
untidy	≠ indisposed	Dk
	≠ untimely	Nl N
unwilling	≠ indignant	D
up	≠ on	Nl
	≠ un-(*with many verbs*):	
to **pack up**	≠ to unpack, etc.	Dk N S
an **updraught**	≠ a dedication; order	Nl
an **upheaval**	≠ a fuss, to-do	Dk
to **uphold**	≠ to delay, detain	Nl Dk N S
an **uproar**	≠ a revolt, rebellion	Nl Dk N S
uproarious	≠ rebellious, mutinous	Nl Dk *N* S
to **upset**	≠ to delay, postpone, put back	Dk
	≠ to pin up, elevate falsely	S
	≠ to set up, establish	Nl Dk N S
	≠ to stuff (an animal)	Nl
to **be upset**	≠ to be keen/bent/set on	Dk N
an **upset**	≠ a plan, design, intention	Nl
upstanding	≠ insurgent, rebel	Nl
urban	≠ urbane	P E I F Dk S
the **urbanisation**	≠ the housing estate	E
	≠ the town rebuilding	I
	≠ the town planning	F Nl
to **urge**	≠ to be urgent, necessary	P E I
	≠ to be (legally) in force	E
an **urn**	≠ a ballot box	P E I F *D* Dk N

usable	≠ liable to wear out with use	F
to **use**	≠ to wear out (esp. clothes)	P E I F
	≠ to exhaust (strength)	F
	≠ to injure (esp. eyes)	F
	≠ to wear, have on (clothes); be in fashion	P E *I*
	≠ to wear	P
to **be used**	≠ to be worn out, shabby, frayed, exhausted	P E I F
utterly	≠ externally, outwardly	Nl

V

the **vacancy**	≠ the holiday, vacation	I F Nl J
vague	≠ lazy	E
	≠ unoccupied, vacant, waste (of land)	P F
	≠ pretty, charming, pleasant	I
vale	See **veil**	
a **valet**	≠ a jack/knave (in cards)	P F Gr
valid	≠ healthy, able-bodied, fit, sound	P F Nl
	≠ favoured	E
	≠ favourite	P
the **valour**	≠ the value, worth	P E I F
vamoose	≠ let's go	P E
a **vapour**	≠ a steamer, steamboat	P E I F Gr
a **variant**	≠ a side road	P
various	≠ several	P E
the **Varsity**	≠ the (Oxford and Cambridge) boat race	Nl
a **vase**	≠ a glass (for drinking)	E
	≠ a vessel, boat, ship	P E
the **vase**	≠ the slime, ooze, mud, silt	P F
	≠ the W.C., loo	P
vast	≠ firm, steady, fixed	Nl
vast areas	≠ determined/fixed areas	Nl
the **veal**	≠ the wheel	Nl
vehement	≠ eager, keen, impetuous	P *E*

a **vehicle**	≠ a jalopy, old vehicle	Nl D
a **veil**	≠ a candle	P E
	≠ a sail	P E I
	≠ a (piece of) fleece	P I
	≠ a (piece of) gauze, crêpe	I
	≠ a mist, fog	I
the **veil**	≠ the sleeplessness, night work	E
the **vein**	≠ the (good) luck	I F
	→ the mood, disposition, talent (for s/th)	E I *Nl*
the **venal price/value**	≠ the market/sale/commercial price/value	P E I F
vendetta	≠ proud, superior, haughty	Gr
the **veneer**	≠ the vinyl	J
to **vent**	≠ to wait	Dk N S
a **vent**	≠ a fellow, chap, bloke	Nl
	≠ a wind	P E I F
	≠ a sale	F
	≠ a nostril	P
a **ventilator**	≠ an electric fan; tyre valve	*Nl* D
a **venue**	≠ an arrival, advent, approach, growth	F
to **verbalise against a conductor**	≠ to take down a driver's particulars	F
the **verbena**	≠ the outdoor (village) party	E
a **verge**	≠ a rod, wand, stick	F
	≠ a virgin	F
	≠ a grill, grating, railing	E
a **verger**	≠ an orchard	F
to **verify**	≠ to fulfil, carry out (orders, etc.)	E
	≠ to examine	P I F Nl
	≠ to audit (accounts)	I F Nl
	≠ to happen, take place	P E I
versatile	≠ fickle, unreliable, unstable	F
a **verse**	≠ a line of poetry	P E I F
versed	≠ altered, modified, garbled	P
	→ experienced, skilled	*P* E I F
	≠ overturned; paid up	F
	≠ poured out, shed (of tears/blood)	I F
	≠ paid in	I
	≠ well-mannered	S

a **version**	→ a translation from a foreign language	P E I F
very	≠ true	I *F*
the **vespers**	≠ the light meals, snacks	D
the **vessel**	≠ the washing-up (liquid), the plates and dishes	F
a **vest**	≠ a jacket	F
	≠ (in BE) a waistcoat	Nl D Dk N S
	≠ a cardigan	I Nl *D*
	≠ a moat	Nl
	≠ a garment	P I
	≠ a dress, gown	I
	≠ a failure (slang)	F
the **vestments**	≠ the clothes (in a general sense)	I F
the **vet**	≠ the law; fat, lard	Nl
	≠ the wager, bet	D
	≠ the brain, wit, gumption	*Dk* N S
to **vet**	≠ to vie, rival; bet	D
	≠ to know	Nl S
a **veteran**	≠ an expert	J
to **vex**	≠ to puzzle, tease	D
	≠ to harass, oppress, persecute	P I
a **vicar**	≠ a curate	E F D
	≠ a substitute, deputy (of people at work)	Dk N S
a **vice**	≠ a pleasure, delight	P
	≠ a failing, malpractice	P
	≠ a bolt	F
	≠ a defect, blemish, flaw	I F
	≠ a habit	E
vicious	≠ depraved (of a person)	P E F
	≠ defective (of a machine)	E F
to **have a good view**	≠ to have good eyesight	F
a **vignette**	≠ a car licence	F
	≠ a badge, emblem	E
a **Viking**	≠ a bacillus	J
the **Viking**	≠ the buffet food, esp. smorgasbord	J
a **villa**	≠ a bungalow	Dk S
	≠ a small town	E
a **villain**	≠ a countryman	P I
	≠ a grill, grating	E
a **viol**	≠ a violin	Nl

a **viola**	≠ a guitar	P
the **violence**	≠ the (mental) shock/ disturbance	E
violent	≠ embarrassing, awkward	E F
a **virago**	≠ a mannish woman	P E
virtuous	≠ masterly, perfect	D S
the **virtuous**	≠ the virtuoso	I
vis-à-vis	≠ opposite, facing	F Nl *D* Dk N S Ch
to **be not visible**	≠ to be not at home to anyone	Dk
to **visit**	→ to inspect, examine	F D
	≠ to search	Nl D
the **visit**	≠ the fee for a doctor's visit	Tr
	≠ the visitor, caller	P E Ch
	≠ the inspection, overhauling, examination	F
a **visitor**	→ an inspector	F
	≠ a customs officer	Nl
the **vista**	≠ the power of sight	P E I
	≠ the intention	E
	≠ the appearance, look	E I
a **voice**	≠ an item (on a list); rumour	I
a **volt**	≠ a thrust with a sword, loop, turn	P
	≠ a time, occasion	I
	≠ a vault (in gymnastics)	F
	≠ a crowd	Nl
voluble	≠ changeable, fickle, unstable	P E I
a **volume**	≠ a book (large, but not in a series)	F
voluntary	≠ stubborn, wilful, obstinate	*I* F
a **vote**	≠ an exam mark/result	I
	≠ a vow, oath, wish, desire, hope	P E I
to **vow**	≠ to wish; fold	Nl
a **vow**	≠ a wish, prayer	F
	≠ a choice	Ch
a **voyage**	≠ a journey, trip	*P E* I F
vulgar	≠ normal, ordinary, everyday	P E *F*
a **vulgar fraction**	≠ an ordinary fraction	P I F
the **vulgarisation**	≠ the popularisation (of knowledge)	E I F
	≠ the translation into the vernacular	E

to **vulgarise**	≠ to spread/divulge (information)	E I
	≠ to popularise	E I F
	≠ to translate into the vernacular	E I

W

a **wagon**	≠ a car	Nl D S
	≠ a railway passenger-carriage (in BE), passenger car (in AE)	*P E* I F Nl S
to **wake**	≠ to be awake; watch (over), keep an eye on	Nl D
a **wake**	≠ a hole in the ice	Nl N S
	≠ a guard, watchman	*Nl* D
a **wall**	≠ a rampart, dam, embankment, dyke, shore	Nl D
to **waltz**	≠ to roll	Nl D Dk S
a **waltz**	≠ a drum, roller, cylinder (in machinery)	Nl D Dk N S
a **wand**	≠ a wall (esp. interior)	Nl D
to **wander**	≠ to hike, travel	D Dk N S
	≠ to walk	Nl D Dk N S
in **a war**	≠ in a mess/muddle/tangle	Nl
a **ward**	≠ an innkeeper, landlord	Nl
a **warehouse**	≠ a (department) store, emporium	Nl D Dk N S
warm	≠ hot	Dk N S
a **wart**	≠ a watch-tower	D
a **washstand**	≠ a clothes-horse	D
to **watch**	≠ to wait	Nl
the **water(s)**	≠ the W.C., loo	E I F
the **waxworks**	≠ the growing pains	Dk
a **way**	≠ a road	Nl D Dk N S
weak	≠ soft, flabby	Nl
a **weapon**	≠ a coat of arms	Nl D N S
the **weather**	≠ the storm, bad weather	D
to **wed**	≠ to bet	Nl
a **weight**	≠ a pair of scales, balance	Dk N
a **well**	≠ a wave (on water)	D
	≠ a spring, fountain	Nl

to **wend**	≠ to turn, reverse	Nl D Dk N S
in **the wet**	≠ in the law	Nl
wet	≠ naive, sentimental, romantic, oversensitive	J
when	≠ if	D
	≠ where	Ar
where	≠ who	D
while	≠ because	*Nl* D
a **whimper**	≠ an eyelash	Nl D
to **whine**	≠ to shriek, scream, whistle, whizz	Dk N *S*
	≠ to weep	*Nl* D
a **whip**	≠ a see-saw	Nl D Dk
a **white shirt**	≠ a shirt (of any colour) worn by a businessman	J
who	≠ how	Nl
wide	≠ far, distant, long	D
a **wife**	≠ a hag, harridan	Nl
the **wild**	≠ the savage	Nl D Dk N S
	≠ the game, deer, venison	Nl D Dk N S
to **win**	≠ to gain	Nl Dk N S
to **wink**	≠ to wave, make a sign	Nl D Dk N S
a **wink**	≠ a sign, nod, hint, tip, suggestion	Nl D Dk N S
a **winkle**	≠ a shop	Nl
	≠ a corner	D
	≠ an angle	Dk N S
a **winner**	≠ a (Japanese) sausage	J
to **wish**	≠ to wipe, rub, mop	D *Dk N*
the **wit(s)**	≠ the pun	S
	≠ the joke	D Dk N
a **womb**	≠ a paunch, big belly	Dk N S
a **worm**	≠ a snake	S
	≠ a whim; little child	D
a **wound**	≠ an injury, hurt, cut	D
	≠ a sore, bruise	Nl
to **wrap s/th up**	≠ to pick s/th up	Nl
a **wreck**	≠ a net, towel rail	Nl
	≠ a shrimp, prawn	N
	≠ a registered letter See also **rake**	S
to **wrinkle**	≠ to jingle	Nl
a **wrist**	≠ an instep of the foot	D Dk N S
	≠ a back of the hand	D

X

a **Xerox**	≠ a bank statement	P

Y

the **yacht**	≠ the hunting	Nl *D Dk* N *S*
yet	≠ now	D
a **yew**	≠ a century	Nl
the **youngest**	≠ the latest, most recent/ up-to-date	Nl D

Z

the **zeal**	≠ the end, finish, aim	D
	≠ the soul, spirit	Nl
a **zebra**	≠ a silly person	P
a **Zeppelin**	≠ any type of airship	D Dk *N*
the **zest**	→ the lemon peel	F
	≠ the heat	Gr
a **zip**	≠ a penis	Ar
the **zinc**	≠ the counter at a bar	F
	≠ the old car	F
the **zone**	≠ the son	Gr
	≠ the belt, girdle (in clothing)	Gr
	≠ the brothel (district)	P *E*
the **zoom**	≠ the squash, juice	E

PART 2

English Meanings

a

abandon B — *v* to give up or leave.

abate C — *v* to get less strong, decrease, or make less. *past participle* **abated**.

abatement C — *n* a decrease or reduction.

abortion B — *n* (c) the removing of the foetus so that it cannot live.

abrade C — *v* to wear away (skin) by rubbing.

absence B — *n* the state of not being (physically) present.

absolute A — *adj* complete, perfect.

absolve C — *v* to pardon someone for doing wrong; free someone from a promise.

abstinence C — *n* (u) usually only refers to not drinking any form of alcohol.

abuse C — *v* **1.** to make wrong use of, esp. in an immoral way. **2.** to use strong or rude words to hurt someone.
n (c) a case of abusing someone or something.

abusive C — *adj* used of comments in sense **2** of the verb.

academic B — *n* (c) a member of a college or university.
adj **1.** concerned with teaching or universities, colleges, etc. **2.** too theoretical, impractical.

access B — *n* **1.** (c) a way or place of entering. **2.** (u) the right to approach or to obtain something.

accessories B — *n* (c; sometimes singular) things that are not essential but go with something larger.

accident A — *n* (c) an event, usually an unpleasant one, which happens without being planned.

acclimatised B — *past participle* adjusted to life in a different climate or surroundings from where one grew up.

accommodate B — *v* **1.** to have room for. **2.** to satisfy the needs of. **3.** to adapt to new conditions.

accommodation A — *n* (u in BE, c in AE) a place to live or spend the night.

accomplishment C — *n* **1.** (u) the act of carrying out something completely. **2.** skill.

accord C — *v* **1.** to agree, fit with. **2.** to grant, allow.
B — *n* used in a few idioms: *of his own accord* without being asked; *with one accord* all together.

accost C — *v* to go up to and speak to someone, esp. a stranger often in an angry or disturbing way.

account A — *n* (c) many meanings, usually connected with money, such as **1.** an amount of money kept in a bank that may be added to or taken from. **2.** a description.

accurate B — *adj* **1.** precise or exact. **2.** (of people) working carefully.

accuse B — *v* to say that someone has done something bad or wrong.

ace C/B — *n* (c) **1.** C a person who is outstandingly good at doing something. **2.** B (playing cards) the card with a single symbol.

achieve C — *v* to finish successfully, accomplish.

achievement B — *n* (c) something successfully finished.

acquaintance B — *n* **1.** (u) knowledge. **2.** (c) someone you know slightly **3.** *make the acquaintance of* to come to know for th first time.

acquit C — *v* to declare innocent in a law court.

acre B — *n* (c) a measurement of area.

act A — *v* A various meanings, but esp.: **1.** to take the part of character in a play. **2.** to behave, take action.

A/C — *n* **1.** (c) A part of a play in the theatre. **2.** *caught in th act* found doing something wrong. **3.** (c) C *The Act* usually refers to the Acts of the Apostles in the Nev Testament. **4.** (c) C *Act of Parliament* the formal phras for British law.

action A — *n* (c and u) various meanings, but not esp. connected wit commerce or business; basically means something done movement.

active B — *n* *the active and the passive* (both *n*) used in grammar t describe the mood of verbs.

adj lively, full of energy and activity.

activist C — *n* (c) a much stronger meaning than the Italian: usually person who is strongly committed to a political move ment, and even a political agitator.

actual B — *adj* real; really existing.

actually A — *adv* truly, really, as a matter of fact.

actuality C — *n* (u) the quality of being real.

addict B — *n* (c) someone who cannot free himself from a seriously ba habit, esp. drugs.

addition C — *n* the action of adding two or more together, somethin added.

address B — *v* **1.** to write an address on a letter, etc. **2.** to speak t someone or an audience.

A — *n* (c) **1.** place to which letters are directed. **2.** a shor speech.

adequate B — *adj* enough, but no more.

adherent C — *n* (c) someone who identifies with a movement or set o ideas, confined mainly to political activities. (It is no usually used of sport or the arts.)

adjourn C — *v* (of a meeting, etc.) to stop for a certain time, postpone

adjudge C — *v* to make a statement or judgment according to the law

adjudicate C — *v* to sit as a judge, esp. in a competition.

adjudication C — *n* (c) a meeting to decide an issue, as in a competition.

adjunct C — *n* (c) something added to the main part of a larger whole

adjustment B — *n* (c/u) a small change to make something more suitable.

admiration C — *n* (u) feeling of respect; a *point of admiration* can only mear a focus of respect.

admired B — *past participle* considered with respect.

adopt B — *v* **1.** to bring a child to one's home to be part of the family legally and permanently. **2.** to choose, start, or accept.

advance B — *v* to move forward; make progress.

n (c) **1.** a move forward; some progress. **2.** a loan o money, usually from a bank.

dventure B *n* **1.** (c) an exciting happening, with danger and risk. **2.** (u) danger and risk.

dvertise A *v* usually only in use in the commercial context of using publicity.

dvertisement A *n* (c) a piece of publicity; notice.

dvise A *v* to suggest what to do; (less strong than *instruct*).

dvocate C *n* (c) **1.** a lawyer who speaks in defence of someone or something in a Scottish court of law. **2.** someone who supports an idea.

eon C *n* (c) an incalculably long period of time.

fair A *n* (c) **1.** a matter or business. **2.** an event; happening. **3.** a sexual relationship between two people who are not married to each other.

fect A/B/C *v* **1.** A to influence. **2.** B to upset; make unhappy. (Other uses of the verb are C and it is not used as a noun.)

fection B *n* gentle love, fondness.

fluence C *n* (u) usually now only used of wealth, money.

fluent B *adj* having plenty of money; rich.

front C *v* to insult or offend, esp. in front of other people.

frikaans B *n* (u) the language derived from Dutch, spoken in Southern Africa.

ter A *preposition* the opposite of *before*, but mostly only used of time not place.

ternoon A *n* (c) the part of the day between lunchtime and evening.

terthought B *n* (c) **1.** something added later, both in conversation or material things. **2.** a child born late in a family.

genda B *n* (c) the list of points to be discussed at a formal meeting.

gent B *n* (c) someone who acts for other people, esp. in business.

gglomeration C *n* (u) the action of things becoming stuck together—not used of buildings.

ggregate B *n* **1.** (c) a whole made up of small parts, more used of things than people. **2.** (u) a kind of building material.

gnostic C *n* (c) someone who neither believes in God nor denies God exists, but says nothing can be known.
adj relating to an agnostic.

gonising C *adj* causing intense pain; also used of mental tension.

gony C *n* (u) intense pain, but not esp. associated with death.

gree A *v* to have the same opinion; approve informally.

greement A *n* the state of having the same opinion as others.

r A *n* **1.** (u) many meanings, but basically the gas mixture round the earth which we breathe. **2.** (c) *give oneself airs* to behave unnaturally and try to impress people.

sle C *n* (c) a passageway between areas in a theatre, church, etc.

arm A *n* **1.** (c) a bell, siren, etc., to warn people of danger. **2.** *alarm clock* a clock with a bell, etc., to wake one. **3.** (u) tension or worry in people when there is danger.

cove C *n* (c) part of a room where the wall recedes, which can be filled with shelves or other furniture, not necessarily in a bedroom.

ias C *n* (c) a false name, esp. of a criminal.

alienated C — *past participle* estranged from, conscious that other peop are unfriendly or hostile.

all day A — *n* the whole of the day.

allege C — *v* to state before having clear proof.

allegro C — *adj* (only used in music) fast or quick.

alley C — *n* (c) a narrow dirty street between buildings; (only rare a path in a park or garden).

alliance C — *n* (c) a group, esp. of countries, joined together for th mutual support.

allure C — *n* (c) an attraction; fascination. (The adjective *alluring* more common.)

almoner C — *n* (c) a social worker who has particular care for people hospital.

alms C — *n* (c; only plural) money given to the poor.

aloud A — *adv* so as to be heard.

also A — *adv* in addition, as well, too. (In BE usually found before t verb.)

alter A — *v* to change; modify in any way.

alterations B — *n* (c) changes; modifications.

alternatively C — *adv* instead, as different possibility.

alternately C — *adv* occurring successively or by turns.

alto C — *n* a man who sings in falsetto; (now often called a *count* ***tenor***). ***adj*** describing the voice of such a person. (woman singing the same notes is a *contralto*.)

amass C — *v* to gather, heap (things) up, esp. money.

amateur B — *n, adj* not (a) professional; an unpaid player.

ambassador B — *n* (c) a man who represents his country in a foreign land.

ambulance A — *n* (c) a vehicle for carrying sick people to hospital.

amendment C — *n* (c) a detailed modification, esp. to a rule or law.

amends C — *n* (c; only plural) *make amends* act in a way so as to cor pensate for rudeness, damage, etc.

amenity C — *n* (c; often plural) a pleasant or useful facility or service.

amorous C — *adj* tending to think of (sexual) love.

amphitheatre C — *n* (c) **1.** a roofless building with open seats that ri above and behind each other to completely surround circular area in the middle. **2.** a half-circle theatr (It is not often used of a modern indoor theatre.)

Amphitryon C — *n* the Theban prince in Greek mythology would be asso ated with gastronomy by only a few English speakers.

ancient A — *adj* old, esp. connected with the Greeks and Romans.
C — *n* (c; usually plural) people who lived long ago, esp. t Greeks and Romans.

androgyne C — *n* (c) mainly used of plants with male and female parts the same flower or on the same plant.

angel C — *n* (c) **1.** a spirit, messenger and servant of God. **2.** (i formal) a very good-hearted person.

anger A — *n* (u) fury; the feeling experienced if you are wronged, et often leading to a wish to hurt someone or to fight.

angina C — *n* (u) short for *angina pectoris*, a heart disease causi severe chest pains.

nniversary B	*n*	(c) the day of the year when something happened.
nnounce A	*v*	to make known to the public; (does not exist as a noun in English).
nnouncement A	*n*	(c) anything announced in writing, print, or on the radio or television.
nnouncer B	*n*	(c) a speaker on radio or television who introduces programmes.
nnoy B	*v*	to irritate; cause to be angry or impatient.
nt C	*n*	(c) one of a number of types of small insects that live in colonies.
ntenna C	*n*	(c) one of the hair-like feelers on the head of an insect. (It is not very commonly used for the wires connected with radio or television reception. Use aerial.)
nticipate B	*v*	to expect something may happen (and take action accordingly).
nticipation B	*n*	*thank you in anticipation* means I hope you can do what I ask (and if you do, I shall not feel obliged to acknowledge it). This may be more polite when writing to ask for something, than writing *thank you in advance* which supposes the thing will definitely be done.
ntiphon C	*n*	(c) one of the pieces sung by a choir during a church service. See also *hymn*.
nxious A	*adj*	**1.** worried, a little afraid. **2.** keen to do something.
part A	*adv*	away from other things, to the side.
C	*adj*	not in very common use except in the phrase *worlds apart* i.e. very different.
partment C	*n*	(c) the usual AE word for the BE *flat*. Used in BE *apartment* is **1.** (only plural) C a set of rooms in a very large house or castle. **2.** (c) C a luxury flat.
pe C	*n*	(c) one of a group of different monkeys including gorillas and chimpanzees, having either no tail or only a short one.
peritive B	*n*	(c) a drink taken before a meal to stimulate the appetite.
plomb C	*n*	(u) the quality of being very self-assured.
pocrypha C	*n*	*The Apocrypha* the collection of religious writings, sometimes printed between the Old and New Testaments.
pology A	*n*	(c) an expression that one is sorry for a fault, etc.
postrophe B/C	*n*	(c) **1.** B a punctuation mark, as in *it's*, *Mary's*; *'cello*. **2.** C a speech or poem, etc., addressed to someone who is dead, or often absent, or to a country or an idea.
postrophise C	*v*	to write or speak (such a speech, etc.).
pparatus A	*n*	(usually u) a machine or equipment for a particular job.
pparent A/B	*adj*	**1.** A clear or obvious. **2.** B seeming.
pparition C	*n*	(c) appearance of a ghost.
ppeal B	*v*	**1.** to ask for help. **2.** to attract.
	n	**1.** a strong request for help. **2.** (u) attraction; interest.
ppear A	*v*	has the same meaning in English as in Portuguese, except English lacks the meaning *mostrar-se; fazer farol*.
ppoint B	*v*	to call someone officially to a position or job; fix a time or place.

appointment A *n* (c) **1.** a time and place for a meeting. **2.** a job position.

appreciable C *adj* enough to be perceived.

appreciate A *v* **1.** to know the worth of. **2.** to be grateful for.

apprehend C *v* (formal) to arrest. (To be filled with apprehension, i fear and *to be apprehensive* are not false friends.)

appropriate C *v* to take and use as one's own; put aside for a speci purpose.

approve A *v* to agree to.

approximate B *v* (of ideas or statistics) to be near. (It is rarely used physical movement.)

apres-ski C *n* (u) evening social activities at wintersport centres.

apt B/C *adj* **1.** B suitable. **2.** B tend to. **3.** C clever, good learning.

aqueduct C *n* (c) a man-built channel for supplying water.

arc C *n* (c) **1.** (geometry) part of a circle. **2.** electric curre which jumps between conductors (electrodes) produci a bright light.

archive C *n* (often plural) a place for keeping old documents and of cial records needed for research and reference.

arena C *n* (c) the open central space in an amphitheatre and figur tively for any place of competition.

argument A *n* (usually c) an exchange of ideas, between a discussion ar a quarrel.

Ark C *n* (c) the large ship built by Noah described in the Bible.

arm B *v* to provide with weapons (also used figuratively).

Armada C *n* the Armada usually refers to the Spanish fleet whi sailed for England in 1588.

armament B *n* (c; usually plural) military equipment, weapon.

armature C *n* (c) the rotating part of a dynamo; an electric motor's coi

aroma C *n* (c) a pleasant smell, e.g. of coffee.

arrange A *v* **1.** to put in order. **2.** to prepare, make plans.

arras C *n* (c) a tapestry or wall-hanging, originally one made Arras.

arrest A *v* to seize legally.
n (c) the act of arresting someone.

arrive A/C *v* **1.** A to reach somewhere, usually the end of a journe **2.** C (informal) to be successful in a career. **3.** A (time) to come.

art A *n* various meanings, esp. academically, but the most ir portant use is in the sense of music, painting, sculptur and drawing.

art nouveau C *n* (u) the name used in English for the style in art ar architecture, etc., current over the turn of the centur known in French as *modern style*.

artist A *n* (c) usually a painter or drawer of pictures.

arty C *adj* trying to impress others that one is artistic.

asbestos B *n* (u) a grey mineral, used to make fire-proof material.

Ascension C *n* the time when Jesus passed from the earth into heave (*Ascent* B any journey upwards.)

sp C — *n* (c) a type of small snake.

sparagus B — *n* (u) a plant of which only the tops are eaten as a vegetable.

spersions C — *n* (c; sometimes singular) attack reputation, say defamatory things: *to cast aspersions on someone* say defamatory things about someone.

spiration C — *n* (c) desire, ambition.

spire C — *v* to have an ambition for, desire.

ss C — *n* (c) **1.** an animal similar to a donkey. **2.** a silly person.

ssault C — *n* (c) an unexpected attack, esp. in legal and military contexts.

ssent C — *v* to agree.
n an official or legal agreement; *by common assent* with everyone in agreement.

ssert C — *v* to declare formally and forcefully.

ssessor C — *n* (c) **1.** someone who makes judgments requiring special knowledge. **2.** someone who evaluates property or establishes an income, esp. for tax purposes.

ssimilate C — *v* to absorb into the mind, the body, or a country.

ssist C — *v* to help.

ssistance B — *n* (u) help; *public assistance* is money given by the state to people out of work, etc.

ssistant A — *n* (c) **1.** someone who helps. **2.** someone who serves customers in a shop.

ssizes — *n* (plural) (in England and Wales until 1971) the meeting(s) of a special court in each county, attended by judges who travelled to different towns.

ssorted C — *adj* consisting of different sorts mixed together.

stute C — *adj* the word has a more favourable meaning in English than in Spanish, though it is still used of a person who quickly sees things to his advantage.

sylum C — *n* originally, a place of refuge or safety, it now usually means **1.** (u) protection and refuge given to a person who has left a country, esp. for political reasons. **2.** (c) a mental hospital.

thenaeum C — *n* a famous gentlemen's club in the West End of London.

thlete C — *n* (c) someone who competes in physical exercises.

tom B — *n* (c) **1.** the smallest unit of any element (as in physical chemistry). **2.** (informal) a very small amount.

ttack A — *v* to go forward to fight against.

ttain C — *v* to manage to do or obtain something.

ttend A — *v* **1.** to be present at. **2.** to pay attention. (*Attend to* B to serve and help someone.)

ttic C — *n* (c) a room under a roof, often used for storage.

ttire C — *v* to dress; (usually used only as a past participle).

ttitude A — *n* (c) **1.** the way someone thinks or feels. **2.** a position of the body.

udience A — *n* (c) **1.** the spectators in a cinema, theatre, or concert hall. **2.** a formal interview, e.g. with the Pope or a monarch. **3.** the people listening to a programme on the radio or watching one on the television.

auditor B — *n* (c) someone who officially examines a firm's account (It is only very rarely used for a listener.)
auditorium C — *n* (c) the place where the audience sit in a theatre, etc.
augury C — *n* (c) a sign of future events; omen.
author A — *n* (c) someone who writes something, usually the writer a book. (Only very occasionally *the author of an action*
average A — *n* (c) the amount found by adding different quantities together and then dividing the total by the number quantities.
avert C — *v* **1.** to turn one's thoughts or eyes away from. **2.** to a in a way to prevent something from happening.
aviator C — *n* (c) (old-fashioned) someone who flies a plane.
avocado C — *n* (c) the pear-shaped tropical fruit.
axe C — *v* **1.** literally, to cut off with an axe. **2.** (informal) t dismiss from employment, reduce spending or service or stop (a project, etc.).
n (c) a tool for cutting (esp. wood), with a short blade right angles to the handle.
axle C — *n* (c) the rod on which a wheel turns.

b

baby foot B — *n* (c) could only mean the foot of a baby.
baby grand C — *n* (c) short for *baby grand piano* a small grand piano.
bachelor C — *n* (c) an unmarried man esp. legal use; (a *Bachelor of Arts*–a B.A.—is a university graduate).
back A — *n* (c) the rear part.
backbone B — *n* (c) the bone down the back; (also called the *spine*).
backside C — *n* (c) (informal, not offensive) the part of the body one si on.
bag A — *n* (c) a container, usually made of soft material, such a paper or cloth.
bagatelle C — *n* (u) a game played with small heavy balls on a board wit holes in it. (Its (c) use meaning 'something unimportan is literary or archaic.)
baggage — *n* **1.** (u) B the usual AE word for *luggage* (BE) but airline in all parts of the English speaking world refer to *passengers' baggage allowance*. **2.** (c) C (occasional) a bad tempered or good-for-nothing woman.
bail C — *n* (u) money deposited at a court for a prisoner to be se free until the trial.
balance B — *v* to maintain equilibrium.
n **1.** (c) a machine for weighing materials, etc. **2.** (u/c equilibrium.
balcony B — *n* (c) **1.** a platform outside an upstairs room, where on can sit. **2.** the upper place for seats in a theatre o cinema, etc.

all A	*n*	**1.** a spherical object, esp. as used in games. **2.** a formal, elegant dance.
allad C	*n*	(c) **1.** a long poem, often set to music. **2.** a romantic song.
alloon B	*n*	(c) **1.** a very light rubber ball used for decorations and for children to play with. **2.** a large ball filled with gas or hot air, often to carry people up.
allot C	*v*	to decide by voting.
B	*n*	(c) the practice or an instance of voting, esp. in secret.
alsa C	*n*	(u) very lightweight wood, esp. used for making model aircraft.
an B	*v*	to prohibit.
	n	a prohibition.
and C	*v*	to put together, unite.
A	*n*	(c) **1.** a flat, thin strip of something. **2.** a range of frequencies or wavelengths. **3.** a group of people with a leader, esp. playing music.
ane C	*n*	(c) something or someone causing much unhappiness.
ank A	*n*	(c) **1.** an institution dealing with money. **2.** the land at the side of a river or other sloping piece of ground.
anquet C	*n*	(c) a large formal meal for many people, often with speeches.
ar C	*v*	to make a barrier, block, or close with a heavy bar.
arb C	*n*	(c) a sharp point, esp. one curved back like a fish hook. See also **barbed**.
arbarity C	*n*	(c and u) very great cruelty.
arbarous C	*adj*	uncivilised.
arbed C	*adj*	most commonly heard in *barbed wire*, wire for fencing with sharp spikes fixed along it.
ark C	*n*	**1.** (u) the rough outer part on a tree's surface. **2.** (c) the sharp noise made by a dog.
armaid C	*n*	(c) a girl/woman serving in (the bar of) a public house.
arn C	*n*	(c) a storage building on a farm.
arracks B/C	*n*	**1.** B (singular or plural verb may follow) building(s) for soldiers to live in. **2.** (c; singular, without *-s*) C a large, ugly building in very bad condition.
arrage C	*n*	(c) **1.** a type of dam built across a river estuary. **2.** a barrier of non-stop gunfire.
arrier B	*n*	(c) type of gate, fence, or bar to obstruct or control the flow of people or things. (Also used figuratively.)
ase B	*n*	(c) **1.** a foundation on which one can build; (literal, not figurative – compare *basis*). **2.** a military establishment.
asin B	*n*	(c) a container, esp. one for water.
asis B	*n*	(c) a foundation on which one can build, esp. figuratively speaking. (plural **bases**)
asket C	*n*	(c) **1.** a lightweight container made of soft thin pieces of wood, for carrying things. **2.** a metal ring with an open net base in basketball.
assoon C	*n*	(c) a musical instrument made of wood, blown through a reed, and giving a deep sound.

bastard B *n* (c) **1.** a person whose parents are not married. (slang) any man, esp. one who is disliked.

bat C *n* (c) **1.** a specially shaped wooden stick used in certa ball games. **2.** a mouse-like animal with wings, oft flying at night.

bathos C *n* (u) a sudden change in literature from a noble subje etc., to an everyday or silly one.

batman C *n* (c) in the army, a soldier who acts as a private servant an officer.

baton C *n* (c) thin stick used by the conductor of an orchestra show the rhythm and expression.

batter C *v* to hit hard and repeatedly, so as to bruise or break.

battery B *n* (c) apparatus used for storing electricity.

bazaar C *n* (c) **1.** a sale, esp. one for a charity. **2.** Eastern stre market.

beach B *n* (c) a sandy area beside the sea.

beam C *n* (c) **1.** a strong piece of wood across the ceiling of room. **2.** a ray of light.

bean B *n* (c) (the seed of) a plant used in food or drink.

beast B *n* (c) **1.** a (large) four-footed animal. **2.** a cruel hateful person.

become A *v* **1.** to grow or develop into. **2.** (of clothes, jeweller etc.) to suit someone. **3.** (with *of*) to happen to.

becoming C *adj* (usually of clothes) that suit one.

bedding C *n* (u) all the sheets, blankets, etc., used to make up a be

bedeck C *v* (old-fashioned) to decorate.

bedstead C *n* (c) the frame of a bed.

beech C *n* (c) a tree with a smooth greyish bark and dark gree leaves.

beef B *n* (u) the meat from cows, bulls, and oxen.

beer A *n* popular bitter alcoholic drink.

befall C *v* (old-fashioned) to happen (to), mostly of something ba

behalf B *n* (u) *on behalf of someone* representing someone.

behold C *v* (old-fashioned) to look (at).

beige C *adj, n* very pale brownish yellow.

believe A *v* to accept as true.

bend A *n* (c) a change of direction, without a sharp angle, in a roa or path, etc.

benefit B *n* (u) something that improves; help or advantage.

Bengali C *n* (c) a person from West Bengal in Eastern India.

benzine C *n* (u) a mixture of liquids obtained from petroleum, use for cleaning.

berate C *v* to speak crossly.

Berliner C *n* (c) someone who lives in or comes from Berlin.

beseech C *v* (rather literary) to ask eagerly or urgently.

beset C *v* (old-fashioned) to be surrounded.

besiege C *v* **1.** to hold (a town) in siege; attack militarily. **2.** t overwhelm.

best man B *n* (c) in a wedding, a friend of the bridegroom who take part in the ceremonies.

bet B — *v* **1.** to risk (money) on the result of a future event, such as a horse race. **2.** (informal) to be sure.

bevel C — *n* (c) a surface cut at an angle, esp. along the edge of a piece of wood or glass.

beware B — *v* (usually used in the imperative) to be cautious; look out: *beware of the dog.*

Bible B — *n* (c) the holy writings of the Christian religion.

bid B — *v* to offer (money) at an auction for something you want to buy.

bide C — *v* old-fashioned except in the phrase *bide one's time* to wait for a good opportunity.

bier C — *n* (c) a type of table or frame used at a funeral, to put the coffin on.

bill A/B — *n* (c) **1.** A a list of items to be paid for. **2.** B the equivalent of a mouth in a bird.

billet C — *n* (c) a place (often a private house) where a soldier lives.

billion C — *n* in BE until recently, one million million, but the AE sense of one thousand million has become increasingly current.

bind C — *n* (c; singular) (informal) something boring and/or irritating.

biography C — *n* (c) the story of someone's life.

biscuit A — *n* (c) a small dry cake made with flour and sugar.

bit A — *n* (c) a small piece or part of something.

bitch C — *n* (c) **1.** a female dog. **2.** (strongly derogatory) a woman.

bizarre C — *adj* very strange.

black A — *adj, n* very dark coloured, opposite of white.

blade C — *n* (c) **1.** the cutting part of a tool or weapon. **2.** a long flat leaf of grass, wheat, etc.

blame B — *v* to place responsibility on (someone) for doing something wrong.

bland C — *adj* showing no strong feelings; (of food) with no strong flavour.

blandish C — *v* (uncommon) to flatter.

blank B — *n* (c) a form which has not been filled in.
adj **1.** having no writing or other marks on. **2.** (of the face) expressionless.

blanket B — *n* (c) a warm bed-covering.

blast C — *n* **1.** (c) a very sudden strong force of wind. **2.** (u) the force of an explosion which damages things.

blaze B — *v* (of a fire) to burn brightly.

bleak C — *adj* cold, without joy, without shelter.

blemish C — *v* (usually passive) to spoil; stain, mark.

blend B — *v* **1.** to mix together. **2.** (of colours) to go well together.
n (c) a mixture.

bless B — *v* to ask God's favour for (someone).

blind A — *adj* unable to see or use the eyes.
C — *n* (c) a covering for a window pulled down from a roller.
B — *v* to cause to lose one's sight.

blink C — *v* to close and open the eyes quickly.

blinkers C	*n*	(c) covers fixed over the eyes of an animal to prevent from seeing to the sides.
blitz C	*n*	(c) (informal) any sudden intensive attack.
block B	*n*	(c) **1.** a piece of wood or stone. **2.** a large building usually of offices or flats. **3.** an obstruction.
blockhouse C	*n*	(c) a strong building giving protection from explosions bombardment, etc.
blot C	*v*	**1.** to soak or dry up (ink). **2.** to spill ink leaving un wanted marks.
blouse B	*n*	(c) similar to a shirt, worn by a girl.
blue A	*adj*	**1.** the colour of the sky. **2.** moody and depressed **3.** pornographic.
A/C	*n*	**1.** (c and u) A the colour of the sky. **2.** (c) C a sports man who has represented or represents Oxford or Cam bridge University.
board A	*v*	to go aboard (a ship or aeroplane).
	n	(c) **1.** a long flat cut piece of wood. **2.** a group o people who administer a company, etc. **3.** a surfac used for a particular purpose.
boat A	*n*	(c) small vehicle for travelling across water.
bobbin C	*n*	(c) a roller on which cotton, etc. is wound.
Boer B	*n*	(c) a South African originating from the Netherlands.
bog C	*n*	(c) **1.** ground so wet that it cannot support muc weight. **2.** (impolite; BE slang) a lavatory.
boil C	*n*	(c) a small eruption on the skin.
boiler C	*n*	(c) a tank in which water is heated.
bomb A	*v*	to drop bombs on, from an aircraft.
	n	(c) **1.** a container with chemicals which can be ex ploded. **2.** *the Bomb* refers to the atomic bomb.
bomber B	*n*	(c) **1.** an aircraft designed to carry and drop bombs **2.** a terrorist using bombs.
bon viveur C	*n*	(c) a person interested in good food and wine.
bonanza C	*n*	(c) something giving prosperity.
bond B	*n*	(c) **1.** a document promising to pay back with interes money lent. **2.** a link between people. **3.** (plural) chain or ropes holding a prisoner. **4.** adhesion.
bone A	*n*	(c) one of the hard white parts of the body, part of th skeleton.
bonnet C	*n*	(c) **1.** (BE) the covering of a car engine. **2.** a hat tie with ribbons under the chin.
book A	*v*	to make a reservation.
bookcase C	*n*	(c) a piece of furniture for holding books.
bookholder C	*n*	(c) not commonly used, but suggests a small stand to hol a book in a position for reading.
boom B	*n*	(c) **1.** the distant sound of an explosion. **2.** a perio of increasing prosperity.
boot B	*n*	(c) **1.** covering for the foot coming above the ankle **2.** (BE) space in a car for luggage.
bore A	*v*	**1.** to be monotonous. **2.** to cut (a round hole).
	n	(c) **1.** an uninteresting person or task.

boss A *v* (informal) to be domineering.
n (c) employer; chief.

bounty C *n* (c) **1.** money which the government gives for special services or as an incentive. **2.** (u) (rare) generosity.

bout C *n* (c) **1.** a short time of activity. **2.** a boxing fight. **3.** an attack, e.g. of influenza.

bow B *v* to bend the body forward to show respect.
n (c) **1.** a bending forward movement of the body. **2.** the front of a boat.

bower C *n* (c) a shaded place in a garden.

bowl C *n* (c) **1.** a round, hollow dish. **2.** (plural) a quiet game played with heavy black balls on closely mown grass.

bowling C *n* (u) a modernised game based on **2** above, usually played indoors.

box A *n* (c) **1.** a container often with a lid. **2.** in a theatre, a private seating place.

boxer C *n* (c) **1.** one who engages in the sport of boxing (i.e. fighting with heavy gloves). **2.** a type of dog.

boy A *n* (c) male child.

brace C *n* (c) **1.** a pair. **2.** a tool for boring holes. **3.** a piece of wire put round the teeth to make them straight. **4.** a piece of metal used in building to strengthen, support, or hold together.

bracket B *n* (c) **1.** the marks { } and ( ). **2.** a support for a shelf.

brag C *v* to boast.

branch C *v* to divide into more than one.
A *n* (c) **1.** one of the main divisions of a tree from the trunk. **2.** a subdivision of family, firm, river, etc.

brand A *n* (c) the commercial name of a product.

branding C *n* (u) the marking of cattle with a red hot piece of metal.

brass C *n* (u) **1.** a yellow alloy, a mixture of copper and zinc. **2.** musical instruments made of this alloy.

brasserie C *n* (c) a bar or a restaurant that serves beer with food.

brassiere C *n* (c) usually called a *bra*, the underclothing for women to support the breasts.

brave A *adj* having courage in the face of pain, danger, or trouble.

bravura C *n* (u) (music) performing well but rather ostentatiously.

breast A *n* (c) the two parts of a woman's body producing milk.

brew C *n* (c) **1.** the amount of liquid (usually tea) made at one time. **2.** flavour.

bribe C *n* (c) money offered or paid to do something, usually dishonest or illegal.

brick A *n* (c) **1.** a block of clay baked in a rectangular shape, used for building. **2.** (informal) a reliable, trustworthy, and good-hearted person.

bride B *n* (c) a woman who is about to be or has just been married.

brief C *n* (c) instructions (usually written) explaining duties, responsibilities, and powers.

briefly B *adv* for a short time.

bright A *adj* **1.** (of a surface or lamp) light or shining. **2.** (of a person

		or face) happy or cheerful. **3.** (of a child) clever or intelligent.
bring A	*v*	to come with, carry to this place.
briquet(te) C	*n*	(c) a kind of fuel made from compressed coal dust.
brochure B	*n*	(c) leaflet, pamphlet, very small book or folder giving information.
bronze C	*n*	(u) an alloy, a mixture of copper and tin.
brood C	*n*	(c) a family of young birds.
brook C	*n*	(c) a small stream of water.
browse C	*v*	to look through a book.
bruise B	*v*	to injure so as to discolour the skin on the body.
brutal B	*adj*	very cruel.
brutalise C	*v*	to make or become cruel.
brute C	*n*	(c) (informal) a cruel and stupid person.
buck C	*n*	(c) **1.** a male deer, hare or rabbit. **2.** (AE slang) a dollar.
bucket B	*n*	(c) a container for liquids.
buckle C	*n*	(c) a fastener on a belt or on a shoe.
bud B	*n*	(c) a leaf or flower before it opens.
Buddha C	*n*	(a statue of) the Asiatic religious leader/teacher.
buffet C	*n*	shares all meanings with French except that for the piece of furniture.
bug C	*n*	(c) **1.** (informal) a germ, infection. **2.** any type of insect. **3.** (informal) a craze; obsessive idea or hobby.
bugle C	*n*	(c) a simple type of small trumpet, esp. as used in the army.
build A	*v*	to construct, put together.
	n	(c) the general shape in proportion and size.
building A	*n*	(c) schools, banks, factories, houses, etc.
bull C	*n*	(c) the uncastrated male of the ox family.
bulldog C	*n*	powerful, smooth-haired breed of dog.
bulletin B	*n*	(c) an official statement or announcement of news.
bungalow B	*n*	(c) a house with only one storey.
burst A	*v*	**1.** to explode from pressure inside. **2.** to go, come, etc., suddenly.
bus A	*n*	(c) a large passenger vehicle.
bust C	*n*	(c) **1.** the upper front part of a woman's body, mainly referring to the breasts. **2.** a statue of head and shoulders.
butt C	*n*	(c) **1.** a target of jokes. **2.** a target at a shooting range.
butterfly C	*n*	(c) an insect with four wings, often prettily coloured, seen in warm and hot weather.
button B	*n*	(c) **1.** a small (round) object used to fasten clothing. **2.** a small round object, esp. for connecting electricity. **3.** (AE) a badge worn on clothing.
by now B	*adv*	already: *I think they must be home by now.*
bypass A	*v*	**1.** to go round the outside of. **2.** to avoid or neglect the complicated part of.
byword C	*n*	(c) a person, place, or thing considered as a perfect or proverbial example of something.

C

cab B	*n*	(c) **1.** (chiefly AE) a taxi. **2.** the part of a large vehicle or locomotive where the driver sits.
cabal C	*n*	(c) a secret intrigue or plot, usually political.
cabaret C	*n*	(c) a programme of entertainment in a restaurant.
cabinet B	*n*	(c) **1.** a cupboard having doors with windows. **2.** the most important members of a government, etc. **3.** the outer case of a television, etc.
cachet C	*n*	(c) **1.** a mark showing something is genuine and of high value. **2.** good reputation associated with something.
cadaver C	*n*	(c) (medical) a dead human body.
cadence C	*n*	(c) (music) harmony at the end of a piece; rhythm (also used of the human voice).
cadet C	*n*	(c) a young person studying to become an officer in one of the armed forces or the police.
cadre C	*n*	(c) some very skilled and active people making an inner group of a political party or an army.
café A	*n*	(c) a small modest restaurant.
cajole C	*v*	to persuade by flattery or deceit.
cake A	*n*	(c and u) a sweet baked food made of flour, butter, eggs, and various other ingredients.
calculate B	*v*	to reckon using numbers.
calendar B	*n*	(c) a list of the days and months of the year.
callous C	*adj*	insensitive, unfeeling.
camel B	*n*	(c) the animal with one or two humps on the back, used for transport in the desert.
Camelot C	*n*	the place where King Arthur is supposed to have had his court.
camera A	*n*	(c) a photographic apparatus for taking pictures.
camp B	*v*	to use a tent, esp. for sleeping away from a house; to holiday in this way.
	n	(c) **1.** a group of tents together. **2.** a place where soldiers live together in small temporary buildings.
Campari C	*n*	(trademark) a kind of aperitive.
camping B	*n*	(u) is the activity described above.
can B	*n*	(c) a simple metallic container esp. for preserving food.
canal A	*n*	(c) a man-made waterway through land.
canalisation A	*n*	(u) the converting of a river into a sort of canal by straightening it, building locks, etc., usually to stop flooding.
canasta C	*n*	(u) a kind of card game, using two packs of cards.
cancan C	*n*	(c) a dance developed in France in the 19th century.
cancel B	*v*	to decide something (a meeting, etc.) will not take place.
candid C	*adj*	direct and truthful, not hiding one's thoughts.
candidate C	*n*	(c) **1.** someone taking an exam. **2.** someone who seeks or stands for an official position.
candle B	*n*	(c) a round stick of wax, burnt to give light.
candour C	*n*	(u) the quality of being candid.

cane C — *n* (c) a piece of bamboo wood, used for furniture or as a light walking-stick or for hitting people as a punishment.

canon C — *n* (c) **1.** a priest in a cathedral. **2.** a kind of repetitive song.

canopy C — *n* (c) a cover (usually of cloth) over something, esp. a bed, or a chair used in important ceremonies.

cant C — *n* (u) language of class or profession, etc., jargon.

canteen B — *n* (c) the restaurant in a factory, offices, educational establishment, etc.

canto C — *n* (c) (literature) one of the main divisions of a long piece of poetry.

cantor C — *n* (c) the leader of a group of singers, esp. in a church or synagogue.

canyon C — *n* (c) a deep cut into the earth's surface made by a river.

cap B — *n* (c) a small hat as worn by sailors, workmen, schoolboys, cyclists, etc.

capacity B/C — *n* **1.** (u) B the amount or quantity that can be held, e.g. by a box, room, or hall. **2.** (c) C position or function. **3.** (c and u) B an ability, power.

cape C — *n* (c) **1.** a piece of outer clothing with no sleeves for the arms; (shorter than a cloak). **2.** a piece of land standing out.

capricious C — *adj* liable to sudden unexpected changes in wishes and behaviour.

car A — *n* (c) **1.** (chiefly BE) a motor vehicle for a few passengers. **2.** (chiefly AE) a passenger vehicle in a railway train.

carbon B — *n* **1.** (u) the non-metallic element in all living matter. **2.** (c) paper used to make copies, esp. in typing.

carbonised C — *past participle* (chemical) converted into carbon by burning.

card A — *n* (c) a piece of stiff paper used for various purposes, e.g. a postcard, a visiting card, a playing card.

cardinal C — *n* (c) one of the Roman Catholic priests who elect a pope.

career A — *n* (c) a person's profession, progress through life.

cargo B — *n* (c and u) goods carried, e.g. on a plane or in a boat.

carillon C — *n* (c) a system of bells on which melodies can be played.

carnation C — *n* (c) a small flower (red, pink, yellow, etc.) with a sweet scent.

carousal C — *n* (c) (a party with) a lot of drinking of alcohol.

carpet B — *n* (c) a soft covering on the floor.

carrot B — *n* (c) an orange-coloured root vegetable.

cart B — *n* (c) a vehicle with two wheels often pulled by a horse.

cartel C — *n* (c) a grouping together of manufacturers to control prices, etc.

carter C — *n* (c) a man whose work is to drive a cart.

carton C — *n* (c) a box or container for goods.

cartoon B — *n* (c) **1.** a humorous or satirical drawing. **2.** an animated film.

case A — *n* (c) **1.** the true state of things. **2.** (esp. with a (u) noun) an example (of). **3.** a container, e.g. a suitcase. **4.** one side of an argument, esp. in a law court.

casement C — *n* (c) a window opening like a door.
cash A — *v* to exchange, e.g. a cheque for money in paper and metal form.
n (u) money in paper and metal form.
casino C — *n* (c) an establishment where gambling (playing for money) takes place.
cask C — *n* (c) (old-fashioned) a barrel.
casket C — *n* (c) a finely decorated box, esp. for keeping jewels.
casserole C — *n* (c) **1.** a deep, heavy cooking container with a lid, usually made of iron or clay. **2.** the food cooked and served in such a container.
cassette A — *n* (c) **1.** a container holding a length of photographic film. **2.** a container holding magnetic recording tape.
cassock C — *n* (c) a long coat-like garment worn by priests.
cast C — *n* (c) the actors taking part in a play or film.
v to throw.
caste C — *n* (c) the system of hereditary classes into which Hindu society is divided.
caster or **castor** C — *n* (c) a small wheel made to turn in different directions, esp. on the base of an armchair.
adj (of sugar) fine.
casual A/C — *adj* A relaxed, (too) friendly, (too) informal, thoughtless of others. **1.** C a person employed for temporary work. **2.** (plural) informal clothes.
casualty B — *n* (c) a person hurt or killed in fighting or an accident.
cat A — *n* (c) the small domestic animal with thick soft fur that catches mice, etc.
catalog(ue) A — *n* (c) a list of items (for sale) with information about them.
catch A — *v* **1.** to stop and hold something which is moving. **2.** to arrive in time for (train, etc.).
C — *n* (c) **1.** the act of catching (a ball). **2.** a hidden difficulty. **3.** a small mechanism for holding a door closed.
category C — *n* (c) a group or division as part of a system dividing things or people.
caterpillar C — *n* (c) the larva of a butterfly or moth, feeding on leaves.
catholic A — *adj* strictly means 'universal', but more commonly used in connection with the Roman Catholic Church.
catkin C — *n* (c) a string-like flower growing on some types of trees in spring.
cause A — *v* to make (something) happen.
caution B — *n* (u) care(fulness).
Cavalier C — *n* (c) one of the group of people in 17th-century England who supported the King in the Civil War.
cave B — *n* (c) a natural hollow place in rocky ground.
cavil C — *v* to look for small mistakes; make unnecessary criticisms or objections.
celebrate B — *v* **1.** to have a party, ceremony, or meeting to mark a special event. **2.** to perform a (solemn) ceremony.
celery B — *n* (usually u) a vegetable of which the stalks are eaten.
cell A — *n* (c) **1.** a small room in a prison. **2.** a small division

of matter. **3.** a part of a battery for making electricity.

cement B *n* (u) clay and burned lime mixed together, used in building.

censor C *n* (c) the person who examines books, films, and letters, for offensive contents.

censure C *v* to show strong disapproval towards.
n (u) the act of expressing that you strongly disapprove of someone or something.

centimetre A *n* (c) a unit of length.

certify C *v* **1.** to declare that something is true. **2.** to declare legally insane.

chair A *n* (c) a seat with a back to it, usually having four legs.

chaise-longue C *n* (c) a long low chair for lying back on, with an arm and back at one end.

chalk B *n* **1.** (u) the soft white rock that allows water to pass through it. **2.** (c and u) a piece of this material (used for writing on a blackboard).

chamber C *n* (c) **1.** (archaic) a room, esp. a bedroom. **2.** the debating and law-making assemblies in government.

champ C *n* (c) (slang) champion.

champion B *n* (c) the winner of a competition because of skill, strength, or appearance.

chance A *n* **1.** (c) an opportunity. **2.** (u and c) probability. **3.** (c) risk. **4.** (u) (very rarely) (good) fortune, luck. **5.** *by chance* unintentionally, accidentally.

chandelier C *n* (c) a hanging ornamental holder for lights.

chandler C *n* (c) someone who sells equipment for ships.

chant C *v* to sing in a special way, as in church (esp. psalms).
n (c) a short melody for singing the psalms.

chap A *n* (c) (informal) man, boy, fellow.

chapel B *n* (c) **1.** the church of a nonconformist group (e.g. Baptist). **2.** a small separate part of a cathedral or other large church with an altar. **3.** a private church, e.g. in a hospital, prison, school, or college.

chaplain C *n* (c) a priest in the armed forces, a hospital, or a college.

character A *n* (c) **1.** a person in a novel or a play. **2.** distinguishing qualities, personality.

characterise C *v* describe the character of.

characteristic B *adj* typical.
n (c) a distinguishing quality.

charge A *n* **1.** (c) the cost or price. **2.** (u) responsibility. **3.** (c) (military) a rushing attack. **4.** (c) (legal) an accusation.

charged A/B/C *past participle* **1.** A asked to pay the sum of. **2.** C given the responsibility. **3.** B accused.

chariot C *n* (c) a type of cart without a seat, used in ancient times.

charisma C *n* (u) a quality enabling someone to influence and inspire others.

charlatan C *n* (c) someone who dishonestly says he has special knowledge and/or skills, esp. as a doctor or dentist.

charm B *n* similar meanings to French except that it is not the name of a tree.

chart B *n* (c) **1.** a diagram or map. **2.** (plural; informal) the lists produced weekly of the best-selling pop records.

chase B *v* to follow in the hope of catching.
n (c) fast pursuit.

chassis C *n* (c) the framework of a vehicle, radio, or television.

chat B *n* (c) a brief informal conversation.

chauffeur B *n* (c) someone employed to drive another person's car.

chef C *n* (c) the head male cook in a restaurant, hotel, etc.

chenille C *n* (u) a kind of material rather like velvet.

chevron C *n* (c) **1.** a zigzag pattern used as decoration, esp. in Romanesque architecture. **2.** a V-shaped mark on a soldier's sleeve, indicating his rank.

chic C *adj* showing good style; elegant; smart; mostly used of women.

chick C *n* **1.** (c) a baby chicken; sometimes also used of other very young birds. **2.** (slang) a girl or young woman, esp. an attractive one.

chiffon C *n* (u) fine almost transparent material used for dresses and scarves.

chiffon(n)ier C *n* (c) a kind of cupboard with drawers.

chimney B *n* (c) the passage from a fire to the roof to carry away smoke and gases.

chin B *n* (c) the part of the face below the mouth.

chips A *n* (c) (BE) small pieces of fried potatoes eaten hot.

chock C *n* (c) a piece of wood shaped specially to fit under a heavy object such as a wheel, to stop it from moving.

choke B *v* (to cause someone) to be unable to breathe by blocking the throat.
n (c) the apparatus in a car engine which controls how much air is mixed with the petrol.

cholera C *n* (u) a tropical disease with diarrhoea, often leading to death.

chore C *n* (c) a routine or difficult task.

chorus B *n* (c) **1.** the group of singers and/or dancers in an opera, film or musical. **2.** a piece of music sung by these singers or the repeated section at the end of a verse of a song.

Christ B *n* Jesus Christ; his followers are called *Christians*.

christen C *v* to name (a baby) at baptism.

Christendom C *n* (u) **1.** all the Christians of the world. **2.** all the Christian countries of the world.

Christmas A *n* (c) the festival on 25 December, celebrating the birth of Jesus Christ.

chrome C *n* (u) **1.** a chromium alloy used for covering things to give a mirror-like surface, such as on cars. **2.** *chrome yellow* a bright yellow colour.

cider B *n* (u) an alcoholic drink made from apples.

cigar B *n* (c) something like a cigarette, but larger and brown-coloured.

cinch C *n* (c) (informal) something easy or certain.

cinder C — *n* (c; usually plural) a piece of partly burnt wood or coal, etc., not yet quite ash, but no longer in flames.

circle A — *n* (c) **1.** a flat ring with a fixed radius. **2.** a group of people with a common interest, etc.

circulate C — *v* **1.** to pass, send, or go from place to place. **2.** to move through a circuit or system.

circulation B — *n* **1.** (u) movement through a circuit or system. **2.** (c) the number of copies of a newspaper or periodical that are distributed.

cite C — *v* **1.** to quote the words of someone. **2.** to call someone to a court of law.

citron C — *n* (c) a fruit similar to a very large lemon.

city A — *n* (c) a large town having special status.

civil C — *adj* **1.** polite. **2.** to do with government.

civility C — *n* (u) politeness.

clairvoyant C — *adj*, *n* (c) (a person) able to see things not normally perceived by the senses, e.g. a spiritualist.

clam C — *n* (c) a sea creature with two shells which are hard to open; a secretive person is sometimes called a *clam*.

clamour C — *v* **1.** to make a great noise. **2.** to demand impatiently and/or noisily.

clamp C — *v* to fix together with a screw and a twisting metal piece.

clang C — *n* (c) a loud ringing sound.

clap B — *v* to beat one's hands together and make a noise.
n (c) **1.** such a noise. **2.** the crash of thunder during a storm.

clapper C — *n* (c) the metal piece hanging inside a bell, striking the bell to make it ring.

class A — *n* a word with many meanings: note esp. that it is not synonymous with *kind*, *type*, or *sort*: *this class of car* would refer to its quality and/or price.

classic B — *adj* the difference between *classic* and *classical* gives much trouble to native speakers: remember *classical music*; *a classic example*.

clavier C — *n* (c) any type of old instrument like a piano or harpsichord.

clay B — *n* (u) a soft substance from the ground used for making pottery and bricks.

clean A — *adj* not dirty. **cleanly** *adv*.

clear A — *v* to remove objects.
adj **1.** free from obscurity or darkness. **2.** not harsh (sound).

clever A — *adj* skilful, talented.

cliché C — *n* (c) used of linguistic style, a phrase that has been used many times before and has no originality.

click C — *v* to make a quick, sharp noise, e.g. with the tongue or the heels.
n (c) such a noise.

cling C — *v* to hold tightly to.

clinker C — *n* (u) partly burnt hard lumps of coal left when a fire has burnt out.

clip B — *n* (c) pieces of metal or plastic to hold together pieces of paper, etc.

cloak C — *n* (c) a piece of clothing with no sleeves (longer than a cape).

cloche C — *n* (c) **1.** a type of woman's hat, fashionable in the 1920s. **2.** (more common) a glass covering for plants in the garden.

clock A — *n* (c) an instrument for telling the time (not so small as a wristwatch). **clock in** *v* to arrive at work and put one's time-keeping card into a machine which prints the time on it.

clog C — *v* usually *clog up*, to become blocked.

cloister C — *n* (c) a covered passage, open one side to a court and often with a garden, esp. at a monastery, convent, or cathedral.

close C — *n* (c) a street with houses and open only at one end.
adj **1.** careful. **2.** not having enough fresh air.
adv near.

closet A — *n* (c) (old-fashioned in BE) a cupboard.

clover C — *n* (u and c) a small plant grown as food for cattle.

clue C — *n* (c) trace or indication helping to find the answer to a problem, esp. used in crosswords and by detectives.

clump C — *n* (c) a group of plants growing close together.

coach A — *n* (c) **1.** a long-distance bus. **2.** (BE) a vehicle in a passenger train; (a *car* in AE). **3.** a sports trainer. **4.** (formerly) a vehicle with four wheels for passengers pulled by horses.

coal A — *n* (u) a black mineral fossil fuel used for fires and from which many chemicals are obtained.

coal tit C — *n* (c) a small bird, with a black head and a white patch on the nape.

coat A — *n* (c) a warm outer garment with sleeves, similar to a jacket or an overcoat.

cobra C — *n* (c) a snake found in Africa and Asia.

cock C — *n* (c) **1.** a male bird of the domestic fowl. **2.** (taboo slang) a penis.

cocktail C — *n* (c) a drink, as drunk at *a cocktail party*.

coda C — *n* (c) the end of a piece of music.

coffer C — *n* (c) **1.** a heavy chest for storing valuable objects, esp. money. **2.** (plural) cash.

cognoscenti C — *n* (plural) people who are specialists in a given subject; similar to *connoisseurs*).

coherent C — *adj* able to make oneself understood in a logical, consistent way.

coin A — *n* (c) a piece of metal used as money.

coincidence B — *n* (c) a notable combination of events happening by chance, without any apparent connection.

cold A — *adj* having a low temperature, the opposite of *hot*.

collaborator C — *n* (c) someone who helps others in their work; (*collaborationist* strictly means someone who helps an enemy occupying his own country, but *collaborator* is often used for this too).

collage C *n* (a work of) art made by sticking paper and other materials onto a surface.

collar A *n* (c) **1.** the part of a coat, dress, shirt, etc. that goes round the neck. **2.** a band to go round a dog's neck.

collation C *n* **1.** (c) a light meal. **2.** (u) the comparing of two texts to find differences between them.

collect C *n* (c) a prayer in an Anglican service.

collector C *n* (c) a person who collects something.

college A *n* the word is used in various ways in connection with higher education; some private boarding schools are called colleges.

collier C *n* (c) a ship used for transporting coal.

collocation C *n* (c) a group of words frequently and naturally found together.

colon B/C *n* (c) **1.** B the punctuation mark. **2.** C the lower part of the large bowel or intestine.

colony B *n* (c) **1.** a country or area settled and controlled by people from a foreign country. **2.** a group of nationals living in a foreign country. **3.** a group of the same sort of plants or animals living together.

colour A *n* red, white, blue, yellow, etc.

coma C *n* (c) a sustained state of unconsciousness.

combination B *n* (c) the joining together of several things.

combine A *v* to join together or unite.

come out A *v* **1.** to appear. **2.** to be published. **3.** to be shown clearly, become apparent.

comedian C *n* (c) someone who tries to make others laugh, esp. in plays, films, on TV or radio.

comedy B *n* (c) an amusing play.

comic C *n* (c) **1.** a children's magazine telling stories with pictures. **2.** a comedian.
adj amusing.

comical B *adj* causing laughter.

comma B *n* (c) a punctuation mark.

commando C *n* (c) a soldier who is trained to make dangerous raids, etc.

commentary B *n* (c) **1.** a collection of writings with explanations and comments on a text, events, or people. **2.** a *running commentary* an explanation given as an event happens.

commissariat C *n* (c) the department in the army in charge of food supplies.

commission B *n* **1.** the authority to do something. **2.** (in military) the rank given to an officer. **3.** the fee given to an agent in business.

commissionaire C *n* (c) a man in uniform at the entrance to a theatre, cinema, or block of flats.

commode C *n* (c) **1.** (very occasional) a piece of furniture with drawers. **2.** a seat with a hole in it used as a lavatory.

commodity B *n* (c) a useful thing, something which can be sold for profit.

commotion B *n* **1.** (c) a great deal of noise (sometimes with movement). **2.** (u) a disturbance.

communal C *adj* shared by a group of people.

commune C *n* (c) a group of unrelated people who live together and share ownership and goods, esp. associated with experimental groups.

commute B *v* to travel to work in a large city but live in the suburbs or beyond. (The original and continental meaning—*to change*—is now C.)

companion A *n* (c) someone who gives company to another person.

compartment B *n* (c) a section of a railway carriage or a passenger aircraft.

compass B *n* (c) **1.** an instrument pointing to the North by magnetism. **2.** a *pair of compasses* an instrument for drawing a circle.

compendium C *n* (c) a book bringing together the main facts on a subject, usually in concise form.

compere C *n* (c) the commentator and introducer at a cabaret or variety show.

competence C *n* (u) skill, ability.

competent C *adj* **1.** (of a person) having the skill to do something satisfactorily. **2.** (of a thing) done adequately.

complacency C *n* (u) self-satisfaction.

complacent B *adj* self-satisfied.

complete A *adj* **1.** having all the parts. **2.** absolute; utter.

complex B *n* (c) **1.** (architectural) a number of buildings grouped together. **2.** (psychology) ideas, emotions, etc., (repressed) causing abnormal behaviour.

complexion B/C *n* (c) **1.** B the natural colour of the face. **2.** C the character, nature.

compliment B *v* to praise (someone) for something.

compose B/C *v* **1.** B to make up or write a piece of music or a poem, etc. **2.** C *compose oneself* become calm.

composition B *n* (c) (in school) an essay; short piece of prose.

compositor C *n* (c) a printer, typographer.

compost C *n* (u) a heap of vegetable and garden waste, left to rot and then used as fertiliser.

comprehend C *v* to understand.

comprehensive B *adj* **1.** including all or much; thorough. **2.** (in BE education) of a school which teaches children of all abilities.

compromise B *n* a solution to a disagreement in which both sides have made concessions.

v **1.** to settle (a disagreement) by making concessions. **2.** *compromise oneself* to leave oneself open to suspicion by what one has done.

comrade C *n* (c) **1.** a friend who shares dangers and difficulties (esp. among soldiers). **2.** (political, esp. communist) a fellow member of the party.

con C *n* (c) **1.** (informal) short for a *confidence trick*. **2.** (usually plural) a person who votes against something. **3.** (also plural) the argument against something.

concept C *n* (c) an idea or thought.

concert B *n* (c) **1.** a programme of musical entertainment. **2.** *in concert* together, in agreement.

concerto C *n* (c) a piece of music for an orchestra and solo instrument.

concession C *n* (c) **1.** a giving in or yielding of something. **2.** land allowed by a government to a company to operate commercially.

concordance C *n* **1.** (c) a book in which ideas and important words are arranged alphabetically with notes and explanations. **2.** (u) a state of agreement.

concourse C *n* (c) a place where many people come together, esp. at a railway station or airport.

concrete C *v* to cover with concrete.

concretely C *adv* materially, not abstractly.

concur C *v* **1.** to agree. **2.** (less common) to happen together.

concurrence C *n* (c) **1.** a coming together. **2.** agreement.

concussion C *n* (u) brain damage caused by shock or a violent blow.

condescend C *v* to agree to do something beneath one's social position, often in a patronising way. (*Condescending* is the adjective.)

condition A *n* **1.** state or circumstance. **2.** stipulation.

conduct B *n* (u) behaviour.

conductor B *n* (c) **1.** director of an orchestra. **2.** ticket collector on a bus. **3.** guard on a train.

conduit C *n* (c) a pipe (usually underground) for carrying water, gas, or electric wires.

cone C *n* (c) a solid form with a point at one end and a round flat surface at the other.

confabulation C *n* (c) a conversation.

confection C *n* (c) (old-fashioned) a sweet flavoured dish.

confectioner C *n* (c) someone who makes and/or sells sweets, chocolates, or cakes.

confer C *v* **1.** to discuss; compare opinions. **2.** to give (a favour, medal, title, or honour).

conference A *n* (c) a formal meeting of an organisation, etc. where ideas and opinions can be exchanged and considered.

confetti C *n* (u) small pieces of coloured paper thrown at a couple at their wedding.

confident B *adj* feeling sure of oneself.

confinement C *n* (c) **1.** being held in a restricted place. **2.** (of a woman) being kept in bed at the time of giving birth.

conflagration C *n* (c) a great fire which does serious damage.

conform C *v* to behave according to rules or accepted patterns of behaviour.

confound C *v* **1.** to confuse or perplex. **2.** *confounded* (old-fashioned) damned, cursed.

confuse B *v* to cause disorder, to mix up. **confusion** *n* the act or state of being confused.

congeal C *v* (esp. of blood or fat) to turn from liquid to solid.

congestion C *n* (u) the condition of being blocked.

conglomerate C *n* (c) a solid mass of various things together.

conjugate C *v* to go through the various forms of (a verb).

conjugation C *n* (c) a group of verbs that have similar forms.

conjunctive C *n* (c) (grammar) a less common word for *conjunction.*
conjure C *v* to produce as if by magic.
conjuror C *n* (c) an entertainer who does magic tricks.
consent C *n* (u) permission, agreement.
v to allow.
consequence B *n* **1.** (c) a result. **2.** (u) importance.
consequent C *adj* resulting.
conserve C *v* to use carefully, esp. fuel or food; keep safe.
n jam or marmalade.
consign C *v* to put into the care of.
consistency C *n* (u) **1.** a logical keeping to the same principles. **2.** degree of firmness, solidity or thickness.
consistent B *adj* logical, having consistency. (**1** above.)
consolation prize C *n* (c) a prize given to a competition entrant who has just missed the proper prize.
consort C *n* (c) the wife or husband of a ruler.
conspicuous B *adj* noticeable; easily seen.
constellation C *n* (c) a group of stars.
constipation C *n* (u) the inability to empty the bowels (regularly). *constipated* in this condition.
constituent C *n* (c) **1.** elector. **2.** one of the pieces which make up a whole.
constructor C *n* (c) a builder.
construe C *v* to interpret the meaning of.
consummation C *n* (u) **1.** the point of perfection and completion. **2.** the completing of marriage by sexual intercourse.
consumption C *n* (u) **1.** the amount used. **2.** (archaic) tuberculosis.
contact A *n* uses are similar in most languages but *contact lenses* are worn to correct eyesight, and a *switch* is used to make electrical connections.
contend C *v* to compete in arguments; enter in competition for, esp. in politics.
contention C *n* (c) a point of view; strong argument.
contest C *v* **1.** to fight competitively for. **2.** to express doubts about the truth of.
B *n* (c) a competition.
contingent C *n* (c) **1.** a group of representatives at a large meeting. **2.** (military) a group of ships or soldiers sent to join a larger group.
continuo C *n* (music) the low notes indicated only in part in the score.
contour C *n* (c) **1.** the outline; silhouette. **2.** short for *contour line* a line on a map joining all the places which have the same height.
contract C *v* **1.** (transitive) to acquire (diseases, illnesses). (Otherwise its uses are similar to the Latin languages.) **2.** (intransitive) to become smaller.
contrast C *v* to bring out the differences in.
contravention C *n* a breaking of the law.
contretemps C *n* (c) strictly (and still sometimes used) in the French meaning of 'an unfortunate event or delay', but increasingly

used for a disagreeable (but probably brief) argument.

contribution B *n* (c) something, usually money, offered to help others.
control A *v* to be in command of, direct.
convene C *v* to call together for a meeting.
convenience B *n* **1.** (u) usefulness; suitability. **2.** (c) a useful device, esp. one that makes life more comfortable. **3.** *at your earliest convenience* as soon as possible. **4.** (c) (BE) a public lavatory.
convenient A *adj* suitable for one's needs.
convent B *n* (c) a religious community of women.
converse C *n* the opposite of something.
convict C *n* (c) someone found guilty of a crime and sent to prison.
convoy C *n* (c) **1.** a large number of ships (esp. in wartime) travelling together. **2.** a group of vehicles (esp. lorries).
cook A *v* to prepare (food) by heating.
n (c) someone who does the cooking.
cooling C *n* (u) the act of making cooler.
coordinates C *n* (c; usually plural) women's clothing (e.g. skirt and blouse) designed to be worn together.
cop C *n* (colloq.) **1.** (c) a policeman. **2.** (u) *it isn't much cop* it isn't much good.
copper B *n* **1.** (u) the soft reddish metal that conducts heat and electricity. **2.** (c) a policeman; (informal, but less vulgar than *cop*).
coquette C *n* (c) a flirting woman.
cord B *n* material thicker than string and thinner than rope.
cordon C *n* (c) (mainly military) a line of soldiers, police, tanks, ships, etc., round an area, to protect it.
cordon bleu C *n* (c) (cookery) a highly qualified cook.
corn A *n* **1.** (u) (BE) any type of cereal and its seeds. **2.** (u) (AE) maize. **3.** (c) a piece of hard painful skin near or on a toe.
cornet C *n* (c) **1.** a musical instrument like a small trumpet. **2.** a cone-shaped biscuit for an ice cream; (also called a *cone*).
corona C *n* (c) the ring of light round the sun, seen when the moon moves in front of it.
coroner C *n* (c) the official who enquires into someone's death if the cause is not evident.
corporation C *n* (c) **1.** a city council. **2.** a kind of large business firm.
corps C *n* (c; plural same) a group of people sharing an activity, esp. in the army or diplomacy.
corpse C *n* (c) a dead body.
corpulent C *adj* (often humorous) fat.
correction B *n* **1.** (u) amendment. **2.** (c) in school, the errors to be corrected.
corrector C *n* (c) anyone who corrects something, but esp. used of people evaluating exam papers.
correspond B *v* **1.** to exchange letters regularly. **2.** to match; be in agreement.

correspondence B *n* (u) the act of exchanging letters or the letters which have been exchanged.

correspondent B *n* (c) **1.** someone with whom one regularly exchanges letters. **2.** a journalist employed to report news.

corridor B *n* (c) **1.** a passage usually enclosed in a building. **2.** a narrow piece of territory across another country.

corsage C *n* (c) **1.** originally, the upper front part of a woman's dress. **2.** (AE, and increasingly in BE) a decoration of flowers fixed to a woman's dress.

cosh C *n* (c) a piece of wood or metal used to hit someone with.

cosmic C *adj* of the (whole) universe.

cosmos C *n* **1.** the whole universe. **2.** (u) a kind of flower.

cost A *v* to have a price.
n (c) the price of something.

costly B *adj* costing much, expensive (also figurative).

costume B *n* **1.** (c) a woman's jacket and skirt in the same material. **2.** (u and c) the clothes worn at any given period or place.

cot C *n* (c) (BE) the bed for a young baby with high sides.

cotton A *n* (u) a plant and also the material made from its seed coverings.

ouch C *v* to express in a certain way.
n (c) a piece of furniture similar to a bed but for sitting on.

ouncil A *n* (c) a group of people chosen to make laws and decisions, esp. for a parish, town, or city.

ountability C *n* (u) (grammar) the quality of a noun having a plural and that can be used with such words as *a* or *an*, *few*, *many*, etc.; (they are marked by (c) in this dictionary).

ountenance C *n* (c) the expression on the face.

ounterfeit C *v* to make a copy or imitation of, e.g. money.
n such a copy.

ountry A *n* **1.** (c) a state or nation, its people and/or territory. **2.** the land outside a town or city.

oupé C *n* (c) a car with a fixed roof, a sloping back, and usually two doors.

ouple A *n* (c) **1.** two of anything. **2.** a few. **3.** two people, esp. a married pair.

oupling C *n* (c) a mechanism connecting two things, esp. railway carriages or wagons.

ourage A *n* (u) bravery; fearlessness.

ourier C *n* (c) **1.** someone who takes special messages. **2.** someone who looks after holiday-makers on a tour, esp. abroad.

ourse A *n* (c) **1.** a number of lessons, lectures, etc., in the study of a particular subject. **2.** a part of a meal. **3.** a way of progressing. **4.** the direction or route taken. **5.** an area on which races are run.

ourt A *n* (c) many meanings, note esp. **1.** an area of ground surrounded by walls or buildings. **2.** the place where legal cases are heard. **3.** the officials, noblemen, and household of a king or queen.

courtier C *n* (c) an attendant at a royal court.
courting C *n* (u) (old-fashioned) the attention a man pays to a woma he hopes to marry.
cove C *n* (c) a small bay on the coast.
cover A *v* largely similar use to the Spanish *cobrir*, except i collocations given in Part 1.
covert C *n* (c) a small area of trees in the country, originally intende to give shelter to foxes.
cow A *n* (c) the fully grown female of the ox family.
cox C *n* (c) someone who guides a rowing boat.
crab C *n* (c) a sea creature that walks sideways.
crack A *n* (c) **1.** a narrow opening. **2.** a sharp sudden nois **3.** a hit or blow. **4.** (informal) a joke, told quickly an spontaneously.
craft B *n* (c) **1.** skilled work done by hands. **2.** (no *-s* i plural) any type of boat.
crafty B *adj* cunning, sly.
crag C *n* (c) a (mass of) high, rough rock.
cram C *v* **1.** to force into a small space. **2.** to work hard befor an examination.
crammer C *n* (c) a school where students are helped to work hard fc examinations, also a book for this purpose.
cramp C *n* **1.** (u) sudden tightening of a muscle giving sharp pai esp. associated with swimming. **2.** (c) (in woodwork a device for holding things together.
crampon C *n* (c) a device attached to boots by mountaineers for climb ing.
crane C *n* (c) **1.** a mechanism for lifting heavy objects. **2.** large bird.
cranky C *adj* (informal) **1.** (BE) eccentric **2.** (AE) bad-tempered.
crass C *adj* stupid, gross.
cravat C *n* (c) a small sort of scarf worn by men in place of a tie.
crave B *v* to desire strongly.
cream A *n* **1.** (u) the top part of milk. **2.** (c) various uses for sub stances of similar consistency.
creation B *n* **1.** *the Creation* the biblical story of the making of th world. **2.** (u) the act of making something. **3.** (c) some thing made, esp. an unusual and imaginative object.
creator C *n* (c) someone who creates or makes something, also use of God.
creature A *n* (c) any being, human or animal.
crèche C *n* (c) a place where very young children can be left in th care of teachers and/or nurses.
credence C *n* (u) belief in something as true.
credit A *n* **1.** (u) the practice of allowing a buyer to receive good and services with payment being made later. **2.** (c) person who has a good reputation, ability, etc.
crème de la crème C *n* the best of the best (people). (This phrase has not d veloped the sarcastic use now common in French.)
crêpe C *n* (u) mostly only understood to mean a thin type of clot

crick C *n* (c) a stiffening of the muscles, usually in the neck, giving some pain.

crime A *n* an immoral or illegal act of any kind.

crippled C *adj* unable to use the legs (or another limb) properly.

crisis A *n* (c) a moment of great difficulty or danger.

crisp B *adj* dry, hard, and easily broken, esp. used of food.

critic B *n* (c) someone who writes reviews, esp. art, plays, music.

crochet C *n* (u) fancy work like lace.

crock C *n* (c) **1.** (infrequent) a simple pot. **2.** (informal) an old car. **3.** (informal) old or feeble person.

crocket C *n* (c) (architecture) a support like a bracket.

crone C *n* (c) an old woman.

crop A *n* (c) a plant grown for food and the food obtained from it.

crotchet C *n* (c) (music) the longest black note.

crowd A *n* (c) a large number of people.

crucial B *adj* of decisive importance.

crude B *adj* **1.** (of materials) untreated, unprepared (not used of food). **2.** vulgar. **3.** poorly finished.

crudity C *n* the quality of being crude in senses **2** and **3** above.

cruise C *v* **1.** to travel by boat for a holiday. **2.** to travel at an economical speed.
n (c) a sea journey as a holiday.

crumb C *n* a small bit of bread, cake, etc.

crummy C *adj* (informal) **1.** of poor quality. **2.** unwell.

crusade C *n* (c) any one of the Christian armies who tried to recapture Palestine from the Muslims (11th–13th cents).

crystal C *n* **1.** (u) natural transparent solid like quartz or ice. **2.** (c) the regularly shaped pieces of substance similar to **1**, e.g. ice or salt crystals. **3.** (u) high quality glass used for lamps, wine-glasses, etc.

cube C *n* (c) **1.** a three-dimensional form, with six equal square sides. **2.** the number made by multiplying a number by itself twice.

cuckoo C *n* (c) a bird named after its call.

cue C *n* (c) **1.** (theatre, films, etc.) a word, action, etc., that serves as a signal for a person to speak. **2.** *take one's cue from* follow the example of.

cuisine C *n* (u) a way of cooking.

cult C *n* (c) **1.** a system of religion and worship. **2.** adoration of a particular person. **3.** a brief fashion or fashionable interest.

culture B *n* the intellectual and artistic development of a society; (there are also C uses in agriculture and science).

cunning B *adj* sly.

cup A *n* (c) a container used for drinking from.

curate C *n* (c) a clergyman who helps the priest of a church and parish.

curator C *n* (c) a person in charge of (usually) a museum or art gallery.

curb C *n* (v) to limit; keep at a low level.

cure A/C *v* **1.** A to make (someone) better. **2.** C to preserve (fooc by smoking, drying, or salting. (c) the act of curing.

current A *n* (c) a flow or stream of water, gas, or electricity. *adj* of the present time. **currently** *adv* at this time.

curse B *n* (c) **1.** word(s) expressing one's anger, wishing punisl ment or destruction on someone or something. **2.** misfortune. **3.** (slang) menstruation.

curt C *adj* speaking with few words so that one seems impolite.

cushion B *n* (c) a bag of soft material filled with a soft substance fc kneeling, sitting, etc.

cylinder B *n* (c) **1.** a container like a short piece of tube closed a one end. **2.** the enclosed space in which a piston mov in an engine.

cynic C *n* (c) a hard-hearted person who sees no good in anythin

cynical C *adj* of or like a cynic.

cynicism C *n* (u) the typical attitudes, opinions, etc., of a cynic.

cyst C *n* (c) an enclosed hollow growth in the body containin liquid matter and giving pain.

d

dado C *n* (c) the decorative band (usually wood and often painte on the lower part of a wall.

dale C *n* (c) (poetic) a valley.

dam B *n* (c) a wall or bank built to hold water back.

damage A *n* (u) **1.** loss or harm causing loss of value. **2.** *damag* (fixed plural) money to be paid for causing damage.

damask C *n* (u) a type of shiny material formerly popular for tabl cloths.

dame C *n* (c) **1.** (BE) a rank of honour given to a woma **2.** (AE slang) a woman.

damp C *v* to make slightly wet. *n* (u) wetness, esp. inside a building, or referring to t climate.

damper C *n* (c) **1.** a device for controlling the amount of air getti to a fire. **2.** a device for making a piano quiete **3.** something or someone who depresses other people.

dance B *n* (c) **1.** a party for dancing. **2.** the steps performed tc given rhythm. **3.** a piece of music for dancing.

dancing A *n* (u) the activity of someone who dances.

dapper C *adj* smart and quick in movement.

data B *n* (u or fixed plural) information, facts.

date A *n* (c) **1.** the time as shown by the day, month, and yea **2.** an arrangement to meet someone, esp. between a b and girl. **3.** (informal) someone one meets in this wa

datum C *n* (c) any fact or piece of information.

daub C *v* to use (paint) in a careless way.
n (c) paint put on in this way.

deal A *n* **1.** (c) quantity. **2.** (c) an agreement, esp. in business. **3.** (u) wood from pine or fir trees.

debit B *v* to deduct from (an account).
n (c) the amount deducted.

debutante C *n* (c) a young woman making her entry into upper-class society.

decade B *n* (c) a period of ten years.

decadence C *n* (u) the fall to a less moral state. **decadent** *adj.*

decani C *n* in a church choir, the singers on the right side, looking to the altar.

deceive B *v* to make (someone) believe something which is not true.

decent A *adj* acceptable socially; respectable.

deception C *n* the act of deceiving or being deceived.

deck A *n* (c) the floor(s) on a boat or a bus.

decorate B *v* **1.** to make pretty or beautiful. **2.** to cover walls with new paint, etc. **3.** to give someone a medal formally.

decoration B *n* (c) **1.** (chiefly plural) ornament(s), esp. at a party or festival. **2.** a medal.

decorator C *n* (c) someone who paints or decorates rooms or houses.

dedicate B *v* **1.** to give much time, effort, etc. to something. **2.** to inscribe (a book, etc.) to someone.

deer B *n* (c; no *-s* in plural) a variety of fast running animals; the males grow big branched horns.

defended B *past participle* protected, esp. from attack.

defiance C *n* (u) open lack of respect (for authority or danger).

defiant C *adj* acting with defiance; openly disobedient.

defile B *v* to make impure.

definition B *n* (c) an explanation of the meaning of a word, as in a dictionary.

deformed C *adj* disfigured, misshaped.

defraud C *v* to cheat, to get dishonestly.

defray C *v* (formal) to pay (the costs).

deft C *adj* skilful, quick (esp. with the fingers).

degradation C *n* the loss of respect.

degree(s) B *n* (c) esp. note among various uses: **1.** the units for measuring temperature. **2.** a title given to successful students by universities. **3.** a stage or step in a rising or falling order (but not used for stairs).

dejected C *past participle* depressed, in low spirits.

dejection C *n* (u) depression; a dejected state.

delay A *v* to cause to be late or slow.
n a case of being slowed down or stopped.

delicate A *adj* **1.** not strong. **2.** in poor health. **3.** (of instruments or the skin) finely made.

delicatessen C *n* (c) (generally the shop selling) unusual or exotic foods.

delicious A *adj* only used of things you can eat or smell. (A person is *delightful or charming*.)

delight B — *n* (something giving) great joy.
delinquent B — *n* (c) a criminal esp. a young offender, called a *juvenil delinquent*.
delude C — *v* to trick (someone).
delusion C — *n* (c) **1.** the act of deluding someone. **2.** a false belief
demagogue C — *n* (c) a leader who excites, appeals to people's feelings rathe than their reason.
demand A — *v* **1.** to claim (something) as if by right. **2.** to need, re quire.
n **1.** (c) the act of demanding or something demanded **2.** (u) the community's desire for something.
demean C — *v* to lower (oneself).
demented C — *adj* mad.
dementia C — *n* (u) any serious mental deterioration.
democracy A — *n* (a country with) government by the people through freel elected representatives.
demur C — *v* to hesitate to approve or do something.
n (u) hesitation or objection.
denomination C — *n* (c) **1.** a religious group. **2.** a class or unit, esp. o money.
denote C — *v* to indicate; mean.
denouement C — *n* (c) the explanation at the end of a novel, film, etc.
denounce C — *v* to give information publicly against (someone).
dentist A — *n* (c) the qualified person who looks after your teeth.
depart B — *v* (esp. of trains and planes) to leave, go away.
departed C — *n* the dead (no change in plural).
department A — *n* (c) a section of a larger organisation, esp. in government universities, business.
dependant C — *n* (c) someone who relies on someone else, esp. for a home and food.
dependence C — *n* (u) the state of having to rely on other people or something, e.g. one's parents or drugs.
deploy C — *v* (military) to spread out (into line) ready for action.
depose C — *v* to remove from a position of authority.
deposit C — *n* (c) **1.** something laid/put down, e.g. mineral or sediment **2.** partial payment to a seller so that he will not sell tc anyone else. **3.** money placed in a bank. **4.** refundabl sum as insurance against loss, damage, etc.
deposition C — *n* (c) the act of deposing.
depot B — *n* (c) **1.** a place for storing goods. **2.** (AE) a railwa station.
deputy B — *n* (c) someone with authority to act for another.
derange C — *v* to disturb, put out of order (usually of the mind).
past participle *deranged* mad, demented.
deride C — *v* to laugh at something as of no value.
derivation C — *n* (c) the origin.
derive C — *v* to originate in; come from.
derogatory C — *adj* showing lack of respect, pejorative.
descend C — *v* **1.** to come or go down. **2.** *descend from* to be connected by a blood relationship with.

escent C — *n* **1.** (c) coming or going down. **2.** (u) being descended, lineage.

escry C — *v* (archaic) to see (at a great distance).

esert C — *adj* in the desert (*desert* as a noun is A).

eserve B — *v* to merit; be worthy of.

esign A — *v* **1.** to plan in the mind. **2.** to draw a plan. **3.** to develop for a specific purpose.
n it has many meanings; if it refers to a drawing, it is to show how something is made.

esk A — *n* (c) a piece of furniture used for writing or reading.

esolate C — *adj* **1.** (of people) lonely and sad. **2.** (of things) empty, abandoned, or ruined.

espot C — *n* (c) a cruel ruler; tyrant.

estination B — *n* (c) the place one is travelling to.

estiny B — *n* (c) the force said to determine what happens.

estitute C — *adj* **1.** lacking the basic necessities of life. **2.** lacking (in certain qualities).

estitution C — *n* (u) the state of being destitute as in **1** above.

etail A — *n* **1.** (c) a small fact or part of something. **2.** (u) attention to small items.

etain C — *v* to keep from leaving.

etention C — *n* **1.** keeping children in school late as a punishment. **2.** military imprisonment.

eter C — *v* to discourage.

etermined B — *adj* firmly resolved, decided on a particular course of action.

etritus C — *n* (u) the rocks, stones, etc., washed down by erosion.

eviation C — *n* a turning away or difference from the normal position, course, or behaviour.

evice A/B/C — *n* (c) **1.** A a piece of apparatus, etc., which does a particular job. **2.** C (literature) a particular form of words. **3.** C (heraldry) a sign, emblem, etc. **4.** B *leave someone to his own devices* to leave someone alone to do as he wants.

evise C — *v* to invent.

evolution C — *n* the giving of authority to someone else.

evolve C — *v* to pass or cause to pass to another.

evout C — *adj* religious.

iabolo C — *n* (c) a type of double cone rotated on a string as a game.

iacritic C — *n* (c) a phonetic sign placed above, under or through a letter.

iagonal C — *adj, n* (c) (of) the straight line joining opposite corners of a rectangle or square.

iagram B — *n* (c) a plan or drawing to explain something.

iapason C — *n* one of the basic stops on an organ.

iary B — *n* (c) **1.** a book in which one writes the events of each day when they have happened. **2.** a book in which one writes down events arranged in advance or things to be done.

iaspora C — *n* the dispersal of the Jews.

iatribe C — *n* (c) an angry verbal attack.

dictate B/C *v* **1.** B to say words for someone to write down. **2.** C t give orders.

C *n* (c) an order which must be obeyed.

differ B *v* to be unlike, different.

difficult A/B *adj* **1.** A not easy to do. **2.** B (of people) not easy to pleas or satisfy; argumentative.

dilapidated C *adj* in poor repair, broken, and old.

dilettante C *n* (c) (derogatorily) someone who likes the arts but ha never really studied them seriously.

adj amateur, not thorough.

diplomat B *n* (c) **1.** someone who officially represents his countr abroad. **2.** someone clever at solving arguments c disputes.

direct A *adj* **1.** straight. **2.** frank; unhesitating. **3.** in an unbroke line of descent. **4.** immediate.

directive C *n* (c) an official order.

director A *n* (c) **1.** one of a group of people who make decisions fc an organisation or company. **2.** the stage manager of play or film.

disagreement C *n* not in agreement, a difference of opinion.

disarm C *v* **1.** to take weapons from. **2.** to take away anger.

disaster B *n* (c) a sudden accident (more intense then in Portuguese

disastrous C *adj* leading to or like a disaster.

disc C *n* (c) something round and flat as a gramophone record.

discharge B/C *v* **1.** B to send out or away. **2.** B to pour out. **3.** C t fulfil an order or duty. **4.** C to shoot (a gun). **5.** C t send away from work or the forces.

disciple C *n* (c) **1.** a direct follower of Jesus. **2.** a follower of great teacher.

discipline B/C *n* (usually u) **1.** B a willingness to obey. **2.** B the orde exercised over soldiers, schoolchildren, etc. **3.** (c) (any subject studied at university. **4.** C a trainin method.

disco B *n* (c) short for *discotheque*, a club where young peopl dance.

discount B *n* a price reduction on goods.

discourage B *v* to make (someone) less inclined to do something.

discourse C *n* (c) a serious piece of writing, conversation or lecture.

discover A *v* **1.** to find out (facts). **2.** to find something which existe but was unknown.

discreet B *adj* tactful or careful.

discretion C *n* (u) the quality of being discreet.

discussion A *n* (c) an exchange of interesting ideas; (more serious than a *conversation*, not angry like an *argument*).

diseuse C *n* (c) a woman entertainer who acts different roles (i monologue).

disgrace B *n* **1.** (u) loss of reputation or favour. **2.** (c) something o someone which causes shame.

disgraced C *past participle* shamed, humbled.

disgraceful B *adj* bringing disgrace or shame.

disgust B *v* to cause a strong feeling of dislike or distaste.
n (u) the strong feeling of dislike or distaste.

dishonest B *adj* not truthful.

dislocate C *v* **1.** to put out of its proper place, esp. of bones. **2.** to disturb, cause chaos.

dislocation C *n* the state of being dislocated.

dismay B *v* to fill with alarm, fear, or hopelessness.
n (u) such feeling(s).

dismount C *v* to get off a horse.

dispatch B *v* to send away (esp. goods for delivery).
n (c) an official government message.

dispensary C *n* (c) the part of a chemist's shop or hospital where medicines are prepared.

dispensation C *n* **1.** distribution, dealing out, esp. in religious contexts. **2.** permission to break a rule.

dispense C *v* **1.** to make up and hand out (medicines). **2.** to deal out (punishment, charity). **3.** *dispense with* to do without.

dispersion C *n* (c) a scattering (technical use).

displace C *v* to move from its place.

displacement C *n* (u) (technical) the amount or weight of water pushed aside by an object.

dispose (of) B *v* to throw away, give away, or get rid of.

disposition C *n* a general tendency of character and way of behaving.

dispute B *n* a quarrel or argument.

disrobe C *v* to take off ceremonial clothing.

distinct B *adj* easily heard, seen, or understood; separate.

distortion C *n* a misrepresentation, a twisting of a true or original meaning or shape; imperfection.

distract B *v* to draw attention away from.

distraction C *n* (c) **1.** something that distracts. **2.** (old-fashioned) something that entertains; diversion. **3.** near madness.

distress C *n* (u) **1.** deep unhappiness. **2.** a state of danger.

dive B *n* (c) **1.** an act of jumping head first into water. **2.** (informal) a café or meeting place with a bad reputation.

diversion B *n* (c) **1.** a temporary re-routing of traffic. **2.** C something turning attention from a more important matter. **3.** C (old-fashioned) something that entertains; amusement.

divert B/C *v* **1.** B to send by a different route. **2.** (old-fashioned) C to amuse; entertain.

divide A *v* **1.** to separate. **2.** to convert into two parts.

division A *n* for the Dutch speakers, this is *(ver)deling*.

divulge C *v* to tell something which was secret.

do up A *v* **1.** to pack together. **2.** (reflexive; informal) to dress oneself smartly. **3.** (informal) to improve, renovate, or redecorate.

dock A *n* (c) **1.** the place in a harbour where ships are (un)loaded. **2.** (informal) hospital. **3.** the place where a prisoner stands in a court.

dog A *n* (c) the common animal often kept as a domestic pet, e.g. spaniel, alsatian.

domain C — *n* **1.** (c) an area of study or knowledge. **2.** a hous (usually old) with land adjoining it.

dome C — *n* (c) a large round roof with a circular base.

domineer C — *v* to tyrannise; force others to do things against thei wishes.

don C — *n* (c) **1.** a university teacher (mainly in Cambridge an Oxford). **2.** a Spaniard's title of respect.

doodle C — *v* (informal) to draw patterns or pictures while thinkin about something else.

doom C — *n* unavoidable fate, death, or ruin.

door A — *n* (c) the movable panel between two rooms, etc.

dormer C — *n* (c) a small upright window in a sloping roof.

dormitory C — *n* (c) a large room for many people to sleep.

dose C — *n* (c) an amount of medicine to be taken at one time.

dot B — *n* (c) a small round mark.

double A — *v* **1.** to become twice as much as before. **2.** (theatre) t take two parts in one play. **3.** to fold in two.
n **1.** (c) a person who looks just like another. **2.** *double.* a game (like tennis) with four players.
adj twice as much.

dove C — *n* (c) the bird, also called a pigeon, a symbol of peace.

Downs C — *n* *the Downs* are the chalk hills in S.E. England.

doze C — *v* to sleep very lightly.

drag B — *v* **1.** to pull something heavy across a surface. **2.** to tak too much time and seem boring. **3.** to search the bot- tom of a lake or river.
n **1.** (c) the apparatus used to drag underwater as in above. **2.** (u) women's clothes worn by men, or vic versa. **3.** (slang) (c) something boring.

dragon C — *n* (c) a mythological creature with four legs and a tail usually breathing fire.

drake C — *n* (c) a male duck.

dramatic B — *adj* **1.** connected with the theatre. **2.** exciting or striking.

draw up A — *v* **1.** to stop, esp. of vehicles. **2.** to prepare in writing. **3.** (reflexive) to straighten oneself.

dress A/C — *v* **1.** A to put clothes on (oneself or another person). **2.** C to add a sauce to (a salad).
A — *n* **1.** (c) a woman's one-piece garment that covers the body from the shoulders to about the knee. **2.** (u) a complete style of clothing.

drift C — *n* (c) **1.** a slow movement, difficult to see. **2.** something piled up by the wind, e.g. *snow*. **3.** the general meaning.

drill C — *v* **1.** to teach by strict exercises. **2.** to make a hole by boring.

drive A — *v* to cause someone or something to move.
n **1.** (c) a journey by road. **2.** (c) a private road leading to a house. **3.** (c) a special effort to do something. **4.** (u) energy and a lot of ideas.

drone C — *v* to make a low monotonous sound, like bees.

dry A — *v* to make or become free from moisture.

	adj	**1.** not wet. **2.** (of drinks) not sweet.
duenna C	*n*	(c) an older woman who supervises the daughters of a family (in Spain, Portugal and Latin America).
dumb B	*adj*	**1.** not able to speak. **2.** (informal) silly; stupid.
dump C	*v*	**1.** to throw down. **2.** to throw away as rubbish. **3.** to sell goods cheaply, usually in another country.
dune C	*n*	(c) a sand hill.
dungeon C	*n*	(c) (literary) a prison.
dupe C	*v*	to trick, cheat, or deceive someone.
Durex C	*n*	(c) (trademark) a sheath contraceptive.
dusk C	*n*	(u) the last light in the sky in the evening.
dusky C	*adj*	dark (in colour).
Dutch A	*adj, n*	of the Netherlands, (also called Holland).
duvet B	*n*	a top covering for a bed filled with e.g. feathers.
dwell C	*v*	(old-fashioned) to live.
dwelling C	*n*	(c) a place where someone lives, i.e. a house, bungalow, flat, etc.; (mainly in legal or formal use).

e

eager A	*adj*	having a strong wish for something.
eagle B	*n*	(c) a large bird of prey.
earl C	*n*	(c) a British nobleman of high rank.
easel C	*n*	(c) a frame for holding a blackboard or a picture that an artist is painting.
easy B	*adj*	**1.** not difficult; simple. **2.** (informal) (of people) not offering objections; ready to accept suggestions.
éclair C	*n*	(c) a kind of pastry cake with cream inside.
economies C	*n*	(c) actions helping one to spend less money.
economise B	*v*	to be sparing; try to spend less money or use fewer resources.
edify C	*v*	to improve the morals or mind of.
edit C	*v*	**1.** to prepare writings for publications. **2.** to plan and direct the publishing of a newspaper or periodical. **3.** to arrange parts of a film or tape-recording into a suitable sequence.
editor B	*n*	(c) someone who edits in any of the above meanings.
editorial C	*n*	(c) an article in a newspaper or periodical written by the editor.
educate A	*v*	this verb is more concerned with teaching and learning at schools and college than behaviour learned at home. *Well-educated* means having learnt much at school and college and *badly educated* means the opposite.
education A	*n*	(u or with indefinite article) like the verb, the noun concerns the teaching and learning in schools and college rather than behaviour learned at home.

effective B *adj* **1.** able to produce the desired result. **2.** impressive ar striking. **3.** (military) ready for war. **effectively** C *ad*

effects C *n* (c; plural only) someone's money and property; (usuall only in legal use).

egg A *n* (c) a round object laid by a female bird, reptile, etc containing a new living being.

egregious C *adj* foolish; shocking.

elaborate C *v* **1.** to add small details to. **2.** to explain in detail.

elaboration C *n* (u) making more detailed.

elastic C *n* (u) cord or string, having rubber woven into it.

elder C *n* (c) **1.** an official in certain religious groups. **2.** a kin of tree with small black berries.

elect B/C *v* **1.** B to choose someone by voting to be a representativ **2.** (rather old-fashioned) C to choose.

election A *n* (c) the process of choosing representatives, esp. fo parliament.

element B *n* coincides with French meanings except for its use c (legal) evidence.

elementary B *adj* very easy, to be taught to the beginner.

embargo C *n* (c) a prohibition of commerce, movement of ships, etc (The verb in English comes closer to the meaning i Latin.)

embarkation C *n* (u) the action of going on a ship for a sea journey.

embarrass A *v* **1.** to cause someone to be ill at ease or ashamed. **2** (very occasionally) to hinder; inconvenience.

embarrassing A *adj* causing embarrassment, shame, and social discomfort.

emission C *n* (c) something emitted or sent out.

emit C *v* to send out (sounds, gases, light, liquids, smells). (No used of broadcasting or the Stock Exchange.)

emotion B *n* strong feelings, such as love, hate, or anger. (The word i less used in English than in the other languages affected and has in English a more intense meaning.)

emphasis B *n* **1.** the giving of special importance to a syllable or word **2.** the giving of importance to a fact, idea, etc.

emphatic C *adj* having emphasis.

employ B *v* to give people work in exchange for pay (very rarely in th French use—very formal).

emporium C *n* (c) a large shop with many departments.

enamel C *n* a type of paint which dries very hard, used e.g. on meta and pottery.

encaustic C *adj* (esp. of bricks and floor tiles) prepared with colour burnt in.

encounter C *v* to meet (usually unexpectedly and often unpleasan things).

encrusted C *past participle* covered with some kind of hard outer surface

energetic B *adj* having, showing, or needing force and vigour.

energy B *n* (mostly u) force, power.

enervate C *v* to weaken; make someone less strong.

enfolding C *adj* (rather poetic) enclosing, wrapping round, usually wit someone's arms.

ngage A/B/C *v* **1.** A to make arrangements to employ someone. **2.** B to make a mechanism work. **3.** (passive) A to agree to marry (and become a fiancé(e)). **4.** C to attack an enemy.

ngaged *adj* occupied, busy.

ngagement B *n* (c) **1.** a formal commitment (usually in writing). **2.** an agreement to marry.

ngrave C *v* to cut (letters or a picture) into a surface, e.g. on a tombstone, or to make a lithograph.

nliven C *v* to make more lively or cheerful.

ntail C *v* to necessitate.

nterprise B *n* **1.** (u) initiative; the courage needed to undertake something new or dangerous. **2.** (c) a business firm. **3.** (c) a project.

ntertain B *v* **1.** to receive people as guests, esp. in one's home. **2.** to amuse and interest. **3.** to have in mind.

ntourage C *n* (c) all the people who travel with (and may work for) someone important.

ntrances and exits C *n* the comings-in and goings-out, suggesting the movements of actors on and off the stage.

ntrée C *n* **1.** (c) a small dish, coming after the fish and before the main course at a formal dinner. **2.** a right to enter.

ntrepreneur C *n* (c) someone directing a commercial undertaking.

nvoy C *n* (c) an official just below an ambassador in rank.

nvy B *v* to wish to have something belonging to another person.

phemera C *n* things (often writing and printing) which will soon be forgotten.

pisode C *n* (c) **1.** one part of a long story (e.g. on television). **2.** an event.

pisodic C *adj* written in the form of a series of separate events.

pithet C *n* (c) an adjective describing a quality, or attribute.

poch C *n* (c) **1.** a long period in history, when something stated was happening. **2.** a notable event which may start a new stage.

qual A *adj* **1.** mathematically of the same value. **2.** having the strength, courage, or ability to manage.

qually B *adv* to the same degree, quantity, or extent.

quip B *v* to supply or furnish.

quipment B *n* (u) things for a certain activity.

quivocate C *v* to be unclear in meaning.

rsatz C *adj* used of something substituted for another, generally second-best; (in English there is a derogatory feel to it).

special C *adj* exceptional; notable.

specially A *adv* **1.** to an exceptional degree. **2.** above all (others). *Specially* (informal) may be used in either of these senses and also for a particular purpose.

ssence C *n* (u) the principal or intrinsic quality of something. (The word is not now much used of perfumes.)

state A *n* **1.** property consisting of land. **2.** *housing estate* a planned area of houses. **3.** *industrial estate* an area of planned factories. **4.** (u)(legal) someone's entire property (i.e. all their assets). For the French, the false friend meanings in Part 1 are archaic in English.

esteem C — *v* (formal) **1.** to respect (someone) very much. **2.** t consider.

etiquette C — *n* (u) the convention for formal behaviour in society o within a given group or profession.

evade C — *v* **1.** to get safely out of the way of. **2.** to avoid.

evangelical C — *adj* relating to mainly Protestant groupings which emphasis the importance of personal conversion and faith in th death of Christ as the means of salvation.

evangelist C — *n* (c) **1.** *the four Evangelists* Matthew, Mark, Luke, an John. **2.** a preacher of the Christian gospel.

evasion C — *n* the act of evading.

even A — *adj* regular, smooth.
adv many uses, but the Dutch and Germans should notic that it is not used to refer to time in English.

event A — *n* (c) **1.** a happening (usually of some importance) incident. **2.** *in the event of X* if X happens. **3.** a singl competition in a programme of sports.

eventual A — *adj* ultimate, coming at the end of something.

eventually A — *adv* finally, in the end, ultimately.

evidence B — *n* (u) reasons, words, actions, etc., that support a belief make something clearer, or prove something.

evidently A — *adv* clearly. (*Obviously* is used of things more plainly indicated, *apparently* of things less plainly indicated.)

evince C — *v* to show (a certain quality) clearly.

evolved C — *past participle* gradually developed.

exaggerate C — *v* to say something was greater, bigger, worse, better, etc. than it really was.

exaggerated B — *adj* made to seem worse, better, etc., than it is.

exalt C — *v* **1.** to praise generously. **2.** to make someone feel very happy and uplifted. **3.** to ennoble.

example A — *n* (c) **1.** something which illustrates a general rule or use of something. **2.** someone or something to be copied. **3.** something taken as representative of others.

exceeded C — *past participle* beyond/past what is lawful, required o expected.

exceptional child C — *adj+n* (c) gifted, intelligent child.

excite A — *v* to provoke strong feelings, esp. of pleasure.

excuse A — *v* **1.** to remove an obligation from someone. **2.** to pardon, justify. **3.** *excuse oneself from* to apologise for no doing something in advance. **4.** *be excused* to leave the room, esp. to go to the lavatory.
n a doubtful reason offered for a fault.

exempt C — *adj* free from an obligation, liability, tax, etc.

exercise B — *v* (military) to cause soldiers to do physical exercises rather than marching practices.
n (c) **1.** activity; drill to improve performance. **2.** (military) manoeuvres.

existence C — *n* **1.** (u) the state of being. **2.** (c) life; living.

exit B — *n* (c) **1.** the way out, esp. of a cinema or theatre. **2.** (of actors) the action of leaving the stage.

exodus C — *n* **1.** (c) a going out. **2.** *Exodus* is the second book of the Old Testament in the Bible.

exonerate C — *v* to clear or free of blame.

expedient C — *n* (c) a plan or action which is advantageous or helpful (though possibly not fair).
adj likely to be good as an expedient.

expedite C — *v* (formal) to make something go faster.

expedition C — *n* (c) **1.** a long journey for a specific purpose. **2.** the people and equipment travelling on such a journey.

experience A — *v* to feel and know something directly, e.g. by observation.
n **1.** (c) something which happens to one. **2.** (u) skill(s) and knowledge acquired practically.

experiment A — *v* to test carefully, to observe results and gain knowledge.
n (c) a test done in this way.

expert A — *n* (c) someone having special knowledge in an activity or profession.
adj skilful; knowledgeable.

expertise C — *n* (u) know-how; expert's knowledge.

expiration C — *n* (c) the date when something comes to an end; expiry.

expire C — *v* **1.** to come to an end. **2.** (poetic) to die.

exploit C — *v* **1.** to operate or make use of someone or something selfishly. **2.** to use something to get full profit.
n (c) a feat or achievement.

explore B — *v* **1.** to travel to find new information. **2.** to examine, investigate.

exposition B — *n* (c) **1.** (chiefly AE) a (large) number of objects shown publicly. (BE almost always uses *exhibition*.) **2.** a careful explanation.

express B — *n* **1.** (c) a fast train, making very few stops. **2.** (u) (BE) a fast mail delivery service.

expression A — *n* **1.** feelings, as shown on the face or in the arts. **2.** a group of words together.

exquisite B — *adj* extremely beautiful.

extension B — *n* (c) **1.** something added. **2.** a lengthening (esp. of time). **3.** an additional telephone within a system.

extenuate C — *v* to make a crime, error, etc. seem less severe.

extra B — *adj* additional, more than usual.

extract B — *n* **1.** (c) anything taken out of something longer. **2.** (a) concentrated form of certain foods.

extraneous C — *adj* not really belonging to the thing it is connected to.

extravagance C — *n* **1.** the wasting of money. **2.** (c) something costing (too) much money. **3.** (very occasional) unreasonable, absurd, or immoderate words. (This is close to the Continental use.)

extravagant B — *adj* **1.** spending a lot of money. **2.** costing a lot of money. **3.** (very occasional) unusual, beyond what is reasonable or rational.

extreme C — *n* (c) **1.** the highest or furthest degree. **2.** either of the two ends of a scale or range.

f

fabric B — *n* **1.** cloth; woven material. **2.** (u) the structure of a building.

fabricate C — *v* **1.** to make up, invent. **2.** to manufacture.

fabrication C — *n* **1.** (c) something false, e.g. a lie or forged document. **2.** (u) (occasional) the making of something.

façade C — *n* (c) **1.** the front of a building. **2.** the outer appearanc of something.

facile C — *adj* too simple, superficial, or hasty.

facilitate C — *v* to make something easier.

facility B/C — *n* **1.** B the ability to do something easily. **2.** (u) C the quality of being easily done. **3.** (plural) equipment advantages.

faction C — *n* (c) a self-interested group, esp. political, who may cause disturbance.

factor B — *n* (c) **1.** one of a number of facts which influence a fina result. **2.** (mathematics) a whole number, which, when multiplied by one or more whole numbers, gives the stated number. **3.** (very occasional) someone who acts for someone else, esp. in business.

factory A — *n* (c) a building where goods are produced by machines.

fad C — *n* (c) a passing interest or enthusiasm for something.

faded B — *past participle* lost intensity, esp. of colours.

fag(g)ot C — *n* (c) **1.** a bundle of dry wood (tied together) for burning **2.** a meat ball. **3.** (AE slang) a homosexual; (ofter shortened to *fag*). (*Faggot* is the BE spelling; *fagot* the AE.)

fail A — *v* **1.** to not do something. **2.** to be insufficient. **3.** to be unsuccessful in an exam. **4.** to judge someone unsuccessful in an exam. **5.** to neglect to do something **6.** to go bankrupt. **7.** to become weak.
n (c) a failure in an exam.

failing C — *n* (c) a weakness.

fair A — *n* (c) **1.** a large exhibition of commercial products **2.** a fun fair.

fairy C — *n* (c) **1.** a small imaginary person with magical powers found in children's stories. **2.** (slang) a homosexual.

fakir C — *n* (c) a beggar considered a holy man, esp. in India.

fall B — *n* (c) **1.** the act of coming down freely. **2.** the distance fallen. **3.** (AE) autumn.

fall in C — *v* **1.** to drop into something. **2.** to collapse. **3.** (military) to take one's place in a line.

fall out C — *v* **1.** to descend or drop out. **2.** (informal) to quarrel.

false A — *adj* not true, wrong, deceitful, not genuine. A more serious connotation in English than Spanish.

fame C — *n* (u) the condition of being well-known.

Headword	Level		Definition
familiar	A	*adj*	**1.** commonly experienced, usual. **2.** knowledgeable (about). **3.** friendly; informal. **4.** more intimate than is acceptable.
famous	A	*adj*	**1.** known to many people. **2.** (old-fashioned) excellent. (The adverb *famously* is more common in this sense.)
fan	B	*n*	(c) **1.** something (hand-worked or mechanical) making a current of air. **2.** a strong supporter.
fang	C	*n*	(c) the long tooth, esp. of dogs or snakes.
fantasy	C	*n*	creation(s) of the imagination (often derogatory).
farce	C	*n*	**1.** (c) a ridiculously funny play. **2.** (u) this style of drama. **3.** (c) absurd events in real life.
fare	C	*v*	(uncommon) to get on.
	A/C	*n*	**1.** (c) A the price of a ticket for a journey. **2.** (u) C food served.
farmer	A	*n*	(c) someone who owns or runs a farm.
fart	C	*n*	(taboo) (c) the noisy passage of gas from the bowels.
		v	to make a fart.
fashion	A	*n*	(c) **1.** a manner of doing something. **2.** the way of doing things which are most admired and imitated at any given time and place, esp. regarding clothes.
fast	C	*n*	(c) a period without eating.
	A	*adj*	**1.** rapid, quick. **2.** ahead in time. **3.** *make fast* secure. **4.** unfading.
	A	*adv*	**1.** deeply (asleep). **2.** rapid.
fasten	B	*v*	to make fast, attach, tie.
fastidious	C	*adj*	hard to please; overprecise; pedantic.
fat	A	*adj*	**1.** having too much flesh. **2.** (of a book) thick; having many pages.
		n	(u) the oily or greasy substance found in animal bodies.
fatal	C	*adj*	**1.** causing death. **2.** as though predestined; inevitable; to be regretted.
fatality	C	*n*	**1.** (c) death caused in a calamity or accident. **2.** (u) deadly influence.
fate	B	*n*	**1.** (u) the irresistable power which is supposed to determine events. **2.** (c) someone's predestined future.
fatty	C	*adj*	having (too much) fat.
fatuous	C	*adj*	very silly.
fault	A	*n*	**1.** (c) an imperfection, esp. mechanical. **2.** (c) a personal weakness. **3.** (u) responsibility. **4.** (c) geologically, a place where rocks slip down or up.
fear	B	*v*	to be afraid of; feel anxious about.
feast	B	*n*	(c) a magnificent meal.
feather	B	*n*	(c) one of the light parts that cover the skin of a bird; necessary for flying.
fee	C	*n*	(c) payment for professional services.
feed up	B	*v*	**1.** to give someone a lot of food to increase weight. **2.** (passive only) to be annoyed or bored.
felicity	C	*n*	**1.** (u) a pleasing way of writing or speaking. **2.** (c) such an expression. **3.** (occasional) contentment.
fell	C	*n*	(c) a hillside, esp. in N.W. England.

fen C — *n* (c) an area of low-lying land, which needs constar drainage; (*the Fens* are the part of England north c Cambridge, south of the Wash).

fern C — *n* (c) a type of flowerless plant with feathery leaves.

fetch A — *v* to go and return with.

fête C — *n* (c) an outdoor festival, usually to raise money for charity.

fetters C — *n* (c; sometimes singular) chains put round the legs of prisoner or horse.

fever A — *n* the condition of the body during illness when the tempera ture goes well above normal, e.g. 42°C.

fibre C — *n* (c) thread, in various meanings.

fiend C — *n* (c) **1.** a very cruel or wicked person (originally, th devil). **2.** someone addicted to something.

fierce A — *adj* **1.** violent; threatening; cruel. **2.** intense.

figure A — *n* (c) a word with many meanings: when applied to humans it refers to the shape of the body.

file A/B/C — *v* **1.** A to keep (papers, etc.) in a folder (see **1** below **2.** B to use a file (see **2** below). **3.** C (of people) t move slowly past in a single line.

A/B/C — *n* (c) **1.** A a system for holding papers, documents notes, etc., in order, esp. in an office. **2.** B a metal toc with a rough surface for smoothing or removing a surface **3.** C a line, esp. of soldiers.

fill up A — *v* to fill to the top.

fillet C — *n* (c) a piece of meat or fish with the bones taken out.

fin C — *n* (c) **1.** a part of a fish used for swimming. **2.** a par of an aircraft, used esp. for changing direction.

final B — *n* (c) **1.** (usually plural) the last series of exams. **2.** th last game or match in a championship.
adj coming at the end.

finally B — *adv* at last.

find A — *v* this is basically the Portuguese *encontrar*.

find out A — *v* **1.** to discover by asking or searching. **2.** to detect crime, etc.

fine B — *n* (c) money to be paid for breaking the law.

fire A/C — *n* (c) **1.** A the burning of fuel to give warmth. **2.** A th burning of a building, etc., causing damage. **3.** C stron feeling(s); excitement.

firm A — *n* (c) a business company.
adj **1.** solid, steady. **2.** not easily influenced.

first A — *n* (c) the highest category in exams.
adj coming before all others.

fish A — *n* **1.** (c; plural usually same) a creature living in water **2.** (u) the food from this animal.

fishline C — *n* (c) the thread used in fishing.

fit B — *n* (c) **1.** a period of activity; attack. **2.** (of clothes) th correct size for someone.

fix A — *v* **1.** to place something so that it will not move. **2.** tc determine, decide on. **3.** (chiefly AE informal) tc arrange something for someone. **4.** to repair. **5.** to arrange a false result. (To *be fixed* exists as a passive in all the above uses.)

n (c) **1.** (informal) a difficult situation. **2.** (slang) a drug addict's injection of a drug.

fixation C *n* (c) an obsession, concentration on one idea or person.

flair C *n* (c) a natural ability or gift.

flamenco C *adj* of or like a type of Spanish dance music for vocal soloist and guitar.

flan C *n* (c) a dish consisting of a pastry case with a (fruit) filling.

flash A/C *n* (c) **1.** A a sudden bright light. **2.** (c) (informal) C a short news announcement. **3.** C (photography) a flashlight photo.

flask A *n* (c) **1.** a narrow container (usually for liquids). **2.** a container which has a vacuum round it, to keep things cold or hot. **3.** the liquid contained in any such container.

flatter B *v* **1.** to overpraise someone in hopes of gaining favours. **2.** to make someone look more attractive than in reality.

lay C *v* **1.** to hit repeatedly so that the skin comes off; (also used of removing skin from animals). **2.** to criticise very severely.

lesh C *n* (u) the soft part of animal and human bodies between the skin and the bones.

lick C *v* to move (usually the hand or wrist) quickly.

n **1.** (c) such a movement. **2.** (plural; old-fashioned slang) the cinema.

lighty C *adj* (mainly of women) unsteady, always looking for pleasure.

lint C *n* (a piece of) hard stone found in chalk used to make fire, and for building in some areas.

lip C *n* (c) **1.** a quick light movement, esp. used to send something into the air. **2.** an alcoholic drink made of egg and sugar.

lipper C *n* (c) **1.** one of the large fins on seals, whales, etc., used for walking and swimming. **2.** either of the rubber pieces worn on one's feet to enable one to swim faster.

lirt C *n* (c) a person who playfully attracts the attention of the opposite sex (*flirtation* is the activity).

loat C *v* to stay on the surface of the water, not sinking.

n (c) **1.** a small object which is attached to a fishing line or net. **2.** a small delivery vehicle.

lock B *n* (c) a group of animals, esp. sheep.

lood C *n* **1.** water overflowing on land which is usually dry. **2.** (c) a great quantity of things. **3.** the flowing of the tide.

loor A *n* (c) **1.** the lower surface of a room on which people stand. **2.** each such level of a building.

lorid C *adj* **1.** (of the face) red. **2.** (of things) having too much decoration.

floss C — *n* (u) a mass of silk threads.

flow C — *n* (c) movement of a current, gas or water, or the tide.

flu B — *n* (u) short for *influenza*.

flue C — *n* (c) the top inside part of a fireplace where the smoke goes to the chimney.

fluent B — *adj* produced in a smooth easy way, esp. of speech and style.

fluke C — *n* (c) an accidental piece of good luck, an unexpected success.

fluster C — *v* to be or cause to be agitated, tense, or upset.

flute C — *n* (c) a wood-wind musical instrument with finger holes played by blowing across a hole in the side.

fog B — *n* thick mist; cloud at ground level.

föhn C — *n* only used in English of the wind over the mountains, as in Switzerland.

folio C — *n* **1.** a very large sheet of paper (of specific size) usually folded in two. **2.** a book of such sheets. **3.** a collection of paintings and drawings by an artist.

folly C — *n* **1.** (u) stupidity. **2.** (c) a stupid or foolish action, habit etc. **3.** (c) a building, usually with a fanciful shape erected for no particular purpose.

fool A — *v* to trick someone.
n (c) a stupid person; (historically also a jester).

footing C — *n* (c) **1.** a firm grip. **2.** the basis or foundation.

forage C — *n* (u) food for horses and cattle.

force A — *n* many uses but as a false friend Italians need to note *he opened the door by force*, i.e. not with a key, etc., but by using physical violence; similarly, for Danish and Norwegian, *he used force to open the door*.

ford C — *v* to cross (a river, brook, etc.) where it is not deep.

foreman C — *n* (c) **1.** a workman in charge of other workers. **2.** the chief member of a jury.

foresee C — *v* to expect; see or know beforehand. (The N. European words refer much more to the actions one takes as a result of expecting something.)

foresight C — *n* (u) the ability to imagine events that may happen in the future, making it possible to prepare for them or even prevent them.

forestall C — *v* to upset someone's plans by doing something before.

foretell C — *v* to say in advance what will happen.

forfeit C — *v* to have something taken from one as a punishment or for breaking a rule in a game.
n (c) something silly or embarrassing to be done in a game.

forfeiture C — *n* (u) the act of forfeiting something legally.

forger C — *n* (c) someone who produces false documents, money, works of art, etc.

forgive A — *v* to pardon.

forgo C — *v* to do without something pleasant.

forlorn C — *adj* **1.** miserable, unhappy. **2.** (of things) abandoned and in poor condition.

form A — *n* many meanings and uses; (the word refers more to the appearance of something than what it was made in).

formal B — *adj* (of people) following rules of society strictly.

format C — *n* (c) the size and shape of a book or periodical.

formation B — *n* **1.** (u) the arrangement or shaping of something. **2.** (military) disposition of troops, aircraft.

formed B — *past participle* given shape or character.

Formica C — *n* (u; a trademark but now often with no capital) a kind of hard plastic made into thin sheets and esp. fitted on tables and worktops.

formidable C — *adj* **1.** causing fear and dread. **2.** difficult to deal with.

formula B — *n* (c) various uses, esp. in science and mathematics; also a conventional fixed phrase for use on social occasions, etc.

forte C — *adj* (music) loud.

fortunate B — *adj* lucky; having or bringing good fortune.

fortune B — *n* **1.** (u) luck, esp. favourable. **2.** a great sum of money.

forward C — *n* (c) a player in the front line of a game of football, hockey, etc.

foul C — *adj* **1.** causing disgust or horror. **2.** *foul play* the breaking of a rule in sport.

fowl C — *n* (c) a domestic hen, etc.

fox C — *n* (c) a wild animal, with a bushy tail, often hunted.

foyer C — *n* (c) the entrance hall in a hotel, cinema, theatre, or restaurant.

fracas C — *n* (c) a noisy disagreement or fight (involving several people).

fraction B — *n* **1.** (c) (mathematics) an amount, not a whole number, written with a number above and below a line. **2.** a very small proportion.

fracture C — *n* (c) a crack or break, esp. in a bone.

franchise C — *n* (u) the right to vote in an election. (Only BE gives false friends.)

frank B — *v* *frank a letter* to put a mark on it to show that postage has been paid.

free B — *v* to release; set at liberty.

freely B — *adv* **1.** readily. **2.** openly. **3.** generously. **4.** without friction.

freeze B — *n* (c) a long period of extremely cold weather.

frequent C — *v* to visit from time to time, not necessarily regularly; (the Latin meaning suggests regular visits).

fresh A — *adj* of many uses; note these. **1.** not stale. **2.** not canned, frozen, or preserved in other ways. **3.** (of water) not salt. **4.** bright, clear; clean. **5.** invigorating; rather strong. **6.** cool or chilly. **7.** having a healthy complexion. **8.** renewed; further, additional. **9.** forward and disrespectful; cheeky; flirting.

friction C — *n* **1.** (u) a force attempting to stop one thing as it moves against another. **2.** (u) the rubbing going with this. **3.** the unfriendliness in a group caused by disagreement.

frigidaire A — *n* strictly a trademark for a refrigerator, now usually shortened to *fridge* in BE; (an *ice-box* in AE).

frisky C — *adj* playful; very active.

frivolity C — *n* (u) the condition of being frivolous.

frivolous C — *adj* silly; making jokes about something other people take seriously; pleasure-loving.

front A — *n* (c) many meanings; used of a person, it can mean the face, opposite of the back, outward appearance.

fruition C — *n* (u) fulfilment or accomplishment.

fugue C — *n* (c) a piece of music in which a theme is repeated on higher or lower notes while it continues.

full A — *adj* replete. (*I'm full* I have eaten quite enough.)

full-blooded C — *adj* **1.** with great strength or conviction. **2.** of unmixed race.

fume C — *n* (c; often plural) the pungent air from such things as new paint, petrol, or burning rubber.

function B/C — *n* (c) **1.** B an event that brings a number of people together for a common purpose, with some ceremony. **2.** B a duty, task, or responsibility. **3.** (mathematics) C a variable quantity which varies as another value varies.

functionary C — *n* (c) an official who has unimportant duties.

fund A — *n* (c) **1.** a supply. **2.** (often plural) money set aside for something.

funk C — *n* (c) a state of fear or lack of confidence.

fur C — *n* various meanings connected with the hairy coat of an animal.

furnace B — *n* (c) an apparatus for holding a large fire, e.g. to produce steam or for treating metals in a factory.

furniture A — *n* (u) the collective word for tables, chairs, cupboards, beds, etc.

fuse C — *n* (c) **1.** a small piece of safety apparatus fitted in an electrical machine or system. **2.** a device used to explode a bomb, shell, etc., or for blasting in mining.

fusion C — *n* the mixing of two or more things, such as metals, races, or organisations.

futile C — *adj* purposeless, useless. (Only very occasionally used of people in the Latin meaning.)

g

gable C — *n* (c) the triangular end of a roof above an upright wall.

gadget B — *n* (c) a small useful piece of apparatus.

gaffe C — *n* (c) the French word in its meaning of a social error.

gaffer C — *n* (c) **1.** (informal) an old man. **2.** (BE slang) a boss.

gag C — *n* (c) **1.** (informal) a funny story or joke. **2.** a band, cloth, etc., fixed over the mouth to stop someone from talking or shouting.

gage C — *n* (c) **1.** short for *greengage*, a green plum. **2.** AE spelling for *gauge*.

gallant C — *adj* **1.** brave, courageous. **2.** (of a man) attentive to women.

gallantry C — *n* (u) **1.** bravery, courage. **2.** attention paid to women.

gallery B/C — *n* (c) **1.** (BE) B a museum. **2.** B a place where works of art are on sale. **3.** B a corridor in a building, esp. with one side open. **4.** B the top floor of a theatre and those who sit in it. **5.** C (closer to the Italian) a passage connecting two caves or two parts of a coal mine.

gallon A — *n* (c) a liquid measurement; BE 4.54 litres, AE 3.78 litres.

galoshes C — *n* (c; but rarely used in the singular) rubber shoes which fit over normal shoes to protect these from the wet.

gang B — *n* (c) **1.** any group of people, friends, children, or those working together. **2.** a group of criminals.

gaol — See **jail**.

garb C — *n* (u) clothing.

garden A — *n* a cultivated, enclosed piece of land for growing flowers, fruit or vegetables.

garnish C — *v* to decorate (food).

garrison C — *n* (c) **1.** a castle or fortification. **2.** the soldiers living in such a building.

gate A — *n* (c) the movable barrier at an opening in a wall or fence.

gauge C — *n* (c) **1.** an instrument for measuring amounts, size, etc. **2.** the distance between the rails of a railway.

gaze B — *n* (c) the act of looking (at something) for a long time.

gazette C — *n* (c) **1.** an official government newspaper. **2** sometimes used in titles of newspapers.

gazetteer C — *n* (c) an alphabetical list (e.g. at the end of an atlas) of place names, countries, rivers, etc.

gelatine C — *n* (u) a clear substance obtained from boiled animal bones, used in cooking.

gender B — *n* (c) the grammatical classifications of masculine, feminine and neuter.

generality C — *n* (c) a vague or general statement.

genial C — *adj* pleasant, kind, good-hearted, agreeable; (a good word for the important false friend *sympathetic*, though not commonly used).

geniality C — *n* (u) the quality of being friendly, sociable, and welcoming.

genie C — *n* (c) a magic spirit in some fairy stories.

genre C — *n* (c) a kind of literature or art, according to the sort of subject.

genteel C — *adj* **1.** exaggeratedly polite in order to impress others. **2.** (becoming old-fashioned) polite, and respectable.

gentle A — *adj* **1.** not violent or harsh. **2.** friendly, patient.

geometer C — *n* (c) **1.** a type of caterpillar with feet-like suckers at the front and back of its body, but none along the middle. **2.** a person skilled in geometry.

German A — *n* (c) someone from Germany.

gestalt C — *n* (psychology) a pattern or whole of something that is different from the sum of its parts.

ghost B — *n* (c) a dead person appearing to the living.

gift B — *n* (c) a present.

gifted C — *adj* talented, very clever, esp. in the arts.

Gillette C — *n* (c) (trademark) a razor or razor blade.

girder C — *n* (c) a strong metal beam used in building.

giro C — *n* a banking system with accounts kept at one centre.

gist C — *n* the essence of something; main part.

give A — *v* **1.** to hand over as a present. **2.** *give out* **a.** to distribute. **b.** to come to an end. **c.** to announce. **3.** *give up* **a.** to be discouraged. **b.** to surrender. **c.** to stop doing (something). **d.** to stop trying to help.

glacé C — *adj* covered with or treated with sugar.

glance A — *v* to look quickly.
n (c) a quick look.

glass A — *n* **1.** (u) the hard matter made from silica, used for windows, etc. **2.** (c) something made of glass, esp. for drinking, or its contents. **3.** (c) a barometer. **4.** (plural) lenses in frames worn to help poor vision.

glass eye C — *n* (c) an artificial eye of glass to replace an injured eye.

globe B — *n* (c) a spherical form, usually one representing the earth.

glorious A — *adj* splendid, marvellous, magnificent; (not much used of people).

gloss C — *n* (c) **1.** a smooth shining surface, e.g. on certain paints. **2.** an explanatory note or comment to a text.

gloss over C — *v* to pass quickly over something unsatisfactory perhaps making excuses for it.

glow B — *n* a warm light.

glue B — *v* to join or stick with an adhesive material.
n (u) the adhesive material used.

glut C — *n* (c) a supply which is too great.

go after A — *v* **1.** to follow. **2.** to leave at a later time than. **3.** to take one's turn in a game after.

go off A — *v* (of people) **1.** to leave, go away. **2.** to fall asleep. **3.** begin to dislike.

goal B — *n* (c) **1.** the place in some sports e.g. football where the ball must go to win a point. **2.** a point won by doing this. **3.** an aim or purpose.

golden A — *adj* **1.** made of or having the colour of gold. **2.** very favourable (opportunity).

golf B — *n* (u) a game played on an open course, the aim of which is to hit a ball with clubs with as few strokes as possible.
adj connected with this game.

gondola C — *n* (c) **1.** a long narrow boat, as traditionally used in Venice. **2.** a small cabin on a mountain cable railway. **3.** a basket hanging from a balloon.

goods A — *n* (c; fixed plural) merchandise, articles for sale.

gorge C — *n* (c) a narrow rocky opening where a river passes through.

gorgeous B — *adj* very attractive or pleasing.

grab B — *v* to seize; snatch rather violently.

gracious C — *adj* (of people) characterised by or showing kindness; courteous and polite, esp. to someone less important.

grade A — *v* to classify or arrange according to size or quality.
n (c) **1.** quality. **2.** (AE) a year's group of pupils or students. **3.** (chiefly AE) the mark or points given for school work. **4.** (chiefly AE) a gradient (on a steep road, etc.).

graffiti C — *n* (plural) writing or drawing(s) on a wall, used only to refer to such writing or drawing when it is humorous, political, or obscene.

grain A — *n* meanings close to the French, but used of seeds usually only when they are for eating, not for propagating the plant(s).

gram A — *n* (c) a unit of weight, a thousandth of a kilogram.

grammar B — *n* **1.** (u) the study and rules used in a language. **2.** (c) a grammar book.

grand A — *adj* wonderful, excellent, splendid.
n **1.** (informal) a thousand (pounds or dollars). **2.** a piano with the strings laid horizontally. **3.** *grandstand* a terraced block of seats at a racecourse, stadium, etc.

grape B — *n* (c) an individual fruit of a bunch from a vine.

graph B — *n* (c) a diagram used in mathematics and statistics, etc., with lines to show comparative changes in two things.

graphic C — *adj* **1.** connected with written signs, esp. letters and symbols. **2.** lifelike, vivid.

grass A — *n* (u) the common green plant growing on the ground. **2.** (slang) marijuana, cannabis.

gratification C — *n* (u) satisfaction.

gratify C — *v* to satisfy, please.

gratis C — *adj, adv* given freely, without payment.

gratuity C — *n* (c) **1.** money paid above salary at the end of someone's employment, esp. in the armed forces. **2.** a tip (money).

grave B — *n* (c) a hole in the ground made to take (a box with) a dead body in it.

grease B — *n* (u) **1.** soft animal fat. **2.** any thick oil-like substance.

grenade C — *n* (c) a small bomb (usually hand-thrown).

grid C — *n* (c) **1.** a network of bars or lines (regularly) crossing one another. **2.** (BE) the system of cables supplying electricity.

grief B — *n* **1.** (u) deep unhappiness. **2.** (c) a cause of grief. **3.** *good grief* a commonly used exclamation of (disagreeable) surprise. **4.** *come to grief* to go wrong, become impossible.

grieve B — *v* **1.** to make someone very unhappy. **2.** to suffer deep unhappiness.

grill C — *v* to cook against direct heat.
n (c) **1.** an apparatus for cooking in this way. **2.** meat cooked this way. **3.** a restaurant serving such food.

grim B — *adj* **1.** cruel, severe, relentless, fierce. **2.** (informal) difficult, tense, busy.

grime C — *n* (u) black thick dirt covering something.

grin B — *v* to smile (showing the teeth).

grip B — *v* to hold something very tightly.
n (c) **1.** a tight hold. **2.** a small soft bag for travelling

gripe C — *v* **1.** to have stomach or abdominal pains. **2.** (slang) to complain constantly.
n (c) (slang) a complaint.

grit C — *n* (c) **1.** small hard pieces of sand or stone. **2.** (less common) courage.

grocer B — *n* (c) someone having a shop selling food such as tea, flour, tinned goods, etc.

groin C — *n* (c) the hollow where the front of the body meets the top of the legs.

groom C — *n* (c) **1.** someone looking after horses. **2.** short for a *bridegroom.*

gross C — *adj* various uses, but when applied to people, it normally means objectionable, offensive, impolite.

ground A — *n* **1.** (u) area of land. **2.** (plural) the parkland or gardens round a large house or hotel, etc. **3.** (plural) reasons, motivation, foundation.

gruesome C — *adj* disgusting, frightful, shocking; (used mostly of events, not people).

guarantee C — *v* **1.** to promise that a product, etc., is of a specified standard or specifications and to promise to repair it with no cost (for a certain period). **2.** to promise that something is correct.

guard C — *v* to protect, be ready for attack.

guardian C — *n* (c) someone who legally takes responsibility for a younger person.

guer(r)illa B — *n* someone who fights on behalf of a small or independant group.

guesthouse C — *n* (c) a private house where visitors pay to lodge and have meals.

guide A — *v* to lead the way, conduct.

guilty A — *adj* not innocent; responsible for doing something wrong or breaking the law.

gulf B/C — *n* (c) **1.** B the deep sea between two areas of land. **2.** C a deep hollow in the earth's surface. **3.** B a great difference of opinion.

gull C — *n* (c) a number of types of birds, usually associated with the sea.

gulley C — *n* (c) a very steep narrow valley, esp. one caused by heavy rain and on a hillside.

gulp C — *n* (c) the action of swallowing something quickly.

gum C — *n* (u) **1.** the sticky substance found on certain plants. **2.** substance used for sticking things together.

gurgle C — *v* to make the sound of water mixed with air.

gusset C	*n*	(c) a triangular piece of material, for widening and strengthening, used in clothing and shoes.
gust C	*n*	(c) a sudden blow of wind of great force; (*with gusto* is sometimes used, meaning enthusiastically).
gymkhana C	*n*	(c) a sports meeting for horse-riding competitions.
gymnasium C	*n*	(c) a large room equipped for doing physical exercises; (a school in some Continental countries is called a *gymnasium*, but not in England).

h

habit A/C	*n*	**1.** (usually c) A tendency, practice or custom. **2.** C the special clothes worn by monks and nuns (but not ordinary priests).
habitat C	*n*	(c) the natural surroundings of a plant or animal.
habitation C	*n*	**1.** (u) the act of living (in a place). **2.** (c) (old-fashioned) a house.
hack C	*v*	to cut roughly.
hag C	*n*	(c) an ugly old woman (sometimes associated with witchcraft).
half A	*n*	(c) either of two equal parts that together make a whole; used of time, 05.30 is correctly spoken as *half past five* but increasingly in informal use, *half five*.
hall A	*n*	(c) **1.** an entrance room; vestibule, esp. in a private house. Compare **foyer**. **2.** a large building or room for meetings, concerts, lectures, etc.
halt B	*v*	to stop.
	n	(c) a stop, pause, or place where one stops.
halter C	*n*	(c) a strap round an animal's neck, to hold it or lead it.
hamburger B	*n*	(c) a roll of bread with a layer of small-cut meat in the middle, eaten hot.
handicap B	*n*	(c) disadvantage, hindrance, something which makes it harder for someone to succeed.
handicraft C	*n*	(c) an art or craft done with the hands.
handle B	*v*	**1.** to hold in the hands. **2.** to deal with something in business. **3.** to control, treat, or manage.
A	*n*	(c) the part of an object by which it is held.
handling C	*n*	**1.** feeling something with the hands. **2.** treatment (of a person, subject or situation).
hang B	*n*	*get the hang of* (informal) to understand, follow.
hang on B	*v*	(informal) to wait.
hangar C	*n*	(c) a large building for housing aircraft.
hank C	*n*	(c) a twisted bundle of string, wool, thread, etc.
harass C	*v*	**1.** to make weak by repeated attacks. **2.** to worry.
hard B	*adj*	similar to the Dutch except when used of sound, it is used of the pronunciation of certain letters: *'g' has a soft sound in 'gentle' but a hard sound in 'get'*.

hardy C — *adj* **1.** (of plants) able to support unfavourable conditions. **2.** (of people) strong; robust. (The word is occasionally used in the French sense of bold or daring, but this now usually sounds old-fashioned.)

hark C — *v* (old-fashioned) to listen; *hark back* to talk of past times.

harm B — *n* (u) hurt, damage, or injury.

harmful C — *adj* hurtful, damaging.

harmony B — *n* although it has the meaning of peacefulness and orderliness, as in Greek, its most common use is in music.

harness C — *n* (u) **1.** the leather and metal frame which goes over a horse's head and neck. **2.** the straps, etc., fastened on a baby to keep it safe.

Harpic C — *n* (u) (trademark) a chemical mixture to clean lavatories.

haste B — *n* (u) quick movement(s), hurry.

hateful C — *adj* disagreeable to experience, detestable.

haven C — *n* (c) **1.** (old-fashioned) a harbour. **2.** a place of quiet and safety.

hazard C — *n* a risk, danger.

health centre C — *n* (c) a building with medical staff where people may go for medical treatment.

hearty C — *adj* (rather old-fashioned) **1.** healthy and strong. **2.** (of a meal) substantial and nourishing. **3.** (chiefly BE) noisy and friendly. **4.** sincere (rare).

heckle C — *v* to shout and interrupt a public speaker, speech, etc.

heckler C — *n* (c) someone who heckles.

hefty C — *adj* **1.** (of a person) big and strong. **2.** (of a thing) heavy and awkward to move.

heinous C — *adj* (of a crime or criminal) atrocious.

helix C — *n* (c) (technical) a spiral.

helm C — *n* (c) the handle in the rudder of a ship.

hen B — *n* (c) the female of any bird, esp. the domestic fowl.

herb C — *n* (c) **1.** a plant used in cooking to add flavour. **2.** a plant grown for medical purposes.

herd C — *n* (c) **1.** a group of animals (esp. cattle). **2.** a large number of people.

heritage C — *n* (u) something which is inherited by each generation, esp. of cultural things.

hide C — *n* (c) a hiding place from which observations are made, e.g. for photographing wildlife.

high collar C — *n* (c) a collar to a shirt or coat, which stands up higher than most collars.

high school B — *n* (c) **1.** (in BE) a grammar school. **2.** (in AE) a school for children over 14 (up to 18 or 19 only).

high street B — *n* (c) the usual name for the main street in a British town or village.

hinder B — *v* to cause delay by obstruction.

Hindi C — *n* (u) a language spoken in Northern India.

Hindu C — *n* a person who follows Hinduism.

hint B — *n* (c) an indirect, subtle suggestion.

hip B — *n* (c) either of the two sides where the legs join the body.

hire C — *n* (u) The use of an object or service for which one pays. (The verb *to hire* is A.)

hiss C — *v* (usually of persons, snakes) to make the sound of the letter 's' esp. as a sign of disapproval or derision.
n (c) this sound.

history A — *n* **1.** (u) the study of past events. **2.** (c) a history book or a study of the events connected with a particular subject, person, nation, etc.

hob C — *n* (c) a metal shelf near a fireplace where things can be kept hot.

hobo C — *n* (c) (AE slang) someone who wanders from place to place and does only casual work.

hold C — *n* **1.** (u) the act of gripping or having in the hands. **2.** (c) a place to hold with hands or feet, esp. in climbing. **3.** (c) the part of a ship where goods are placed. (The verb *to hold* is A.)

hold out B — *v* **1.** to put forward. **2.** to offer. **3.** to endure or last.

hold over C — *v* to postpone.

hold under C — *v* to keep below (i.e. below the surface of a liquid).

hole A — *n* (c) an opening.

homage C — *n* (u) formal signs of deep respect.

home A — *n* (c) the place where one lives.

homely B — *adj* **1.** (BE) pleasant, simple; friendly. **2.** (AE) (of people) unattractive, not good-looking.

honest A — *adj* truthful, not lying.

honesty B — *n* (u) the quality of being honest.

hood C — *n* (c) **1.** a soft head covering for the head, often attached to e.g. a coat. **2.** (BE) a cover which folds over something, esp. a car. **3.** (AE) the cover over a car engine.

hook B — *n* (c) a piece of curved metal to catch or hang things on.

hoop C — *n* (c) a circular band of wood or metal, used esp. to go round a barrel, or as a children's toy.

hoot C — *n* (c) **1.** the sound made by an owl, and by a car or ship's horn. **2.** (informal) something very funny; *it was a hoot.*

hop C — *v* **1.** to jump on one leg only. **2.** to *hop it* (slang) to go away.
n (c) **1.** a jump on one leg. **2.** (informal) a dance. **3.** a plant with green flowers, used to flavour beer.

hope A — *v* to wish (that something will happen).
n such a wish.

horn B — *n* (c) **1.** either of the two pointed growths on the head of cattle, goats, etc. **2.** a musical instrument now usually made of brass.

hose C — *n* **1.** (c) a long flexible pipe for watering a garden or putting out a fire. **2.** (u) stockings, tights.

host B — *n* (c) **1.** a man who entertains others to a meal, etc.; (a woman doing so is a *hostess*). **2.** a very large number.

hotel A — *n* (c) a (large) building, designed for people to eat and sleep in when they travel.

hound C — *n* (c) a dog used for and in hunting.

hour A — *n* the period of time of 60 minutes.
hourglass C — *n* (c) a glass containing sand which takes an hour to pas from top to bottom through a narrow opening.
house B — *v* to provide with shelter or a house.
A — *n* (c) building for people to live in.
householder C — *n* (c) a person in charge of a house, usually the owner.
houseman C — *n* (c) a junior doctor (in Britain, living in a hospital) wh has not yet finished his training.
housemaster C — *n* (c) a teacher who is responsible for a school boardin house.
housework A — *n* (u) work, such as cleaning, to be done in the house.
huddle C — *n* **1.** (c) a group of things or people close together. **2.** *g into a huddle* (informal) to meet together to discus something.
hue C — *n* **1.** (c) a colour. **2.** *to raise a hue and cry* to shout warning that a criminal is being chased, to protes against wrong or injustice.
hug C — *v* to hold tightly, esp. in showing love.
n (c) a loving embrace.
huge A — *adj* enormous, very big.
hulk C — *n* (c) **1.** formerly, an old ship used as a prison, now an ship too old to go to sea. **2.** a big clumsy person.
hulking C — *adj* big, clumsy, and awkward.
human A — *adj, n* (c) (of) man (in contrast to animal).
humour C — *n* (u) **1.** the ability to amuse. **2.** the ability to be amuse (the French use is very formal and old fashioned).
humane C — *adj* being kind-hearted, and having the qualities of a civilise person.
hurl C — *v* to throw wildly and/or violently.
hurt A — *v* to give pain, injure, distress.
adj **1.** upset; saddened. **2.** (bodily) injured.
n (u) harm.
hush B — *n* (c) silence.
C — *v* (in imperative) be quiet: *hush!*
hustler C — *n* (c) **1.** (BE) an active person who does things quickly **2.** (AE slang) a prostitute.
hut B — *n* (c) a small simple building (esp. one made of wood).
hymn B — *n* (c) a song, consisting of several verses, sung usually by th church congregation.
hypothesis C — *n* (c) an idea put forward as a possible explanation fo something, but which has not yet been proved. (Much les common in English than other languages.)

cing C — *n* 1. (u) the accumulation of ice, esp. on the wings of an aircraft. 2. the hard sugar covering on a cake.

conography C — *n* (u) the study of the development of the themes and symbols used by artists and writers.

diom A/C — *n* (c) 1. A a phrase whose meaning cannot be deduced from the separate words in it. 2. C (old-fashioned) a language.

diosyncrasy C — *n* (c) a way of behaving or form of expression unique to an individual or a group.

diotic C — *adj* stupid, foolish.

dle B/C — *adj* 1. B not working, unemployed, lazy. 2. C meaningless, worthless.

gnore B — *v* to pay no attention to, to refuse to observe.

llumined C — *adj* (poetic) made bright.

llusion C — *n* (c) false belief. (Spanish speakers should note that *illusion* is not a verb.)

llustrate A — *v* 1. to make pictures or drawings for books, newspapers, etc. 2. to give examples to help people to understand something.

llustrated C — *past participle* 1. shown in the picture. 2. having pictures.

llustration B — *n* (c) 1. a picture; photograph. 2. an example.

mage B — *n* (c) 1. a picture in one's mind. 2. the picture formed by a mirror or a lens. 3. a figure or statue worshipped as a god. 4. the reputation or character of a person or thing as held by the public. 5. (informal) someone who looks just like someone else.

mago C — *n* (c) (technical) the final form of a moth or butterfly when it has emerged from its chrysalis.

nbecile C — *n* (c) a very stupid person; (the English is stronger than the Latin use, and less frequently heard).

nbibe C — *v* 1. (formal) to absorb knowledge, ideas, etc. 2. to drink, esp. alcohol.

nmediate B/C — *adj* 1. C without anything coming between (it is more used of people than things). 2. B occurring at once.

nminent C — *adj* expected at any moment.

nmortal C — *n* (c; usually plural) 1. the gods of ancient Greece and Rome. 2. someone who will never be forgotten, e.g. a great writer.

npasse C — *n* (c) a situation with no solution; (very occasionally used of a street with no way out, but this use seems to be declining).

nperative C — *n* (c) the verb form giving orders.

nperfect C — *adj* not perfect, having a fault in its manufacture.

npetus C — *n* 1. (u) the force by which a moving object continues to move. 2. in human contexts, a driving impulse or force.

impinge C *v* to have an effect or impact on.

implicit C *adj* **1.** implied but not expressed. **2.** absolute; withou doubts.

import A *v* to buy from another country.
n (c) an article brought into a country from abroad.

important A *adj* **1.** having great value. **2.** worthy of time and attention **3.** having influence and authority.

impose C *v* **1.** to force something on someone. **2.** to force onesel onto the company of others. **3.** to take advantage o

imposition C *n* (c) **1.** an action taking advantage of someone. **2** (becoming uncommon) a school punishment.

impostor C *n* (c) someone who tries to make people believe he i someone else.

impotent C *adj* **1.** (of a man) unable to perform sexual intercourse **2.** unable to take action.

impregnable C *adj* which cannot be conquered in attacks.

impressario C *n* (c) someone who presents or arranges entertainment i theatres, concert halls, etc; (the word is not used outsid this context).

impress B *n* (c) a mark or imprint made by putting pressure on some thing.

impression C *n* *make an impression* to have a strong or favourabl effect on.

improper C *adj* **1.** suggesting indecency. **2.** (occasional) not suitable **3.** (occasional) incorrect, in matters of language.

impropriety C *n* the state of being improper, sense **1**, or an imprope action.

inadequate B *adj* **1.** insufficient, not enough. **2.** incapable of lookin after him/herself socially.

inadmissible C *adj* which is not to be considered or allowed.

incarnate C *adj* (placed after the noun) in the form of a body, not a spiri

incendiary C *n* (c) short for an *incendiary bomb*, a bomb which causes fire.

incensed C *past participle* made furiously angry.

incessantly C *adv* continually; without stopping.

incident B *n* (c) **1.** a small event, esp. as part of a narrative. **2.** more violent happening which may get into the news.

incitement C *n* (c) a stimulus or encouragement to others to do some thing (not usually positive or good).

inclination C *n* **1.** a liking, wish. **2.** a tendency (there are also som technical uses).

incline B *v* **1.** to lean at an angle. **2.** to be disposed (to), have tendency (to).

inconsequent C *adj* not logically following what was said before, irrelevant

inconsistent C *adj* not consistent, esp. in argument; contradictory.

incontinent C *adj* **1.** unable to control the bladder. **2.** (now rare) lackin self-control.

inconvenience C *n* something which gives trouble and/or does not suit one' needs.

indelicate C *adj* without refinement or modesty.

index B *n* (c) **1.** the alphabetical list at the end of a book giving page references for all the subjects mentioned in it. **2.** a similar list for reference, e.g. in a library or an office. **3.** a *cost of living index* an indicator of the rate of inflation. **4.** the *index finger* the finger next to the thumb.

indicate B *v* to show by clear signs.

indication B *n* (c) a sign.

indicative C *n* the usual verb form, contrasted with the subjunctive, (as a noun, only used in grammar).

indicator C *n* (c) **1.** a hand, needle, or pointer on the dial of a machine. **2.** a flashing light on a vehicle showing the driver's intention to go left or right. **3.** (less common) something which indicates.

indifferently B *adv* **1.** in a mediocre way, poorly. **2.** without being interested.

indignant B *adj* showing or feeling anger.

indignity C *n* something causing humiliation and loss of dignity, or the state of feeling this.

industrial action B *n* (u) action, such as a strike or go-slow, taken by employees as a protest against working conditions, pay, etc.

inexcusable C *adj* that which cannot be forgiven or pardoned.

infatuation C *n* **1.** a strong unreasonable (and esp. not lasting) love for someone. **2.** (c) the person so loved.

infect C *v* to fill with germs; to pass a disease to someone else. (*Infect* is not an adjective in English.)

inferior B *adj* lower in position or quality.

infirm C *adj* physically and/or mentally feeble.

inflammable C *adj* There has been confusion over this word because BE and AE had opposite meanings; it is better to avoid it by using the newer recommended forms which are *flammable* burnable; *non-flammable* non-burnable. (In older use, *inflammable* (BE) burnable; (AE) non-burnable.)

influenced B *past participle* affected; swayed.

influenza C *n* (u) an illness, like a very serious cold; (often shortened to *flu*).

inform B *v* to give information to; tell.

informal B *adj* casual, relaxed, not formal, not following any special rules.

information A *n* (u) facts and knowledge passed on or made available to others; (not concerned with current affairs like the *news*).

infusion C *n* (c) **1.** a drink made by putting something into hot water, usually for medical purposes. **2.** (figuratively) a contribution.

ingenious B *adj* **1.** (of a person) clever, full of new ideas. **2.** (of things) cleverly made.

ingenuity C *n* (u) the quality of being ingenious or skilful.

inhabited B *past participle* lived in, occupied; (the *in-* is prepositional; the negative is *uninhabited*, i.e. empty, deserted, or abandoned).

inhale C — *v* to breathe in.

initiation C — *n* (c) an introduction ceremony, esp. in religious or anthropological contexts.

injure B — *v* to hurt (usually physically, but occasionally used of someone's feelings).

injurious C — *adj* harmful, hurtful.

injury B/C — *n* **1.** (c) B a physical hurt; a place damaged and giving pain. **2.** *add insult to injury* C to cause further offence after one has already caused harm in another way.

inn C — *n* (c) usually, an old public house in a village or the country.

innings C — *n* (c; no change in plural) **1.** (cricket) the turn of a player or team at batting. **2.** (figurative) a time when someone is active; period in office or in power.

insane C — *adj* mad, mentally ill.

inscribe C — *v* to write (one's name), usually with a message, e.g. in a book given as a present.

inscription C — *n* (c) the words written on a monument or a coin or in a book given to someone.

insensate C — *adj* having no feelings, senseless.

inset C — *v* to put something into a larger whole, esp. used in printing.
n (c) (*insert* is more usual) something put into a page in this way.

insight C — *n* the understanding of the real nature of something, to see the real significance.

inspiration B — *n* **1.** (u) the act of inspiring. **2.** (c) a clever idea which suddenly comes to one. **3.** (c) something which inspires.

inspire B — *v* to give someone better feelings; move someone to do something, esp. something good.

instance A — *n* (c) an example, case.

instant B — *adj* immediate, which happens straight after something else.

instantly B — *adv* immediately.

institute B — *n* (c) an organisation or society formed for a specific purpose; (not necessarily educational, though often for research).

instructor C — *n* (c) someone who teaches skills but usually not in a school.

intact C — *adj* remaining unbroken/unspoilt.

insulate — *v* See **isolate**.

intend A — *v* **1.** to plan, propose. **2.** (passive) to be meant for.

intensive B — *adj* concentrated and giving much attention in a short period (*Intense* is especially used of strong feelings or sensations.)

interested A — *adj* having a desire for knowledge, fascinated. (It is not often used in the sense of biased, self-seeking.)

interesting A — *adj* stimulating, fascinating.

interloper C — *n* (c) someone in a place where (s)he has no right to be.

intern C — *v* to restrict someone's movement (usually in prison) for political reasons or in wartime.

interpret B/C — *v* **1.** B to translate orally. **2.** C to perform as in **2** opposite

interpretation C — *n* (c) **1.** the meaning of something put into simple language; (but not using a different language). **2.** a performance; rendering (in acting or music).

nterpreter B *n* (c) someone who can translate orally. (*Translating* usually refers to writing not speaking.)

nterrogation C *n* (c) a long examination by questioning, esp. by the police.

nterrupter C *n* (c) someone who interrupts a conversation, etc., or something that interrupts mechanically; (but not used for an ordinary electric switch).

ntervene B *v* **1.** to come between. **2.** to interfere so as to change a result, esp. in a dispute.

ntervention C *n* (the act of) coming between two sides of a dispute, usually to try to stop them fighting.

ntimate B *adj* **1.** private, usually not revealed to people uninvolved. **2.** having sexual relations with.

ntoned C *past participle* sung on a single note, esp. of prayers by a priest.

ntoxicating C *adj* **1.** causing drunkenness. **2.** exciting, stimulating.

ntoxication C *n* the state of being drunk.

nvent A *v* to create something which has not existed before.

nventory C *n* (c) a list of all the goods in a house or a storehouse.

nversion C *n* (the act of) putting something upside down, back to front, or in its opposite order.

nvest B *v* usually, to use money in hopes of making a profit.

nvestigation B *n* (c) an enquiry or search, esp. by the police or other authorities.

nvestment B *n* (the act of putting) money into something.

nvolved A *adj* **1.** concerned, connected. **2.** complicated.

rritate B *v* **1.** to make annoyed, cross, or angry. **2.** to cause pain or discomfort.

sland A *n* (c) a piece of land surrounded by water; (note that *-s-* is not pronounced here, nor in the older form *isle*).

solate B *v* to place apart or at a distance from other things. (*Insulate* is to cover something with materials which prevent the loss of heat, the passage of sound, or electricity; *insolation* C is the amount of sunshine recorded.)
n (u) *isolation* the act or instance of isolating.

sotherm C *n* (c) a line on a map joining places with the same temperature.

ssue B *n* (c) **1.** the sending out; publication. **2.** an important question for discussion.

alian B *n* **1.** the Italian language. **2.** (c) someone from Italy.

em B *n* (c) anything appearing in a list.

j

jabber C *v* to talk very fast and not clearly.

jack C *n* (c) **1.** a machine for lifting up one side of a vehicle, es to change a wheel. **2.** a playing card in rank between ten and a queen.

jacket A *n* (c) **1.** a short coat of any type, with sleeves. **2.** th skin of a potato.

jail B *n* (c) a prison; (also written *gaol*).

jargon C *n* (u) the specialised language concerned with a particula subject or profession.

jealousy B *n* (usually u) the feeling of resentment towards someon who has something one wants oneself.

jejune C *adj* **1.** (esp. of writings) insipid, uninteresting. **2.** (AE childish.

jelly C *n* **1.** a sweet made with gelatine, sugar, and fruit juic which shakes when moved. **2.** a jam of similar con sistency. **3.** any substance similar in texture to these.

jest C *n* something that makes people laugh; *in jest* not seriousl

Jew A *n* (c) someone of the Jewish faith or race.

joint A *n* (c) **1.** a device where two things join, esp. bones. **2.** large piece of meat for roasting. **3.** (slang) a plac where people go to amuse themselves.

jolly B *adj* happy, cheerful.
adv (BE only) very.

journal B *n* (c) a periodical (e.g. monthly) dealing with a serious sub ject, usually professional.

journey A *n* (c) the act of moving from one place to another.

joy B *n* **1.** (usually u) happiness. **2.** (c) something giving hap piness.

jubilation C *n* (u) great happiness and excitement.

jubilee C *n* (c) (the celebrations to mark) an anniversary of an even

jug C *n* (c) a pot with a handle for holding liquids.

jumper C *n* (c) **1.** an athlete or horse specialising in jumpin **2.** (BE) a garment put on over the head, for warmt usually made of wool.

junkman C *n* (c) (chiefly AE) someone who travels round collecting ol articles (i.e. junk) which he hopes to sell; (a *rag-and-bon man* in BE).

junta C *n* (c) a government (usually military) which has come int power in a revolution.

Jura C *n* *the Jura* the hills in East France and North and We Switzerland.

jurist C *n* (c) someone who is an authority on the law (esp. civ law) but the name denotes no specific status.

just B *adj* having justice; fair, merited. (The adverbial uses of *ju* are A and very complex.)

justly C *adv* with justice and fairness.

K

kaffir C *n* (c) a black African; (used in Southern Africa as a term of abuse).

kayak C *n* (c) a small narrow covered boat, originally those used by Eskimos.

keel C *n* (c) the bar along the middle and bottom of a boat, to which its sides are fixed.

keen A *adj* **1.** enthusastic, eager; fond (of), interested. **2.** sharp, sensitive.

kerb C *n* (c) the line of raised stones along the edge of the pavement by the road.

kernel C *n* (c) **1.** the inside part of a nut, which can be eaten. **2.** (very occasional) the essence (of a question, problem, etc.); (also called the *core*).

kettle B *n* (c) a container with a lid, for boiling water, with a handle at the top and a spout.

kick A *v* to hit with the foot.
n (c) **1.** such a movement. **2.** (informal) strength, stimulant effect. **3.** (plural) excitement.

kicker C *n* (c) a person or animal that kicks, esp. a horse.

kid B *n* (c) **1.** a young goat. **2.** (BE slang, AE informal) a child, young person.

kill A *v* to cause the death of.

killer C *n* (c) **1.** something which kills, usually a disease. **2.** someone who kills; murderer.

kind A *n* (c) a sort, type.

kindly C *adj* friendly, pleasant.

kinky C *adj* **1.** not straight, twisted. **2.** (u) (informal) perverted, having a strange way of behaving or character.

kip C *n* (c) (BE informal) **1.** a sleep. **2.** a place to sleep.

kipper C *n* (c) a herring that has been salted and smoked.

kiss A *n* (c) a touch or caress made with the lips.

kit C *n* (c) all the equipment needed for an activity, job, or sport.

kitchen A *n* (c) the room in a house where food is prepared and cooked.

knack C *n* (c; only singular) **1.** a skill. **2.** habitual action.

knickers C *n* (c; plural only) (old style) woman's underpants.

knight C *n* (c) (history) a noble soldier. **2.** (BE) a man given the rank as an honour, adding the title *Sir* before his name. **3.** (chess) the piece with a horse's head.

knob C *n* (c) a round handle.

knock B *n* (c) **1.** a hit on something (hard, making a sharp sound) esp. on a door. **2.** (informal) a piece of bad luck.

knoll C *n* (c) a small round hill.

knot B *n* (c) **1.** parts of string, rope, etc., tied together to make a fastening. **2.** a hard piece in wood, where a branch has grown. **3.** a unit of speed used by ships and aircraf about 1853 metres per hour.

knuckle C *n* (c) the outer joints of the hand at the base of the finger

l

label B *n* (c) a piece of material (e.g. paper or card) attached to a article to show where it comes from, where it should go what it is, etc.

laborious C *adj* (used only of things) requiring hard work and effort.

labour B *v* **1.** to work with difficulty; try hard. **2.** to work out i too much detail. **3.** to move slowly.

n (u) **1.** work. **2.** work force. **3.** the act of givin birth.

Labour Party B *n* political party representing the interests esp. of workers

labourer B *n* (c) a man whose work needs strength rather than skill.

lack B *n* the absence of something; deficiency.

lacquer C *n* (u) a kind of varnish used to give a hard shining surface

lad C *n* (c) a young man (colloq. *a bit of a lad* is a rather wild one

ladder B *n* (c) **1.** two pieces of wood or metal with cross pieces (usually portable), used for climbing against a wall, tree etc. **2.** a fault in a stocking, looking like a ladder.

lager C *n* a sort of light beer.

lagoon C *n* (c) a body of water separated from the open sea by bank of sand or rock.

lamb B *n* **1.** (c) a young sheep. **2.** (u) meat from young sheep.

lame C *adj* **1.** unable to walk evenly. **2.** (of story, excuse) un convincing.

lament C *v* to feel or express great sadness for.

lamp A *n* (c) any apparatus for giving light.

lance C *v* to cut into the flesh with a medical knife.

n (c) **1.** a long spear used formerly by soldiers on horse back. **2.** a long spear used formerly for catching fish

land A *n* (u) **1.** the surface of the earth on which we live. **2** ground owned as property. **3.** (old-fashioned) nation country.

landsman C *n* (c) a man who is not a sailor.

lane B *n* (c) **1.** a simple road, often rough and in the country **2.** a route used regularly by ships or aircraft. **3.** one of the parallel parts of a wide road for a single line o traffic.

lap C *v* **1.** to overtake or lead in a race by one or more circuits **2.** *lap up* (informal) **a.** to drink or eat. **b.** to accep uncritically.

n (c) the circuit of a racetrack.

ard C *n* (u) purified pig fat, used in cooking.

arge A *adj* of great size; (a less emotive word than *big*, but very close in meaning).

arva C *n* (c) the stage in the life of an insect, after leaving its egg.

ast A *pronoun* **1.** the final thing or person in a series; (this can be a singular or plural with no *-s*.) **2.** the one before the present. (Notice these are not nouns but may well sound like them to North Europeans.)

C *n* (c) the shoe-shaped block used by a shoemaker or shoe repairer.

atin B *n* **1.** the language of ancient Rome. **2.** someone who speaks a language descended from Latin.

attice C *n* (c) **1.** a frame for plants to climb; (more commonly called a *trellis*). **2.** the diamond-shaped strengthening framework in constructions.

auds C *n* the traditional morning prayer of the Western Church.

avatory A *n* (c) the W.C. or the room containing it.

avender C *n* (u) a stiff plant with strongly aromatic violet flowers.

ay out B *v* **1.** to arrange or spread out. **2.** to spend (money), esp. in an extravagant way.

earn A *v* to absorb knowledge.

earner C *n* (c) someone who is learning, esp. to drive a car; (more correctly called a *learner driver*).

ease C *v* to allow someone to make use of a house or land for a given period, by legal agreement.
n (c) the duration of such an agreement.

eather jacket C *n* (c) **1.** a jacket made of leather. **2.** a type of large beetle.

ecture B *n* (c) **1.** a formal talk given to a group of people, esp. as a method of teaching in universities. **2.** a long spoken warning.

eek C *n* (c) a vegetable of the onion family.

eer C *v* to give a disagreeable, impolite or sly look, often suggesting sexual desire.
n (c) a look of this kind.

eg A *n* (c) **1.** the limb of the body used for walking. **2.** a section or part of a course, race, or journey.

egal B *adj* **1.** conforming to the law. **2.** connected with the law.

egend C *n* (c) **1.** a story from the past. **2.** (old-fashioned) an inscription on a map or coin.

egs A *n* the plural of *leg*.

emon B *n* (c) a small yellow citrus fruit with sour juice.

.ent B *n* the 40 days before Easter.

entil C *n* (c) the small round seed of a plant used for food.

et up C *v* to stop gradually.

etter A *n* (c) **1.** a written message usually sent in an envelope. **2.** any of the signs of the alphabet.

evee C *n* (c) **1.** (chiefly AE) a high bank along a river to prevent flooding. **2.** (old-fashioned) a morning reception with a noble person.

lever C *v* to move or lift something heavy with a bar, turning on fulcrum.
n (c) a bar used as a tool to move or lift something heavy i this way.

liaison B *n* **1.** (the action of) working with someone else to ex change ideas, esp. used of different sections of an arm working together. **2.** (becoming old-fashioned) an ill cit love affair.

libel B *v* to publish something false or unfair which damag someone's reputation.
n (mostly u) something printed containing such materia

liberation C *n* the setting free, esp. from enemy occupation.

libertine C *n* (c) someone who leads a sexually immoral life.

library A *n* (c) a building or room where books are kept for readin or reference.

libretto C *n* (c) the text of an opera or oratorio.

licence B *n* (AE spelling: *license*) **1.** (c) an official document givin permission to marry, to drive, to own a television, et **2.** (u) the wrong use of freedom. *Licensed* (or *licencec* is the past participle meaning authorised.

lid B *n* (c) the movable cover for a box, suitcase, saucepan, et

lieder C *n* (c; plural) in English used only of the serious Germa songs mainly of the 19th and early 20th century.

life A *n* translates the Dutch *(het) leven* in most contexts.

lift A *v* to raise something to a higher level; (the Swedish ha come from the phrase *to give/offer a hitchhiker a lift*).

light article C *n* (c) *light* here means entertaining to read.

like A *v* to find enjoyable or pleasant.

lime C *n* (c) **1.** a yellow-green citrus fruit, smaller than a lemor **2.** a tree with yellow sweet-smelling flowers, not produc ing the fruit in **1** above. **3.** the white material used i cement.

limp B *v* to walk unevenly because of pain or injury.
n (c) a walk like this.
adj not stiff, without strength.

line A *n* (c) basically the German *Leine* though with man meanings and idioms.

ling C *n* (u) heather.

lingerie C *n* (u) women's underwear; (usually used only to name th department selling women's underwear in a large store)

links C *n* (no change in plural) **1.** the sand hills by the sea **2.** a golf course.

lino C *n* short for *linoleum*, a type of floor covering.

lint C *n* (u) soft linen material, used for covering cuts an wounds.

liquidation C *n* (c) **1.** the closing down of an unsuccessful business an payment of its debts by selling all its goods. **2.** killing

lira B *n* (c) the unit of money in Turkey and Italy.

list A *v* to write down a number of things in a column.
n (c) a number of items written in this way.

sten A — *v* to pay attention by hearing.

hograph C — *n* (c) a picture made by lithography.

igate C — *v* to bring (an action or claim) to a law court.

vid C — *adj* extremely angry. (The original meaning was pale blue-grey, but this is falling into disuse.)

ving B — *n* **1.** (c) the means by which one lives. **2.** the manner in which one leads one's life. (The *cost of living* is the cost of providing for such basic needs as food, clothing, shelter, and fuel.)

ad B — *n* (c) **1.** something which must be carried, esp. if heavy. **2.** (figuratively) worries. **3.** (plural; informal) lots.

an B — *n* (c) **1.** something lent, esp. money. **2.** the act of lending.

cal A — *n* (c) (informal) short for **1.** a local newspaper. **2.** a local pub(lic house). **3.** a local (village) inhabitant; (the plural would most commonly refer to meaning **3**).

calise C — *v* to confine to a small area.

cality C — *n* (c) a place; area.

cation C — *n* (c) **1.** a place; locality. **2.** a place where a film is made, away from a studio.

ch C — *n* (c) a lake or sea inlet in Scotland.

ck A — *v* **1.** to close or fasten with a key. **2.** *lock up* **a.** to make safe by locking. **b.** to put into prison.
n (c) **1.** a mechanism used for fastening in this way. **2.** a system of gates in a canal or river where there is a change in the level of water.

cket C — *n* (c) a small container hung round the neck, holding a picture or a small piece of someone's hair, etc.

co C — *n* (c) (informal) short for a (railway) *locomotive.*

comotive B — *n* (c) a railway engine; (the word only has this meaning in English).

cum C — *n* (c) a priest or a doctor who carries on the duties of another who is away on holiday or ill, etc.

cust C — *n* (c) **1.** any of various African and Asian species of winged insects, which do great damage to plants. **2.** a kind of tree.

dge C — *n* (c) **1.** a small house for a gatekeeper at the entrance to the grounds of a large house. **2.** a meeting place for Freemasons. **3.** a house used for the hunting season only. **4.** one or more rooms used as a porter's office at the entrance to an institution.

dger C — *n* (c) someone paying for a room or rooms in a private house.

ft C — *n* (c) an attic, or room under the roof, used esp. for storage.

gical C — *adj* according to the rules of logic.

ng A — *adj* having a large measurement from one end to another in space or time.

ngueur C — *n* (c) (writing) a very slow-moving passage of a text.

ok A — *v* **1.** to use one's eyes (and try to see). **2.** *look after* to take care of.

loom C — *n* (c) a machine for weaving cloth.

loop C — *v* to produce a figure (in e.g. string) by doubling round ar crossing over.
n (c) such a figure; (to *loop the loop* is said of an aircra flying up, over, and down again).

loose C — *v* to make free; (loosen is B); *loosen up* to exercise one muscles, e.g. before a race.

lore C — *n* (u) traditional knowledge.

lorgnette C — *n* (c) a pair of glasses with a long handle to hold up to th eyes.

lose A — *v* **1.** to have (something) no longer, to be deprived o **2.** not to win. (There are many other uses and idioms

lot A — *n* of many uses, note **1.** the whole quantity. **2.** (c) great quantity. **3.** (informal) a great deal; muc (There are a number of A uses; the meaning of 'fate' now rather formal.)

lotion C — *n* (c) a liquid mixture used on the skin for medical c cosmetic purposes.

lotto C — *n* a kind of game, now played publicly as *bingo*.

lovely A — *adj* charming, pleasing, agreeable.

low C — *n* (c) **1.** (meteorology) an area of low pressure. **2.** period of feeling depressed. **3.** a position, degre stage, etc., which is low.

loyal C — *adj* faithful to one's friends, country, etc.

loyalty C — *n* the quality of being faithful to someone or something.

luck A — *n* (u) fortune; success.

lucky A — *adj* having good fortune.

lump B/C — *n* (c) **1.** B a mass with no specific shape. **2.** B a swelling **3.** (informal) C a dull person.

lunatic C — *n* (c) a mad, crazy, and mentally abnormal person.
adj **1.** mad, insane. **2.** eccentric, foolish.

lunch A — *n* (c) a meal eaten in the middle of the day; (called mor formally *luncheon*).

lure C — *n* (c) something which attracts or tempts.

lurid C — *adj* **1.** intensely coloured. **2.** shocking and unpleasant.

lust C — *n* strong desire, esp. applied to sex.

lustre C — *n* (u) **1.** the quality of a bright polished surface, e.g. pearl. **2.** distinction.

lusty C — *adj* **1.** full of sexual desire. **2.** cheerful, strong (similar t **hearty** definitions **1** and **3**).

lute C — *n* (c) a stringed instrument, esp. associated with Renaissance music.

luxurious B — *adj* providing luxury.

luxury A — *n* **1.** (u) the condition of having unnecessary or costl things that give pleasure and comfort. **2.** (c) ar unessential thing giving enjoyment.

lyrical C — *adj* expressing a fullness of emotion.

m

macabre C *adj* causing fear, usually because of reference to death; (strictly an adjective but also used in such phrases as *Tales of the Macabre*).

machine A *n* (c) a man-made apparatus, using power to do work. (There are various C uses.)

Madeira C *n* (u) wine produced in the island of Madeira.

maestro C *n* (c) the conductor of an orchestra.

magazine A/C *n* (c) **1.** A a periodical of general interest; (in contrast to a *journal*). **2.** C a building where explosives are kept. **3.** C the part of a gun holding bullets before being fired.

maggot C *n* (c) a small worm-like creature.

magistrate C *n* (c) the equivalent of a judge in the lowest court of law (e.g. a police court).

mains current C *n* (u) **1.** electricity supplied from a power station into a building. **2.** its rate of flow in amperes.

major A *v* (AE) to graduate (in college in a particular subject).
A/C *n* (c) **1.** A an officer of middle rank in the British Army or the U.S. Air Force. **2.** C someone of 18 or over who is legally a grown-up. **3.** (AE only) A a student's main subject of study in university.
A *adj* important, significant.

make A *n* (c) the (commercial) name of the manufacturer.

make out A *v* to understand.

make up A *v* of many uses, note **1.** to devise or construct. **2.** to put cosmetics on. **3.** *make up one's mind* to decide.

maker B *n* (c) any manufacturer.

malice C *n* (u) a feeling that you want to hurt someone.

malicious C *adj* full of ill-will.

mammy C *n* (only in AE or Irish) mother, mummy.

Man B *n* (usually with a capital but no article) the human race or representative(s) of it.

manage A *v* **1.** to be able to do something despite difficulties. **2.** to direct and organise. **3.** to live with little money; (close to the French usage).

management B *n* **1.** (u) the control and directing of a firm. **2.** (c) the directing group of a firm; the managers collectively; (usually used with a plural verb).

manager A *n* (c) **1.** a person who directs or controls an organisation, shop, etc. **2.** a person who organises the business affairs of an actor or entertainer. **3.** a person who directs the training of a sports team or player.

mangle C *n* (c) the equipment used (formerly) for squeezing the water out of washed clothes between two rollers.

mania C *n* (c) an obsession; (a far stronger word in English than in the Latin languages, often suggesting madness).

maniac C *n* (c) **1.** someone violent to others because of men illness. **2.** (informal) wild person.

manifestation C *n* (c) **1.** a sign, indication, or display. **2.** a ghost.

manoeuvres C *n* **1.** (c; sometimes singular) military exercises. **2.** mov or plans performed to trick someone or to get out of awkward situation.

mansard C *n* (c) a roof that has two slopes on each side, the lower pa being steeper than the upper.

mansion C *n* (c) a very large house.

mantle C *n* (c) **1.** a type of loose cloak. **2.** (rather old-fashione a shelf above a fireplace. **3.** (poetic) a covering. **4.** t part of a gas lamp which gives out a bright light.

manufacture C *n* (u) **1.** the act of producing goods, esp. by machiner **2.** the method(s) used in this. (The verb is A.)

manufacturer C *n* (c) a person or firm that produces goods by machiner

map A *n* (c) a representation of part of the earth's surface, as se from above, and in scale.

march B *v* to walk in step (sometimes to music) as of a group soldiers.

n (c) **1.** the action of walking like this. **2.** music f marching. **3.** *March* the third month of the year.

mare C *n* (c) a female horse.

margin C *n* (c) **1.** the empty space round the writing or printi on a page. **2.** the difference between the buying ar selling price in business. **3.** the amount over what needed. **4.** the outer part of something.

marginal C *n* (c) short for a *marginal seat* a constituency where th winning candidate only has a small majority of votes.

marina C *n* (c) a harbour for holiday boats.

marine C *n* (c) **1.** a soldier serving on a naval ship. **2.** th *merchant marine* a country's fleet of ships (non-military

mark A *v* **1.** to make a sign. **2.** to evaluate and correct.

n (c) there are many meanings, esp. note **1.** a stain o spot. **2.** a number, letter, or percentage as a grade i academic work. **3.** a sign or indication. **4.** a type o brand. **5.** a desired or required standard.

marmalade B *n* (u) a preserve (similar to jam) made of any citrus frui usually bitter oranges.

Marmite C *n* (u) (trademark) a well-known food produced from yeas

marmoset A *n* (c) any of various types of hairy large-eyed America monkeys.

marmot C *n* (c) a small European mammal, related to the squirrel.

maroon C *adj, n* a deep red colour like Burgundy wine, definitely no the orange-brown colour suggested in most language

v to isolate or abandon.

marquess (quis) C *n* (c) a nobleman of high rank.

marsh C *n* (c) an area of nearly flooded ground, usually uncultivate

martinet C *n* (c) someone who demands total obedience.

mascara C *n* (u) eye cosmetic for thickening the eyelashes.

mash C *v* to crush (esp. potatoes) to a soft mass.

ıask C *n* (c) **1.** a covering for the face to make it difficult or impossible to identify the wearer. **2.** special breathing equipment to put over the nose and mouth.

ıass A *v* to crowd together in large numbers.
n (c) **1.** a large amount of matter, things, or people. **2.** the amount of matter in a body, measured by how much power is used in changing its movement. **3.** *Mass* the communion service in Catholic and Orthodox Churches, also the music written for this; *High Mass* is the main such service held in a church.

ıassive C *adj* exceptionally large, enormous.

ıasticate A *v* to chew or bite up food.

ıat C *n* (c) **1.** a strong protective piece of material on the floor. **2.** a tablemat used to protect a wooden table from hot plates.

ıat(t) C *adj* not bright or shining.

ıatador C *n* (c) the bullfighter who is appointed to kill the bull.

ıatch A *n* (c) a lot of meanings, note **1.** a game or sports competition. **2.** a thin strip of wood with a tip that is set alight when struck. **3.** a person who provides strong competition.

ıaterial A/C *n* **1.** A woven cloth for making clothes, etc. **2.** A something used for making other things. **3.** *raw materials* the natural substances things can be made from. **3.** C knowledge, information.

ıaterialise C *v* to become real.

ıaterialist C *n* (c) **1.** someone who believes in no form of spiritual life. **2.** someone who wants a lot of possessions.

ıaternity C *n* (u) motherhood, the process of becoming a mother.

ıatinée C *n* (c) only used in the theatrical meaning of an afternoon performance.

ıatriculate C *v* to be successful in an exam qualifying for university entrance.

ıatrimony C *n* (u) the state of marriage or of being married.

ıatter A *n* many meanings similar in use to the Latin languages but not used of subjects studied in education; basically matter is material substance.

ıattress C *n* (c) the part of a bed filled with rubber, springs, hair, etc., on which people sleep.

ıaturity C *n* (u) the quality of being mature.

ıeagre C *adj* (of quantities) insufficient or very small.

ıean A *v* **1.** to express; try to convey or say. **2.** to propose, intend. **3.** to have as a result. **4.** (passive only; BE) to be supposed to.

neaning A *n* (c) **1.** the significance or sense. **2.** the value, purpose.

neat A *n* (mainly u) the flesh of dead animals, eaten as food.

nechanic C *n* (c) someone who specialises in repairing engines and/or machinery.

ıedicine A *n* **1.** a substance swallowed to prevent, alleviate, or cure a disease. **2.** (u) the science of treating ill-health.

Medusa C — *n* one of the Gorgons in Greek mythology (used of jellyfish only in scientific usage).

meet A — *v* to come together, often by prior arrangement.

meeting A — *n* (c) people coming together usually for some purpos or occasionally by accident.

melissa C — *n* an aromatic plant known as lemon balm.

melon C — *n* (c) a type of fruit with a hard thick skin and soft water flesh.

memoir C — *n* (c; usually plural) an autobiography. (In the singular may be biographical, but this is much less common.)

menu B — *n* (c) the list of all the food and drink offered in a restauran showing the prices.

mercy C — *n* **1.** (u) a willingness to forgive. **2.** (c) something fortun ate.

mere C — *n* (c) a (small) lake.

mess B — *n* (c) **1.** a state of disorder. **2.** trouble. **3.** the buildin where soldiers, sailors, or airmen eat.

metaphor C — *n* (c) the non-literal use of a word.

metaphrasis C — *n* (u) the putting of poetry into prose.

meter B — *n* (c) a machine for measuring (units of time, electricit etc.).

metre B — *n* (c) a unit of length.

metropolis C — *n* (c) the largest city in a country, usually the capital.

midday B — *n* twelve o'clock; noon.

middle A — *n* (usually only singular) the centre (but less precise).

mid-week C — *n* usually Tuesday, Wednesday and/or Thursday.

middle-aged B — *adj* (of people) from about 45 to 60 years of age.

millipede C — *n* (c) a kind of small creature with a worm-like bod having up to 200 pairs of legs.

mime C — *v* to act with movements but no speech.
n the practice of doing this.

mimic C — *n* (c) someone who copies the behaviour and speech c another person, to make others laugh.

mine B/C — *n* (c) **1.** B an excavation in the ground to obtain minerals **2.** C a kind of bomb in the ground, which will explod when walked on or driven over. **3.** C a kind of bom at sea, which will explode when a ship hits it or passe near it. **4.** C a valuable source (esp. of information)

mint B — *n* **1.** the plant in the family mentha. **2.** the place wher coins are made by government authority; (a coin i perfect when it leaves the Mint hence the term *mir condition*).

minute B — *v* to write the minutes (**2** below) of a meeting.
n (c) **1.** the period of time of 60 seconds. **2.** a para graph written as a record of a decision made at a forma meeting, kept in a *minutes book*.

minutely C — *adv* **1.** by a very small amount. **2.** in great detail. (Thi comes from an adjective *minute*.)

mire C — *n* (old-fashioned) deep mud, marsh.

miscreant C — *n* (c) (now old-fashioned) a rogue, someone who behave in an evil way.

niser C — *n* (c) someone who tries to keep all his money and possessions.

niserable B — *adj* a word covering quite a number of meanings, though it most commonly means 'unhappy'; (occasionally it covers some of the Continental meanings: wretched, vile, unfortunate, sordid, rotten).

nisericord C — *n* (c) a kind of elaborately shaped seat for a priest to lean back on in a long service.

niss A — *v* **1.** to be sad because of the absence of (someone). **2.** to fail to catch, meet, find, etc. **3.** to fail to hit.

nission C — *n* (c) **1.** a group of people who go abroad for a specific purpose. **2.** the journey such people make and its purpose. **3.** the building(s) used by a religious group for teaching, etc. **4.** the work someone believes God wants them to do.

nist B — *n* thin fog.

nixer B — *n* (c) a machine which mixes different ingredients.

nnemonic C — *n* (c) a method of helping one remember something.

noan C — *n* (c) a deep sound made by someone in pain or unhappiness.

nobile C — *n* (c) a decorative hanging device which moves round in air currents.
adj able or designed to move.

nobilise C — *v* **1.** to prepare for a war or other crisis by organising (men, resources, etc.). **2.** to organise for a purpose.

nock C — *v* to make fun of.

nodality C — *n* (linguistics) the use of words (esp. modal verbs) to show emotions, attitudes, etc.

node C — *n* (c) (formal) the way of living, doing something, etc. (also various technical uses, esp. in music).

nodern style B — *n* can be used of any style which is considered up-to-date.

noleskin C — *n* (c) the skin of a mole (French, *taupe*) formerly used to make clothing.

nolest C — *v* to annoy or attack, used now principally for a dog which attacks sheep or a person who assaults someone sexually.

noment B — *n* (c) *from the moment* from that time onwards.

noney A — *n* (usually u) coins or paper printed with values on them, used in buying and selling; (the French, *argent*).

nonster C — *n* (c) **1.** an abnormally mis-shaped creature (also imaginary and mythological). **2.** a very cruel person.

nontage C — *n* **1.** (u) the cutting and arranging of cinema film. **2.** (c) a piece of art made by joining several other pictures together.

nonument B — *n* (c) **1.** something built to remind others of someone's life or an event. **2.** an old building or ruin preserved for historic interest.

nood B — *n* (c) someone's feelings at any given moment.

noody B — *adj* **1.** having quickly changing moods. **2.** irritable, unhappy.

noonshine C — *n* (u) **1.** fantastic and totally absurd ideas or conversation. **2.** (AE) alcoholic drink produced illegally.

moor C *n* (c; often plural in BE) **1.** an area of acid soil where plants grow and of little agricultural value. **2.** *Moors* historically, the Arabs of N.W. Africa.

moose C *n* (c; plural same) (AE) a large type of deer; (*elk* in Europ

mop C *v* to wash with a device consisting of a handle and heac string or sponge.

n (c) the tool used for this.

moquette C *n* material used for upholstery or carpets.

moral B *n* (c) **1.** the simple lesson to be learned from a stc **2.** (plural) rules of behaviour.

morale C *n* (u) good spirits and confidence, esp. in difficult sit tions.

morality C *n* (u) purity of action; rightness.

morbid C *adj* unnaturally interested in disagreeable matters, e death.

morgue C *n* (c) (chiefly AE) the building where the authorities h dead bodies until they are identified.

morning dress C *n* (u) formal clothes worn by men for some ceremor such as elegant weddings.

morning service C *n* (c) a church service held in the morning, esp. matins.

morose C *adj* sullen, not cheerful or good-tempered.

Morse C *n* (u) short for *Morse code*, the system of sending messa using dots and dashes.

mortal C *adj* quite a number of meanings, most of them connec with death.

mortified C *adj* deeply ashamed and/or embarrassed.

motel B *n* (c) a hotel consisting of separate units for travell motorists with space for their cars.

motif C *n* (c) **1.** a repeated element in a design or recurrent the in a piece of music. **2.** the main subject in a work art.

motion A *n* **1.** (u) the state of moving. **2.** (c) a separate moveme **3.** (c) a proposal put formally to a meeting.

motivate C *v* to give a reason for doing something.

motive C *n* (c) the reason why someone acts in a given way, esp. u of crimes; (a far more restricted use in English than other languages).

motor B *n* (c) **1.** a machine that converts power into moveme **2.** (BE only; now old-fashioned) a car.

motorist B *n* (c) someone who drives a car.

mould C *n* (spelt *mold* in AE) **1.** (c) a hollow form in which mel metal or other material is put to cool into the sha required. **2.** fungi growing on old bread, cheese, e **3.** (u) soil rich in decayed vegetable matter.

mount C *v* **1.** to climb onto a horse or bicycle. **2.** (formal) climb. **3.** to put (a picture) on a frame. **4.** to prep (an attack). **5.** to present (a play) at a theatre. **6.** provide with or place on a horse or bicycle.

little mouse C *n* (c) a small mouse!

mousse C *n* (c) a cold whipped cream sweet/pudding.

movement of humour C *n* (c) an amusing movement of some sort.

muck C *n* (u) **1.** farmyard manure. **2.** (informal) anything disgusting or useless.

muff C *n* (c) **1.** a tube-shaped piece of fur for keeping the hands warm. **2.** someone who fails to do something easy.

muffler C *n* (c) **1.** (old-fashioned) a type of short neck-scarf. **2.** (AE) a vehicle's silencer.

mug C *n* (c) **1.** a type of cup with a handle but without a saucer. **2.** (informal) a silly person.

multitude C *n* (c) **1.** a large number of things. **2.** (uncommon) the common people.

mum B *n* (c) (informal) mother, esp. used when talking to her.

mundane C *adj* boring, dull, uninspired.

municipal credit C *n* while not a recognised phrase, suggests a system of credit (providing funds) offered by some municipal authority.

murder A *n* **1.** (c) the crime of killing someone. **2.** (informal) something very tiring or irritating.

murmur B *v* **1.** to speak very quietly and often unintelligibly. **2.** (old-fashioned) to complain in private.

muse C *v* to be deep in thought.

music A *n* (u) an art form; arrangement of sounds, having a definite harmony and rhythm.

music hall C *n* (c) a theatre where the entertainment consists of light songs, comedians, and other special acts.

must C *n* (c) (informal) something necessary.

muster C *v* to gather or call together.

myrrh C *n* (u) a tree gum used in perfume and incense production.

mystification C *n* **1.** (u) the state of being confused. **2.** (c) something which confuses or puzzles (rare).

mystify C *v* to confuse; cause incomprehension.

n

nag C *v* to complain and/or criticise continually.

nap C *v* to sleep for a short time, esp. during the day.

B *n* (c) a short (day-time) sleep.

nappe C *n* (c) (geology) folded-over rocks.

national A *adj* concerning the whole nation.

nationalise B *v* to take over an industry and put under state control.

natural C *n* (c) someone who learns something very quickly or is certain to succeed.

nature B *n* there are several meanings, but the word is far less used in English than the corresponding word in other languages. **1.** the whole of creation and the study of what is in it. **2.** personality.

nave C — *n* (c) the longer part of a church, where the congregatio sit.

navigation C — *n* (u) the art of directing the course of an aircraft or shi

Nazi C — *n* (c) someone belonging to the political party of Ado Hitler in Germany.

near A — *adv, preposition* at or to a place or time not far away.

neat B — *adj* **1.** arranged in good order. **2.** (AE) excellent. **3.** (c alcoholic drinks) not mixed with soda water or ice (*straight* in AE).

necessary C — *n* (c) what is needed. (This word is rarely used as a noun

necessitate C — *v* to need, make necessary.

neck A — *v* (slang) to kiss.

C — *n* (c) **1.** the part of the body joining the head to th shoulders. **2.** something shaped like this. **3.** a nar row strip of land, projecting into water.

necrology C — *n* (c) a list of people (recently) dead.

needle C — *n* (c) a pin with a hole at one end for the thread.

negligee C — *n* (c) a woman's light dressing gown, esp. one matching nightdress.

negro C — *n* (c) a member of the dark skinned race originating i Africa.

nervous A — *adj* in BE usually it means 'afraid'. (Much less commonl and in AE, it approaches the Continental meaning as i *nervous energy*.)

net A — *n* material made of knotted thread or string.

nettly C — *adj* filled with nettles (urtica).

niche C — *n* (c) **1.** a hollow space in a wall in which a statue coul be placed. **2.** a suitable place in an organisation.

nick C — *v* **1.** (BE informal) to steal (unimportant things). **2.** (A informal) to charge too high a price for.

nickel C — *n* **1.** (u) the hard white metal. **2.** (c) a five-cent coin i the U.S.A.

night A — *n* (c) the part of the 24 hours when it is dark.

noble B — *adj* **1.** of high moral quality; worthy; courageous. **2.** o high social rank.

noise A — *n* a loud (unpleasant) sound.

noisome C — *adj* (old-fashioned) very irritating and unpleasant.

noisy A — *adj* loud; causing a lot of noise.

nomination C — *n* (c) the putting forward of someone's name for an office o position (to be confirmed or voted by a committee, etc.)

normal school C — *n* (c) a school in no way marked as different from others.

normalised C — *past participle* returned to its normal (usual) state.

Norman C — *n* (c) one of the French people who conquered England i 1066.

not A — *adv* used to give the negative; only mentioned here for the signs *Notausgang* and *notuitgang* which to the English speaker appear to mean 'not the way out'!

notch C — *n* (c) **1.** a V-shaped cut as made in wood by a knife **2.** (AE) a narrow way between mountain peaks. **3.** (informal) a degree (in quality).

note A — *n* (c) **1.** a short informal letter. **2.** (BE) a piece of paper money; (a *bill* in AE). **3.** (often plural) things written down which you need to remember. **4.** a musical sound, usually of a specific frequency. **5.** a written sign for a sound in music. (A *notebook* is a book of lined or blank paper on which one can write notes in sense **3** above.)

notice A — *n* **1.** (u) *take notice of* to observe, pay attention to. **2.** (u) warning of something which is going to happen. **3.** (c) a written statement to inform people of events, etc.

notoriety C — *n* (u) the quality of being famous for something bad.

notorious C — *adj* well-known for some bad quality.

noun A — *n* (c) (grammar) the name of someone, something, a quality, action, etc.

novel A — *n* (c) a work of fiction, printed as a book.

now A — *adv* at the present time; (notice this is not an adjective).

nude C — *n* (c) a (painting of a) human without clothes on.

number A — *v* to attach a number to.
n (c) **1.** numerical quantity (1, 2, 3, etc.). **2.** a piece of music. **3.** an issue of a periodical.

nut A — *n* (c) **1.** a hard dry fruit with a seed (often edible). **2.** a four- or six-sided piece of metal which screws onto a bolt. **3.** (informal) someone who is crazy. **4.** (AE taboo slang) a testicle.

O

obituary C — *n* (c) a short biographical article in a newspaper, printed just after someone's death.

obligations C — *n* social, moral, or political duties, but not usually referring to someone's work.

obliteration C — *n* (u) total destruction.

obscure B/C — *adj* **1.** B not clearly expressed, and therefore not easy to understand. **2.** B not well-known. **3.** C dark; without enough light.

obscurity C — *n* (u) the quality of being obscure.

obsequious C — *adj* appearing too keen to help or serve.

obstetrics C — *n* (u) the branch of medicine concerned with childbirth.

occasion A/B — *n* (c) **1.** A a time when something happens. **2.** A a suitable time for something to happen. **3.** A a special event. **4.** (u) B a reason.

occasionally A — *adv* from time to time, now and then.

occult C — *adj* supernatural, astrological.

occur A — *v* **1.** to happen. **2.** to come to mind.

occurrence C — *n* (c) an event.

occurring C — *present participle* happening; (with no adjectival use).

of A — *preposition* usually the Dutch *van*.

off A — *adv, preposition* usually the Dutch (*er*)*of* or *weg*.

off day C — *n* (c) a bad day because someone does not feel well, doe not work well, or is in a bad mood, etc.

offer A — *v* **1.** to give someone a chance to accept something. **2.** t say one is willing to; volunteer.
n (c) **1.** something which is offered. **2.** the statemen offering something.

office A — *n* (c) a place of business and where a service is provided esp. connected with writing.

official B — *n* (c) someone working in a government or some othe responsible position.

officious C — *adj* interfering, too keen to show authority.

offset C — *v* to balance, compensate for.

old-timer C — *n* (c) someone who has done something or been somewher for a long time.

omnibus C — *n* (c) **1.** (old-fashioned) a bus. **2.** a book containin several works by one author.

one B — *pronoun* includes the speaker (first person) and may includ the hearer(s); a substitute for *I* or *me*; (*man* is similar t *one* in North European).

one man A — *n* as in: *I could see one man in the street but no women o children.*

onslaught C — *n* (c) a wild attack; often used figuratively.

ooze C — *v* to move very slowly, esp. used of thick liquids.
n (c) muddy thick liquid.

opera B — *n* (c) only used in the musical sense.

operate A — *v* **1.** (of a machine) to work. **2.** to make something work **3.** to do a surgical operation. **4.** (of laws) to be effective

operations room C — *n* (c) a room where military information is collected and orders are given out.

opportunity A — *n* (c) a favourable time.

opposition B — *n* **1.** (u) the resistance to something or someone. **2.** *the opposition* the political group(s) against the party in power.

oration C — *n* (c) a formal public speech.

oratorio C — *n* (c) a long musical work with singing based on a biblical story, but not acted.

ordeal C — *n* (c) a difficult or fearful experience which cannot be avoided.

ordinance C — *n* (c) a formal order.

ordinary A/B — *adj* **1.** A usual, commonly found. **2.** (chiefly AE) B of poor quality, inferior.

ordination C — *n* (c) the ceremony of making someone a priest.

ordnance C — *n* (u) **1.** heavy guns and military supplies. **2.** *Ordnance Survey* the organisation that officially produces maps in Britain.

ore C — *n* rock from which metal is obtained.

organ B — *n* (c) **1.** any part of an animal or plant with a specific function. **2.** a publication, radio, or television, considered as expressing opinions. **3.** a (large) musical instrument (esp. in a church).

orgasm C *n* (c) the climax of sexual intercourse.

orientate C *v* (chiefly BE) to give direction to.

original B *n* (c) **1.** a genuine painting or sculpture; not a reproduction. **2.** the original language of a text. **3.** (occasional) an eccentric character.
adj (of people) unlike other people because not copying others.

ostensible C *adj* seeming (but probably not) true, apparent.

ostensibly C *adv* in an ostensible way.

outbuilding C *n* (c) a smaller building attached to a larger one.

outcast C *n* (c) someone who has been thrown out from society, his friends, or his family.

outcome C *n* (c; but singular only) the result.

outdo C *v* to do better than another person.

outfall C *n* (c) a place where water leaves a lake or reservoir.

outing B *n* (c) an excursion.

outlandish C *adj* strange, odd, or unusual; unconventional.

outlay C *n* (c) the amount of money spent on something (for a specific purpose).

outlet B *n* (c) **1.** a place where a liquid or gas can leave a container. **2.** a way in which someone can release his feelings and energy.

outrage C *n* (c) an act which makes the general public very angry.

outrageous B *adj* shocking; giving offence.

outset C *n* (c) the beginning.

outspoken C *adj* saying exactly what one thinks, without much tact.

outstanding B *adj* **1.** exceptionally good. **2.** which has not yet been dealt with, still awaiting attention.

oven B *n* (c) an enclosed space, heated for the cooking of food.

over C *n* (c) (cricket) a set of six balls bowled.
A *adv*, *preposition* **1.** straight above though not touching. **2.** up and across and down again: *he jumped over the fence.* **3.** down from the edge of. **4.** finished. **5.** during. **6.** more than; older than. **7.** throughout.

overall C *n* (c) protective clothing worn over one's normal clothes.

overbearing C *adj* insisting on obedience in an insensitive way.

overbook C *v* to take bookings (i.e. reservations) for more people than there are places.

overbooking C *n* (c) a situation where too many reservations have been made.

overcome B *v* **1.** to defeat. **2.** to make someone ill.

overdo C *v* to use too much of, go too far in, etc.

overdrive B *n* (c) a special high gear on some cars.

overflow C *n* (c) an outlet for liquid if the container becomes too full.

overhang C *n* (c) a projection of rocks with a hollow below it, offering some shelter but an obstacle to climbers.

overhaul B *v* to examine very carefully and do any necessary repairs to.
n (c) the act of doing this.

overheads	B	*n*	(fixed plural in BE; c in AE) regular expenses in running a business.
overhear	C	*v*	to hear what someone is saying, without their knowledge.
overload	B	*v*	to load too heavily.
		n	(c) the fact of loading too much.
overplant	C	*v*	to plant too much in (a garden).
overreach	C	*v*	to try too hard, so that one fails.
override	C	*v*	to pay no attention to or contradict another person's orders.
oversee	C	*v*	to watch over and direct, e.g. in a factory.
oversight	C	*n*	(c) **1.** an unintended failure to do or notice something. **2.** supervision.
overspill	C	*n*	(c) (chiefly BE) people who leave a large town for a (new) smaller one.
overtake	B	*v*	to move or progress faster and pass.
overture	C	*n*	(c) **1.** the opening piece of music to an opera, or concert. **2.** (plural) initial contacts made with someone.
overwind	C	*v*	to tighten a spring too much.
overwork	B	*v*	to work or make work too hard.

p

pace	B	*n*	(c) **1.** one single step. **2.** the distance covered by this. **3.** the speed of movement. (Compare **tempo**.)
pack	A	*v*	**1.** to put into suitcases or boxes for storage or travelling. **2.** to crowd into a space. (There are a number of other uses; to *pack up* is an extension of **1** above.)
	B	*n*	(c) of many meanings, note **1.** a number of things tied or wrapped up, or put in a case for carrying, esp. on the back. **2.** a collective word for groups of dogs, thieves and playing cards.
package	B	*n*	(c) a number of things carried together, with their container; (like a *parcel*).
packet	A	*n*	(c) a small parcel.
packing	C	*n*	(u) **1.** material loosely fitting round an article (in a box). **2.** the action of filling luggage.
pact	C	*n*	(c) a formal agreement.
pad	B	*n*	(c) **1.** something filled with soft material for protection. **2.** a block of paper for letter writing, etc. **3.** (slang) the room where someone lives.
padre	C	*n*	(c) a priest serving the Armed Forces; (also called a *chaplain*).
pail	B	*n*	(c) a water container with a handle; bucket.
pain	A/B	*n*	**1.** A sharp physical discomfort, worse than an ache. **2.** B suffering or anxiety.

pal C *n* (c) a (school) friend.

palace B *n* (c) a large elegant house used by a monarch and family, a bishop, or occasionally a noble family.

palaver C *n* (informal) a lot of unnecessary talk or trouble.

palette C *n* (c) the small board used by an artist to hold and mix the colours.

pallet C *n* (c) **1.** a board used when storing or moving goods with a fork-lift truck. **2.** (formerly) a simple kind of bed.

pamphlet B *n* (c) a small book with paper covers (non-fiction); booklet.

pan A *n* (c) a metal cooking container with a handle, short for a *saucepan*.

panel B *n* (c) **1.** a wooden board, esp. in a door, or along the wall of a room. **2.** an instrument board with dials. **3.** a group of speakers answering questions from an audience. **4.** (BE) a group of doctors working in a given area, in the National Health Service.

pannier C *n* (c) each of a pair of baskets or containers to carry goods on a horse or a bicycle.

pant B *v* to breathe quickly, esp. after a great physical effort.
n (plural) **1.** short underclothes for men. **2.** (AE, and BE informal) trousers.

panties B *n* (plural) a pair of women's underclothes.

pantomime C *n* (c) (BE only) a theatrical production for children based on a fairy story; (originally, acting without words, now called *mime*).

pantry B *n* (c) a small room in a house where food is stored; (also called a *larder*).

pants B *n* (c; plural) **1.** (BE) underclothing fitting over the legs and up to the waist. **2.** (BE colloq. and AE) trousers.

panzer C *n* (c) a German tank (in World War II).

pap C *n* **1.** (u) liquid-like mixture (esp. food for a baby). **2.** (u) (AE) light reading matter. **3.** (c) a woman's nipple.

papa C *n* (old-fashioned) father.

paper A *n* **1.** (u) a substance made from wood and cloth. **2.** (c) a single piece of such material, esp. for writing or printing on. **3.** (c) a newspaper. **4.** (c) a set of examination questions. **5.** (c) an academic essay or dissertation.

parade B *n* (c) **1.** a wide street (esp. at the seaside). **2.** a gathering of troops for inspection and/or marching.

paraffin B *n* (u) (BE only) a liquid fuel made from oil, used for heating and lighting; (*kerosene* in AE).

paragraph B *n* (c) **1.** a division of writing starting on a new line. **2.** a short piece of news in a newspaper.

paraphernalia C *n* (u) **1.** a collection of articles, esp. those needed for a specific activity or skill. **2.** (informal) unnecessary articles.

parasite C *n* (c) **1.** an animal or plant that lives off another. **2.** (informal) a person who does no work, but lives off others.

pare C *v* **1.** to cut away the outer layer of (e.g. cheese). **2.** *pare down expenses* to reduce expenses to a minimum.

parent A *n* (c) the mother or father.

park A *n* (c) **1.** the gardens or land open to the public. **2.** the land in which a large country house stands; (not used of a large private garden of a normal house).

parking B *n* (u) the action of leaving one's car parked.

parole C *n* (u) **1.** a promise made by a prisoner, to behave lawfully when set free before the official imprisonment term has ended. **2.** the time covered by this promise.

parquet C *n* (u) a type of wooden floor.

parsimonious C *adj* miserly; over-cautious about spending money.

parsimony C *n* (u) the (bad) quality of being parsimonious.

part A *v* **1.** to (cause to) divide or separate. **2.** to separate one's hair.
n (c) many meanings, esp. note **1.** a piece or section. **2.** an actor's role in a play. **3.** *take part in* to share or participate in.

partake C *v* take a share (in something, esp. food).

participate C *v* to join in an activity.

particular A *n* (c; usually plural) one's name, address, and other details.
adj **1.** worthy of notice; unusual. **2.** being too much concerned over unimportant details. **3.** *in particular* more than anything else.

particularly A *adv* in a way different from others; very (much).

partisan C *n* (c) **1.** a secret soldier fighting an occupying army. **2.** a fanatical supporter of a political party or some movement or plan.

partita C *n* (c) only of music in English: a type of suite.

partition C *n* (c) **1.** an internal wall between two rooms. **2.** the division of a country into two parts. **3.** (occasional) something formed by dividing.

partner A *n* (c) a companion or ally; a person who shares in the same activity.

party A *n* (c) **1.** a political group with similar ideas. **2.** a group of people doing something together. **3.** a celebration. **4.** each of the people or sides in a legal dispute.

Paschal C *adj* **1.** of Easter. **2.** of the Jewish feast of the Passover.

pass A *v* a verb with many meanings; note esp. **1.** to move past. **2.** to spend (time). **3.** (of time) to elapse; go by. **4.** *pass the time of day* to have a brief conversation. **5.** to exchange or transfer. **6.** to gain a sufficient mark to be successful in (an exam). **7.** to accept. **8.** to allow to go without comment. **9.** to cease. **10.** *pass water* to urinate.
n (c) **1.** a permit. **2.** a success in an exam (esp. at the lowest level). **3.** a way through mountains.

passage A *n* (c) **1.** a corridor. **2.** a section of text or music considered on its own. **3.** a long sea journey. **4.** a way through.

passé C — *adj* old-fashioned.

passe-partout C — *n* (u) **1.** adhesive material used in making frames for small pictures. **2.** (rare) a master key or pass key.

passive C — *n* (c) (grammar) the voice of verbs expressing an action done to the subject of a sentence, in contrast to the *active*.

past B — *n* *the past* times gone by.

pasta C — *n* (u) a collective name for the food made from flour, such as spaghetti and macaroni.

paste C — *n* (c) a soft mixture in any of various combinations, e.g. for sticking wallpaper, making pastry, toothpaste, etc.

pastel C — *n* **1.** (the materials used for making) pictures in pale colours. **2.** any such colours as made with chalk.

pat C — *n* (c) a soft touch made with the palm of the hand, e.g. *give him a pat on the back*.

patch B — *n* (c) various meanings connected with a small part of a larger area. (The German use seems to be linked with the phrase *go through a difficult patch* in which some adjective is essential in English.)

paté C — *n* meat paste.

patent B — *n* (c) the right given by a government to make or sell an invention.
adj obvious, clear, or plain.

pathetic B — *adj* **1.** causing sadness. **2.** (common informal) useless, totally without success.

pathos C — *n* (u) (literature) the quality causing pity or sorrow.

patio C — *n* (c) a small open paved space by a house for eating meals, etc.

patron B — *n* (c) **1.** someone supporting a cause, art, a charity, etc. **2.** a regular customer to a shop, hotel, restaurant, etc.

pause B — *n* (c) a very short break/interruption (a briefer time than in other languages).

pavement B — *n* (c) (BE) a path beside a road for people to walk along; (a *sidewalk* in AE).

pavilion C — *n* (c) **1.** (BE) a building at a sports ground, esp. cricket. **2.** a temporary building or tent esp. at an exhibition.

peach B — *n* (c) a round soft juicy fruit.

peaked C — *past participle* fitted with a point.

pear B — *n* a sweet juicy fruit, narrower at the top than at the bottom.

pearl C — *n* (c) a jewel, formed inside an oyster.

peculiar B/C — *adj* **1.** C belonging to, or found only in one individual or place. **2.** B strange, odd, unusual.

peep C — *v* **1.** to look cautiously. **2.** to make a high small sound like a small bird.

peg C — *v* **1.** to fix with a piece of sharp wood. **2.** to stabilise at a given level, e.g. prices.

pen A — *n* (c) an instrument for writing, originally using ink.

penalise C — *v* **1.** to put someone in an unfavourable position. **2.** (in sport) to punish for breaking a rule.

penalty B — *n* (c) a punishment.
pencil A — *n* (c) graphite in a wood or metal case, used for writing or drawing.
pendulum C — *n* (c) a weight swinging freely from a fixed point, e.g. to regulate a large clock.
penetrated C — *past participle* entered; forced a way into.
pension B — *n* (c) a sum of money paid to someone who has retired; (for a boarding house, *pension* is not used with an English pronunciation).
pensioner C — *n* (c) someone receiving a pension, usually an *old-age pensioner*.
people A — *n* (plural; singular is *person*) the normal word for men and women, not derogatory.
per se C — *adv* considered on its own, not for any other reason.
perceive C — *v* to come to know of something through the senses, esp. sight.
perception C — *n* (u) the ability to understand deeply.
perfect A — *adj* of several uses, esp. note **1.** excellent; of the highest level; faultless. **2.** utter or absolute. **3.** (grammar) a tense of verbs.
perfume C — *n* (c) **1.** a pleasant smell; aroma. **2.** a concentrated liquid giving a pleasant smell.
periodical C — *n* (c) a publication which comes out at regular intervals, usually weekly or monthly. See also **journal**.
perk C — *n* (c) something received at work in addition to the salary (short for *perquisite*, but this is now hardly ever used).
permanence C — *n* (u) the quality of being permanent.
permission C — *n* (u) the state of being allowed to do something.
persecution C — *n* (u) the action of treating cruelly, or annoying.
person A — *n* (c) an individual human; (the normal plural, esp. in BE, is *people*, which is not derogatory).
persona C — *n* (literature) used of the speaker in a poem, i.e. the first-person narrator.
personality B — *n* **1.** (c) the character of an individual. **2.** (u) unusually interesting character. **3.** a well-known person.
personage C — *n* (c) (pompous/humorous) an important person.
personification C — *n* (c) someone who is a perfect example of a given quality.
perspective C — *n* (u) **1.** the geometry used in drawing objects correctly. **2.** thinking of something (e.g. a problem) from all points of view.
persuaded B — *past participle* made to believe by argument or begging.
persuasion C — *n* similar in meanings to the Latin cognates, except when meaning 'conviction', it sometimes refers to religious belief.
Peru B — *n* only used of the South American nation.
pest C — *n* (c) a nuisance, cause of irritation.
pester C — *v* to keep irritating by demanding things.
pestle C — *n* (c) an instrument with a round end, used for crushing something in a bowl (used in laboratories and in cooking).

pet B — *v* to touch lovingly.
n (c) **1.** an animal kept as a companion. **2.** someone (esp. a child) who is much loved.

petrol A — *n* (u) the fuel used to power motor vehicles.

petroleum C — *n* (u) the mineral oil from which petrol and paraffin are made.

petulant C — *adj* irritable, easily getting cross over very small matters; (similarly, though less common, the u noun *petulance*).

phone A — *n* (c) short for a *telephone*.

photo A — *n* (c) the usual informal word for a *photograph*.

photograph B — *n* (c) a picture produced by means of a camera.

photographic apparatus C — *n* any equipment needed for photography, not only a camera.

photography B — *n* (u) the activity of producing photographs.

phrase B — *n* (c) **1.** a group of words forming part of a sentence but without a finite verb. **2.** a few notes of music.

physic C — *n* (c) (old-fashioned) a medicine or drug. (Note that *physics* is the science concerned with the study of matter and natural forces.)

physical A — *adj* **1.** concerning material things in contrast to spiritual ones. **2.** *physical geography* the study of the earth's surface. **3.** concerning the body. **4.** according to the laws of nature.

physician B — *n* (c) a medical doctor.

physiognomy C — *n* (u) the study of the human face and head and the attempt to judge character from this.

physique C — *n* (c) the form of the human body.

piano B — *n* (c) a musical instrument, formerly known as *pianoforte*.

piccolo C — *n* (c) a small flute, playing very high notes.

pick A — *v* of many uses, note **1.** to gather or pluck. **2.** to choose or select. **3.** to remove loose parts from; clean with something sharp, e.g. to pick one's teeth with a toothpick.
n (c) **1.** a sharp pointed tool. **2.** the action of choosing. **3.** a selection of the best.

pick-up B — *n* (c) **1.** the needle and the arm of a record player. **2.** a small open lorry.

picket C — *n* (c) **1.** group of soldiers on a special kind of guard duty. **2.** an individual or group, often from a trade union, who prevent workers from entering their place of work during a strike.

pickle C — *n* **1.** a strong flavoured mixture, esp. of vinegar and preserved vegetables. **2.** (informal) a difficult situation or condition.

pie C — *n* (c) food cooked in a pastry case.

piece A — *n* (c) of many meanings, note **1.** a part that is separate from others; bit (esp. used with u nouns). **2.** an object that is part of a set. **3.** one of many parts to be fitted together. **4.** (BE only) a coin with a certain value.

piety C — *n* (u) **1.** respect for God. **2.** *filial piety* respect for a parent.

pigeon B — *n* the Italian *piccione*.

pile A — *v* to heap up in a regular fashion.
n (c) a regularly shaped heap.

pill B — *n* **1.** a small hard piece of medicine to be swallowed. **2.** *the pill* the oral contraceptive taken by women.

pillow B — *n* (c) a soft cushion used in bed to support the head.

pilot B — *n* (c) **1.** someone who flies an aircraft. **2.** someone who guides ships into a river or harbour, taking the captain's place.

pimp C — *n* a man who provides prostitutes.

pin B — *n* (c) a short thin piece of metal, esp. used for joining pieces of paper or cloth. (In technical use, it may mean something larger and of different material, but it still refers to something which holds things together.)

pincers C — *n* a tool consisting of two short connected arms used for picking something up or pulling something out.

pinch B — *v* **1.** to squeeze between the thumb and the first finger. **2.** (informal) to steal, something unimportant.
n (c) **1.** the action of pinching (**1** above). **2.** *at a pinch* if really necessary.

pineapple B — *n* (c) a tropical fruit.

pinion C — *n* (c) **1.** feathers at the end of a bird's wing. **2.** a wheel with teeth used in machinery.

pink B — *v* (BE) to make a tapping sound when a car is driven in too low a gear; (to *ping* in AE).
n, adj red and white mixed.

pint B — *n* (c) **1.** a liquid measurement=0.57 litre; (a *pinta* is informal for a *pint of milk*).

pipe A — *n* (c) **1.** a tube for carrying gas or liquids. **2.** a simple musical instrument. **3.** a tube in a (church) organ. **4.** an object in which tobacco, etc., is smoked.

piqued C — *past participle* irritated because one's pride has been hurt.

piscina C — *n* (c) a small stone basin near a church altar, used during the Mass.

piss B — *v* (vulgar, near taboo) to urinate.
n urine.

piston C — *n* (c) the sliding part of a pump in a pipe and the similar part in an engine.

pit C — *n* (c) **1.** a deep hole in the ground. **2.** a coal mine.

pitch C — *n* **1.** (u) black material used to block holes in a boat. **2.** (c) the height or depth of a voice or musical note. **3.** the angle of a roof to horizontal. **4.** (c) an area of ground used for a sport, with lines marked out.

pittance C — *n* (c) a very small amount, esp. of money.

placard C — *n* (c) a large notice, usually carried about, e.g. in a demonstration.

place A — *n* (c) of a wide range of meanings, note **1.** a point or part of space on a surface. **2.** a usual or proper position. **3.** the part of a text being read. **4.** one's rank or position. **5.** a house, flat, room, etc. **6.** a point in an argument:

in the first place. (In the meaning of a town square, you are only likely to find a *market-place*; there are no important (u) uses except in idioms.)

plague C — *n* (c) **1.** one of the (historic) diseases which killed many people. **2.** (informal) a nuisance or annoyance.

plaid C — *n* a long piece of woollen cloth with a Scottish tartan design, worn over the shoulder.

plain B — *n* (c) a wide area of flat country.

plan A — *n* (c) **1.** a diagram of a building showing the arrangement of rooms. **2.** a scheme, proposal, for future activities.

plane B — *v* to cut away the surface of wood with a special tool.
n (c) **1.** short for an *aeroplane*. **2.** a completely flat surface, as in mathematics. **3.** a tool for smoothing wood.

plank C — *n* (c) a flat piece of wood; board (no specific purpose).

planking C — *n* (u) a collective word for planks, esp. referring to a floor.

plant B — *v* **1.** to place, put (something) somewhere (esp. horticulturally). **2.** (derogatory) to place unsuitably. **3.** to place ideas in someone's mind.
n **1.** (c) a living thing with leaves and roots, growing in soil. **2.** (u) the heavy equipment needed for a special task. **3.** (c) a factory (rare).

plantation C — *n* (c) **1.** a large area of land where one crop is cultivated. **2.** trees planted together for wood production.

plaque C — *n* (c) a flat inscribed plate fixed to a building.

plaster B — *n* **1.** (u) a mixture used in building which dries very hard. **2.** (c) cloth treated medically to fix over a cut, etc.

plastic A — *n* a strong synthetic material made chemically from coal or oil.

plate A/C — *n* (c) **1.** A a flat dish with a raised edge for serving food. **2.** A a full-page illustration in a book, mostly coloured. **3.** A a circular flat piece as used in machines. **4.** (u) C silver or gold vessels used in church or kept as antiques (compare Spanish).

plateau C — *n* (c) **1.** a flat area of country with higher land around it. **2.** a period of time when no progress is made.

plausible C — *adj* **1.** seeming reasonable and convincing but not proved. **2.** (of people) clever at convincing others in argument.

play A — *n* (c) a theatrical presentation of a story. (There are also some C u uses.)

plectrum C — *n* (c) the small piece of metal or wood used in playing guitars, etc.

pliant C — *adj* **1.** easily conforming to the orders and wishes of others. **2.** (materials) easily twisted or bent.

plight C — *n* (c) a dangerous or unhappy situation or state.

plinth C — *n* (c) the base of a pillar or statue, usually a stone block.

pluck C — *v* **1.** to pull out the feathers from a dead bird, eyebrows, etc. **2.** (music) to pull on the strings of a violin, etc. **3.** (literary) to pick (flowers and fruit).

plume C — *n* (c) a large feather.

plump C *adj* a little fat; (not generally derogatory).

plunder C *n* (u) goods, stolen esp. by a victorious army.

ply C *v* **1.** (of ships, buses, or taxis) to travel regularly on a given route. **2.** (old-fashioned) to work at one's trade.

pneumatic C *adj* containing or working with air under pressure.

po C *n* (c) (old-fashioned slang) a pot kept in the bedroom for urine. (The correct word is *chamber pot*; a small one for children is called a *potty*.)

pochard C *n* (c) a kind of duck.

pocketbook C *n* (c) **1.** a small book for keeping notes. **2.** (AE) a paperback book small enough for the pocket; (not a false friend for the Scandinavians). **3.** (AE) a woman's handbag. **4.** (formerly) a wallet.

point B/C *v* **1.** B to indicate with the finger. **2.** B to aim (a gun). **3.** C to make (a pencil) sharp. **4.** B to stretch (the toes and feet) forward. **5.** B to fill cracks between bricks with mortar or cement.

B *n* (c) there are many meanings, esp. note **1.** the sharp end of a pin or needle. **2.** an element in an argument or discussion. **3.** a reason. **4.** an important purpose or reason. **5.** *decimal point* the full stop between a whole number and parts of a number. **6.** a socket for electrical fixtures.

poke C *n* (c) the action of pushing with something pointed.

police A *n* (always takes a plural verb) the public officials who maintain law and order.

policy B *n* (c) **1.** a document, certificate. **2.** a course of action to follow.

politic C *adj* tactful, diplomatic.

politics B *n* (plural) **1.** the activity of politicians and practice of government. **2.** political opinions.

political C *adj* concerned with politics.

polo C *n* **1.** (u) a sport played on horseback with two teams, hitting a ball with long hammers. **2.** (trademark) (c) a peppermint sweet.

polygon C *n* (c) (geometry) a flat shape with five or more straight sides.

pomp C *n* (u) solemn ceremonial for some official occasion; also used derogatorily.

pond B *n* (c) a small area of still water (man-made or natural).

ponder C *v* to think about something for some time.

pony C *n* (c) a kind of small horse; (a *pony-tail* is a woman's or girl's hair tied back so it falls in a tail).

pool B *n* **1.** (c) a small area of water. **2.** (c) a swimming pool. **3.** (c) a quantity of liquid on a surface. **4.** (c) a shared supply of things or people. **5.** (c) the accumulation of bets from which prizes are paid, esp. in the football pools. **6.** (u) (AE) a game similar to billiards.

port A/C *n* **1.** (c) A a town with a harbour. **2.** (u) A a strong red wine from Portugal. **3.** A the left-hand side of a ship, looking forwards. **4.** C *a porthole* the round window in the side of a ship.

portal C *n* (c) an imposing entrance (door).

portent C *n* (c) a sign of something to happen in the future.

porter A *n* (c) **1.** someone who carries luggage. **2.** (BE) a kind of doorman, e.g. at a hotel, hospital, or hostel.

portfolio C *n* (c) **1.** a large flat case for carrying drawings. **2.** a collection of drawings or paintings. **3.** the list of commercial shares held by someone. **4.** the duties of a minister of state.

portion B *n* (c) **1.** a share or division of something. **2.** the amount of food for one person.

portmanteau C *n* (c) a very large case for clothing, esp. one opening into two parts.

pose C *n* (c) **1.** the position of the body, esp. for a painting or photo. **2.** a false attitude presented by someone.

posse C *n* (c) **1.** a group of people acting together with a common purpose. **2.** (AE) a group of men helping a sheriff to keep order.

possibility B *n* **1.** (u) a state that could exist or occur. **2.** (c) likelihood. **3.** (c) potential.

possibly C *adv* **1.** in accordance with what is possible. **2.** perhaps.

post A *n* **1.** (c) a job. **2.** (c) a piece of wood or metal upright, e.g. to support a fence. **3.** (u) (BE) the system of sending letters and parcels; (*mail* in AE). **4.** (u) (BE) the letters, etc., so delivered. **5.** (n) the place where a soldier is on duty.

post bus C *n* (c) a public bus which also carries letters and parcels for the Post Office.

poster B *n* (c) a large printed notice for publicity.

postman B *n* (c) someone who delivers the post.

pot A *n* **1.** (c) a container, esp. one made of baked clay. **2.** (u) (slang) cannabis or marijuana. **3.** (AE) money put together by a group of people, e.g. to buy food; (there are various other C uses).

pot-load C *n* (c) suggests a load which could be put into a pot.

potency C *n* (u) the effectiveness or strength of something, esp. medicines or alcoholic drinks.

pouf(f)e C *n* (c) **1.** a drum-shaped object to sit on. **2.** (BE slang) homosexual (also written *poof*).

pout C *v* to push the lips forward showing irritation.

practice A *n* there are many meanings, esp. note **1.** a habitual action. **2.** the repetition of an exercise to increase one's skill. **3.** the actual performance of something, as compared with the theoretical idea behind it. **4.** the people using the services of a doctor or lawyer.

practise B *v* **1.** to act according to beliefs. **2.** to repeat an activity to improve one's skill, etc. **3.** (esp. of a doctor or lawyer) to do regular professional work.

pragmatic C *adj* dealing in a practical way; (*pragmatically* is the adverb).

pragmatics C — *n* the method of dealing with something pragmatically.

pram B/C — *n* (c) **1.** (BE only) B short for a *perambulator* a small carriage, in which a baby can be taken out; (a *baby carriage* in AE). **2.** C short for a *pram dinghy*, a very small rowing boat.

precarious C — *adj* dangerous, because not firm or stable.

precious A — *adj* **1.** of great value. **2.** valued for emotional reasons. **3.** (of manners, speech, etc.) overrefined, affected.

precise B — *adj* **1.** exact. **2.** careful about small details.

precisely C — *adv* **1.** exactly.

precision C — *n* (u) exactness.

precocious C — *adj* developing at an unusually young age; (often derogatory and mainly used of children).

predicament C — *n* (c) a difficult situation.

predict B — *v* to foretell; describe something in the future before it happens.

prefect C — *n* (c) a senior pupil in a school, given some disciplinary responsibility over younger pupils; (the French meaning is occasionally heard in Britain).

pregnant B/C — *adj* **1.** B carrying an unborn baby in the womb. **2.** C full of (hidden) meaning.

prejudice B — *v* to cause someone to think in a particular way, persuade. (*Prejudiced* often means having fixed ideas, esp. against people of a different race or religion.)

n (u) **1.** opinion based on ignorance, not rational thinking. **2.** in law, harm which may come from some judgment or action. (**1.** is more commonly heard than **2.**)

premium C — *n* (c) **1.** the amount paid regularly to an insurance firm to maintain a policy contract. **2.** an extra charge made for something, above the normal value. **3.** *at a premium* difficult to obtain and therefore in great demand or of a high value. (The idea of a prize is only found in BE in *Premium Bonds*, the national weekly lottery tickets.)

preoccupy C — *v* to absorb one's mind.

preparation B — *n* (c) **1.** the act of getting ready. **2.** (often plural) arrangements, e.g. for a journey. **3.** a chemical mixture. **4.** (BE only) homework; (usually shortened to *prep.*).

preposterous C — *adj* absurd, totally unreasonable.

prepared A — *past participle* **1.** ready in advance. **2.** willing.

presbytery C — *n* (c) **1.** the part of a church near the altar. **2.** the house where a Roman Catholic priest lives. **3.** the committee of elders in charge of a Presbyterian church.

presents B — *n* (c) things given, gifts.

preservative C — *n* (c) a substance added esp. to food to preserve it.

president B — *n* (c) **1.** the head of state of a republic. **2.** the head of certain organisations, firms, colleges, etc. (A *chairman* is the head of a committee.)

press B — *n* **1.** (c) an apparatus which keeps something flat. **2.** newspapers and periodicals in general. **3.** (c) a printing machine, and by extension, a printing firm.

pressing C *n* (c) (technical) a gramophone record. (Note *give my trousers a press*, iron them; *pressing* would not be used.)

prestige C *n* (u) distinction, good reputation; (the English associations are more serious than in French).

presto C *adj* **1.** (music) fast. **2.** *hey presto!* an exclamation.

pretend A *v* **1.** to give a false impression, trying to make others believe something which is not true. **2.** (game) to make believe.

pretensions C *n* (c; sometimes singular) statements of claims (often false).

pretty A *adj* pleasant, attractive to the eye or ear.

prevaricate C *v* to hide the truth by giving elusive answers.

prevarication C *n* the act of prevaricating.

prevent A *v* to act in advance so that something does not happen.

prevention C *n* (u) the act of preventing something from happening.

preventive C *n* (c) something, esp. in medicine, to prevent something from happening.

prick C *n* (c) **1.** a small hole made in a surface. **2.** the action of making such a hole. **3.** a small sharp pain. **4.** (taboo slang) a penis.

prickle C *n* (c) a sharp point such as on a bramble.

prim C *adj* showing dislike of anything rough or rude.

primate C *n* (c) **1.** a priest of the highest rank. **2.** a member of the highest order of mammals.

prime C *n* **1.** the period when someone or something is at its highest stage of development and/or performance. **2.** the second church service of the day as held in Catholic monasteries, etc.

primer C *n* (c) **1.** an elementary school book. **2.** a kind of paint used under ordinary paint. **3.** a kind of exploding device in a bomb, etc.

primitively C *adv* in a way that is related to the earliest or least developed ways of doing things.

primrose C *n* (c) a small pale yellow wild flower.

principal A *adj* leading, chief, or most important.

principality C *n* (c) a country ruled by a prince, e.g. Liechtenstein.

principle B *in principle* **1.** according to rules and theories, but not in practice. **2.** in general but not in detail.

print B *n* **1.** (c) a photograph. **2.** (u) *in print* printed in a newspaper.

priority C *n* **1.** (c) something needing attention before other matters. **2.** (u) the right of coming before others.

private A *n* (c) a soldier of the lowest rank.
adj belonging to the individual; not public.

probe C *v* **1.** to search deep into something. **2.** (by extension) to investigate.
n (c) a careful search, esp. to discover what is wrong.

proboscis C *n* (c) normally only used of the tube-like mouth part of insects; (only a zoologist is likely to refer to an elephant's trunk as a *proboscis*).

proceeds C — *n* (c; plural) money produced from a sale or some activity for money raising.

process A/B/C — *v* **1.** A to treat something so as to preserve it. **2.** A to develop and print photographs. **3.** B to put information through a computer. **4.** C to move in a procession.

B/C — *n* (c) **1.** B a series of connected actions. **2.** C the whole of an action in law.

procure C — *v* (formal) to obtain.

Prodigal Son C — *n* the youth in the parable by Jesus, who spends all his inheritance and returns home penniless.

product A — *n* (c) something which is produced, esp. by man; (in contrast to *produce* (u), fruit and vegetables).

profane C — *adj* showing a lack of respect for God, esp. by blaspheming.

professor B — *n* (c) **1.** (BE) a senior teaching position in a university department. **2.** (AE) anyone teaching at a college or university.

proffer C — *v* (very formal) to offer.

program(me) A — the uses in English are similar to those in other languages except for the academic use: *what are the books on the syllabus?* (*Programme* is the BE spelling, *program* the AE).

prole C — *n* (c) (derogatory) a member of the proletariat.

promenade C — *n* (c) **1.** a wide walking place parallel with the beach at a seaside resort. **2.** a walking step in certain dances.

promiscuous C — *adj* changing often from one sex partner to another.

promise A — *n* (c) a spoken or written commitment to do something.

promoted C — *past participle* **1.** moved up in position, esp. in a firm or a profession. **2.** supported, financed. **3.** given publicity.

promoter C — *n* (c) someone who supports or introduces something or someone publicly.

promotion C — *n* **1.** (c) a move to a higher position. **2.** the action of trying to get something better known by publicity.

proof A — *n* **1.** the evidence that shows something to be true or correct. **2.** (c) a stage in printing in which corrections can still be made.

prop C — *v* to support and keep in the right position.

n (c) **1.** short for an aircraft's *propeller*. **2.** something which supports. **3.** (often plural) anything used on the stage for the production of a play; (but not the scenery itself).

propaganda C — *n* (u) (the action taken, esp. by a political party, to spread) information to influence what people think and believe (often used derogatorily; very rarely used of commercial publicity).

proper A — *adj* **1.** correct, suitable. **2.** (informal) total, thorough. **3** real. **4.** (following the noun) in the exact sense of the word.

properly A — *adv* correctly, suitably.

propose A — *v* **1.** to offer marriage. **2.** to suggest for consideration esp. at a meeting. **3.** to announce a toast (i.e. a drink) to someone.

roposition C *n* (c) **1.** an offer in business. **2.** a suggestion to be considered.

roprietor B *n* (c) the owner of a shop, business, or invention.

ropriety C *n* (u) suitable or fitting behaviour.

rosecute C *v* to charge someone in a court of law; (the Spanish and Italian meanings are very occasionally found in English but are old-fashioned).

rosecution C *n* (mainly legal) the action of prosecuting or those who prosecute; (again the Continental meaning is old-fashioned).

rospect A *n* **1.** (c) something expected or hoped for. **2.** hope, possibility. **3.** (rather old-fashioned) (c) a view. **4.** (c) (AE) someone whom one hopes will buy something for sale.

rotection A *n* **1.** (u) the act of keeping safe or being kept safe. **2.** (c) something which protects. **3.** (u) the state of being insured against accidents.

rotocol C *n* **1.** (u) the fixed rules of behaviour, esp. between officials of different states. **2.** (c) (very rare) the first draft of a treaty.

rove A *v* **1.** to supply proof of. **2.** to be found (to be).

rovidence C *n* (u) God, or some force, viewed as caring for and protecting his creatures; (note there is no plural use).

rovision A *n* **1.** (u) the act of providing or supplying. **2.** (u) careful preparation taken for what may happen later. **3.** (plural) supplies of food.

rovoke B *v* **1.** to make angry. **2.** to cause someone to do something.

rovoking B *adj* causing anger or irritation.

rudish C *adj* too correct or modest.

rune B *n* (c) a dried plum.

salm C *n* (c) the poems or songs by David in the Bible.

ublic A *n* **1.** people in general. **2.** a group of people interested in a particular thing.

ublic school C *n* (c) in England a private fee-paying school as opposed to a state school; (for Scotland and the U.S.A. the phrase is not a false friend).

ublish A *v* **1.** to produce and issue (books, etc.). **2.** (very occasional) to announce or make public.

uce C *n, adj* intensely bright deep pink.

udding A *n* **1.** sweet dish served after the main course of a meal. **2.** *black pudding* a kind of sausage. **3.** *steak and kidney pudding* meat covered with pastry.

uddle C *n* (c) a small area of water left after rain.

ueblo C *n* (c) the community of houses as built by certain Amerindian tribes in South Western U.S.A.

uff C *n* (c) a small amount of wind, air or gas.

uffer C *n* a child's word for a *steam locomotive*.

pull A	*v*	to draw along; (the opposite of *push*). *n* (c) the action of pulling.
pulley B	*n*	(c) a wheel with a rope or chain round it, used for liftir things.
Pullman C	*n*	(c) **1.** an especially comfortable railway coach. (AE) a sleeping car of greater comfort than usual.
pulp C	*n*	**1.** a near liquid mass, usually edible. **2.** the so mass of material (wood, etc.) used for paper man facture.
pulpit C	*n*	(c) the raised structure in a church from which a sermc is given.
pulse B	*n*	**1.** the regular beating of blood in the body which can l felt at the wrist. **2.** a small electric charge. **3.** (usually plural) the seed of a plant (e.g. the bean) eaten food.
pump B	*v*	**1.** to force (a gas or liquid) through an apparatus. **2.** work such an apparatus.
B/C	*n*	(c) B **1.** the apparatus doing this work. **2.** C a lig shoe for dancing.
punctuation B	*n*	(u) the marks used in writing indicating stops, questior etc.
puncture B	*n*	(c) a small hole, esp. in a vehicle's tyre.
punt C	*n*	(c) a long straight boat as used on some rivers (esp. Oxford and Cambridge).
puny C	*adj*	small and too weak.
pupa C	*n*	(c) the middle stage in the development of an insect wh it is inside the chrysalis.
pupil B	*n*	(c) **1.** a child being taught at school. **2.** the dark pa in the centre of the eye.
pure A	*adj*	there are various uses similar to D and NL, but of u mixed drinks, *neat* is used.
purple B	*n, adj*	between red and blue, but closer to red than violet.
pursue B	*v*	**1.** to follow in order to catch. **2.** to carry on wi studies, plans, etc. **3.** to follow persistently (of som thing unpleasant).
pursuit C	*n*	(c) the act of pursuing **1.** occupation, hobby. **2.** stud
pus C	*n*	(u) yellow thick matter from an infected part of t body.
push A	*n*	(c), *v* (to make) a pressure away from one; (the opp site of *puxar*).
put oneself out B	*v*	to make a special effort.
pygmy C	*n*	(c) though it can be used of anyone (or an animal) smaller than usual, it usually relates to one of a shc race of men who live in the central African forests.
pylon C	*n*	(c) **1.** a large metal tower for carrying electric wir **2.** a tower or post at an airport, used to guide aircraft.
pyre C	*n*	(c) a pile of wood used for burning a dead body.

q

quadrille C — *n* (c) an old dance for four couples.

quake C — *v* to shake; tremble.

Quaker C — *n* (c) a member of the Society of Friends.

qualification B — *n* (c) **1.** a document showing that one has fulfilled certain requirements, esp. that one has passed examinations. **2.** something which restricts a statement.

qualify A — *v* **1.** to be trained and have been successful in final examinations, esp. in a profession. **2.** (of a statement) to limit or make less general.

quality A — *n* **1.** (high) degree of goodness. **2.** characteristic of someone or something.

qualm C — *n* (c) doubt or anxiety about one's actions.

quark C — *n* (c) (physics) the smallest possible piece of material that forms the substance atoms are made of.

quart C — *n* (c) a liquid measurement; =2 pints or 1.136 litres.

quarter A — *n* (c) one of four equal parts. **2.** a section or area of a town. **3.** (plural) (military and naval) lodging, somewhere to live.

quay C — *n* (c) the solid part of a harbour where ships can be tied and (un)loaded.

queer B — *adj* **1.** strange, odd, peculiar. **2.** (informal derogatory) homosexual.

question A — *n* (c) **1.** (part of) a sentence asking for information. **2.** doubt, uncertainty. **3.** a problem.

quell C — *v* to put down, suppress.

queue B — *n* (c) **1.** a line of people waiting. **2.** a column of vehicles waiting to move on.

quid B — *n* (c) (plural same) (informal) a pound sterling.

quiet A — *adj* **1.** making very little sound. **2.** free from worry and trouble. **3.** (colours) not bright. **4.** inconspicuous. **5.** secret; *keep it quiet*, i.e. don't tell other people.

quill C — *n* (c) **1.** the stiff feather of a bird, formerly used for writing. **2.** the spine of a porcupine.

quit B — *v* **1.** to stop, leave.

quota C — *n* (c) **1.** the quantity of goods or number of people allowed to enter a country (each year). **2.** the amount of work required to be done.

r

race A — *n* (c) **1.** a group of men descended from the san ancestors, with distinct culture, appearance, etc.; (us far more of humans than animals). **2.** a contest to s who can do something faster than others. **3.** (plura the running of horses in such a contest; (a *racehorse* one which runs races).

rack C — *n* (c) **1.** a frame on which to keep things. **2.** a type torture. **3.** a bar with teeth on one side, into which th teeth of a wheel fit.

racket B — *n* (c) **1.** the instrument used in playing tennis; (als written *racquet*). **2.** a great noise. **3.** a dishonest wa of making money. **4.** hurry and social activity.

raclette C — *n* (u) only used of the cheese dish in English.

racy C — *adj* lively, amusing, sometimes a bit shocking.

radio A — *n* **1.** (u) the method of sending and picking up sound b electric waves through the air and space. **2.** (c) a apparatus used to receive such signals and convert the to sound.

raffle C — *v* to put up an article as a prize; (similar to a lottery
n (c) the selling of articles in such a way.

rag C — *n* (c) **1.** a piece of torn cloth. **2.** a number of show etc., organised by students to raise money.

rage B — *n* **1.** (c) furious temper. **2.** *the rage* the latest fashion.
v **1.** to show great anger. **2.** (of storms, fires, etc.) t be very violent.

raid B — *v* to attack suddenly.

raider C — *n* (c) someone or something making an attack.

rain A — *n* (usually u) water coming from the clouds.

raise A — *v* to put up, lift up, increase.
n (c) (mainly AE) an increase, esp. of prices or salaries.

raisin C — *n* (c) a dried grape, usually brown.

rake C — *n* (c) **1.** a gardening tool having teeth at the end of a lon handle. **2.** a man who spends all his money on wome and wild living.

ram C — *v* to push into something with great force.
n (c) **1.** a male sheep. **2.** a machine used to hit som thing repeatedly and forcefully.

ramp C — *n* (c) **1.** a man-made slope to connect two levels witho steps. **2.** (very occasional) the same as *racket* in sense

rampant C — *adj* **1.** growing wildly. **2.** (heraldry) standing on back leg

ranch B — *n* (AE) a farm; (the word is rarely heard in BE).

Rand C — *n* only used in connection with South Africa. **1.** th standard monetary unit. **2.** the area where Johanne burg is.

range C — *v* **1.** to move freely in a given area. **2.** to extend betwee limits.

rank C — *adj* **1.** thickly growing/covered. **2.** smelling or tasting ba

ansack C — *v* 1. to search through thoroughly. 2. to steal indiscriminately, as in a conquered town.

ant C — *v* to speak loudly and wildly.

ape C — *n* 1. the crime or act of having sexual intercourse with a woman against her will. 2. (u) a yellow-flowered plant grown for its oil and as cattle food.

aped C — *past participle* forced to have sexual intercourse.

apids C — *n* (c; sometimes singular) a shallow rocky section of a river where the current is very fast.

apine C — *n* (u) the removal of goods by force (esp. by an enemy); plunder.

apporteur C — *n* (c) someone who is delegated to report back to the main session of a meeting from a smaller group.

approchement C — *n* (c) the improvement of relations between two former enemies.

are A — *adj* not frequently found; uncommon.

ash C — *adj* acting too hastily with no thought for the consequences.

at B — *n* (c) animals similar to mice but larger.

ate C — *v* to estimate the value of.

A — *n* 1. (c) speed, tempo. 2. (plural) (BE only) local property tax. 3. (c) many phrases, e.g. *the birth rate*.

avish C — *v* 1. to thrill; delight. 2. (old-fashioned) to rape.

ay B — *n* (c) a line of bright light.

ayon C — *n* (u) a man-made material, looking like silk.

aze C — *v* to destroy, e.g. buildings so that they are flat on the ground; (also sometimes written *rase*).

eactor B — *n* (c) 1. short for a *nuclear reactor*, a machine producing atomic energy. 2. an apparatus for a chemical reaction.

eader B — *n* (c) 1. someone who reads. 2. an elementary textbook. 3. a lecturer at certain universities.

eal A — *adj* truly existing, genuine, not in the imagination.

ealisation C — *n* (u) 1. understanding, awareness. 2. the getting of money by selling property. 3. becoming real; (similar to *realise* in sense **2**). (*Total realisation* could occur in sense **1**.)

ealise A/C — *v* 1. A to be aware of, understand fully. 2. C to convert into reality, esp. plans, ambitions. 3. C to get money by selling.

eason A — *n* 1. (c) the explanation or cause. 2. (c) the basis for an action. 3. (u) the power to think clearly and form opinions. 4. (u) good sense.

ebate C — *n* (c) the returning of part of a payment (esp. of income tax).

ebound C — *n* (c) the action of springing back.

ebus C — *n* (c) a puzzle in which words or sentences have to be guessed from pictures or letters.

ebut C — *v* to show the incorrectness of, disprove.

eceipt A/C — *n* (c) 1. A a declaration that something (usually money) has been received. 2. (plural; bookkeeping) C money received. (A *prescription* is a doctor's instructions to a pharmacist about medicine etc.; a *recipe* gives instru tions for the preparation of food.)

recension C *n* (c) a critical revision or correcting of a text.

recherché C *adj* (esp. of words) unfamiliar, obscure.

recipient C *n* (c) someone who receives something.

recite B *v* to repeat esp. poetry from memory.

reckon up B *v* to calculate, estimate.

reckoning C *n* (u) the act of calculating.

reclaim C *v* **1.** to ask for the return of something as a right. **2.** bring back or convert land for cultivation; (*reclaimi* is occasionally used as a gerund for these uses, but no that *reclaim* does not exist as a noun).

reclamation C *n* (u) bringing land (back) into agricultural use.

recollection C *n* **1.** (c) something in one's memory. **2.** (u) the ability remember the past.

recommend A *v* **1.** to speak in favour of. **2.** to advise. **3.** to mak (something) attractive.

reconnaissance C *n* (u) the activity of reconnoitring.

reconnoitre C *v* (usually military) to go and find out about the size an locality of the enemy.

record A *v* **1.** to set down for later reference, e.g. in a book or o tape. **2.** to indicate.

n (c) **1.** written information. **2.** facts about the pas **3.** a vinyl disc used on a gramophone, esp. to play musi (only called a *disc* informally). **4.** (esp. in sport) th highest level of performance.

recoup C *v* to recover (one's losses or expenses).

recourse C *n* (u) mainly in the phrase *have recourse to*, to turn for he to.

recover A/C *v* A **1.** to get back (the use of). **2.** to get back to goo health. **3.** to become normal again. (To *re-cover* to cover again.)

recreation B *n* **1.** (c) a pastime. **2.** (u) free time.

rector C *n* (c) a clergyman in charge of a parish is a *vicar* or a *recto* the head person of a school or college is called a *rect* only in very few such institutions: in a school, *headmast* and *headmistress* (often just the *head*) are usual and th *principal* in most colleges.

recuperate C *v* to get back strength after an illness or being very ex hausted.

recycling B *n* (u) the re-using of materials after treatment.

redoubt C *n* (c) a small fort, part of a larger fortification.

redress C *v* to put right an injustice, grievance; (English has onl taken this meaning).

reduced B *past participle* Italian, *ridotto*.

reed C *n* (c) **1.** a big grass-like plant growing in wet place **2.** the material (usually wood) in a wind instrument whic vibrates when air is blown over it.

refer A *v* **1.** to pass to someone in higher authority. **2.** to spea of.

efined C — *adj* **1.** (of materials) purified. **2.** (of people) cultured, without vulgarity.

eformed C — *adj* **1.** formerly bad but now made good. **2.** (of institutions) modified by improving. **3.** relating to a Protestant Church, esp. Calvinist. (*The reformed* could be any group of people who have been improved or altered.)

efrain C — *n* (c) the repeated lines at the end of a song.

efrigeration B — *n* (u) the freezing or cooling (esp. of food to preserve it).

egale C — *v* to give someone pleasure (often used sarcastically).

egalia C — *n* (u) the ceremonial ornaments worn to show someone's official position.

egard B — *v* to consider. (There are other C uses of *regard*.)

egatta C — *n* (c) a meeting for boat and yacht races.

egime/régime — *n* (c) **1.** a method of government. **2.** (old-fashioned) a diet.

egiment B — *n* (c) in modern English mainly used to mean a military unit.

egister A — *v* **1.** to give one's name. **2.** to send letters and parcels by special post to insure against their loss. **3.** to make a formal record of. **4.** to show.
n (c) **1.** an official list. **2.** the extension of someone's voice (e.g. in singing) or of a musical instrument. **3.** (language) the style of speech, i.e. informal, formal, slang, etc.

egistrar C — *n* (c) someone who keeps official records.

egress C — *v* to go back to a less advanced or satisfactory condition; (often in emotional contexts).
n (c) the state of regressing.

egular A — *adj* **1.** symmetrical, arranged evenly. **2.** occurring at the same interval. **3.** (informal) complete, thorough. **4.** (grammar) having the usual changes. **5.** (esp. AE) usual, ordinary, normal. **6.** permanent.

eign C — *v* to rule as a monarch.

ein C — *n* (c; often plural) the leather strap held when riding a horse.

eiterate C — *v* to say several times.

ejoin C — *v* **1.** to return to (a group) one had been with before. **2.** to say in reply; answer or retort.

elate B — *v* **1.** to tell a story. **2.** to establish a connection.

elation A — *n* (c) **1.** a relative; member of the same family. **2.** a connection. **3.** (plural) connections or dealings between two people or groups.

elent C — *v* to become less harsh; show pity.

elevant C — *adj* connected with what is being considered.

elief B — *n* **1.** something which brings comfort. **2.** extra transport needed to deal with more passengers than usual. **3.** a change from monotony. **4.** someone replacing another on duty. **5.** (c) a flat type of sculpture (as on a coin). **6.** (u) the comparative amount of high and low land in a landscape. **7.** (u) help for people in trouble.

rely A — *v* to depend confidently on.

remark A — *v* to make a comment; (very rarely used in the French sens and better avoided).

remedy B — *n* (c) **1.** a healing treatment. **2.** a way of putting some thing right.

remission C — *n* **1.** (u) the forgiving of sins by God. **2.** the shortening c time in prison for good behaviour. **3.** a period when chronic disease is less severe.

remit C — *v* to send money by post; (other uses are uncommon).

remittance C — *n* (c) money sent by post, e.g. a cheque or postal orde

rend C — *v* to divide or pull apart with force.

render B — *v* **1.** to give, esp. help. **2.** (accounts) to send in. **3.** t cause to be. **4.** to perform (music).

rendition C — *n* (c) the performing of music.

renovation B — *n* the restoration of old buildings.

rent A — *v* **1.** to allow land or buildings to be used by others i return for regular payment. **2.** (esp. AE) to hire (a ca cycle, etc.).
n the money paid for the use of land, property, etc.

rentable C — *adj* that which may be rented.

repair A — *v* to mend.

reparations C — *n* (plural) money paid by a defeated country to the con queror after a war.

repeal C — *v* to annul (a law).
n (c) the act of annulling (a law).

repeat A — *v* to do or say again.

repel C — *v* **1.** to drive back forcibly. **2.** to disgust.

repent C — *v* to feel very sorry and ashamed for having done wrong

repertoire C — *n* (c) all the pieces, plays, music, etc., that a performer o group can present.

repetition B — *n* the repeating of something.

replica C — *n* (c) an exact copy of something, esp. a work of art o something old (e.g. clothing or a locomotive).

report A — *v* **1.** to give an account of. **2.** to present oneself some where as ready for work. **3.** to complain about.
n (c) **1.** an account or statement of what has happened o been seen. **2.** the noise of an explosion, esp. of a gun

repose C — *v* (rather old-fashioned) **1.** to rest. **2.** to place (trus or confidence) in someone.
n (c) **1.** quiet, peaceful behaviour. **2.** sleep.

represent A — *v* **1.** to be or give a sign or picture symbol of. **2.** to speak for (officially); (there are other C uses).

representation C — *n* **1.** (u) the state of representing other people (as in 2 above). **2.** a sign or symbol of something.

representative C — *adj* typical.

repugnance C — *n* (u) intense disgust; (far stronger in English).

require A/C — *v* **1.** A to need. **2.** C to order, demand.

requisite C — *n* (c) something needed for a given activity.

requisitions C — *n* (c) things formally required, esp. by the army.

resent B — *v* to feel angry about.

eserved B — *adj* **1.** kept for someone else. **2.** kept for a special purpose. **3.** (of people) not showing feelings or opinions readily; (not particularly pejorative).

esolution B — *n* **1.** (u) determination, firmness in character. **2.** (c) a decision made formally by voting, e.g. on a committee. **3.** (c) something you decide to do. (There are other C technical uses.)

esonance C — *n* (u) the quality of having or reproducing deep or clear sound(s); (there are various technical uses connected with sound in physics and music).

esort B — *v* to turn (to something, often something bad).
n (c) **1.** a holiday place. **2.** *as a last resort* or *in the last resort* if all else fails.

espond B/C — *v* **1.** B to react. **2.** C to answer.

esponsibility A — *n* **1.** (u) the state of being responsible. **2.** (c) something you are responsible for.

esponsible A — *adj* **1.** having authority or control; (the English use is more positive than the Latin use, which especially refers to things going wrong). **2.** having many responsibilities.

est A — *v* **1.** to relax and be still. **2.** to place for support.
n **1.** (plural same) the remainder. **2.** (a period of) no movement. **3.** (c) a period of being quiet and peaceful. **4.** a silent pause in music.

estless B — *adj* unable to relax and keep still; (*restlessly* is the adverb).

esult C — *v* to happen as a consequence.

esume B/C — *v* **1.** B to continue after a pause. **2.** C to occupy again.

etain A — *v* to continue to have (there are other C uses).

etarded B — *adj* (of a child's development) held back; developing more slowly than others.

etinue C — *n* (c) the servants, etc., travelling with someone of high rank; (now also used of anyone travelling in employment of another, e.g. a pop star).

etire B — *v* note this verb is only intransitive in English. **1.** to give one's job up when one is old. **2.** to move to a quiet place. **3.** to go to bed.

etreat B — *n* **1.** (c) movement back (esp. of an army); withdrawal. **2.** (c) a peaceful place or a time spent there (esp. in a religious establishment).

etribution C — *n* (u) punishment (esp. in a moral or religious sense).

eturn A — *v* **1.** to travel or move back (to a former position or condition). **2.** to send/hand/pass back.

eunion C — *n* (c) a gathering of old friends or a family after a long period of separation.

eunite C — *v* to bring or come together again; (but in a narrower sense than the Latin use).

evel C — *v* **1.** to take part in noisy activities; make merry. **2.** to have much happiness.

evelation C — *n* (c) the disclosure of something surprising or important.

evenge B — *n* *in revenge* from a desire to punish someone who has hurt one.

reverberate C *v* to echo, fill with sound.

reverse B *v* **1.** to move backwards. **2.** to change round.
n **1.** (c) the opposite. **2.** (u) the position of a vehicle' controls in which it will move backwards; other uses ar C.

revise B *v* **1.** to examine and bring up to date. **2.** (BE) to go ove work before a test or exam.

revision B *n* **1.** (c) a corrected edition of a book, etc. **2.** (u) the ac of revising a book, etc. **3.** (u) re-reading schoolwor before a test or exam.

revolted C *past participle* disgusted, shocked.

revolve C *v* to turn round.

rhapsody C *n* (c) **1.** a piece of music of no specific form. **2.** (plural expressions of great enthusiasm.

rice A *n* (u) the white grain widely planted and eaten in Easter countries.

rich food B *n* (usually u) food with more than usual amounts of fa cream, etc., likely to be difficult to digest.

ride A *v* to travel on a horse, cycle, etc.
n (c) **1.** a journey on a horse or other animal, or in vehicle (of any type, in contrast to the use of the verb) **2.** a turn on equipment at a fairground .

rider C *n* (c) **1.** someone who rides a horse. **2.** something ad ded as a comment or qualification to an official statemen

rind C *n* the thick skin of certain fruit, e.g. lemon, and on chees and bacon.

ring A *v* **1.** to surround. **2.** to telephone (someone).
n (c) **1.** a circle. **2.** a metal band worn on the finger **3.** a bell-like sound. **4.** (informal) a telephone call.

ring road C *n* (c) a road going all round the outside of a town connect ing the roads going out beyond it; (a *bypass* is usuall elliptical and round one side only).

riotous C *adj* rather wild, noisy, and often very amusing.

risk A *v* to expose (oneself) to danger.
n the possibility of danger.

risky B *adj* having the possibility of danger. (*Risqué* is used in Englis with the French meaning.)

road A *n* (c) a paved way for vehicles to travel on.

road show C *n* (c) **1.** entertainment given by a disc jockey in a singl programme (with mobile equipment) to an audience, the moving on.
2. (formerly) any performance given for one night only by a group of entertainers.

roar B *n* (c) the sound made by a lion, big waves, a great wind, etc

roast C *n* (c) **1.** a piece of roasted meat. **2.** (AE) a meal eaten and cooked out of doors.

rob B *v* to steal from.

robber C *n* (c) a thief; someone who robs.

robe C *n* (c) **1.** a long flowing garment. **2.** (plural) ceremonia clothes. **3.** (AE) a rug (usually fur) to use when sitting out of doors.

rock A — *n* **1.** (c) a large piece of stone. **2.** (u) short for *rock-and-roll music*. **3.** (BE) a hard brightly coloured stick-shaped sweet.

rodeo C — *n* (c) in N. America, an open-air performance of riding, lassooing, etc., with competitions; (the original meaning was 'a cattle round-up' as in Spanish and Portuguese).

role B — *n* (c) the part taken by someone in a play or film; the function of someone or an institution.

roller C — *n* (c) **1.** one of a number of smooth long cylinders placed under something with no wheels, to move it. **2.** a heavy apparatus for making a lawn smooth.

Roman C — *n* (c) someone who lives in or comes from Rome.

romance C — *n* **1.** (c) a story of adventure and love, usually fictional. **2.** (c) a love affair. **3.** (u) adventure, excitement, and mystery.

romanesque C — *adj* used of Continental architecture for the building style in Britain known as Norman, used between the 10th century and the beginning of Gothic.

romp C — *v* **1.** (esp. of children and dogs) to play wildly. **2.** to win a race easily.
n (c) the activity of romping.

roof A — *n* (c) the covering on a building, car, etc.

rook C — *n* (c) a large black bird.

room A — *n* **1.** (c) an enclosed space in a building. **2.** (u) space for something.

rooster C — *n* (c) (AE) a domestic cock.

rope A — *n* (u) thick strong cord.

rostrum C — *n* (c) a small raised platform for someone making a speech or for a conductor of an orchestra.

rot C — *n* (u) **1.** (informal) rubbish, nonsense. **2.** something that has disintegrated or decomposed.

rota C — *n* (c) a list of people's names showing who is on duty and when; (also called a *roster*).

rouge B — *n* (c) the cosmetic used to colour the cheeks.

roulette C — *n* (u) a gambling game using a ball on a numbered wheel.

route A — *n* (c) the way planned or taken for a journey.

routine B — *n* (u) the regular way of doing something, esp. one that does not change.

rove C — *v* to move from one place to another.

rover C — *n* (c) someone who moves from place to place.

row C — *v* **1.** to make a noise. **2.** to have a quarrel; (different pronunciation gives different meanings).

royal A/C — *adj* **1.** A connected with the king and/or queen. **2.** C splendid; (close to the Dutch but used only in a few phrases).

rub A — *v* to move two surfaces against each other, using pressure.

rubric C — *n* (c) **1.** the instructions on a test or exam paper. **2.** the similar instructions in a prayer book or missal.

ruby C — *adj* deep red colour, similar to burgundy.

rudder C — *n* (c) the movable blade at the back of a boat to control its direction.

rude A — *adj* impolite.
rudely A — *adv* impolitely.
rudiments C — *n* (c; plural) the essential parts (of a subject).
rue C — *v* to be sorry about, regret.
ruff C — *n* (c) **1.** a stiff collar that stands out, esp. as worn in the 16th century. **2.** a shore bird.
ruffian C — *n* (c) a wild (often violent) youth or man.
ruffle C — *n* (c) a kind of frill or ruff (in sense **1** above).
rug B — *n* (c) **1.** a piece of material to put on the floor (thicker than a mat). **2.** a piece of warm material to wrap round one's shoulders or legs in cold weather. Compare **plaid**.
Ruhr C — *n* *The Ruhr* the industrial area in West Germany.
ruin A — *n* **1.** (c; often plural) a ruined building. **2.** (u) a state of destruction, decadence, or decay.
rum C — *n* (u) **1.** strong alcoholic drink made from sugar cane. **2.** (AE) any sort of alcoholic drink.
rumour C — *v* (usually passive) to report unofficially.
B — *n* (c) stories or gossip without a basis of certainty or truth.
rump C — *n* (c) the part of an animal above the back leg.
run B — *n* (c) a period of running.
running B — *n* (u) **1.** the action of having a run. **2.** the organisation and management. **3.** *in* (or *out of*) *the running* with (or without) hope of winning.
rush B — *n* (c) the state of being in a hurry; great activity.
rusk C — *n* (c) a kind of hard biscuit for babies.
rust B — *v* (of certain metals) to oxidise, corrode.
rusty B — *adj* covered with rust.
rye C — *n* (u) a cereal.

S

sabotage C — *v* to destroy as an act of sabotage.
n (u) secret damage to machines, buildings, etc., to weaken an enemy or opponent.
sable C — *n* **1.** (c) a small dark animal. **2.** (u) fur from this animal.
saccharin B — *n* (u) a chemical sweetener.
sack A — *v* (BE informal) to dismiss from work.
n **1.** (c) a large bag. **2.** *give someone the sack* (BE informal) to dismiss someone from work.
sag C — *v* to hang down in the middle because of weight.
saga C — *n* (c) **1.** a traditional story, as of the Vikings. **2.** (informal) a long tedious story.
sage C — *n* **1.** (c) a wise old man. **2.** (u) a herb, the leaves of which are used in cooking.

Sahara B — *n* used only of the great desert in Africa from the Atlantic coast to the Red Sea.

Saint T(h)eresa C *n* used only of the woman Saint.

salad A/C — *n* **1.** A (c) a dish of mixed vegetables served cold and mostly raw. **2.** A (AE) a sort of sandwich. **3.** (u) C green vegetables grown for salad (esp. lettuce).

salamander C — *n* (c) **1.** a kind of amphibious lizard. **2.** a lizard-like creature supposed to have lived in fire.

salary A — *n* (c) payment for (professional) work, paid monthly by cheque; (*wages* are usually paid weekly; *fees* or a *fee* is payment made once for professional services).

saloon C — *n* (c) **1.** the passengers' sitting room on a large ship. **2.** short for a *saloon car* a car for several passengers and having a fixed roof. **3.** (AE) a bar. **4.** (BE) a part of a public house.

salt A/C — *n* **1.** (u) A the white substance used in cooking, etc. **2.** (c) C a sailor.

salute B — *v* to greet formally as in the army (also with flags or firing guns).

salvo C — *n* (c) **1.** a salute made with a number of guns firing together. **2.** a number of bombs dropped together.

n (c) the action of saluting.

same A — *adj, pronoun* not different.

sanatorium C — *n* (c) a kind of hospital for those needing a long rest, fresh air, and sunshine.

sanction C — *v* to permit, approve.

sand A — *n* the fine-grained material found in deserts and by the sea.

sandwich A — *n* (c) two slices of bread and the filling between.

sane C — *adj* **1.** mentally healthy. **2.** (of ideas, etc.) reasonable.

sanguine C — *adj* optimistic, hopeful; (the association with blood is literary).

sauce B — *n* **1.** the (usually) thick liquid served with various foods, sweet or savoury; (but not made from meat juices, which is *gravy*). **2.** (BE) impoliteness, answering back; (*sass* in AE).

saucy C — *adj* (BE) answering back; (*sassy* in AE).

savage A — *adj* **1.** uncontrollably violent and cruel; ferocious. **2.** uncivilised.

save A — *v* *save oneself* to succeed in making oneself safe in a dangerous situation.

scab C — *n* (c) the hard dried blood which forms over a cut on the skin.

scald C — *v* to burn the skin in hot liquid or steam.

n (c) a burn of this kind.

scale A — *n* (c) **1.** the hard flat pieces on the body surface of a fish, etc. **2.** a series of marks placed at regular intervals. **3.** a series of numbers or standards for comparing or measuring. **4.** the proportion of size, e.g. of a map. **5.** (music) (usually) eight notes.

scalpel C — *n* (c) a special knife used in surgery, biology, etc.
scandal B — *n* an event which shocks or angers people.
scandalise C — *v* to shock.
scandalous C — *adj* shocking, likely to cause a scandal.
scatter B — *v* to cover an area with small pieces.
scenario C — *n* (c) **1.** the written outline of a plot of a play or film. **2.** the description of a possible course of events.
scene A — *n* (c) a word with many meanings: in the theatre, it usually means the place represented on the stage by the backdrop rather than the stage itself.
sceptical C — *adj* full of doubt; reluctant to believe or trust others.
scheme A — *n* (c) a plan or system.
scholarship C — *n* **1.** (c) money provided for study. **2.** (u) exact and serious study.
schooling C — *n* (c) education at school.
schottische C — *n* (c) a round dance, a kind of slow polka, or music for such a dance.
scissors A — *n* (fixed plural) a cutting instrument with two moving blades; (also called a *pair of scissors*).
scold C — *v* to express anger in words, to reprimand; (to *tell someone off* is now more usual).
scope B — *n* (u) **1.** opportunity. **2.** the area within the limits of an action or subject.
scorch C — *v* to burn slightly, changing colour but not destroying.
n a burn of this type.
Scotch B — *n* (u) Scottish whisky.
scout C — *n* (c) **1.** a member of the (Boy) Scout Association; (girls may be *guides*). **2.** a person, ship, or aircraft which goes ahead to reconnoitre.
scowl C — *n* (c) an angry expression on the face.
scratch C — *n* (c) **1.** a small cut on the skin, e.g. made by a thorn. **2.** the act of scratching.
scrupulous C — *adj* **1.** careful to observe rules (and one's conscience). **2.** paying minute attention to very small details.
scrutinise C — *v* to examine very carefully.
scrutiny C — *n* (u) **1.** the careful examination of something or some-one. **2.** (BE only) the re-counting of election votes, when the results are too close.
scum C — *n* (u) **1.** undesirable filmy covering on the surface of a boiling liquid. **2.** dirt on the surface of water. **3.** (very derogatory) the most inferior part of society.
scurrilous C — *adj* (language) full of abuse, impoliteness, or evil.
sea A — *n* (c) the salt water covering much of the earth's surface.
seal C — *n* (c) **1.** a fish-eating sea animal. **2.** any of various kinds of devices attached to documents, letters, etc., to show their authenticity.
seance C — *n* (c) almost exclusively used of a spiritualist meeting with a demonstration.
search A — *v* to look through hoping to find something.
seawards C — *adv* towards the sea.

secret A — *n* (c) **1.** a piece of information to be known or shared by few people. **2.** a hidden or unexplained cause. **3.** something unexplained so far; mystery. **4.** *in secret* secretly.

sect C — *n* (c) a group of people who share opinions or beliefs (esp. religious ones) different from a larger (religious) group.

section A/C — *n* (c) **1.** A one of the parts which make a whole. **2.** C a piece cut off like a slice.

secular C — *adj* of the ordinary world, in contrast to the spiritual.

security B — *n* **1.** (u) freedom from danger and violence. **2.** (plural) documents (showing ownership) of stocks and shares. **3.** (c) something taken in exchange for a loan.

sedan C — *n* (c) (esp. AE) a type of saloon car.

seduce C — *v* **1.** to persuade to have sexual intercourse. **2.** to persuade to do something (undesirable).

see into B — *v* to investigate, examine, probe.

segment C — *n* (c) **1.** strictly, the area in a circle between its edge and a straight line cut across it. **2.** a section.

self C — *n* one's own personality and interests.

sell A — *v* to exchange for money.

semaphore C — *n* **1.** (u) the method of sending a message by holding the arms in various positions to represent letters. **2.** (c) (correctly, a *semaphore signal*) on the railways, a signal with an arm which moves up and down; (now becoming obsolete in Britain).

semester B — *n* (c) (mainly AE) half the university year.

semi B — *n* (c) short for a *semi-detached house*, one of two built side by side.

seminar C — *n* (c) a small class of students discussing a subject with their teacher.

seminary C — *n* (c) a training college for priests.

send up C — *v* **1.** to deliver to a higher floor in a building. **2.** (slang) to make a parody of.

sender C — *n* (c) someone who sends a letter or parcel.

senna pod C — *n* a laxative from a tropical plant.

sense A — *n* of many meanings, note **1.** purpose or reason. **2.** an ability to perceive. **3.** (c) a meaning. **4.** (u) *common sense* sound practical judgment.

sensed C — *past participle* felt.

sensible A/C — *adj* **1.** A reasonable, showing good judgment and common sense. **2.** C aware.

sentence A — *v* to announce a sentence (in sense **2** below).
n (c) **1.** (language) a group of words forming a question, exclamation, command, or statement, usually containing a finite verb. **2.** a punishment announced in a court for a criminal.

sepia C — *n* (u) (printing and photography) a brown colour.

sequel C — *n* (c) **1.** something that follows something else, esp. as a result. **2.** a film or book which carries on the story of an earlier one.

sequester C — *v* **1.** to keep apart from other people (esp. in a quiet place). **2.** to sequestrate.

sequestrate C — *v* to take legal control of (goods) till debts have been paid.

serene C — *adj* **1.** calm, composed. **2.** clear.

series A — *n* (c; plural same) **1.** a group of things coming in sequence. **2.** *in series* in an ordered arrangement.

serin C — *n* (c) a small wild bird, wild canary.

serious A — *adj* **1.** solemn, in earnest, sincere. **2.** having possible dangers.

Serpentine C — *n* *the Serpentine* the long curving lake in Hyde Park, London.

servant B — *n* (c) someone who works for another for a wage, esp. in the house.

service A — *n* of many meanings, note esp. **1.** (u) the act or manner of serving customers or guests in a shop, restaurant, etc. **2.** (c) work done. **3.** (c) the public supply of water, gas, etc. **4.** (c) a department of public employment. **5.** (c) a branch of the armed forces.

serviceable C — *adj* (used only of things) capable of providing good service.

serviette B — *n* (c) a square of paper or cloth to keep clothes clean while eating.

set A — *n* **1.** a group of things going together. **2.** a radio or TV receiver. **3.** a group of games won in tennis.

set out B — *v* **1.** to leave, start a journey. **2.** to lay out on display.

shackles C — *n* (c; plural) **1.** rings joined by a chain to fit round a prisoner's ankles. **2.** anything which prevents the freedom of an individual.

shade A — *n* **1.** an area protected from bright light or heat. **2.** the degree of intensity or darkness of a colour. **3.** something which gives protection from bright light, esp. an eyeshade or a lampshade. **4.** a degree of difference.

shame A — *n* **1.** (no plural) something regretted. **2.** (u) feelings of dishonour or guilt.

shape C — *v* **1.** to give form to. **2.** to develop.

shaping C — *n* (u) the action of giving something shape.

sharp A — *adj* **1.** which cuts well. **2.** distinct. **3.** piercing. **4.** abrupt. **5.** quickly perceiving things. **6.** pointed.

shawl C — *n* (c) a piece of material worn by women over the shoulders or for wrapping a baby in.

shears C — *n* (fixed plural) like large scissors, for use in the garden (also called a *pair of shears*).

sheen C — *n* (c; no plural) a bright reflective surface.

shell B — *n* (c) of several meanings, notice esp. **1.** the hard outer layer of an animal or an egg. **2.** an explosive for firing from a large gun. **3.** the outside structure of a building.

shellfish C — *n* (plural same) **1.** (c) any water animal with a shell but no backbone. **2.** (u) any of these animals eaten as food.

shield B — *n* (c) **1.** the part of armour carried on the arm, now also used in heraldry. **2.** anything which protects something else; (a metal plate is a *shield* only if it protects).

shift B — *v* to move, change position (to *shift one's clothes* can only mean move them from one place to another).

shin C — *n* (c) the bony front part of the lower leg.

shine C — *n* the quality of reflecting light or the cause of this; polishing.

ship A — *n* (c) a large (seagoing) boat.

shock A — *v* to cause to feel surprise, disgust, horror, or anger.
n (c) **1.** something which gives a shock. **2.** the phrase a *shock of hair* is the only use parallelling the German meaning.

shocking A — *adj* giving or causing shock.

shoe cream C — *n* thick liquid used for cleaning shoes.

shoot A — *v* **1.** to fire a weapon. **2.** (BE) to hunt (with guns). **3.** to move very fast. **4.** to kick a ball towards the goal. **5.** to make a film.

shop A — *n* (c) (chiefly BE) a (part of) a building where goods are sold; (a *store* in AE).

shorts B — *n* (c; plural) **1.** (esp. BE) trousers ending well above the knees. **2.** (AE) underpants for men; (in both senses also called a *pair of shorts*).

show A — *v* to present something or someone so that it can be seen or demonstrated; (there are many other similar uses, usually referring to the activity of someone who demonstrates, not the person who watches).

shower A — *n* (c) **1.** a short period of rain. **2.** an apparatus for washing in a bathroom, under small jets of water. **3.** the use of such an apparatus. **4.** (AE) a party when people bring presents. **5.** (BE slang) a group of useless people.

shriek B — *v* to make a high cry.

side A — *n* (c) of many meanings and uses, note **1.** either of two surfaces of a flat object. **2.** the area at the edge of a room, road, etc. **3.** a district or part of a town, etc., considered from a central point. **4.** a position in an argument or game. **5.** a part or aspect to be viewed. **6.** a line of descent in the family. **7.** the area around the waist of the body.

sidesman C — *n* (c) (BE) a man who shows people to a seat in church.

siege C — *n* (c) the action of surrounding a town in order to capture it, block its supplies, etc.

sierra C — *n* (c) a mountain in Spain or S. America.

sieve C — *v* to pass (food, etc.) through a fine wire net.

sigh A — *v* to let out a long breath, esp. of satisfaction, tiredness, or sadness.

sign A — *v* to write (one's name) as signature.
n (c) **1.** a symbol. **2.** a signal made to someone (e.g. by lifting the hand. **3.** a notice giving instructions, warning, etc. **4.** indication.

signal B — *v* **1.** to send a message by means of a sign or gesture. **2.** to be an indication of.

signature A — *n* (c) the way a person regularly signs his name.

silly A — *adj* stupid, foolish.

simple A — *adj* **1.** (of things) not giving difficulty, easy. **2.** (of ma chines) uncomplicated. **3.** plain, not highly developed **4.** (of people) not sophisticated, innocent. **5.** (o people) easily deceived, inexperienced.

sin B — *n* (c) **1.** a wrong action according to religious teaching **2.** anything considered wrong.

sinew C — *n* (c) the cord which joins a muscle to a bone; tendon.

sinful C — *adj* wicked, wrong.

sinus C — *n* a cavity in the face bones, opening into the nose.

siren C — *n* (c) **1.** an apparatus for making a loud prolonge sound of warning, used on fire engines, police cars etc.; (note that a *hooter* is not prolonged and a *foghor* is a siren only used during fog). **2.** (Greek mythology one of the singing women who caused shipwrecks b distracting the sailors. **3.** a dangerously attractiv woman.

site A — *n* (c) **1.** a piece of land for building on. **2.** a plac where something existed or happened in the past.

sixpence C — *n* (c) an obsolete British coin with a face value of six ol pennies.

skate B — *n* (c) **1.** the metal blade fitting on the bottom of a boo with which to move fast on ice; (*roller skates* are similar fitted with wheels). **2.** a kind of large flat fish.

skin A — *n* **1.** the outer covering of a body. **2.** the detached cover ing of an animal.

skip B — *v* to move with a hop and run with each foot alternately **2.** to miss out in reading. **3.** to be absent from. **4** to jump over a rope that swings under one's feet.

skirt A — *n* (c) a woman's outer garment that hangs from the wais down.

skive C — *v* (BE slang) to avoid doing work.

sky A — *n* (c) the space above the earth.

slab C — *n* (c) a flat piece of material.

slack C — *n* (u) **1.** coal dust. **2.** the part of a rope or wire whicl hangs loose.

slacken C — *v* **1.** to make a rope or wire less tight. **2.** to make les intense.

slag C — *n* (u) the glass-like waste which remains when metal ha been separated from its natural rock (ore).

slang A — *n* (u) the informal register of language not considere standard English; not often written, often only used by a particular group of people (esp. the young).

slap C — *v* **1.** to hit with the hand and make a sharp sound. **2.** tc put carelessly, roughly.

slate C — *v* **1.** to cover (a roof) with slates. **2.** (BE slang) tc reprimand or blame severely. **3.** (AE) to propose o plan.
n (c) a tile made of a smooth grey material, used to cove roofs.

Slav B — *n* (c) a person of one of the Slavonic nations.

slave C — *n* (c) **1.** a person who has no freedom and belongs to another person. **2.** someone who works very hard. **3.** a person controlled by something or a habit.

slay C — *v* (old-fashioned) to murder, kill.

sleep A — *n* **1.** (u) the natural state of resting when the body is unconscious. **2.** (c) a period of this.

A/C — *v* A **1.** to be in a state of sleep. **2.** *sleep in* C to sleep late in the morning. **3.** *sleep out* to sleep away from home or in the open air.

sleet C — *n* (u) a mixture of rain and snow.

slick C — *n* (c) a large area of oil, floating on the sea.

slim A — *adj* **1.** not fat; pleasingly thin. **2.** slight.

slime C — *n* (u) **1.** dirty semi-liquid mud. **2.** the thick sticky liquid left by snails, slugs, etc., when they move.

sling C — *v* **1.** to throw forcefully. **2.** to lift (a load, etc.) with ropes as round a barrel.

slip A/B — *v* A **1.** to move by sliding. **2.** to put on or take off clothes. **3.** to move without being noticed. **4.** *slip up* B **a.** to fall down. **b.** to make a small mistake.

A — *n* (c) **1.** an undergarment worn by women. **2.** a small mistake. **3.** the act of slipping or sliding. **4.** a sloping surface where a ship is built. **5.** a narrow strip of paper. **6.** *the slips* a specific place in a cricket field near the wicketkeeper.

slope C — *v* to be inclined at an angle.

slot C — *n* (c) **1.** a narrow straight opening. **2.** a space in a list or between programmes on radio or TV.

sluice C — *n* (c) a kind of gate across a river to hold back the water at a certain height.

slump B — *v* **1.** to collapse. **2.** (business, etc.) to decline.

n (c) a period when business declines; (*the slump* usually refers to the American depression in the 1920s).

slur C — *v* to pronounce indistinctly.

slut C — *n* (c) a dirty or immoral woman.

smack C — *v* **1.** to hit with the hand, esp. as a punishment.

n (c) **1.** the action of smacking. **2.** a small fishing boat.

small A — *adj* not big; little.

smart C — *v* to give or feel a sharp pain, esp. on the skin or in the eyes.

C — *n* (c) a sharp pain.

A — *adj* **1.** quick at understanding, clever. **2.** (of clothes) fashionable or elegant.

smear C — *n* (c) **1.** an oily-looking mark or stain. **2.** a small piece of body tissue, taken for medical examination. **3.** unfounded information circulated about someone to spoil their reputation.

smell A — *n* **1.** the sense centred on the nose. **2.** (c) scent.

smelt C — *v* to melt ore to get the metal out.

smite C — *v* **1.** (archaic) to hit. **2.** *be smitten with* (informal) **a.** to be ill with. **b.** to be attracted to, in love with.

smoking A — *n* (u) the activity of using a pipe, cigar, or cigarette.

smut C — *n* **1.** (c) a small particle, esp. from a fire that may mark th skin. **2.** (u) filthy talk. **3.** (u) a disease of cereals.

snack B — *n* (c) a quickly eaten small meal.

snail B — *n* (c) a small creature with a shell on its back and noted fo moving slowly.

snake B — *n* (c) **1.** a reptile with no legs, of which many species ar poisonous. **2.** a system of allowing the currency c certain countries to make moderate changes in thei rates of exchange.

snap B — *v* **1.** to break with a clear sound. **2.** to speak sharply **3.** to make a sharp sound.

n (c) **1.** a short sharp sound. **2.** an informal photc **3.** (occasionally used as in Japanese) a snap fastener (this is more usually called a *press stud*).

sneer C — *v* to show contempt in speech or by facial expression.

snob C — *n* (c) a person who believes he is socially superior to mos other people and who acts in this way; (*snob* is not a adjective in English).

snobbish B — *adj* like a snob.

snore C — *v* to breathe noisily when sleeping.

n (c) a noise of this kind.

snout C — *n* (c) **1.** an animal's nose. **2.** something of this shape esp. in a machine.

snub C — *v* to treat with contempt, esp. in refusing an offer.

snug C — *adj* warm and comfortable, cosy.

so A — a word with too many uses to list here, but in this sen tence *he missed the bus so he took a taxi*, *so* means 'fo this reason' (*then* would mean 'after that').

soap A — *n* the substance used for washing the skin in water.

social A — *adj* many meanings, so only misunderstandings are given in English it is more concerned with society in general a *social reason* suggests a reason based on how societ will react; *social news* means news of high society weddings, etc.

sock B — *n* **1.** (c) a covering for the foot and lower leg, worn insid a shoe. **2.** (informal) a hard blow, hit.

soffit C — *n* (c) the undersurface of a projection on a building.

soil A — *n* earth; ground in which plants will grow.

sole C — *n* (c) **1.** a flat sea fish. **2.** the underside of the foot **3.** the underside of the front part of a shoe.

solicit C — *v* **1.** (formal) to ask someone for something. **2.** (legal to beg for money. **3.** to advertise oneself as a prostitute

solicitude C — *n* (u) the quality of showing care for someone's comfort welfare, health, etc.

solid A — *adj* there are too many uses to give them here: note that it i rarely used of people, but mostly of things.

solitaire C — *n* **1.** (u) a game for one player with a board and small ball or pegs. **2.** (u; chiefly AE) a card game for one player **3.** (c) a single jewel (in a piece of jewellery).

solo B — *n* (c) a performance by one person, esp. in music or flying

sophisticated B *adj* **1.** (of people) cultivated to a high level. **2.** (of things) complex.

sort A *v* **1.** to separate into groups. **2.** to resolve.
n (c) a kind, type.

sortie C *n* (c) **1.** a short military (or air) attack made from a position of defence. **2.** an action made by an organisation into an unfamiliar area.

soul C *n* (c) the part of man believed to live on after death; (there are other allied uses of the word).

sound C *v* *sound someone out* to try to discover someone's opinions/ ideas; (less intense than the Latin meaning).
adj **1.** in good health, fit. **2.** dependable, firm. **3.** based on good judgment and reasoning. **4.** (of a person) having good judgment. **5.** (of sleep) deep and undisturbed.

English soup C *n* (c) any kind of soup associated with England.

sour B *adj* **1.** not sweet, of acid taste like vinegar, or lemon. **2.** having or showing a bad temper.

source A/B *n* (c) **1.** A the place where something comes from. **2.** B the place where a river or stream originates.

souvenir B *n* (c) something bought in a place to remind one of one's visit.

spa C *n* (c) a place where there are natural mineral waters.

spade B *n* (c) an implement for turning over soil.

span B *v* **1.** to stretch from one side to the other (esp. said of a bridge). **2.** to cover (esp. of activities, hobbies, or time).
n (c) **1.** the distance between supports of a bridge. **2.** a period of time.

Spanish A *adj* connected with Spain; (with no idiomatic meanings).

spank C *v* to hit as a punishment, esp. on the bottom.

spanner C *n* (c) (BE only) a tool for turning a nut (a six-sided piece of metal with a screw hole); (a *wrench* in AE).

spar C *n* **1.** (c) a pole which has a ship's sail fixed to it. **2.** (u) a type of light-coloured mineral.

spare A *v* to have or be free for (something).

spark C *n* (c) **1.** a small bit of burning material thrown out by something burning or caused by the rubbing of two hard surfaces. **2.** a flash of light produced by the passage of electricity through the air.

speak against B *v* to oppose, speak critically.

speak out C *v* to say openly and boldly.

speaker B *n* (c) someone who speaks, esp. in public.

spear C *n* (c) a long narrow weapon with a pointed end, for throwing.

special A/B *adj* **1.** A specific, not general. **2.** B unusual.

specious C *adj* seeming correct but in fact wrong.

spectacle C *n* **1.** (c) something notable which is seen. **2.** (plural) (old-fashioned) glasses for the eyes.

speeder C *n* (c) (informal) someone who moves very fast.

speedy B *adj* moving fast.

spell B — *v* to give the letters used in writing a word.
n (c) **1.** a short period of time. **2.** (words used to put) magic power (on someone). **3.** fascination.

spend A — *v* **1.** to pay (money) for. **2.** to pass time.

spendable C — *adj* (rare) which can be spent.

spender C — *n* (c) someone who spends.

spent C — *adj* exhausted.

sperm C — *n* (c) the generative cell produced by the male.

sphere B — *n* (c) **1.** a ball shape. **2.** an area of (someone's) interest, knowledge, or activities.

spider B — *n* (c) any of various kinds of creature with four pairs of legs and which make silk.

spiel C — *n* (c) (colloq.) a long persuasive or complaining tirade.

spike C — *n* (c) a long pointed shape.

spill B — *v* to cause liquid to flow accidentally (over an edge).
n (c) **1.** a fall from a cycle, horse, etc. **2.** a thin twisted piece of paper or wood for lighting tobacco, etc.

spine C — *n* (c) **1.** the backbone. **2.** a prickle on a plant or animal. **3.** the back of a book.

spire C — *n* (c) a pointed structure on a building (esp. a church).

spiritual C — *adj* **1.** of the spirit or soul, in contrast to material matter. **2.** religious, sacred.

spleen C — *n* **1.** (c) a small organ near the stomach that makes changes in the blood. **2.** (u) anger, irritation.

splice C — *v* **1.** to join the ends of rope, film, etc. **2.** (informal use; passive) to get married.

splint C — *n* (c) a flat piece of metal or wood to keep a broken bone in position for healing.

split B — *n* **1.** (c) a division along the length of something. **2.** (plural) the acrobatic position with the legs open and touching the ground in their whole length.

sportive C — *adj* (old-fashioned) playful, jolly, jocular; (*sport* has a more competitive connotation in German than in English).

spot A — *v* **1.** to manage to see, recognise. **2.** to rain very slightly.
n (c) **1.** a small mark (of dirt). **2.** a place, locality. **3.** a small blemish on the skin. **4.** a drop (of rain).

spotter C — *n* (c) someone who watches for planes, cars, etc.

spring A — *v* to jump; leap.
n (c) of many meanings, note **1.** the season following winter. **2.** a device, such as a coil or bent strip of metal for suspension or power as in e.g. a clock.

spur C — *n* (c) **1.** a ridge of land projecting from a larger mass. **2.** a small wheel with spikes fitted on the back of riding boots. **3.** something which urges one to action.

squalid C — *adj* very dirty, not cared for.

square A — *n* (c) **1.** a shape of four equal sides and 90° corners. **2.** an open area in a town. **3.** (informal) someone who is conventional or old-fashioned. **4.** (mathematics) the result of multiplying a number by itself.

stab C — *n* (c) **1.** a wound caused by a pointed weapon. **2.** the striking or wounding of someone with such a weapon.

table C *n* (c) a building where animals, esp. horses are kept.

adium B *n* (c) a large building where sports are organised.

taff A/C *n* (c) **1.** A the people who work together in a firm, etc. **2.** (old-fashioned) C a heavy stick for walking with or for defence.

tage A *n* (c) **1.** in a theatre, the raised part where the acting is done. **2.** a level of development.

aircase B *n* (c) the whole length of stairs with all supports.

take C *v* **1.** to support with strong posts. **2.** to risk (esp. money) in betting. **3.** to make a claim to something.

taking C *n* (u) **1.** strong posts for making a fence. **2.** the activity of putting in stakes or claiming (sense **3** of the verb).

tall B *v* **1.** to (cause to) stop. **2.** to delay in giving an answer.
n (c) **1.** a space for a single animal. **2.** a special seat in a church (esp. near the choir). **3.** (BE only) a table for an open shop. **4.** (BE only; plural) the seats in a theatre at the lowest level.

tamp A *v* **1.** to put down the foot with force. **2.** to put a postage stamp on a letter. Compare **frank**. **3.** to print.
n (c) **1.** a small piece of paper with an official mark to stick on letters, etc. **2.** an instrument for printing on a surface. **3.** a mark made by this. **4.** a sign characteristic of something or someone.

ampede C *n* (c) **1.** a rush of frightened animals. **2.** a wild rush of people.

and B *n* (c) of various uses, note **1.** a position of defence. **2.** a piece of furniture on which to put items such as hats or sheets of music. **3.** a stall or space at an exhibition, etc. **4.** a raised stage at a public gathering. **5.** (AE) a witness box in a court.

andard A *n* (c) most uses coincide with French, except the telephone use given.

anding C *n* **1.** reputation, rank. **2.** *of long standing* of long duration.

aple C *v* to fasten together with a U-shaped piece of metal, esp. wood or paper.
n (c) the metal piece used to hold things together in this way.

ar A *n* (c) **1.** one of the bodies shining in the night sky (excepting the moon and planets). **2.** a symbolic representation of a star as in the U.S. flag. **3.** a leading performer in a film, play, or other entertainment.

ar map C *n* (c) a map showing the night sky with the constellations, etc.

ark C *adj* without decoration, bare; (*stark naked* completely without clothes).

art A *n* (c) **1.** a beginning. **2.** a sudden movement.

arter B *n* (c) **1.** someone who starts a race. **2.** the instrument in a motor to make it start.

starve C *v* to die because of lack of food.

stasis C *n* (u) (medical only) the stoppage of circulation of the bloo

state A *n* **1.** (c) the condition of someone or something. **2.** (a nation. **3.** one of the partly self-governing sections certain nations. **4.** (u) ceremony connected with a rule **5.** *in a state* (informal) in a state of agitation or tensio

station A/B/C *n* (c) **1.** A a place where passengers enter or leave trains buses. **2.** C a position in society. **3.** B a place whe a service is provided, e.g. *a police station.*

stature C *n* (u) **1.** importance. **2.** height or size.

status C *n* **1.** position or rank in relation to others; prestige. the state of affairs.

statute C *n* (c) a formally accepted law of a country.

stave C *v* to break a hole in something.

stay A *v* **1.** to remain. **2.** to keep. (There are many other uses

steak B *n* a thick piece of meat or fish for frying, etc.

steal A *v* **1.** to take something belonging to someone else. Com pare **rob**. **2.** to move quietly, secretly.

steel A *n* (u) the hard alloy made of carbon and iron.

steer C *n* (c) a castrated bullock.

stem B/C *v* **1.** B to originate; come from. **2.** C to stop the flow of liquid, etc.

B/C *n* (c) B the thin upright part of a plant; (there are a fe other C uses).

stench C *n* (c) a very unpleasant smell.

step B *v* to place one foot down after the other as for walkin (In modern English the verb has no connection wit dancing.)

Stepney C *n* a part of East London.

stern B *n* (c) the back of a ship.

stick A *v* **1.** to (cause to) fix with adhesive material. **2.** to b fixed and unmoving. **3.** (informal) to bear, stan **4.** (slang) to stay, wait. **5.** to push something pointe into.

n (c) a small thin piece of wood or a rod or tool of thi shape; (but not one carried when riding a horse).

stickle C *v* to insist or argue over small detail.

sticky B *adj* **1.** tending to adhere to other things. **2.** (informa difficult.

stigma C *n* (c) **1.** the part of a plant which receives the polle **2.** a stain or mark on one's character.

stile C *n* (c) a set of steps over a fence or wall.

stiletto C *n* (c) **1.** the very pointed heel on women's shoes. **2** (rare) a small dagger.

still C *n* (c) an apparatus for producing alcohol.

A/C *adj* **1.** A motionless; at rest. **2.** C (of wines or drinks without gas.

sting B *n* (c) **1.** the pain caused by poison from a snake, insect, o plant. **2.** the pointed organ on an insect which inflict this.

tink C *n* (c) a very unpleasant smell; (this is a more informal and slightly offensive word compared with *stench* – clearly a cognate).

tipend C *n* (c) a salary, esp. of a clergyman.

titch B *n* (c) **1.** (of embroidery and knitting) one pass of a thread. **2.** the result of this. **3.** a pain in the side caused by running.

tock A *n* too many meanings to be given here; the basic uses are **1.** (c) the total goods kept in a shop or business. **2.** (u) farm animals; livestock; cattle.

tomach C *v* **1.** to swallow. **2.** to accept, tolerate.

tomp C *v* to walk or dance heavily.

tool B *n* (c) a simple chair without a back.

top A *v* **1.** to (cause to) cease movement; come or bring to an end. **2.** to block payment (of a cheque).
n (c) **1.** a place where something stops, esp. a bus. **2.** a state of no movement.

toppage C *n* (c) **1.** a blocked condition, preventing normal functions. **2.** the action of stopping work as in a strike.

topper C *n* (c) something like a cork which fits into an opening, esp. of a bottle.

tore A *v* **1.** to keep ready for use. **2.** to keep in a safe place.
n (c) **1.** a shop. **2.** a supply of something kept for when needed. **3.** a place where anything is kept (not just for sale).

torm C *v* to attack.
A *n* (c) **1.** A a period of wild weather, with heavy rain, thunder or strong wind. **2.** C an expression of strong feelings.

tormy B *adj* **1.** characterised by a storm. **2.** showing strong feeling.

tout C *adj* **1.** (of people) rather fat. **2.** (of things) strong. **3.** (old-fashioned) brave, courageous.

tove B *n* (c) a closed apparatus, using fuel, for heating and cooking.

traight A *adj* without curves; not changing direction.

trand C *n* (c) **1.** (old-fashioned) a beach, river bank, shore. **2.** a single string or wire from which a rope is made.

trange A *adj* **1.** odd or peculiar. **2.** surprising.

tranger A *n* (c) **1.** someone one does not know. **2.** someone from another town. **3.** someone unaccustomed to something. **4.** (fig.) a friend whom one has not seen for a long time.

trap C *v* **1.** to fix with a strap. **2.** to hit with a strap as punishment.

tream A *n* (c) **1.** a small river. **2.** a steady flow, e.g. of traffic, blood or people. **3.** a group of schoolchildren, divided according to their ability to learn.

tride B *v* to walk with long steps.
n (c) a long step.

trident C *adj* (of sound) loud, harsh, shrill.

trife C *n* (u) the state of conflict and quarrelling.

strike A/B *v* **1.** A to hit. **2.** A to refuse to work. **3.** A to indica (the time) by hitting a bell. **4.** A to come to the min of. **5.** B to find, discover. **6.** *strike up* (of a band c orchestra) to begin to play.

strip C *n* (c) a long, flat, and often narrow piece of something.

stripe B *n* (c) a band of colour. (*Strip* lays less emphasis on colour

stroke A *v* to caress.

n (c) **1.** a blow (e.g. with a weapon). **2.** a sudden illne damaging part of the brain. **3.** the sound of a bell in clock. **4.** the single movement of a piston up and dow a cylinder. **5.** an arm movement (as in swimming c rowing).

strong A *adj* **1.** powerful in body. **2.** (of things) solid; not easi broken. **3.** affecting the senses powerfully (but not *strong noise*). **4.** (of drink) concentrated.

strophe C *n* (c) a group of lines in a poem.

strudel C *n* (c) the Austrian speciality made with apples and pastr

strut C *v* to walk aggressively or proudly.

stub C *n* (c) the end of something left after use, usually a cigaret or cigar, also a pencil, and the counterfoil of a chequ See also **talon.**

stud C *n* (c) **1.** a double button, esp. used on a shirt-front c collar. **2.** a kind of nail, esp. on sports shoes or boo to prevent slipping. **3.** horses kept for breeding; plac where they are kept. **4.** (AE) a male horse kept fc breeding.

studio A *n* (c) the establishment where an artist, photographer, etc works.

study A *v* **1.** to spend time learning. **2.** to examine carefull **3.** to give careful thought to.

stuff A/C *n* (usually u). **1.** A material substance not clearly seen c recognised. **2.** (c) C woven cloth, e.g. satin. (There ar various other informal uses.)

stuffy B *adj* **1.** lacking fresh air. **2.** (informal) dull, old-fashionec or conventional.

stump C *n* (c) **1.** the part of a tree left above the ground when th rest has been cut down. **2.** the remaining part of a amputated limb. **3.** a small upright post in cricket.

stupid A *adj* silly; (not so strong as German).

stylus C *n* (c) **1.** a pointed instrument used for marking a surface **2.** the needle-like instrument on a record-player.

suave C *adj* with smooth manners, usually suggesting that they hid a suspicious character.

subject C *v* to rule (usually rather cruelly).

A *n* (c) **1.** something to be talked or written about o studied. **2.** (grammar) the word or phrase about whic the verb states something. **3.** any member of a stat except the ruler.

subsistence C *n* (u) **1.** what one lives on. **2.** *subsistence level* livin with little food or money.

suburb A *n* (c) an area on the outer part of a city.

succeed A/C *v* **1.** A to manage to do what is attempted. **2.** C to take the place of another.

success A *n* **1.** (u) the act of succeeding (in sense **1** above). **2.** (c) someone or something that has been successful.

successive C *adj* coming one after another.

sucker C *n* (c) **1.** a person or thing that sucks, or uses suction. **2.** a stem or shoot growing from a root of a plant. **3.** (informal) someone easily tricked or attracted to something.

sud C *n* (c; usually plural) a soap bubble.

suede C *n* (u) soft leather made from goatskin, used in clothing.

sufferance C *n* (u) *on sufferance* with permission but not welcome.

sufficiency C *n* (u) (old-fashioned) a sufficient quantity.

sufficient B *adj* enough.

suffocated C *past participle* unable to breathe, and possibly killed.

suggest A *v* **1.** to put an idea into someone's mind. **2.** to propose formally. **3.** to be a sign of.

suggestion A/C *n* **1.** (c) A an idea put forward. **2.** (c) A a slight sign. **3.** (u) (psychology) C the process of putting an idea in the mind by association with other ideas.

suggestive C *adj* **1.** originally, giving suggestions. **2.** (informal) suggesting sex.

suit A *n* (c) **1.** a jacket and trousers or skirt of the same material. **2.** one of the four sets in playing cards. **3.** a case in a law court.

suitcase A *n* (c) a case for carrying clothes.

suite B/C *n* (c) **1.** B a set of several matching pieces of furniture. **2.** B a group of private rooms in a hotel. **3.** B a number of musical pieces joined together under one title. **4.** C the followers (servants, etc.) of an important person.

sum up A *v* **1.** to give the essential points of. **2.** to evaluate (a situation).

sump C *n* (c) **1.** a place at the bottom of something, such as a yacht, where water collects. **2.** the bottom part of an engine, holding the oil.

superb C *adj* magnificent, exquisite.

superficial C *adj* not deep, on the surface only (esp. of ideas).

superior A *adj* **1.** of better quality. **2.** snobbish.

supply A *v* to provide.

support A/C *v* **1.** A to bear the weight of. **2.** A to help and encourage. **3.** A to provide money, etc. **4.** C (old-fashioned) to stand, tolerate.

surname A *n* (c) the name shared by all members of a family, usually the same as the *family name*.

surrogate C *n* (c) (very limited use) someone replacing another person, esp. a bishop or judge.

survey B *v* **1.** to make a map. **2.** to examine and give the value of a building. **3.** to look at from a height; to view the whole of something.

susceptible C *adj* **1.** easily influenced. **2.** sensitive. **3.** easily inclined t fall in love.

swamp C *n* (c) an area of very damp unstable ground; bog.

swarm C *v* to rush or crowd together.

swerve C *v* to change direction suddenly, e.g. round a corner.

swim A *v* to move through water using the limbs, fins, tail, etc (*My head is swimming* C is close to the Scandinavia usage.)

swing B *v* **1.** to hang freely, moving from side to side. **2.** to tur quickly. **3.** to ride on a swing (hanging seat).

Swiss A *adj* of or relating to Switzerland or its dialects.
n an inhabitant of Switzerland (plural unchanged).

sycophant C *n* (c) someone who flatters another.

syllabus C *n* (c) the list of things to be studied on a course.

sympathetic B *adj* being kind and helpful to someone with problems understanding and compassionate.

sympathise B *v* to show or feel sympathy.

sympathy B *n* (u) **1.** the ability to share others' feelings, esp. sadness **2.** pity.

symposium C *n* (c) a conference of formal meetings where specialists rea papers on their subject(s); a book of such papers.

syncope C *n* (c) **1.** the omission of certain sounds or letters in word. **2.** (medical use only) unconsciousness in a faint

syndicate C *n* (c) a group of people working together with a specifi aim. There is no connection with trade unions.

syringa C *n* a shrub with scented white flowers.

syringe C *n* (c) a small pump for spraying plants by hand or fo injecting liquids into the body.

systematise C *v* to arrange carefully according to some system or se method.

t

tab C *n* (c) **1.** a small cloth label with someone's name (esp. sewn inside clothing). **2.** a small projecting label to help find something easily.

table A *n* (c) **1.** a flat horizontal board supported by legs. **2.** a collection of information presented in a book in lines and columns.

tableau C *n* (c) short for a *tableau vivant*, a representation of a scene by a person or group remaining silent and not moving.

tablet A/C *n* (c) **1.** A a small medical pill. **2.** C a board with writing commemorating an event or person; plaque.

tack C *n* (c) **1.** a small nail with a flat head. **2.** (technical) movement in sailing to take advantage of the wind. **3.** a (new) course of action. **4.** loose stitching.

tackle B — *v* **1.** to deal with. **2.** to attack an opponent, esp. in football.

tact B — *n* (u) the ability to say or do the right thing at the right moment.

tag B — *n* (c) **1.** the same as a *tab*. **2.** a price label. **3.** a question tag, for example *can he* in *he can't understand, can he?*

tail A — *n* (c) **1.** the part of an animal at the base of the spine, often prolonged from the body. **2.** the back of some objects, esp. an aircraft. **3.** the reverse side of a coin.

tailor C — *n* (c) someone who makes clothes to order, esp. for men.

taint C — *n* (c) a trace of decay or some other bad quality.

take A/B — *v* **1.** A to carry or lead away. **2.** *take on* B **a.** to accept a responsibility. **b.** (rather old-fashioned) to be upset. **c.** to start to employ. **d.** to start a quarrel with. **3.** *take place* A to happen.

talcum C — *n* (u) short for *talcum powder*.

tale A — *n* (c) **1.** a story, esp. a traditional one. **2.** a lie. **3.** an incorrect rumour or piece of gossip.

talent B — *n* **1.** an aptitude for doing something. **2.** (u) a person or people who can do things skilfully.

talk A — *n* (c) a conversation, discussion.

talon C — *n* (c) the sharp curved nail on the feet of hunting birds.

tampon A — *n* (c) a mass of absorbent cotton material fitting into a woman's vagina to absorb monthly bleeding.

tan C — *n* (c) the browning of the skin by the sun.

tang C — *n* (c) a strong taste or smell.

tangent C — *n* (c) **1.** a line touching (but not intersecting with) the edge of a circle. **2.** *go off at a tangent* to change one's line of conversation or action.

tap B — *v* **1.** to strike lightly and repeatedly. **2.** to draw liquid from a barrel. **3.** to use (resources). **4.** to listen to a phone conversation by means of a secret apparatus.
n (c) **1.** an apparatus for starting or stopping a flow of liquid or gas from a pipe. **2.** a short light blow.

tape B/C — *v* **1.** C to do up a parcel with sticky paper or strips of plastic. **2.** B to record on magnetic tape.

tapestry C — *n* cloth with a woven picture or design especially used as wall-hangings.

tappet C — *n* (c) a small arm-shaped piece on a motor or engine.

target B/C — *n* (c) **1.** B a board with concentric rings, used for shooting at. **2.** B an aim for which people work. **3.** C someone who is made fun of.

tart B — *n* (c) **1.** a kind of cake made with pastry and jam or fruit, etc. **2.** (informal) a woman who is regarded as having a sexually immoral character; prostitute.

task B — *n* (c) **1.** something which has to be done. **2.** (AE) school homework.

tassel C — *n* (c) a decorative bunch of string or wool tied together at the end of a cord, etc., or attached to a flag.

taste A — *v* **1.** to have a certain flavour. **2.** to experience th flavour of. **3.** to test the flavour by taking a little o

n **1.** (c) a flavour. **2.** (u) the experience of flavour. **3.** (the ability to enjoy and choose the best in art, et **4.** a personal liking for something.

tattoo C — *n* (c) **1.** a great military pageant. **2.** a special beatin of drums (as a signal). **3.** a dyed pattern on the ski

tatty C — *adj* (informal) of poor quality, untidy, dirty.

tax A — *v* **1.** (of a government) to charge money to raise revenu **2.** to tire (by making demands on).

n (c) money to be paid by law on one's income, purchase profits, etc., for government funds.

taxi A — *n* (c) a car with a driver for hire.

teasel C — *n* (c) a spiny wild flower.

technical A — *adj* having or requiring specialised knowledge, esp. in scientific sphere.

technique B — *n* (c) a method of doing something.

telephone A — *n* (c) **1.** the apparatus used for a telephone call. **2.** *b on the (tele)phone.* **a.** to have a telephone in the house flat. **b.** to be telephoning someone at a given moment.

tell A — *v* **1.** to inform. **2.** to indicate. **3.** to know, distinguish

teller B — *n* (c) **1.** (in AE only) a bank cashier. **2.** a person wh counts votes in a parliament, assembly, etc.

temper A — *v* **1.** to make less severe. **2.** to make (metal) the require hardness.

A/C — *n* **1.** A a mood, state of mind, esp. with respect to anger **2.** (c) C the hardness and strength of a metal.

tempera C — *n* (u) a thick kind of paint used occasionally in art.

temperament A — *n* the personality of an individual.

tempest C — *n* (c) (literary) a violent wind or storm.

temple C — *n* (c) **1.** the flat area on the side of the head between ey and ear. **2.** a place of worship; (not usually used o a Christian church).

tempo C — *n* (u) **1.** (music) the speed of the main beat. **2.** th speed of activity of life; (*pace* is more usual in sense **2**)

temporal C — *adj* not spiritual.

tend A/B — *v* **1.** A to be inclined to. **2.** B to look after.

tender C — *v* to present or offer.

n (c) **1.** the (document stating the) price at which ser vices would be done. **2.** the short wagon carrying coa and water behind a steam locomotive. **3.** the money which must lawfully be accepted for payment.

tennis A — *n* (u) refers only to the sport.

tent A — *n* (c) a shelter made of canvas, etc., esp. as used by campers

term A — *n* (c) **1.** a determined period of time. **2.** the time of study at a school, college, etc., contrasted with the holi- days or vacations. **3.** the similar period of activity in the law courts. **4.** (plural) the conditions in a contract, etc. **5.** the state of a relationship. **6.** a way of expres- sion or words used.

terminus B *n* (c) the end of a bus or train route.

terrace B *v* to level sloping ground to make terraces.
n (c) **1.** a levelled area along sloping ground. **2.** a line of houses.

terrible A *adj* has kept its older meaning in English: causing terror; very serious or extreme. (Colloq. use as a mere intensive like *awful*.)

test A *v* to examine in order to establish the value, quality, or contents of.
n (c) the examination or trial to do this; (academically an *exam(ination)* is longer and more important than a *test*).

testament C *n* (c) **1.** *the Old and New Testaments* sections of the Bible. **2.** (legal, rare and formal) a will.

textbook C *n* (c) a book used to study from, esp. at school.

than A *conjunction* used in comparisons: *I am older than you.*

theatre A *n* (c) **1.** a building for the presentation of plays, dramatic productions, etc. **2.** *the theatre* that type of entertainment, in contrast to the cinema or TV. **3.** a place where important events occur. **4.** a room in a hospital equipped for surgical operations.

theme B *n* (c) **1.** a subject. **2.** a recurring melody in a piece of music. **3.** (AE) a student's essay or composition.

thermos C *n* (c) short for a *thermos flask*, the trademark of a type of vacuum flask.

thesaurus C *n* (c) a book of words arranged according to their similarity of meaning; (usually not alphabetically).

thesis C *n* (c) **1.** a reasoned argument presented by someone; (less commonly used than in German). **2.** a long piece of writing presented by a student as work for a degree.

thick A *adj* **1.** a comparatively large distance between opposite surfaces. **2.** dense. **3.** strong. **4.** stupid. **5.** (slang) unreasonable.

thus C *adv* in this way, by this means; (not usually used in spoken language).

tick B *v* **1.** to make the sound (as) of a clock. **2.** to mark as correct. **3.** *what makes someone tick* what motivates a person.
n (c) **1.** the sound of a clock. **2.** a minute bloodsucking parasite. **3.** (informal) a moment. **4.** a sign indicating 'correct'. **5.** a very small spasmodic movement.

tide B *n* (c) **1.** the daily rise and fall of the sea along the coast, caused by the sun and moon. **2.** the general trend of thought and opinion.

tidy A *adj* good order or neat arrangement.

tiger B *n* (c) the large fierce animal of the cat family found in Asia (not in Latin America!).

tights B *n* (c; plural only) stockings with the tops joined together and made to fit up to the waist used by women and ballet dancers.

tile B — *n* (c) a hard thin piece of ceramic used on rooves, walls or bathrooms, fireplaces, etc.

till A — *preposition, conjunction* far more limited use than the Scandinavian word: mainly used of time: *I'll work here till I go home.*

timbre C — *n* the quality of sound, esp. as made by different instruments or voices.

time A — *n* there are too many uses to list here fully, but esp. note **1.** (u) sufficient interval to do something. **2.** (c) a period described in a particular way. **3.** (c) an occasion or instance. **4.** duration. **5.** the hour by the clock.

timely C — *adj* opportune, happening at a suitable time.

tin A — *n* **1.** (u) a metal, found esp. in Bolivia and Malaysia. **2.** (c in BE) a metal container for preserving food, the inside of which is covered with a thin layer of tin; (a *can* in AE).

tint B — *v* to add a small amount of colour to.

n (c) **1.** a colour mixed with white; any pale colour. See **hue**. **2.** a colour (dye), used esp. to give colour to the hair.

tinted C — *past participle* very slightly coloured.

tip A/C — *v* **1.** C to tilt. **2.** A to give money for service. **3.** C to give advice and suggestions esp. on how to invest or win money in betting, etc.

tipple C — *v* to drink alcohol as a habit.

tippler C — *n* (c) someone who drinks too much alcohol.

tirade C — *n* (c) an angry speech.

tire A — *v* to weary or exhaust (someone).

tissue B — *n* **1.** thin light cloth. **2.** thin soft paper for cleaning the nose or skin. **3.** (u) thin light paper for wrapping things; (also called *tissue paper*). **4.** (u) cells in bodies or plants.

title A — *n* (c) **1.** the name given to a book, film, etc. **2.** the manner of addressing someone, e.g. Lord, Mrs, Dr, etc.

toad C — *n* (c) an amphibian, similar to but larger and rougher than a frog.

tobacco A — *n* (u) **1.** the dried leaves of a plant which can be smoked or chewed. **2.** the plant used for this.

toenail C — *n* (c) a nail on any of the toes.

toga C — *n* (c) the robe worn by men in ancient Rome.

toil C — *n* (u) heavy or hard work.

toilet C — *n* **1.** (c) (a room containing) a W.C.; (commonly called a *loo*). **2.** (u) (old-fashioned) the act of getting dressed and ready. **3.** (u) (old-fashioned) someone's appearance in style, clothing, hair, etc.

toll C — *n* (c) **1.** money paid to use a section of road, bridge, harbour, etc. **2.** the cost in injuries or deaths in road accidents, etc.

tollhouse C — *n* (c) a building used by someone who collects tolls (sense **1** above).

tombola C	*n*	a sort of raffle with a drum holding tickets from which prize winners are selected.
tone C	*v*	to give a particular sound or colour to.
A/C	*n*	(c) **1.** A any sound considered with reference to its pitch, loudness, strength, etc. **2.** A the general nature and character of something. **3.** C a quality of a particular colour, changed by the addition of white or black; shade, tint.
tongue B	*n*	(c) **1.** the movable piece inside the mouth, detecting flavour. **2.** (rare) a (spoken) language.
top A	*n*	(c) various uses, essentially the upper part of something, the highest position.
topic A	*n*	(c) a subject, e.g. of an essay or discussion.
topical B	*adj*	interesting and important now. Compare **actual**.
torment C	*n*	(something or someone causing) great pain or worry.
torrent C	*n*	(c; often plural) a violent rush (usually of liquid).
torso C	*n*	(c) the central section of the human body.
toss C	*n*	the act of throwing something up.
tot C	*n*	(c) **1.** a small amount of alcohol or spirits. **2.** a very small child.
toto C		*in toto* altogether, totally.
touch C	*v*	**1.** A to (cause to) be physically in contact. **2.** C to eat or drink; (usually used in the negative). **3.** C to affect the feelings of; (used esp. in passive). **4.** C to equal in quality.
A	*n*	(c) **1.** the act or feel of touching. **2.** a slight amount of. **3.** the style of playing a musical instrument.
tour A	*n*	(c) a journey or walk round a place or region.
tourniquet C	*n*	(c) something twisted tightly against the skin to stop bleeding.
town A	*n*	(c) basically, Dutch *stad.*
toy B	*n*	(c) a plaything, usually for children.
trace B	*v*	*trace a line* to copy a line onto thin paper from a line on paper underneath (e.g. copying a map from an atlas).
	n	(c) a very small quantity.
tract C	*n*	(c) **1.** an article or small pamphlet, esp. one dealing with a religious subject. **2.** an area of land. **3.** (biology) a group of related organs in the body.
traction C	*n*	(u) **1.** the power needed to pull something along. **2.** the sort of power used by this.
traduce C	*v*	to speak damagingly of someone, to slander.
traffic A/C	*n*	(u) **1.** A the movement and circulation of vehicles. **2.** A the movement of passengers using public transport. **3.** C trade, usually illegal.
train B	*v*	**1.** to instruct. **2.** to study to be. **3.** to get ready for a competition, esp. in sport. **4.** to cause (esp. a plant) to grow in a particular way.
trainer C	*n*	(c) someone who prepares a sportsman for a competition.
training B	*n*	(u) the activity of preparing someone for a competition, esp. in sport; (a *training pack* has no clear meaning).

trait C *n* (c) a distinguishing characteristic.

traitor C *n* (c) someone who is disloyal to a friend, his country, etc.

tramp C *v* to walk slowly and heavily.
n (c) **1.** (BE) someone who does no work and has no home but wanders from place to place, begging. **2.** the sound of heavy walking.

trampoline C *n* (c) an apparatus with elastic material across a frame on which gymnasts can do exercises; (but not used for diving at a swimming pool).

trance C *n* (c) a state of seeming to be asleep, which may be induced by hypnosis or drugs.

transcend C *v* to go further than, be better than.

transcendence C *n* (u) the quality of going beyond ordinary limits of earthly knowledge.

transit C *n* (u) the action of passing across or through a place.

translate B *v* to give the equivalent of in another language.

translation A/C *n* **1.** (u) A the putting of one language into another. **2.** (c) A a book or text given in a different language from its original. **3.** (c) (technical) C the movement of an object from one place to another.

translator A *n* (c) somebody who translates.

transpire C *v* **1.** to become known, esp. gradually. **2.** (informal) to happen. **3.** (technical) to produce liquid or waste matter (used mainly of plants).

transporter C *n* (c) a vehicle which carries some large object(s), esp. one which carries cars on two levels.

trap A *v* to catch in a trap or by a trick.
n (c) an apparatus used for catching (animals).

trapeze C *n* (c) a swinging bar used by acrobats, etc.

trapper C *n* (c) someone who traps animals, esp. for their furs.

trauma C *n* (c) a severe emotional upset often causing mental illness.

travel A *v* to go from one place to another; move.

traverse C *v* to move across.
n (c) **1.** a place where a climber crosses a slope without a change of height. **2.** something that crosses something else, such as a bar or a beam.

treasure C *n* **1.** money, gold, silver, or jewels. **2.** something which is highly valued. **3.** someone loved.

treatment A *n* **1.** (u) the way of dealing with or behaving to someone or something. **2.** medical attention.

treaty B *n* (c) a legal agreement between nations and signed by their representatives; (a *treaty of union* suggests a political agreement bringing union to formerly separate nations).

tree A *n* (c) a kind of plant with a wooden trunk that rises to branches at a height off the ground.

trefoil C *n* (c) any of a number of small plants with leaves divided into three.

trek C *v* to walk or go a long way.
n (c) a long walk or journey; (also *pony-trek*, to ride a pony across country).

tremendous B *adj* **1.** impressively large. **2.** strong, powerful. **3.** (informal) marvellous.

trench C *n* (c) a long ditch dug in the ground.

trepidation C *n* (u) fear, worry, or anxiety.

trespass C *v* **1.** to go on privately owned property without permission. **2.** to take advantage of.

tribunal C *n* (c) a group of people who have authority to make judgments on certain disputed matters such as the level of rents.

tribune C *n* (c) **1.** a platform on which a speaker stands. **2.** often used as the name of a newspaper.

trill C *v* to make a rapidly alternating sound of two notes, esp. used of birds and in music.
n (c) a sound of this kind.

trim C *v* **1.** to make tidy and neat. **2.** to balance something, esp. a boat, better, by distributing the weight evenly. **3.** to reduce.
adj compact, neat.

trimming C *n* **1.** (u) ornament on the edge of clothes. **2.** (c; plural) additions.

tripe C *n* (u) **1.** the casing of the stomach of cows, eaten as food. **2.** rubbish, nonsense.

trivial C *adj* of little importance, easily forgotten.

trombone C *n* (c) a metal wind instrument with a sliding U-shaped tube.

trooper C *n* (c) **1.** a cavalry soldier of the lowest rank, also in an armoured regiment. **2.** (AE) a state policeman.

troops C *n* (plural) soldiers.

trophy C *n* (c) **1.** a prize. **2.** something kept as a sign of success, e.g. after hunting.

trouble A *n* there are many meanings: note there is no particular idea of movement or speed; of disorders, it is confined to political, social, or medical spheres; in the plural, it is the cause of anxiety rather than the worry in the mind itself.

troupe C *n* (c) a group of dancers, actors, etc.

trousers A *n* (plural) (BE) outer clothing, worn from the waist and covering both legs to the ankles; (*pants* in AE).

trousseau C *n* (c) the clothes, linen, etc., collected by a girl before and for her marriage.

truant C *n* (c) **1.** a child who misses school without permission. **2.** someone who fails to go to work.

truck A *n* **1.** (c) a simple vehicle for carrying goods (esp. one pulled by hand). **2.** (c) (BE) an open railway vehicle for freight. **3.** (c) (esp. AE) a lorry. **4.** (u) (AE only) vegetables or fruit grown to be sold in a market. **5.** *have no truck with* to have nothing to do with.

truculent C *adj* rebellious, resentful, and unrepentant.

true A/C *adj* **1.** A not false; correct. **2.** C faithful, loyal.

truly C *adv* **1.** *yours truly* used at the end of some formal letters before the signature. **2.** truthfully, really. (Notice thi is not an adjective.)

trump C *n* (c) **1.** (old-fashioned) the sound of a trumpet. **2.** th playing-card suit chosen in some games to have th highest rank.

trumpery C *n* (u) things or ideas of no value, though seeming impressive

trunk B *n* (c) **1.** a large suitcase. **2.** the main upright part of tree. **3.** the long round nose part of an elephant. **4** the middle part of the body. **5.** (plural) shorts, esp. fo swimming.

trust A *v* **1.** to rely on; have faith in. **2.** to hope or expect.
n there are many meanings, esp. note **1.** faith; reliance **2.** (u) care or charge. **3.** the management of somethin for the advantage of someone else. **4.** (c) a group o people (*trustees*) holding money and or property fo others; (a *foundation* in AE).

tub C *n* (c) a large round container like a barrel.

tuba C *n* (c) a deep-sounding brass instrument.

tug C *v* to pull something heavy.

tumbler C *n* a flat-bottomed drinking glass with no handle or stem

tumult C *n* **1.** noise made by a disorderly crowd. **2.** mental con fusion.

tumulus C *n* (c) a burial mound as used in prehistoric times.

tune B *v* **1.** to adjust a musical instrument to the correct pitch **2.** to adjust an engine so it runs perfectly.
n (c) a melody.

tunnel A *n* (c) a hollow space under the ground, e.g. for vehicles people, etc. to pass.

turbulent C *adj* disorderly, wild; (but not often used of individuals).

turf C *n* **1.** (a piece of) soil having grass with its roots, for makin a lawn. **2.** (c) a horse-racing track. **3.** (u) hors racing.

turkey B *n* **1.** (c) a large non-flying bird kept for meat, eaten esp. a Christmas and American Thanksgiving Day. **2.** (u the meat from this.

Turk's Head C *n* a comparatively common name for a hotel or restaurant and often painted on a sign.

turn A *v* there are too many uses to give here: the primary meanin is to move round a point; change direction; Portugues speakers should notice *he turned angry*; *the weathe turned cold* are not reflexive.
n (c) German speakers should note *go for a turn* C mean to go for a short walk.

tusk C *n* (c) the long pointed tooth of an elephant, walrus, etc.

tutor C *n* (c) **1.** (BE) a university teacher who directs a numbe of students through their studies. **2.** (occasional) a private teacher.

twin B *n* (c) one of two children born of the same mother at the same time; (the Japanese use is a shortening of the phras *twin beds*).

twist C — *v* the meanings are all connected with turning in a spiral, except *twist someone's words* to force words out of their true meaning.
n **1.** (c) a spiral shape. **2.** (u) any of certain types of thread. **3.** a loaf of bread in a twist or plait. **4.** a particular tendency in the character (usually bad).

type A/B/C — *n* (c) **1.** A a sort; kind. **2.** B a small block of metal or wood with a letter on for printing. **3.** C a person, usually derogatory.

typical A — *adj* characteristic.

tyrant C — *n* (c) an unjust cruel ruler.

U

U.S.S.R. A — *n* the Union of Soviet Socialist Republics.

ult(imo) C — *adv* (used only in very formal business letters) of the previous month.

ulterior C — *adj* only likely to be heard in *ulterior motive* a hidden reason.

ultimate C — *adj* at the end of something, happening finally, sometimes after some uncertainty.

ultimately C — *adv* in the end, finally.

unconscious B — *adj* **1.** not aware (of). **2.** in a faint.

unconsulted C — *adj* (rare) not asked for an opinion.

under A — *preposition* in a lower position, directly below.

underarm C — *n* (c) more correctly the *armpit* the underside of the joint connecting the arm to the body.

undertake C — *v* to agree (to begin) to do something.

undertaking C — *n* (c) (a promise to do) a task.

underwrite C — *v* (commercial) **1.** (of a person or a firm) to agree to buy all the shares of a company which remain unsold to the public. **2.** (insurance) to take responsibility for fulfilling a payment in case of a large claim.

unedited C — *adj* (of books, films, etc.) not prepared, in their original condition. See **edit** sense **1**.

unhomely C — *adj* lacking a friendly atmosphere; unwelcoming.

unique B — *adj* being the only one of its kind.

unkindly C — *adv* lacking kindness and consideration.

untidy B — *adj* disorganised, messy.

unwilling B — *adj* not disposed, not willing.

up A — *preposition* Dutch/Flemish speakers should note the difference between *on the roof* and *up on the roof*: Scandinavians should note *up* in English gives the meaning '(put) together': *we packed up the suitcases.*

updraught C — *n* (c) an upward moving current of air.

upheaval C — *n* (c) a violent disturbance; much stronger in English tha Danish.

uphold C — *v* to maintain (principles/a point of view).

uproar C — *n* (c) a wild disorderly activity, esp. with shouting; (les strong than the N. European words).

uproarious B — *adj* noisy, esp. involving laughter.

upset A — *v* **1.** to cause to be unhappy. **2.** to spill. **3.** to make ill
n (c) something which causes unhappiness.
adj anxious, unhappy, tense, cross, etc.; (a useful word t express the Continental word *nervous*).

upstanding C — *adj* **1.** honest, reliable. **2.** well-built, tall; (in both sense used of people).

urban B — *adj* belonging to the town.

urbane C — *adj* courteous, refined.

urbanisation C — *n* (u) the (gradual) change from being rural to bein urban.

urge A — *v* to persuade; press; plead; (not an impersonal verb i English, where it is replaced by *it is urgent*).

urn C — *n* (c) **1.** a large container for liquids, esp. to keep then hot. **2.** a vase shaped like an urn. **3.** a container fo the ashes of a cremated body.

usable C — *adj* suitable or fit for use.

use A — *v* **1.** to make use of, employ. **2.** *use up* to finish. **3.** *b used* to be employed. **4.** *be used to* to have the habit of be accustomed to.

utterly C — *adv* totally, absolutely.

V

vacancy C — *n* (c) an empty space, ready to be filled or occupied.

vague B — *adj* not precise, unclear, inexact.

vale C — *n* (c) an older word for *valley*.

valet C — *n* (c) a man who looks after another's clothes as a persona servant or in a hotel.

valid B — *adj* **1.** legally acceptable, as usable. **2.** well-founded.

valour C — *n* (u) great courage, esp. in fighting.

vamoose C — *v* (imperative; slang) clear out! go away! (Taken fron *vamos*.)

vapour C — *n* the gas-like form of a normally liquid or solid sub- stance.

variant C — *n* (c) different form of a word, story, etc.

various A — *adj* of several different kinds.

varsity C — *n, adj* (informal) university.

vase B — *n* (c) a container made of clay or glass, esp. for holdin flowers.

vast B — *adj* immense, huge, very great.

veal C *n* (u) meat from a calf.
vehement C *adj* with strong feeling, passionate.
vehicle B *n* (c) something in which people and/or goods are moved, usually having wheels.
veil C *n* (c) a thin cloth, covering the face.
vein C *n* (c) **1.** a tube carrying blood to the heart. **2.** a line on a leaf or insect wing. **3.** an ore-filled crack in rock. **4.** a mood; (but requiring an adjective preceding it).
venal C *adj* (of person) willing to accept bribes, acting unscrupulously for gain.
vendetta C *n* (c) a blood feud between families; (the word is not an adjective in English).
veneer C *n* (c) **1.** a thin layer of fine wood covering poorer material. **2.** an outer appearance hiding an unpleasant reality.
vent C *v* to express feelings esp. of anger, impatience, etc.
n (c) **1.** a hole for gas or liquid to pass through. **2.** an opening at the back of a jacket. **3.** an outlet for feelings.
ventilator B *n* (c) an apparatus for changing air in a room, etc.
venue C *n* (c) a place where people agree to meet.
verbalise C *v* to express thoughts in words.
verbena C *n* a garden plant.
verge B *n* (c) **1.** the edge or extremity of something, esp. a road, wood, or lawn. **2.** *on the verge of* on the point of.
verger C *n* (c) an official in a church.
verify C *v* to test or show the truth of.
versatile C *adj* **1.** (of things) having many different uses. **2.** (of people) able to perform well at many different things.
verse B *n* (c) **1.** a group of lines in a poem. **2.** one of the short paragraphs into which the chapters of the Bible are divided. **3.** (u) poetry in general.
versed C *adj* having skill in something, esp. in the phrase *well-versed in*.
version B *n* (c) **1.** someone's personal account of something which has happened, esp. compared with someone else's. **2.** a different form or variant of something. **3.** (occasional) a translation.
very *adj* A absolute, exact; (the C use is as an adverb).
vespers C *n* (c; plural) an evening church service.
vessel C *n* (c) **1.** any type of ship or boat; (similar to **craft** sense **2**). **2.** any container for liquid, e.g. a barrel or cup.
vest A *n* (c) an undergarment worn on the upper part of the body, next to the skin.
vestment C *n* (c; often plural) clothing worn by a priest during religious services.
vet C *v* (informal) to examine carefully, in order to discover if something or someone is acceptable.
n (c) **1.** (BE informal) short for a *veterinary surgeon.* **2.** (AE) short for a *veteran*; (see sense **2**).
veteran C *n* (c) **1.** someone who has had a long experience doing something, esp. as a soldier. **2.** (AE) anyone who was formerly a soldier.

vex C — *v* to annoy or irritate.

vicar C — *n* (c) a fully ordained Anglican priest, of similar status to a rector; (but not a curate).

vice B — *n* (c) **1.** an apparatus used for holding wood while it is being shaped, etc. **2.** a bad or evil habit.

vicious C — *adj* dangerous, cruel, and bad-tempered.

view B — *n* (c) *have the/a good view* to have a good vantage point.

vignette C — *n* (c) **1.** an ornamental pattern used in printing or building. **2.** a picture with the edges fading out (as in some early photographs). **3.** a concise, effective description of someone or a scene.

Viking C — *n* (c) Scandinavian trader and sailor of the 8th to the 10th centuries.

villa C — *n* (c) **1.** a large house away from a town, in its own garden. **2.** a holiday house, esp. in the Mediterranean area. **3.** (in former times) a large country house built by the Romans.

villain C — *n* (c) a bad person, esp. in a story.

viol C — *n* (c) a medieval string instrument similar to a violin.

viola C — *n* (c) a large kind of violin.

violence B — *n* (u) forceful physical behaviour or action.

violent B — *adj* **1.** involving or resulting from extreme physical force; dangerous and causing damage. **2.** extreme e.g. temper.

virago C — *n* (c) an extremely bad-tempered woman.

virtuous C — *adj* full of goodness, righteous; worthy, trustworthy; (*the virtuous* could be used in a religious context to describe righteous people).

vis-a-vis C — *preposition* in relationship to, compared with.

visible B — *adj* clear and easy to see, apparent.

visit A/C — *v* **1.** A to go and see (a person or place). **2.** C to examine on an official inspection. **3.** (AE) to stay at a hotel. **4.** (AE only) A to chat (with someone).
n A (c) a time or act of visiting.

visitor B — *n* (c) someone who visits.

vista C — *n* (c) a distant view with closer objects making a frame to it.

voice A/C — *n* (c) **1.** A the sound produced by someone speaking or singing. **2.** C an opinion expressed as a vote. (There are other meanings, presenting few problems.)

volt B — *n* (c) only refers to a unit of electrical force.

voluble C — *adj* talking a lot, garrulous.

volume B — *n* **1.** (c) a book, esp. one which is part of a series. **2.** (u) cubic measurement. **3.** loudness of sound. **4.** an amount, quantity.

voluntary B — *adj* **1.** done without being forced. **2.** done without payment.

vote B — *n* (c) **1.** the expression of one's choice in an election or on a committee. **2.** the decision resulting from the act of voting.

vow C — *v* **1.** to promise in a religious way. **2.** to resolve firmly.
n (c) a promise or declaration of these kinds.

voyage B — *n* (c) a long sea journey, esp. one visiting several parts on the way; (the verb is also occasionally used for the same idea: *to voyage round the world*).

vulgar B — *adj* **1.** lacking good taste; rude; socially unacceptable. **2.** *vulgar fraction.* See **fraction** sense **1**.

vulgarisation C — *n* (c) the act or result of making something vulgar; spoiling.

vulgarise C — *v* to spoil; make vulgar.

W

wagon B — *n* (c) **1.** a vehicle pulled by horses. **2.** (BE) a goods truck on a railway. **3.** a little table fitted with wheels, from which food and drink may be served.

wake B — *v* to come to consciousness after sleeping.

C — *n* (c) **1.** the waves or track where a ship has passed through water. **2.** *in the wake of* behind, following. **3.** a gathering of people overnight to pray round a corpse before a funeral. **4.** a party held after a funeral.

wall A — *n* (c) **1.** an upright construction made of brick, stone, wood, etc., used to enclose or divide something. **2.** an upright mass, e.g. of rock.

waltz B — *v* to dance in triple time.

n (c) a dance of this kind.

wand C — *n* (c) a thin stick used by magicians and conjurors.

wander B/C — *v* **1.** B to walk without aim. **2.** C to proceed irregularly; meander. **3.** C (of the mind or thoughts) to lose direction, lack concentration.

war A — *n* (c) is the Dutch *oorlog*.

ward C — *n* (c) **1.** a room for patients in a hopsital. **2.** a political division of a town. **3.** a young person, looked after by a guardian.

warehouse C — *n* (c) a building where goods are stored.

warm A — *adj* the word(s) used in Scandinavian refer to greater heat than the English words.

wart C — *n* (c) a small hard growth on the skin.

washstand C — *n* (c) (old-fashioned) stand for washing (hands).

watch A — *v* **1.** to observe, look at. **2.** to guard.

water A — *n* **1.** (u) the clear liquid without taste, colour, or smell, found in impure form in rain, rivers, the sea, etc. **2.** (plural) mineral waters from a spa. **3.** (plural) the sea near to a (named) country. (The full form *water closet* is now almost never used: say *lavatory*, *WC*, or in BE, *loo*.)

waxworks C — *n* (plural) an exhibition of wax figures.

way A/C — *n* **1.** (c) A the route to reach somewhere. **2.** (c) A a distance travelled. **3.** (c) A a method. **4.** (c) A a habit. **5.** (c) A a type of behaviour. **6.** (c) A a course; path. **7.** (u) C momentum.

weak B — *adj* **1.** not strong. **2.** in poor health, frail. **3.** poor in academic ability.

weapon B — *n* (c) instrument used in fighting.

weather A — *n* (u) the meteorological conditions.

wed C — *v* (old-fashioned) to get married (to).

weight A — *n* **1.** (u) the measurement of heaviness in kilos, etc. **2.** (c) something of a fixed heaviness to balance against other things on a pair of scales.

well B — *n* (c) a deep hole in the ground from which water, oil, or gas is taken.

wend C — *v* *wend one's way* to go or leave; (rather old-fashioned).

wet A — *n* damp weather or rain.
adj **1.** covered with water. **2.** (slang) silly, weak, lacking in initiative.

when A — *adv, conjunction* at what time.

where A — *adv, conjunction* at, or in, what place.

while A/C — *conjunction* **1.** A during the time that. **2.** C though.

whimper C — *n* (c) a small cry of distress.

whine C — *v* **1.** (esp. of a child) to make a lot of complaints. **2.** to make unhappy cries.

whip C — *n* (c) a stick with a piece of cord or leather on the end, used for hitting e.g. a horse.

who A — *interrogative and personal pronoun Who is she? She is the child who was wounded.*

white shirt B — *n* (c) a shirt which is white.

wide A — *adj* broad, not narrow.

wife A — *n* (c) a married woman.

wild C — *n* (often plural) an area of land where few people live, in its natural uncultivated state.

win A — *v* to be the best in, come first: e.g. you win a competition/a war/a prize/a race/a game/money (esp. from betting). (Note that *gain* is used of mostly abstract things: *to gain a reputation/knowledge/experience/weight/height/favour*; and to *earn wages/a salary*.)

wink C — *v* to close one eye briefly.
n (c) an eye movement of this kind.

winkle C — *n* (c) a small kind of sea animal that lives in a shell, eaten as food.

winner C — *n* (c) someone or something that has won, or is expected to be successful.

wish A — *v* **1.** to have a desire which at present cannot be satisfied. **2.** to express a hope.

wit C — *n* **1.** (u) an ability to say clever and amusing things. **2.** (c) someone who can do this. **3.** (plural) intelligence; *use your wits*; *keep your wits about you*, i.e. be ready to act as necessary.

womb C — *n* (c) the part of a woman's body where a baby grows before its birth.

worm C — *n* (c) **1.** a small boneless, legless creature (esp. an earthworm). **2.** any of various kinds of similar creatures which are parasites.

wound C — *n* (c) a severe hurt to body tissue, esp. as a result of an attack; (*injury* is more usually used when caused by an accident).

wrap up B — *v* to make into a parcel by covering with paper, etc.

wreck C — *n* (c) **1.** something which has been badly damaged (and usually abandoned). **2.** someone in very poor health.

wrinkle C — *v* to have folds in the skin.

wrist B — *n* (c) the joint connecting the hand to the arm.

Xerox C — *n* (c) (trademark) a process that makes a photographic copy (of a document, picture, etc.).

yacht C — *n* (c) a sailing boat.

yet A/C — *adv* note the following uses. **1.** A up till now; up till then. **2.** C still, e.g. *I have yet to see one.*

C — *conjunction* but, nevertheless; (there are a few other C uses).

yew C — *n* (c) an evergreen tree with small red berries.

youngest B — *adj* the least old; (used mostly of people; animals; compare *the latest news/ideas/fashions/information*, etc.).

Z

zeal C — *n* (u) enthusiasm, keenness.

zebra C — *n* (c) a horse-like animal with black and white stripes.

Zeppelin C — *n* (c) a German airship used in World War I and into the 1930s; (no other airships were given this name).

zest C *n* (u) **1.** a feeling of keen pleasure. **2.** an attractive stimulating quality. **3.** (occasional) the original French meaning, lemon (peel) flavouring.

zinc C *n* (u) the bluish-white metal used in making alloys and covering metal objects with a surface that gives protection against rust.

zip C *n* (c) (strictly: zip fastener) a device with metal teeth used for closing two edges in clothing, etc.

zone B *n* (c) an area or region, esp. one with a particular purpose, use, or characteristic.

zoom C *n* (c) **1.** (no plural) the sound of an aircraft when taking off. **2.** short for a *zoom lens*, a photographic lens that can move continuously between a distant and a close-up view while keeping a sharp image.

APPENDIX

Uncountable nouns

The countability of nouns in English is as important a classification as noun gender in many other languages. These lists give nouns found to be countable in one or other of the languages covered by this dictionary but normally uncountable in English.

To prevent the lists from becoming too long, the following cases are omitted:

1. Those abstract nouns which, though uncountable, may occur in the plural for nuances of meaning or style, e.g. *miseries*.
2. Similarly, abstract nouns which may very occasionally be used with the indefinite article plus an adjective, e.g. *filled with a great happiness*. Admittedly this pattern is less common in English than in some West European languages, but see type 3.
3. The usual words for food, substances, etc., where commercial usage accepts *a very cheap butter*; *a poor quality zinc*.

Foreign students are advised to go through the lists carefully (as far as the section appropriate to their level), underlining all the nouns which, when translated, can be used in their own language as countable nouns.

Type 1. These nouns are straightforward uncountables. Do not use them with *a*(*n*), numerals, or in the plural.

A words:

bread	luggage	shopping
clothing	machinery	smoking
dancing	music	snow
fun	news	soap
furniture	parking	sunshine
information	pay	tennis
laughter	photography	weather (except in the phrase, *in all weathers*)
luck	propaganda	

Languages are all uncountable (never say: *He speaks a good English*).

B words:

alcohol	golf	lightning
anger	handwriting	macaroni
behaviour	harm	publicity
camping	harness	refuse
cardboard	hospitality	rheumatism
cash	housework	rubbish
chaos	importance	safety
chess	jeopardy	scenery
chewing gum	knitting	seaside
commerce	legislation	shipping
conduct	leisure	slang

cookery/-ing
co-operation
courage
entertaining
etiquette
equipment
evidence
mass production
moonlight
overtime
permission
pollution
postage
prejudice
spaghetti
sterling
strength
stupidity
tobacco
training
violence
waste paper
zinc

C words:

ammunition
appendicitis
armour
arson
arthritis
artillery
asparagus
blackmail
booty
bribery
bronchitis
cajolery
celery
cement
china
confetti
constipation
crochet
crockery
croquet
cutlery
debris
destruction
dirt
distress
embroidery
fencing
fluff
fodder
foliage
footwear
forage
gossamer
hay
homage
hunting
icing
impertinence
imprudence
impudence
influenza/flu
irrigation
jargon
jewellery
kitsch
lava
linen
livestock
loot
magic
merchandise
mistletoe
mud
nationalisation
negligence
non-fiction
peel
percussion
pneumonia
pomp
porcelain
postage
posterity
produce
rigging
salvage
scaffolding
sewing
shrapnel
silver
sleet
sophistication
spinach
stamina
stubble
subsistence
sunburn
surf
teamwork
trash
tripe
tuberculosis/TB
undergrowth
underwear
unrest
urgency
vegetation
vigour
webbing
willpower

Type 2. It is not usual to use these words as countables in modern British English (except in some specialised uses or in American English).

A words:

accommodation
advice
aggression
coal
data
food
grass
homework
money
nonsense
pardon
progress
steam

B and C words:

apparatus
forsythia
garlic
gorse
granite
gravel
greenfly
heather
jasmine
libel
mail
melancholy
mimosa
punishment
research
seaweed
semaphore
slander

Type 3. These words do not occur in the plural but sometimes appear in the pattern: a(n) + adjective + noun.

aid
applause
confusion
countryside
dust
education
hunger
knowledge
peace
poetry
resistance
revenge
thirst

Type 4. These words to a variable extent change their meaning, depending on their use as countables or uncountables. Their uncountable use is easily overlooked. You should consult a good EFL dictionary very carefully.

A words:

attention
business
care
company
condition
damage
duty
experience
fruit
grammar
hair
health
help
history
intelligence
love
post
service
string
stuff
success
toast
traffic
wealth
work

B words:

atmosphere
capital
confidence
corn
correspondence
energy
exhaust
fiction
gossip
humour
litter
nature
plant
spray
thunder
timber
transport
treatment

C words:

baggage
broom
bunting
coke
consumption
disorder
gear
grain
hail
initiative
lace
paraphernalia
property
royalty
shingle
tackle